P9-DTU-974

ALSO BY PATRICK N. HUNT

Ten Discoveries That Rewrote History

When Empires Clash: Twelve Great Battles in Antiquity

HANNIBAL

Patrick N. Hunt

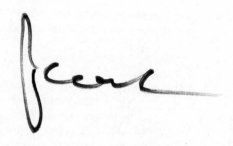

SIMON & SCHUSTER

NEW YORK   LONDON   TORONTO   SYDNEY   NEW DELHI

Simon & Schuster
1230 Avenue of the Americas
New York, NY 10020

Copyright © 2017 by Patrick N. Hunt

All rights reserved, including the right to reproduce this book or
portions thereof in any form whatsoever. For information, address
Simon & Schuster Subsidiary Rights Department,
1230 Avenue of the Americas, New York, NY 10020.

First Simon & Schuster hardcover edition July 2017

SIMON & SCHUSTER and colophon are registered trademarks of Simon & Schuster, Inc.

For information about special discounts for bulk purchases, please contact
Simon & Schuster Special Sales at 1-866-506-1949 or business@simonandschuster.com.

The Simon & Schuster Speakers Bureau can bring authors to your live event.
For more information or to book an event, contact the
Simon & Schuster Speakers Bureau at 1-866-248-3049
or visit our website at www.simonspeakers.com.

Interior design by Ruth Lee-Mui
Maps by Paul J. Pugliese

Manufactured in the United States of America

1   3   5   7   9   10   8   6   4   2

Library of Congress Cataloging-in-Publication Data
Names: Hunt, Patrick, author.
Title: Hannibal / Patrick N. Hunt.
Description: First Simon & Schuster hardcover edition. | New York : Simon & Schuster, 2017. |
Includes bibliographical references and index.
Identifiers: LCCN 2016051474| ISBN 9781439102176 | ISBN 1439102171 |
ISBN 9781439109779 (ebook)
Subjects: LCSH: Hannibal, 247 B.C.–182 B.C. | Generals—Tunisia—Carthage (Extinct city)—
Biography. | Punic War, 2nd, 218–201 B.C.—Campaigns. | Carthage (Extinct city)—Biography.
Classification: LCC DG249 .H86 2017 | DDC 937/.04092 [B] —dc23 LC record available at
https://lccn.loc.gov/2016051474

ISBN 978-1-4391-0217-6
ISBN 978-1-4391-0977-9 (ebook)

To great soldiers of the world who have waged just war,
who know the agonizing questions of battle.

"War may too often issue from the bowels of hell
but even heaven has its war trumpets."

PATRICK N. HUNT

CONTENTS

PREFACE

Hannibal has loomed large in my imagination since my youth. Over the decades, as I have read about his exploits and the history of his time, I attempted to follow in his footsteps across three continents. As I discovered, ambiguities abound. Ancient sources provide often contradictory or problematic interpretations of his motivations and actions. Should we expect anything else, given the passage of time?

My archaeology fieldwork has concentrated for decades on Hannibal. Every year for the last twenty years I have stood at the summits of Alpine passes, ascending and descending rocky footpaths and road surfaces in every calendar season. Whether in biting wind and flurries of snow—not uncommon above 8,000 feet even in August—or on gusty, sunnier days, I have marveled at the challenges Hannibal faced on his intrepid marches and campaigns, especially when I climbed for hours to reach a spectacular vista as the almost vertical crags descended into forested slopes and plains far below. With more questions than answers over time, I have traveled to Carthage, where at the Secret Harbor I once picked up an old murex shell—the source of the famous Punic (Carthaginian) purple dye—before carefully placing it back on the sand. Many times I have traipsed through the remains of Punic Cartagena, the walled terraces of Saguntum, and western coastal Spain as well as across the eastern Pyrenees, through what was ancient Gaul and now is France, and then up the Rhône and Isere Valleys. I have walked back and forth across all the Italian battlefields important in Hannibal's military campaigns and various Hannibal sites elsewhere in Italy. On multiple occasions in Turkey, standing along the sun-glimmered Sea of Marmara around Gebze has made me reflect on Hannibal's last days. Many times with teams of Stanford students and more than a few times with engineers and geologists, I have carefully investigated at least thirty Alpine summits to try to determine where Hannibal crossed the Alps. I could never be an armchair historian: I have to see and try to understand what I write about.

The ancient historian Polybius has so often been my guide—literally in my hands—that my copy of his *History* is nearly worn out. I believe, as did he, that it is best to visit as many locations as possible if one wants to better understand historical events. Attempting to match text and topography has been my touchstone wherever possible. Other ancient historical accounts I have consulted include Livy's ample and colorful texts—even though his geography is often suspect—augmented by Appian, Plutarch, Diodorus Siculus, Virgil, Horace, Juvenal, Frontinus, Cornelius Nepos, Ammianus Marcellinus, Valerius Maximus, Strabo, Dio Cassius, Vegetius (listed here not necessarily in chronological order, but in order of importance to my research), and many other fragmentary sources, as much in the original languages of Greek and Latin as possible. From these sources I infer that Hannibal was one of history's greatest military minds because of his changing tactical responses to extraordinary challenges. That Hannibal has been a riveting topic for millennia, and continues to be so even as he remains a conundrum, explains why so many writers continue to ponder him from different angles. How I wish I could have met Hannibal and asked him the questions that to this day still defy authoritative answers.

Stanford, 2017

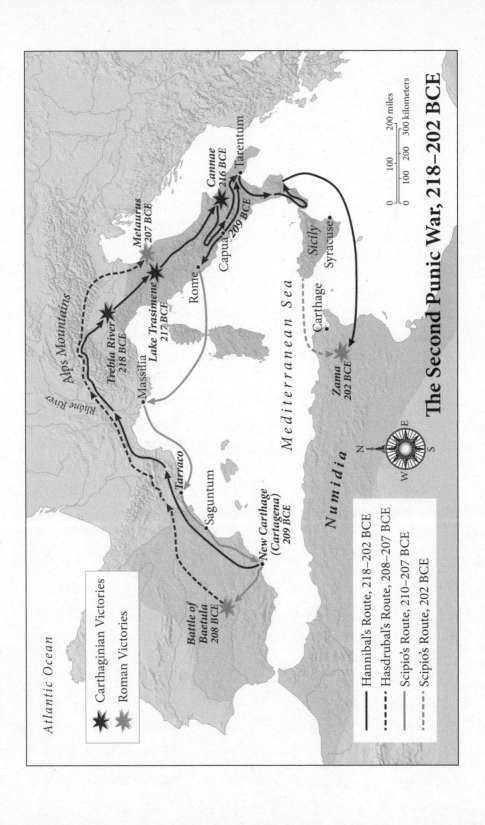

The Second Punic War, 218–202 BCE

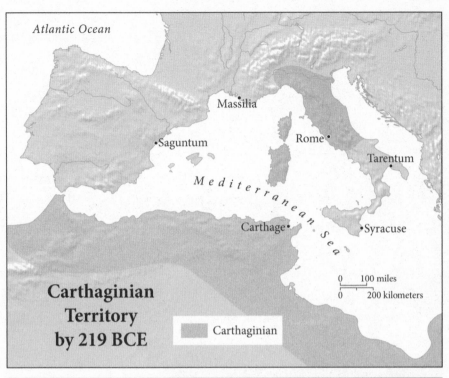

Carthaginian Territory by 219 BCE

Atlantic Ocean

Massilia

Saguntum

Rome

Tarentum

Mediterranean Sea

Carthage

Syracuse

| 0 | 100 miles |
| 0 | 200 kilometers |

Carthaginian

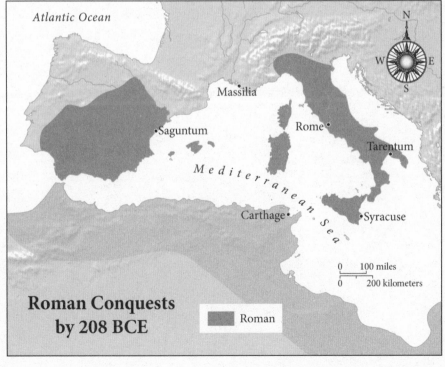

Roman Conquests by 208 BCE

Atlantic Ocean

Massilia

Saguntum

Rome

Tarentum

Mediterranean Sea

Carthage

Syracuse

N
W E
S

| 0 | 100 miles |
| 0 | 200 kilometers |

Roman

AUTHOR'S NOTE

All dates are BCE unless indicated otherwise.

HANNIBAL

One

THE VOW

The Roman historian Valerius Maximus tells a story about the young Hannibal. As a boy in Carthage, Hannibal and his younger brothers would wrestle one another. Their father, Hamilcar Barca, would boast proudly to his guests, "My boys are lion cubs reared for Rome's destruction." Whether this actually happened, we don't know, but we can imagine the young Hannibal wanting to please his father and taking pride in Hamilcar's boast.[1]

Hannibal was born around 247 BCE during a long war between Carthage and Rome that often took Hamilcar, a famous general, away for extended periods of time. Hannibal's parents gave him a name rich in religious meaning; "Baal be gracious to me" or "Baal be merciful to me." Baal was a great Carthaginian god of fertility who manifested himself in thunderous storms; in naming him so, Hannibal's family tied the boy's future to his personal god and thus to his destiny. With sacrifices to the gods made at his birth, Hannibal had a long military tradition to follow.

Carthage in North Africa had been deliberately chosen for its location by the Phoenicians, who had founded the city in what is now Tunis. They thought it was perfectly situated for trade. A natural bay and man-made harbors offered shelter to Carthaginian ships that traded with fertile Sicily, only a short voyage away.[2] Trade also extended to Spain and over much of the Mediterranean Sea. Although Carthage's docks were secreted behind a high wall, protected from the prying eyes of the outside world, young Hannibal would have frequently seen his city's renowned double harbor. He would have walked with family members, maybe elder sisters or servants, passing through exotic markets of redolent spices alongside the famous port. The Phoenicians who established Carthage around 814 BCE were most likely refugees from Tyre who fled from Assyrian invaders swarming like locusts from their Mesopotamian lands in the east. As Carthage's mother city, Tyre was famous for its mercantilism and its far-flung trade, as the prophet Ezekiel scorns in his tirade against Tyre in Ezekiel 23:7–8: "whose footsteps led her abroad to found her own colonies, whose traders were princes, whose merchants the great ones of the world." Like mother, like daughter.

As a boy, Hannibal would have heard many times that for a half millennium, Carthage had ruled the western Mediterranean sea unchallenged. In addition to its mercantilism, Tyre bequeathed to Carthage the Phoenician alphabet and the Phoenician language, which in the Carthaginian dialect was known as Punic. (Both languages are extinct.)

After centuries in the Mediterranean, Carthage had no rivals until Rome began to flex its newfound power.[3] Now there was a growing shadow from Italy. With an agrarian mindset, the upstart Romans were much more acquisitive than the Carthaginians, constantly seeking to bring new territories under their sway. Carthage had colonies in Spain and elsewhere, but these were largely mercantilist enterprises. Carthage was uninterested in making the Celtiberians of Spain and other colonies into Carthaginians, whereas Rome wanted its colonies to think of themselves as Romans, and indeed it made Roman citizenship a possibility. So long as goods and treasure flowed back to Carthage as expected, the city-state was content to let the colonies organize themselves politically however they wished. In contrast, in the Roman world, even slaves could become wealthy, and in time they might even become free. The available evidence does not indicate that slaves in Carthage ever had such opportunities.

Hannibal's family was aristocratic, descended from military leaders and merchant princes.[4] Hannibal lived in one of his family's villas, likely atop one of the hills where Carthage caught afternoon breezes from the sea. But Carthage's harbor was the city's pride and joy. It possessed the best naval berths the world could offer. The outer rectangular harbor's water glinted around a merchant fleet and quays that could berth up to 220 sailing ships. The inner circular harbor often bristled with warships and many-oared triremes and quinquiremes, their bronze shields reflecting sunlight. Perhaps the young Hannibal wished to sail in a warship to one of the great naval battles he heard about often.

HANNIBAL'S FAMILY

Hannibal's family was the Barcid clan, landowners of vast farms a few days' journey to the south around the Sahel region of North Africa, where wheat was then plentiful, well watered by the forested eastern Atlas Mountains.[5] More important, his immediate ancestors were generals and legendary fighters. Because the Barcids were natural leaders in the old pattern of Phoenician aristocracy,[6] during his early life Hannibal would see his father only between engagements in Sicily, where he fought the hated Romans. From snippets of household conversations, the boy might have grown to understand that the Romans were now challenging Carthage over which power would control the great island. His father often moved so fast between lightning-strike battles along Sicily's northern coast that messengers from Carthage would arrive on each other's heels. The year of Hannibal's birth, 247, was also about the time that Hamilcar Barca received his military commission to lead much of Carthage's forces.

Not much is known about Hannibal's mother. We do not even know her name, but she would have likely descended from a similar aristocratic family of Carthage and would have wedded with a dowry of silver, land, and slaves, as was common for aristocratic families at the time. In between engagements, when his father would return with Carthaginian fleets for a few months, Hannibal's mother bore two other boys, Hasdrubal and Mago. His mother and father already had three daughters before Hannibal, although their names, too, have been lost to history. Hannibal's parents guaranteed that their daughters would marry well, usually into other leading military families. The eldest married a man named Bomilcar, who would become admiral over a Carthaginian fleet. The second daughter would marry Hasdrubal the Fair, who later helped Hamilcar conquer and govern Iberia, as much of Spain was known then. The third daughter later wed outside the Carthaginian aristocracy, marrying a local chief of nearby Numidia for a political alliance. Thus, the Barcids were a well-connected family in Carthage.

Hannibal's education would have been similar to that expected for a young aristocratic boy. Not much can be said other than that he had a Greek tutor in literature named Sosylos who must have taught him some of Homer's epics and probably how to read. Sosylos may have taught him from Aristotle's *Logic*, because Hannibal knew much about Aristotle's famous pupil Alexander the Great and his military exploits. The boy may well have known about Odysseus because Hannibal shared the cunning character of this Greek hero, full of stratagems. We do not know when Hannibal's education started, but Sosylos even accompanied Hannibal later on his military campaigns in Italy.

END OF THE FIRST PUNIC WAR

But everything changed in 241 BCE when Hannibal was six years old. Military disaster struck the Carthaginians as events near the end of the First Punic War reversed earlier successes. Although the enemy Romans had lost fleet after fleet, more than seven hundred ships, and up to a hundred thousand men in a series of naval disasters starting in 264 BCE, when war had broken out, they refused to give up. Carthage had a very different leadership after 244 BCE. Its Council of Elders—the Gerousia—increasingly opposed the long Punic War that had dragged on for twenty years. (*Punic* was the Roman word for Carthage, a possible abbreviation of the Greek word

Phoinikes, which may have originally meant the people of "red dye."[7] This important cloth dye derived from shellfish was a commodity in which the Phoenicians had a trading monopoly for centuries.) The Romans had refused to surrender during two decades of bad outcomes and had only the final naval victory in their favor. But Carthage was already intimidated by Roman mobilization of endless resources.

The Gerousia was Carthage's governing body. According to Aristotle's *Politics*, Carthage had a form of constitution and elected magistrates. The Gerousia was not as powerful as the contemporary Roman Senate, but like the Roman Senate, it was oligarchic in nature. In Carthage, the upper class consisted of wealthy merchants and landowners, and so the Gerousia sought to protect commercial interests. As a consequence, the Gerousia tended to be conservative and cautious about military action. Military families such as the Barcas were often at odds with the Gerousia if there was not an imminent threat. We should remember, too, that much of Carthage's military was made up of mercenaries, who might not have even been Carthaginian by birth.

The leaders in Carthage wrongly assumed that the last Sicilian battle at Drapanum (now Trapani) in 249 BCE had been such a complete victory for Carthage that the Romans would soon relinquish their claim to western Sicily, traditionally Punic territory. Led by Hanno, a great landowner rather than a military man, the now-dovish Gerousia began recalling and dismantling the fleets. In demobilizing their great navies, the Carthaginians turned many back into merchant vessels and sent them out again on far-flung trade. Hanno believed the future of Carthage lay in Africa and not overseas. Hamilcar Barca still led forces of thousands in Sicily and even raided South Italy in quick attacks, but Carthage's Senate wanted peace so much that it blindly underestimated Roman tenacity of will.

The blow that Hamilcar Barca anticipated was slow to develop but quick to strike. The Roman Senate heard from its well-placed spies that Carthage was sending ships home. In Italy, southern Campanian senators and rich landowners had always had the most to lose from a close Carthaginian presence in Sicily. These wealthy Romans formed an unusual plan. Because Rome was either unable or unwilling to finance a new fleet, they dug deep into their own pockets and absorbed all the costs. Even borrowing against their land, they took advantage of the downsizing of Carthaginian naval power and paid for outfitting as many new ships as they could. Smart businessmen, these rich Romans asked for reimbursement only in the event of victory. Back in Carthage, Hamilcar was dismissed as a hawk. The general's messengers who conveyed his warnings about the piles of fresh cut timber on the wharves and quickly growing hulls in Italian harbors went unheard.

After many Roman losses at sea, one naval battle decided the outcome of this struggle between Carthage and Rome. The Romans had recently dredged a storm-wrecked Carthaginian ship's hull out of the Sicilian water to be examined by their carpenters and shipwrights. To their surprise, the Italian ship builders discovered an amazing fact: every piece of wood on the Carthaginian ship was numbered. The Romans were not long in figuring out that the Carthaginian boats were easily assembled from timbers according to a template. This made shipbuilding easier, since all the wood dimensions were predetermined and merely slotted into place and caulked. It was hardly necessary to have a master shipwright in charge of building each boat. Many ships could be assembled simultaneously. The practical Romans quickly duplicated the technique, accelerating the usual time needed to build a navy.

On March 10, 241 BCE, in the Battle of the Aegates Islands west of Sicily, Rome's new fleet completely outmanned the small and hastily prepared Carthaginian fleet. Once the mightiest power on the seas, Carthage's navy was destroyed. Demoralized by its first naval defeat—an unthinkable event—the Council of Elders negotiated a quick surrender that infuriated Hamilcar. The terms of surrender left nothing to Carthage and everything to Rome. This was partly because the Hanno-led Carthaginian Senate was not interested in maintaining maritime power—unlike Rome, which understood its destiny in the need to expand. Hanno's Senate faction thought only of its status quo control of African territory. The Treaty of Lutatius in 241, so named after the victorious Roman consular admiral Gaius Lutatius Catulus, was a permanent blow to Carthaginian maritime might and apparently also a personal affront to Hamilcar Barca. It was a disaster, demonstrating Roman intents that Hamilcar could never forgive. In one treaty, Carthage's traditional monopoly of the seas was lost forever. Hamilcar Barca even refused to come to the negotiating table with Rome.

The Greek historian Polybius, who wrote about the rivalry between Rome and Carthage, carefully recorded the terms of surrender. First, Carthage would have to remove every Carthaginian citizen from Sicily and give up all claims to this huge, fertile island. Second, all Punic ships and men were to withdraw from the many islands around and between Sicily and Italy. These had been convenient places where Carthaginian ships had harbored for centuries. Third, Carthage would also have to cut off all ties with Siracusa, a powerful city-state in Sicily that the Romans wanted badly to control because of its superb harbor. Hamilcar saw correctly that this treaty would end Carthage's historic claims to sail and trade in the western Mediterranean. Finally, Carthage would have to pay an indemnity of 3,200 talents of silver, a total of almost 10 million shekels, a third of it due immediately because Rome demanded war reparations. In the short term, accepting these circumstances was dire enough, but over the long haul, this could be a death sentence to Carthage, however slow the squeeze would be. Hamilcar knew it and was enraged. He believed Carthage could rise again.

HAMILCAR'S RETURN TO CARTHAGE

A bitter Hamilcar Barca came home from Sicily, reluctantly obeying the recall mandate from Carthage, and the troops soon followed. So many mercenaries were unpaid, however, that they rebelled in 239 BCE, and the weak city elders hesitated to make any restitution. Carthage itself was now under siege from its Libyan and other alien mercenary veterans who rightly demanded their promised back pay. After brutal decimation of men on both sides, including generals such as Gisco, who had led some of Carthage's armies in Sicily, Hamilcar defeated the rebellious mercenaries, some of whom had even fought with him in Sicily. As the battle advantage fluctuated between the rebels and the city, many died a cruel death by crucifixion. Both rebels and Carthaginians were tortured and nailed in public view

along roads and on city walls. Hamilcar finally prevailed and trampled the
rebel leaders with war elephants. The general's popularity rose due to his
leadership, which broke the siege and saved Carthage.

About this same time in 238 BCE, young Hannibal lived through a new
crisis when Rome annexed the island of Sardinia. This was not one of the
territories ceded to Rome in the Treaty of Lutatius of 241, yet Rome took advantage of Carthage's siege and a Punic economy weakened by the rebel war.
Rome had long been uneasy about the island of Sardinia, with its centuries-
old Phoenician colonies such as Tharros. One Roman description even referred to Sardinia "as a long ship anchored against Italy's side."[8] But when
Rome seized Sardinia, Carthage could do nothing except send ambassadors
to Rome to protest. The Senate of Rome responded that any hostile action
by Carthage would be considered an act of war. Making matters worse,
Rome added a new clause to the treaty. Long after the fact, it demanded an
additional fine against Carthage of 1,200 more silver talents. Even the pro-
Roman Polybius writes in his histories that Rome made Hamilcar Barca
more of an implacable enemy by this cavalier action, and that the results
would be nothing short of calamitous for a soon desperate Carthage.[9] The
frustration in Hamilcar's voice must have now carried through his house
as he raged against both Rome and the shortsightedness of his own people.
The general also unleashed tirades against his rival Hanno for leading the
Carthaginian Senate into appeasing a Rome that would never be satisfied.

When young Hannibal, now between the ages of around five and eight,
watched quietly or heard his family's heated conversations between 241 and
238 BCE, he would have formed opinions likely modeled after his father's.
Weighing most heavily on Hamilcar's mind was revenge against the Romans. Young Hannibal would have heard such sentiments frequently.

HANNIBAL'S VOW TO HIS FATHER

In 237 BCE, at age nine, Hannibal's life was altered irrevocably. Hamilcar
had finally persuaded the Carthage Council of Elders to let him go to Spain,
where Carthage could more quickly raise money to pay the penalties Rome

had imposed. Spain's silver mines were fabulously rich, and the more democratic Hamilcar was fed up with the ruling oligarchy under Hanno and more than ready to leave Carthage. The Hanno faction, meanwhile, saw an opportunity to keep a popular opponent at a distance where he could not stir up trouble against Rome so easily. Like many boys, young Hannibal must have adored and worshipped his father. Surely his parents would have talked about Hamilcar's and the family's options. If his father had talked about not wanting to return to Carthage, the boy would not have wanted to wait in futility. Hannibal would have done anything in his power to accompany his father.

According to Polybius and the later Roman historian Livy, Hamilcar took young Hannibal with him to a place that could forever haunt the boy. Some of the sacred precincts of Carthage, including the Temple of Baal, a place of possible ancient human sacrifice, and the sacred cemetery called the *tophet*, often were interpreted as a repository for human sacrifice. Whether Carthaginians still practiced human sacrifice is a contentious subject. That there could be original Canaanite or Phoenician antecedents of likely child sacrifice—as the modern scholar Brody maintains from fairly recent *Iron II* (1000–550 BCE) *tophet* contexts at the *tombolo* (sandy "mound") of Tyre[10]—does not necessarily mean full continuation into Punic culture in the West. The Semitic word *tophet* as a cremation burial place itself may even relate to a Greek word, *taphos*, meaning both funerary rites or a tomb and burial place.[11] The debate about *tophet* practices still embroils scholars in heated arguments and equally acrimonious counterarguments. This story of human sacrifice is hardly new, because historians such as Diodorus Siculus had made this assertion long ago, although more than a few interpret it mostly as propaganda against Punic religion.[12] While Polybius says nothing about the element of human sacrifice, he does emphasize this event as the defining moment of young Hannibal's life.

Hamilcar and Hannibal went to the precinct of the Temple of Baal, entering through the gates and doors where priests waited. Beyond the sacred threshold of a temple, a quiet hush would have surrounded the visitors. Hannibal's name may be a clue to what happened next, if the story is true.

We are told in Hannibal's own words—repeated much later in his life—that his father brought his young son to the place of sacrifice. Hamilcar likely made his son ascend the altar and there place his hand on the sacrificial victim in order to make a vow. As the animal tied to the altar breathed away its last few minutes, Hannibal would have felt the warm flesh rise and fall. Placing his hand on the sacrificial victim—the exact words of Polybius[13]— in making his vow, this physical act would have fused a clear connection in the boy's mind between himself and the victim. Hannibal would have known that such vows made before gods such as Baal were unbreakable. That a living creature died in witness of a vow to the gods was the most serious part of this sacrifice ritual.

Thus, Hannibal's own destiny was both "sacrificed" and consecrated to Baal, his god. Hannibal must have soon realized that his own life owed all to the god's mercy; he must have comprehended that an animal died while he lived in order to make this vow.

At the climax of this momentous event, Hannibal's father asked him to swear undying hatred to Rome, and Hannibal did so. Even though the boy might not have grasped the meaning, its sense would grow on him throughout his life. If Polybius and others have related this story accurately, Hannibal would remember the details until the end of his life, telling it to Antiochus III, another enemy of Rome in the East, only a few years before his death. In a way, the child Hannibal died that day. He would increasingly come to know thereafter that he lived only to see Rome's destruction.

Livy claimed later that Hannibal was impious and *nulla religio*, "without religion." This is not true. While Hannibal respected Roman oracles later in his military campaigns—naturally taking advantage when the Roman omens were against Roman victory—he was certainly also religious with respect to Carthaginian gods. Apparently the Romans would never fully understand what Hannibal's devotion meant. They did not comprehend the implications of Hannibal's childhood vow.

A few months later in the same year of 237 BCE, Hannibal prepared to accompany his father in their departure from Carthage. Hannibal was about to leave his mother, older sisters, and younger brothers behind. Hasdrubal and Mago were too young to make this hard journey to Spain, but they would come years later. Perhaps his mother had too many ties to Carthage, including her other children and relatives, as she did not accompany them. We hear nothing about her again.

HANNIBAL MOVES TO SPAIN

In 237 BCE, either during spring when the sea-lanes reopened after winter or in summer when the land was dry enough to march across, Hamilcar and his young son left Carthage accompanied by a small retinue of loyal soldiers, junior officers, and slaves. Dawn was usually the best time to begin traveling as many possible miles in a day. The city was probably not yet awake except along the harbor markets where the fishnets were already being hauled in with their morning catch. The Barcids were also followed by an unknown number of thousands of Carthaginian troops, proud cavalry from Numidia, the adjacent kingdom (mostly modern-day Algeria) allied to Carthage, and many Libyan and other mercenaries—as well as pack animals, traveling metalsmiths, cooks, suppliers, civilian quartermasters (paymaster and supply officer), and camp followers, as well as the usual stragglers and hawkers of wares and human vices.

Several routes to Spain lay open to the army, including by land or sea. Hamilcar and Hannibal could have taken a ship out of the bay and sailed along the Maghreb coast west toward Spain, as Diodorus Siculus claims. Polybius, on the other hand, implies that they marched overland in Africa with the army toward the coast opposite Gibraltar.[14]

Young Hannibal, perhaps excitedly wide awake the first night due to the novelty, must have enjoyed the traveling spectacle of the noisy army, uncountable soldiers of every size and garb, with tribal and clan outfits alongside recognizable Carthaginian armor. It was certainly unusual for a general to take along his ten-year-old son. Hannibal would have heard coarse jokes, camp songs, and daily reports to his father, and been amazed at the spectrum of decorum and behavior. Most of all, the boy would have seen and soaked up the army's respect for his father as chief general at the pinnacle of his soldierly world.

Finally leaving Africa by sea, they would have crossed the Strait of Gibraltar and the legendary Pillars of Hercules, where headlands rose to windblown cliffs. As would have been customary, after landing on the Spanish shore, Hannibal likely followed his father and a few of his chosen guards up a path to one of the windy and rocky points—maybe up Gibraltar Rock itself—where an altar to the god Melqart stood in this forlorn but sacred place. Hamilcar's journey required the blessing of Melqart, once the city god of Tyre in the old Phoenician homeland and now also the god of new ventures. In addition, Melqart was Hamilcar Barca's personal god—the deity his father's own name honored.

Whatever guarded thoughts Hamilcar had, he knew there was no turning back. From high up on Gibraltar, the boy would have enjoyed a magnificent view of the blue Mediterranean in one direction eastward and the often gray Atlantic Ocean in the other direction westward. Doubtless, Hannibal would have looked back toward Africa, which he would not see again for a long time. Hannibal could have also seen where the silver-rich Sierra Morena Mountains beckoned northward, now a blue horizon in the shimmering distance across the water and the curving coastline.

Two

YOUNG HANNIBAL

It is no wonder that the "indignant" Hamilcar, "unvanquished in spirit" by the war's outcome in Sicily, as Polybius tells,[1] had been ready to leave contentious Carthage for a new land where he could do almost as he wanted and better use his military acumen. Carthage, like its Phoenician parent, was not highly militarized but a commercial society dependent on mercenaries.[2] Spain on the other hand, was a mountainous land, possessing an incredibly rich bounty in precious metals such as silver and additional wealth in game in its forests and abundant fish along its long coastline. Its deep soil was fertile and full of agricultural promise for its Punic colonizers.

Hannibal must have been just beginning to understand how important this fact of Spanish resources was to his father. Although he might not have seen all the implications for Carthaginian independence from the penalties of the Roman indemnity assigned by the Treaty of Lutatius, he would not have been able to avoid hearing about the potential for independence in Spain's wealth.

Historians in antiquity had mentioned Spanish mining wealth since the sixth century BCE. If Hannibal visited the silver mines near the Sierra Morena with his father, as he probably did, he would have seen that they continued for miles in all directions. The boy would also have heard the clang of iron and bronze on rock, hammers and picks seeking the glint of silver. Wooden ladders descended down into the pits all around, each of them echoing with ringing staccato blows and a din of voices. Man-made hills of ore would have been piled everywhere and the air filled with rock dust. The keen eyes of Hamilcar Barca would have missed nothing, as he likely calculated the time and labor required to amass a treasure of silver bullion.[3]

If in a few short years after 237 BCE Hamilcar was able to revive the old Phoenician silver mining operations, it would have been because he was intensely driven to pay back the Carthaginian indemnity to Rome as well as to build a new war chest against Rome. Even if he might not live to see it, he would make sure that Hannibal would. Hamilcar traversed Andalucia from east to west not just to reinvigorate the mining of silver but also to visit the Celtiberian tribes, which had a fragile alliance with Carthage.

The Phoenicians had been exploring this southern region of Spain for centuries. At first beaching their ships where wide rivers flowed out along the steep and cliff-indented coast, the Phoenicians had carefully scouted the land. Trading with the Iberian tribes that had slowly been processing the ubiquitous iron, the Phoenicians were always looking for metal and indigenous mining operations they could assimilate. Phoenician merchants had expanded their network of small trading posts, bringing finished products such as Near Eastern and Greek pottery, colored glass beads, and luxury items such as Egyptian ivory, spices, ostrich eggs, purple-dyed textiles for the ladies, and rough but practical textiles along with farming tools for the men in exchange for Iberian mineral and other goods. The Phoenicians were careful not to arm the Iberians with weapons that could be turned against them. The local agricultural products and the teeming fisheries off the coast of Andalucia were also part of the Iberian network of natural wealth. Many fish-processing villages lined the Gulf of Cádiz coast. The island of Ibiza had been the site of a huge fishing industry since the seventh century BCE.

Posidonius the Greek philosopher wrote that the Phoenicians founded the colony of Gadir (also known as Gades, or Cádiz) around 1100 BCE. In Hannibal's day, it was a thriving city, the center of all Phoenician mining trade in the region. Offspring of Phoenicians here were as proud of their early Temple of Melqart as their Carthaginian cousins were of the Temple of Eshmoun towering above Carthage on Bursa Hill. Along the coast, the local Iberians had also borrowed or adopted the gods of their masters the Carthaginians or joined them to their own deities. Symbols of the Carthaginian goddess Tanit could be seen painted on tombs or pebbled into pavements, her triangular skirt easily recognizable as a Punic religious icon, seen later in a mosaic at Selinus in Sicily.

On the frontiers of Andalucia were the hostile tribes of the Turdetani or Turdulli, who would give Hamilcar much grief. The Celtiberian north was still filled with fierce tribes and clans that were always threatening to muster enough men and weapons for raids on Phoenician outposts. Hamilcar had well-armed groups of trained veterans placed in forts and towns along the frontier that would communicate any unusual tribe movements to him on a regular basis. Messengers regularly went back and forth between the command centers such as Gades and the outposts, since communication was vital and protecting the mines was crucial. Sooner or later Hamilcar would have to move deeper into the interior and deal with the Celtiberian tribes.

Within two years after he left Carthage, Hamilcar Barca founded the Carthaginian colony of Akra Leuke on the Mediterranean coast of northern Andalucia, northeast of the city of Murcia. Akra Leuke sat below looming white plateaus, and its Greek name, meaning "white high place," later became *Alicante* in Arabic during the medieval Moorish kingdom of al-Andalus.

In Akra, his new base of operations, from 235 BCE onward, Hamilcar seems to have assigned another teacher to his preadolescent son. While Sosylos continued to teach Hannibal about the ancient Greeks, a new tutor would have trained Hannibal in manly weaponry. Hannibal's new tutor was most likely a grizzled veteran with only one job: to instruct him in swordsmanship and archery with real weapons instead of toy ones.

Because he went everywhere with his father, Hannibal was already saddle hardened and tanned from the sun. As a soldier in training who had been partly raised in military camps, Hannibal probably rode a horse with skill and ease. A legendary leader who knew his men extremely well, Hamilcar knew that Hannibal must have been ready to fight very early.

HANNIBAL LEARNS WAR

Although Livy does not agree with the epithet, he sarcastically mentions Hamilcar's reputation among his admirers as a "second Mars" as a war commander.[4] Hannibal would have learned an officer's sense of authority and how the chain of command worked both in peace and in war. Hamilcar's force was usually a mobile, well-trained force, and divided into experienced officers on horseback and many hundreds or thousands of foot soldiers. Hamilcar would have surrounded himself with handpicked Carthaginian veterans and have chosen Numidian cavalry officers, among others. The Numidians were famous horsemen and were allies of Carthage. Hannibal would have learned to think of himself as a unit with his horse, learning both on horseback and on foot how fast an army could march in different terrain—and he would have done it himself to test and develop his youthful stamina. He would have learned from the Numidians how to pretend to retreat but instead fight even harder facing backward in a surprise feint when the enemy least expected it. Hannibal eventually earned his own battle experience, including slight wounds from grazing arrows or skirmishes.

Most of all, Hannibal would have learned from his father how to lead by example and how to be fair with every soldier; when to encourage and when to express justifiable anger. Judging from later military experiences, young Hannibal seemed to have picked up quickly not to be impetuous or to let anger rule him, when to engage and when to disengage, how to choose the terrain on which to fight, and how to lead men to respect him not only because of his father but also due to his own developing sense of strategy and battle logic. Hannibal's childhood passed into adolescence far from his mother and family females to coddle him.

If Hannibal loved or was infatuated with anyone in the passions of adolescence, history has not preserved any names. His loves and concubines throughout his long life must have been fairly private, because other than a brief mention of a Spanish wife named Imilce, we never learn their names, not even when he lived with a courtesan in Salapia. Nor do we know whether he had any children, which is not as unusual as it might seem. On the other hand, Hannibal lived a military life without ever being tied down to one place long enough to develop relationships outside of his family (and mistresses) and his eventual close circle of military advisors. That is not to suggest that young Hannibal was lonely while surrounded by his military comrades and his father's officers. Seldom in history has any young man been so devoted to one thing alone: the art of war, and that was due greatly to his father, probably the best general of his generation.

After founding Akra Leuke, Hamilcar turned his full attention to bringing the people between the rest of Andalucia and even western Valencia under his control in several military campaigns between 235 and 231 BCE. Near the Gulf of Cartagena, the Batuli tribes around Cape de Palos were assimilated as a conquered people fairly quickly by Hamilcar, who was accompanied by his son-in-law Hasdrubal the Fair (husband of Hannibal's older sister) around 236 BCE. Hasdrubal the Fair had also founded Cartagena in one of the best natural harbors in the Mediterranean, adjacent to land rich in silver ore a few miles to the east. Shipping from this deep harbor, well protected against raids, could hardly have been easier. Here Hasdrubal built a fort, as well as several temples and a thriving colony with stone structures whose foundations still remain—no doubt with Hamilcar's military assistance or the supervision of his military engineers.

A new minting of silver coins was apparently stamped with Hamilcar's visage, much of it sent to Carthage from the fine, deep port and the rest stockpiled for the general's future campaigns. Hamilcar must have also taught Hannibal the value of silver for military negotiation with locals for food and supplies or paying an army's mercenaries. When the Romans sent a deputation to inquire around 231 BCE about the purpose of the Punic silver mining activity, Hamilcar's answer must have referred to repaying the war indemnity from 241 BCE.[5] Apparently the Romans accepted this answer and left him alone.

The Mastetani tribe near Murcia, just north of Cartagena, was also soon within Hamilcar's military vision, apparently a mostly successful campaign, and in 229 BCE Hamilcar was attempting to conquer the area of Helike, near modern Toledo to the north. This was where the Celtiberian Vettoni tribe was located, northern allies of the warlike Turdulli and Turdetani. Unfortunately for Hamilcar, this interior location deep in Spain—where negotiations were set to take place—was quite far removed from his long supply lines on the coast. The Celtiberian Oretani tribe marched south from the Manchegan plains to help defend the Vettoni until Hamilcar was greatly outnumbered, the main body of his army having been left a few miles to the east while he went to negotiate. However, the Vettoni feared and respected Hamilcar's leadership too much to attack the entire Carthaginian army. Hannibal would have been alongside his father in almost every campaign, and was certainly near his father at this one.

HAMILCAR'S DEATH

One source, Diodorus Siculus, writing a couple of hundred years later, says that while Hamilcar was negotiating with the treacherous Vettoni, accompanied by only a few officers, he was ambushed. This went completely against the protocols of ancient warfare, because there was a truce during negotiations. But the Celtiberians were more chaotic barbarians than a unified army.

Hamilcar feared for Hannibal, who led a small scouting detachment also removed from the larger army. Hannibal would have been around nineteen, and his younger brother Hasdrubal was with him in this small force. According to the ancient sources, Hamilcar diverted attention from the small force with his sons during the ambush and sacrificed himself to save them. Diodorus has Hamilcar drowning in the Júcar River, probably wounded, but a terse account by Polybius has him surrounded and fighting the Vettoni down to his last man and then being killed himself. Finally, Cornelius Nepos, a Roman biographer who lived in the first century BCE, writes that Hamilcar engaged at first with the Vettoni but then drowned in the Tagus River.[6] Taken all together, an ambush by the Vettoni seems likely, and Hamilcar, severely wounded, managed a partial escape only to drown. Furthermore, considering how good a soldier he was and a master tactician, sacrificing himself for his sons was in keeping with Hamilcar's character.

Hannibal was now bereft of his father before he was twenty. But enough of his father's will and experience had been imparted that Hannibal would have been prepared to lead, however premature the timing seemed. While Hannibal must have deeply mourned the loss of his father privately, he was by now every inch a warrior, and soldiers are supposed to be emotionally and psychologically steeled for sudden death in battle. Knowing that good decisions must be made despite personal loss, there is little time for sentiment, as soldiers are taught to put the deaths of their comrades behind them and move on. Hannibal already had years of dedicated military training at his father's side, in which he had been prepared for leadership. He must have been ready to take his father's mantle as well as carry out the life-changing promise he had made back in Carthage: the vow to hate Rome.

Three

SPAIN

Hamilcar's unexpected death was a great blow to Carthaginian affairs abroad and to Hannibal personally, although we can only guess his reaction because there was no word about it from Carthage or Hannibal himself.

How the news of Hamilcar's death was received in Africa depended on whether the majority in the Gerousia, the Council of Elders, had sided with the charismatic and popular general or with his dovish enemies such as Hanno, who wanted to stay close to home and not venture out so boldly to provoke Rome.

Hasdrubal the Fair, now sole commander of the colonies, administered Carthaginian Spain effectively for a half decade from 228 to 221 BCE, consolidating positions held already while his adjutant Hannibal served him militarily across southern Iberia, expanding new territories under Carthaginian control. As war chief and virtual ruler, Hasdrubal was more inclined to administer Spain through diplomatic pragmatism than had Hamilcar, who'd carved out territory by military force and ruthless tactics that made him feared among the Celtiberian tribes. In this regard, Hasdrubal was more similar to the traditional rulers of Punic Carthage, who were less inclined to military power and more to commercial consolidation.[1] Polybius refutes the charge of the contemporary Roman historian Quintus Pictor Fabius that Hasdrubal was ambitious and power hungry and that his policy in Spain was an underlying cause for the Second Punic War. Polybius maintains that it was Hamilcar who had "contributed much to the origin" of the Second Punic War but instead relates Hannibal's admiration for Hasdrubal's leadership.[2] Under Hasdrubal, most of the southern half of Spain gradually fell under Carthaginian hegemony or at least operated with varying degrees of autonomy under its shadow. From Gades in the hot South along the Atlantic side of Gibraltar, to New Carthage (modern Cartagena) in the east along the Mediterranean coast, to the forested Sierra Morena northward, and soon even into central Spain along the Tagus Valley, Carthage was unchallenged by any cohesive foe, least of all Rome, which could only look on with envy at this time. Able troops spread throughout garrisons in Spain now complemented Carthaginian mercantile and engineering acumen.

The overall policy that Hamilcar had established would continue. Although Hannibal no longer had his father for counsel or further military training, the young commander had enough natural leadership ability that he was given increasingly more responsibility over the soldiers, moving ever farther north and west into the Spanish frontiers. Probably due to Hasdrubal's skill at parleying with the Celtiberians, Hannibal now acquired a Spanish wife: the princess Imilce from the Punic ally of Castulo on the upper Gaudalquivir River, although we have no surviving accounts about her other than she might have later borne Hannibal a child, possibly a son.[3]

In the meantime, the silver mining operations and other Iberian trading ventures were enormously successful, and through spies and a network of informants and trading partners—colonies such as Massilia at the mouth of the Rhône River in Gaul (roughly modern-day France)—Rome could not help but notice that the Carthaginians were not suffering as much as they would have preferred under the chafing war indemnity imposed on them from the Treaty of Lutatius. By now, Rome was certainly also wishing it had some of the silver wealth of Spain for itself. Rome was waiting to reduce Carthaginian power and wealth in Spain.

ROME MAKES A CLAIM TO SPAIN

Finally, the Romans, having subjugated some of the Celts who were living just south of the Po River Valley of Lombardia, Northern Italy, decided that Carthage's hold over Spain was becoming too profitable and too close to Roman interests for comfort. In 226 a small envoy of Roman diplomats visited Hasdrubal, probably at Cartagena, and demanded that he draw the Punic boundary at the Ebro River. If the diplomatic mission was indeed at Cartagena, the Roman envoy would not have failed to notice the wealth of local silver flowing through the port city.

However much dissembling took place on both sides, a minor treaty was signed between the Spanish Carthaginians and the Romans that Carthage acknowledged this Ebro River boundary—and that Carthage would not cross the Ebro "for the purpose of waging war." The Ebro River merely divides the eastern seaboard of Spain's long coastline into two-thirds to the south and one-third to the north—not a natural boundary like the jagged Pyrenees Mountains. For Hasdrubal and Hannibal, this uneven treaty also played the Roman hand, showing its designs on the rest of Spain above the Ebro. Hasdrubal acquiesced nonetheless, although we don't know whether he did it to buy his people time or to assuage Rome of Carthaginian ambitions about the rest of Spain.

But Hannibal and surely Hasdrubal would have remembered the disasters of the Treaty of Lutatius and how Rome had taken advantage of the Carthaginian desire for peace and continuity of its maritime trade after years of war—forcing Carthage to relinquish claims to any kind of toehold in Sicily even for shipping. They also would have remembered how Rome soon assimilated Sardinia not by battle victory or diplomacy and treaty, since Sardinia was not even part of the Lutatius treaty—instead, Rome had taken Sardinia by outright duplicity, clandestinely arming a revolt in its favor and landing an army on the island for peacekeeping, claiming it had been invited. It was an old ploy that has usually worked throughout history. Hasdrubal and Hannibal would surely have suspected that the Romans could not be trusted over the Ebro boundary. The treaty must have satisfied Rome, which left Spain alone for a few more years.

CHANGING OF THE GUARD

Once again circumstances changed for Hannibal. After ruling Spain for a little more than five years, Hasdrubal the Fair was killed in battle by insurgent Celtiberians in the far north in 221 BCE. The shock would have been far greater had not Hannibal been prepared to step into his natural role as general over the assembled forces. Now he was quickly elected commanding general. The trained Carthaginian military presence in Spain consisted not only of Carthaginians, Numidians, and other Libyans but also assimilated Iberians, Celts, Balearic Islanders, and others from Ibiza or islands such as Mallorca and Menorca, as well as friendly tribes spread throughout the Spanish peninsula. Livy marks the transition as one of destiny. Even Hannibal's physical likeness to his father was a factor:

> [The armies] imagined that Hamilcar himself had been restored to him as he had appeared in youth. They observed in his face the same intense expression and penetrating gaze, the same confidence and strong-willed countenance. But Hannibal had not needed time to prove his resemblance to his father was not just physically superficial and this mirror image was the least important in gaining the support of the army. Never before was there a more suited genius for commanding respect and obedience from his men . . . Nor did any other leader fill his men with courage and boldness . . . In addition he was indefatigable in body and spirit and took no comforts or pleasures beyond those of his men, in fact could often be found at night sleeping wrapped in a blanket like one of his merest scouts. The things that set him apart were not his clothes, which were identical to those of his

men, but his horses and weapons and above all his position to be first into battle and last out.[4]

In this text, it is hard to miss the egalitarian role Hannibal encouraged regarding the lives of his soldiers, whose loyalty he carefully gathered and possibly manipulated, as Livy suggests. He inspired confidence not just in his unswerving military prowess but also in his personal virtues. He was not motivated or spoiled by luxuries like so many of his historical counterparts in Rome or elsewhere.

It is not unlikely that Hannibal's physical toughness was influenced by the stories of Alexander the Great he knew through his tutors.[5] En route to his victories in Persia, Alexander was often said to be more austere and unmovable like a Spartan—and his teacher Leonidas had trained him in his adolescence—when it came to personal comfort. Hannibal's decades with his father, Hamilcar, had also strengthened his self-discipline. Sharing his soldiers' daily hardships would cement the bond between Hannibal and his men even further.

When it came to "obedience"—Livy's grudging choice of words for the soldiers' response—Hannibal would come to expect his men to follow him unfailingly even when it appeared counterintuitive and dangerous. But Hannibal's strategies would prove to be trustworthy to his armies. This was one of the greatest strengths of a Hannibal-led army, such that history has rarely if ever seen its equal before or after. It wasn't a disregard for danger, as Alexander often displayed, thinking himself to be a demi-god or a heroic avatar, but an ability to understand and exploit others' weaknesses. Livy is forced to describe Hannibal as a military "genius" because how else could Hannibal wreak such destruction on Rome's armies unless he had genius? Livy's only other explanation is that Hannibal was treacherous—a characteristic that the Roman historian wants his readers to infer.

HANNIBAL'S LEADERSHIP IN SPAIN

In 221–220 BCE Hannibal immediately set out to establish his authority and test his military power by starting to rein in the tribes on the fringes of Spain in the West, including the Turdetani and Turdulli, and the Cynetes, and tribes to the north such as the Lobetani, Veitones, Vaccaei, and Olcadi. Learning much from Hasdrubal's policies, Hannibal also knew that Spanish silver would have to be spread around the peninsula. Hamilcar had also been careful to pay his mercenaries according to expected standards augmented by loot from conquests, and Hannibal had learned firsthand from observing his father in the 240–238 BCE Mercenary Wars back home in Carthage[6] how important it was to take care of mercenaries. Fortunately, there was ample silver to be spread around Spain.

Basing himself in Cartagena, as had Hasdrubal, Hannibal carefully acquired the best possible army of trained soldiers—on the one hand, buying the loyalty of some veteran mercenaries; and on the other, offering other mercenaries the opportunity to share loot from his Spanish conquest as he subjugated the peninsula in lightning attacks and sieges. Although he still visited Akra Leuke, where his father had colonized and set up a military command just outside Andalucia, Hannibal seemed to always return to Cartagena and its silver as the primary Punic base of operations and also the primary link back to Carthage. He always made certain that the leaders in Carthage had favorable reports of his success to accompany the silver shipments, although the silver bullion spoke the loudest and underscored his reports with convincing evidence.

THE FOUNDING OF CARTAGENA

The fort that Hasdrubal the Fair began on the Cerro del Molinete hill closest to the harbor was made of worked stone in Punic style: carved blocks with detailed borders and many building foundations whose traces still line the hill with remnant walls. From the heights of this hill, one can still see across the blue harbor or across to the summits of the other hills that also housed urban forts or temples to Carthage's gods. Carthaginian silver coins were also minted here from the nearby mines, and the local archaeological museum has a silver Punic coin of Tanit, the goddess consort of Baal, so there also may have been a Tanit shrine, or *tophet*, in or near Cartagena as well as in other Iberian colonies, especially since other early sanctuaries have been found in Sardinia and Sicily.[7] The natural harbor has been so valuable historically over millennia that it was the primary Mediterranean port for the Spanish Empire of the fifteenth through twentieth centuries and more recently that of Spain's submarine fleet.

CARTAGENA'S TOPOGRAPHY AND HISTORY

As one arrives by boat into the Cartagena harbor, the jagged coastline here gives way to many smaller bays under looming plateaus, and panoramic remains of seventeenth-to-nineteenth-century cannon emplacements can be glimpsed that solidified Cartagena's reputation as among the most impregnable ports of the historic world. That this port was also only a few miles from the richest silver mines in Spain demonstrates how canny and practical the Carthaginians were in carefully choosing locations of their maritime colonies for maximum trading convenience. The Archaeological Museum of Cartagena displays Punic amphorae—vessels for shipping oil or wine—and household pottery of all shapes and sizes. Quite a bit of it was imported from Carthage or Greek colonies, and the rest local copies; all evidence of a substantial Punic population of several thousand people, although there also would have been a constant flow of people back and forth from the mother city of Carthage. Archaeological exploration of more of Cartagena's perimeter and survey of even some of the higher local peaks may yet uncover additional sanctuaries to Baal and Tanit and additional support communities outside the known walls. The now-dry lagoon to the immediate southwest of Cartagena could have accommodated an entire merchant fleet or warships. Unfortunately, when the Romans conquered Spain a few years later under the Scipio family, the Carthaginian buildings and the Punic stamp on the city was mostly obliterated—deliberately.[8]

From 230 to 220 BCE, there would have been a steady procession of mule trains down into Cartagena from the rusty red hills of the peninsula to its immediate east: sturdy pack animals on whose backs the piled silver ingots came by the hundreds. Carthaginian accountants and quartermasters kept a close watch on the bullion, and the Cartagena mints were busy stamping out silver coins, probably most of them with Barcid dynasty images. Hannibal could have become incredibly wealthy from this glut of Spanish silver but instead chose to focus his economic policy on military matters. The few surviving Punic silver coins found to have been minted in Cartagena—since the Romans later took them out of circulation and melted them down partly to avoid reminders of Hannibal's victories—seem to show the older, bearded face of Hamilcar Barca or the younger, beardless Hannibal on one side. The peering profiles look as if these gifted Punic generals could see to the edge of the world and had their eyes on the future. On the reverse side of the portrait profile, some of these new Barcid family silver mints often portrayed an army elephant brought from Syria, where they had been bred for generations. Hannibal's apparent first victorious use of elephants was in Spain against the Carpetani tribe, when he employed forty pachyderms stampeding along the Tagus River to trap and crush resistance after an uprising. These animals might have been many of the same elephants he took with him two years later to Italy.

Hannibal's elephants are perhaps the most enduring image of his intrepid story. These huge beasts are what nearly everyone visualizes on the march—the picture made all the more impressive by the crossing of the Alps, where elephants are a visual oxymoron. Many famous depictions show the elephants with Hannibal's army in the snow, often surrounded by rocky peaks.

Hannibal marched with elephants because they were so frightening and destructive. The best war elephants were trained to enhance their natural instincts to gore with their wicked ivory tusks, often sharpened or tipped with razor-sharp metal. They could lift and toss with these tusks, using them as we use pitchforks. They also had very thick outer skin, often one and a half inches or even thicker, especially in places where skin folds or calluses occur—hence the descriptive Greek name for them, *pachyderm*, meaning "thick skinned." Often airborne projectiles such as spears and arrows could barely penetrate their skin unless used at very close range (and who would want to be that close?). Furthermore, nearly all cavalry horses— even the Numidian horses with Hannibal—hated the beasts' unique smell and often stampeded away even when trained for battle.

The Celtiberians and later the Gauls were seeing elephants for the first time. Polybius says that the ragged Gauls in the snowy Alps avoided Hannibal's elephants at all costs, never attacking or ambushing anywhere near them.

Everyone wants to know what kind of elephants Hannibal had. None of the ancient sources, primarily Polybius and Livy, record this detail. Instead, these historians tell us only that Hannibal crossed Gaul and the Alps with about thirty elephants (the historic estimates range from twenty-seven to thirty-seven). To this day, no one knows for certain which species Hannibal employed, but the primary candidate is the Asian or Indian elephant, *Elephas maximus*. Four or five subspecies of this elephant have been bred and used for millennia in labor and battle in Asia and Southeast Asia. The Asian elephant is highly trainable—although never really tamed. It had to be forcibly trained in warfare to charge and trample enemies either singly or in ranks. A herbivore, the adult can easily eat 10 percent of its weight in vegetable matter (up to five hundred pounds) and drink, on average, thirty gallons of water daily. Its maximum pace is generally about fifteen miles per hour unless charging, although it generally prefers a lumbering walk of about two to three miles per hour.

Historically, the Asian elephant was probably first encountered by Alexander the Great when he fought with the Persians at the Battle of Gaugamela in 331 BC and again farther east on the Indus River frontiers of India around 325 BC in his battles with King Porus—where he faced almost a hundred war elephants at the Battle of the Hydaspes River. Asian elephants were subsequently imported from India and bred in Syria by Alexander's Seleucid successors and also used in Macedonia by King Pyrrhus of Epirus in 280 BC.[9] In the third century BCE, elephants were expensive but fairly common imports from Alexandria to Carthage, where they were also bred for war.[10]

In antiquity, there was a smaller species of elephants inhabiting the Atlas Mountains in North Africa, *Loxodonta africana pharaoensis*, now believed to be extinct. It is possible that this elephant species also was used by the Carthaginians, given its geographical proximity, and some historians think this may have been Hannibal's elephant.

For two years, from 221 to 219 BCE, Hannibal slowly strengthened his leadership and trained his men into the best fighting unit in the world, a great achievement considering their multicultural backgrounds and the different languages they spoke, although their different commanders would have all spoken sufficient Punic to be able to relay commands from Hannibal downward. In the meantime, a waiting Hannibal stockpiled weapons and silver for his next step toward ultimate revenge against Rome, whether his allies in Spain or back home in Carthage understood or even guessed his long-term goal.

SPAIN'S CELTIBERIANS

Some of Hannibal's knowledge was acquired by his direct observation from military campaigns, with other information coming from a network of paid informants and intelligence gathered from his scouts in outposts, and some from merchants who doubled as spies.

Hannibal's trained ability to make accurate assessments and observations was no doubt instigated and encouraged by his father when Hannibal was a young adolescent in Spain. He would apply this lesson throughout his subsequent engagements for the next decade as he marched through Gaul and into Italy. Hannibal reasoned rightly that if he could harness their strengths and address their weakness, these Celtiberians and their kin could make able allies or, at worst, could be the frontline buffer for his troops against the Romans. If he could both win their trust and simultaneously exploit their desire for independence while adding to their suspicions of Roman intents, Hannibal could amass an unusual military force that would more than give the Romans pause. Some of these very Celtiberians who came over to the Punic side would later accompany Hannibal into Italy and form a vital core of his most resolute veterans.

What Hannibal could glean from Celtic culture—especially weapons of good Spanish steel and their bravery in war—would also be a huge boon in his burgeoning dealings with far more of their kind as he moved ever closer to Roman Italy. That Hannibal was far more successful than the Romans with the Celts and their close kin in Spain and Gaul—observing and learning how best to deal with them in war and peace—is likely proof that his time spent in Spain was a necessary step toward invading Italy.

Hannibal's continued successes in Iberia worried some Romans but did not much faze the Senate, which was more concerned at the time with Illyria. The aggregate people making up the Illyrians included the territories of modern Croatia, Serbia, and Albania on the Dalmatian coast. The Romans had to quickly deal with the Illyrians on their northeastern flank as a higher priority than this young Carthaginian upstart in Spain. Increasing Illyrian piracy had made the Adriatic Sea unsafe for Roman shipping for several years, and the Roman recourse to this danger was to invade Illyria with sufficient legions at the expense of any other interests. Roman ambitions for Spain were mostly postponed for the time being. This overcommitment to the Illyrian distraction would also prove to be a severe Roman mistake in 219 BCE regarding Saguntum.

Four

SAGUNTUM

The Romans had demanded that the Carthaginians respect the Ebro River as a boundary. The town of Saguntum was many leagues to the south of the river, outside the Roman boundary and roughly midway between Cartagena and the Ebro. Saguntum, however, was also a Roman ally, commercially tied to the Roman colony of Massilia in Gaul. By 219 BCE, the Romans were apparently using Saguntum to keep an eye on Hannibal and possibly to divide Spain. As far as we know, Saguntum had not even been mentioned in the Ebro River boundary treaty between Hasdrubal and Rome, but the Romans evidently believed they could grandfather it.

Whatever the case, Saguntum provided the spark to the Second Punic War. Even as Rome engaged with the Illyrian pirates in the Adriatic Sea in 220 BCE, it paid a little attention to Spain.

SAGUNTUM AS ROME'S ALLY

Polybius says that the Saguntines had placed themselves under the protection of Rome long before Hannibal's time.[1] It is uncertain what Polybius meant specifically about Saguntum being under official protection, as he was likely biased toward Rome. The nature of Saguntum's relationship to Rome and when it commenced has been long debated—whether it was a formal alliance (*foedus*, in Latin) or a dependency for protection (*deditio in fidem*). Polybius calls it an alliance (*symmachia*), while Livy says that Saguntum and Rome had the obligations of allies (*fides socialis*). The connected question is whether Saguntum's alliance began before or after Rome's Ebro River declaration of 226 BCE, because Saguntum's location outside the Roman boundary would provoke Punic interests.[2]

Around 220, Rome inserted itself into a political fracas in Saguntum, claiming that it had been invited to arbitrate between the Saguntines[3] and a tribe, the Turboleti, that lived in the montane highlands to the west. The Turboleti traded with the Carthaginians to the south and probably favored them over the coastal Saguntines.[4] The Romans, now decisively involved south of the boundary they had earlier set up with Hasdrubal the Fair, continued the expansionist policy they had adopted with Sicily in 264 BCE and Sardinia just after 240 BCE. This full Roman intrusion into Saguntum could mean only one thing to Hannibal: with Carthage burned two times over losing Sicily and Sardinia, he wasn't about to let it happen again. It didn't take a soothsayer to predict that Rome would challenge Carthage over Spain. If Hannibal chose to intervene in Saguntum, he could claim that he was merely defending the interests of his Turboleti trade allies. According to Polybius, Hannibal had multiple incentives to act: depriving Rome of further Spanish conquests, inspiring terror in the Iberian tribes, and amassing and distributing booty that would raise his troops' morale and pacify Carthage back home.[5] According to one historian, this was the turning point of Hannibal's life[6]: Would he accept Roman interference at Saguntum or call the Romans' bluff?

HANNIBAL'S SIEGE OF SAGUNTUM

Once he consulted with his commanders, whose men were on winter leave, Hannibal acted fairly swiftly in the early spring of 219 BCE and assembled an army, marching from Cartagena on Saguntum in about a week. The distance would have been about 140 miles if he took the more direct route north from Akra Leuke (modern-day Alicante), or about 200 miles if he followed the coastal route northeast and then north along the Gulf of Valencia.

The Saguntines must have heard from their scouts that an army was entering the plain of Valencia. Watching from their high walls, they would have seen with trepidation the dust of the thousands of troops along with horses and supplies. No doubt Hannibal added some local troops en route and also stocked up on food and supplies taken from local people. The Saguntines, however, well defended behind their natural cliffs with added stone ramparts, had already driven all their farm animals, livestock, and horses into the citadel. As the army loomed closer on the plain, they would have just had time to send news northward to allied Massilia and onward to Rome itself, fully expecting Rome to march to their aid. Hannibal wasted no time cutting off the fortress from its surrounding agricultural territory and the well-watered valley of the Palancia River immediately north of the plateau.

In laying siege to Saguntum in 219 BCE, Hannibal surely knew there would be no turning back. Polybius suggests that this act was a *casus belli*, or "cause of war," as the Romans interpreted history. But as far as Hannibal was concerned—and Polybius acknowledges this was a somewhat valid Carthaginian interpretation[7]—the Romans having taken Sardinia without a treaty was his primary justification. Many modern scholars agree that Rome initiated relations with Saguntum in order to block further Barcid expansion in Spain.[8]

By choosing to force the Romans' hand over Saguntum, Hannibal knew he would have to act boldly if he were to influence the Celts in Spain and Gaul even as he gambled on the Roman response. Could he make the

Romans look weak to the Celts if Rome—already engaged in Illyria—didn't send an army to stop him? Could he thus prove that the Romans would not abide by their treaties with enemies such as Carthage, but if they abandoned Saguntum, they would also prove unfaithful to their allies?[9]

In 219 BCE Saguntum was a fortified oppidum (hill fort) of about twenty acres on top of the plateau about two-thirds of a mile from the shore, where the steepest cliffs rise almost vertically coastward but are much shallower on the landward approach from the west. Like any good fortress, Saguntum's deep wells and cisterns could provide water in a siege for a few months during dry seasons and possibly longer during winter rains when water collection was possible in the cisterns. Its later stout silhouetted battlements such as El Ciudadillo and Castillo are still very much in evidence from when the Moors ruled Spain as Al-Andaluz between 711–1492 AD/CE. With its many terraced vestiges of ruined walls going back millennia, Saguntum is as unforgettable today as it was when it was built.

The siege of Saguntum lasted about eight months, if Polybius and Livy are right. The siege was prolonged because the upper walled city was mostly impregnable on three sides—east, north, and south—and the walls were formidable on the western sloping side. Food would be the greatest issue, since Hannibal had marched and attacked just after spring planting. The winter's larders or food supply would already have been thinner than was optimal for a long survival.

The Saguntines probably had a type of defensive fire-throwing weapon, the *falarica*, which projected heavy iron javelins smeared with gobs of burning tar. The sharpened tips were a meter long and rained down on Hannibal's surrounding siege army from various wall ramparts. Some later Roman writers on Saguntum, such as Silius Italicus, maintain that the *falarica* missiles were "launched by catapult."[10] While the Saguntines found it impossible to escape or bring in food supplies under the eyes of the enemy troops, the daunting high walls were apparently unassailable for more than a half year. Hannibal himself was said to have been wounded in one foray by a javelin in his thigh.

ROME'S RESPONSE TO THE ONGOING SAGUNTINE SIEGE

Once they had word of the siege and had debated in the Senate how to handle it, the worried Romans sent envoys by ship to land on the Spanish coast. They demanded immediate cessation of all military engagement against Saguntum and claimed that Hannibal had breached the Treaty of Lutatius, which banned all hostilities against Roman interests. Hannibal appears not to have even received them personally, but his word came via adjutants that he was merely righting wrongs against Carthaginians and that Saguntum had never been mentioned in any previous treaty. Polybius allows that Hannibal was wrong in attacking Saguntum because the Treaty of Lutatius purportedly protected allies as well,[11] but, as discussed, Hannibal would not have seen it that way. When told by the Romans not to get involved in Saguntum, Hannibal also— apparently in the heat of anger—retorted that the Romans had already broken trust by executing a few Saguntines and locals who were friends of Carthage and that they had contravened their own Ebro River boundary treaty.

Having been snubbed outside Saguntum, the diplomatic envoys sailed straight to Carthage. Hannibal had prepared for this situation by sending advance word to the pro-Barcid faction of the Gerousia, laying out the real Roman agenda for Spain. In Carthage, the Hanno faction voted to stop Hannibal as a warmonger, but the Council of Elders was decidedly pro-Barcid for the time being—possibly influenced by Spanish silver. The Roman envoys were sent packing to their ships.

Back in Rome, the Senate debated what to do for its Saguntine *amici populi Romani*, or "friends of the people of Rome."[12] The Illyrian campaign was just concluding at considerable expense and casualties, and the conservative Fabii clan was always loathe to pursue another war. Two opposing families, the old Aemilii and another great patrician family that would become glorious through the Punic Wars, the Scipiones, wanted action. While Saguntum suffered, Rome dithered.

During the summer of 219, Hannibal took a brief respite from the long siege to put down a revolt, marching a small part of his army northeast to Manchegan and Castilian territories, where portions of the Oretani and Carpetani tribes had rejected Punic recruiting attempts. It is also likely at about this time, as some argue,[13] that Hannibal received an invited envoy from Gaul over the Pyrenees. These were Celts from the Volcae tribe near Roussillon. The Celts would have observed for themselves what was happening at Saguntum, and they would later remember it. It appears that Hannibal was already thinking long term and preparing for the future, wanting to assess loyalties and to understand how the Romans were perceived in Gaul. He seems to have been already looking for allies when the time came to challenge Rome directly.

The siege went on for month after month, the spirits of the Saguntines flagging as their resources dwindled. Hannibal concentrated his efforts on the west of Saguntum, massing his troops there. This was Saguntum's most vulnerable flank because the plateau rises gradually there. Today the ruined towers of the much-later western Moorish citadel can still be seen, some of which were later exposed to Napoleonic cannonry. No doubt Hannibal's final assaults took place from more than one location, but the strength of the famine-stricken Saguntines was decisive. When the volley of stones flung from the fort at Hannibal's army gradually began to peter out, Hannibal knew the city could not last. The successful final attack occurred during early fall 219.

THE FALL OF SAGUNTUM

The end was gruesome, whether later legend has exaggerated the details or not. We are led to believe by the propagandizing Romans after the fact that the starving Saguntines, having consumed all their livestock and then their horses and all other animals, broke one of the ultimate social taboos and engaged in cannibalism. We are told by more than one ancient authority—eliciting both sympathy for the Saguntines as intended and moral outrage at Hannibal—that the broken Saguntines at last began to eat their own children, whether dead or alive. Famine had already reduced many families, not stopping at the houses of the poor but now affecting the entire aristocracy—its gold and silver useless because there was no food to purchase.

At the end of the eight-month siege, the last outer walls were breached and the remaining weakened defenders were slaughtered, allowing the army to pour into the city unhindered. But a horrible sight met the eyes of Hannibal's army gathering at the dead heart of Saguntum. Holding their noses at the smell, the arriving troops saw an endless pyre of slowly burning corpses, many of the last emaciated Saguntines having thrown themselves on the inferno to die in the flames after killing their own starved, half-skeletal children. Even Hannibal must have been taken aback, however accustomed to the horrors of war as he was by now. But perhaps to offset blame and guilt or to quell too many questions other than to blame Rome, after disposing of the dead, he quickly set the conquering army to divide the rich spoils of gold, silver, and other precious treasures.

Hannibal and his officers oversaw three divisions of the Saguntine spoils of war. First there were survivors, many of them slaves; and then precious objects that could be sold; and, finally, materials of gold and silver, including bullion and coin. How many Saguntines defended the city and how many died has always been inexact, but fatalities may have been at least several thousand, given the booty that Hannibal took away, with the rest of the Saguntines now enslaved. Hannibal's army had its share of loot, and he set apart a considerable bulk of the precious objects to be sent to Carthage, partly to buy off dissent. Hannibal apparently did not skim off any loot for his own personal wealth but instead put aside a considerable sum for the campaign against Rome he now clearly planned. His mercenaries, loyal soldiers, and officers were happy with their overall portions, a promise of future gains should they continue conquering.

Hannibal returned to Cartagena for the winter of 219 BCE with his loyal troops to plan for the expected Roman retaliation.

The awful word about Saguntum's end spread quickly across Spain and over the Pyrenees to Gaul and soon even to Rome. Across the Alps and in Spain, many of the Gauls certainly got the message, repelling repeated Roman entreaties via Massilia to have no dealings with Hannibal.

Hannibal was laying a ground plan he would follow for years: if you wished to be Rome's ally, think long and hard.

Five

OVER THE PYRENEES

Hannibal wasted little time guessing the Roman response to Saguntum. War was now a reality: Rome had already begun to assemble old and new legions under its consuls Publius Cornelius Scipio and Tiberius Sempronius Longus. The former was a cautious and seasoned military veteran, and the latter, a hotheaded political appointee. Hannibal's army assembling at Cartagena was a combined force of Carthaginians, Numidians, Libyans, and Celtiberians, a considerable number of them mercenaries.

This initial army of around 90,000 soldiers and 12,000 cavalry—if we are to believe Polybius and other sources—was large but nothing like the Persian armies under Xerxes I and Darius III, where even conservative numbers suggest around 300,000 soldiers leaving Sardis on the Aegean coast with Xerxes in 480 BCE (the fifth century BCE Greek historian Herodotus claimed 2 million) and 100,000 soldiers under Darius III at the Battle of Issus in 333 BCE.[1] Hannibal's army contained speakers from four or five language groups, but standard Punic was the dominant tongue. He had read lessons from Alexander the Great as a model for unconventionality and mobility and knew that it required great logistical skill to successfully manage such a large army of culturally diverse soldiers.

With their spies reporting that Hannibal was almost on the move toward the Ebro, the Romans planned to send an army by ship under Longus to lay siege to Carthage. They also readied another army to sail to Spain under Scipio to stop Hannibal at the Ebro River.[2]

PLANNING THE MARCH TO INVADE ITALY

Through the spring of 219 BCE, Hannibal recalled troops from all over southern Spain. Outfitting them properly entailed another few months of tasks, such as blacksmithing and leatherworking on top of basic training. In the end, the huge force melded into an army. He made sure his troops knew their objectives: march to Italy and perhaps ultimately toward Rome's heart. Some soldiers would have been daunted and deserted quickly. Others would have found the great distance a lure for adventure and, as Hannibal would have promised, plenty of loot along the way as a magnetic pull.

The Celtiberians and other Spanish recruits would have required great discipline to bring them up to an acceptable standard of military preparedness. It is likely that after discovering how much drudgery was involved in a march, more than a few Spanish mercenaries also melted away from the camps by night during the midspring march of about 288 miles from Cartagena to the Ebro crossing. It is likely that Hannibal's army crossed the river in the late spring of 218 BCE, possibly not long after its high-water mark at the end of the spring snow melt in Cantabria to the far west and while much of the wetlands would still be flooded or at least saturated.

THE EBRO RIVER

The Ebro River crossing was an important indicator of Hannibal's historical resolve. As a major Spanish river flowing east to the Mediterranean sea, in nearly any season it could not be forded easily. Coastal swamps would have forced Hannibal's army a few miles inland, probably to cross near the Celtiberian village of Dertosa (now Tortosa). Here the river became mainly nonnavigable upstream because of the rapids descending from the plateau above the town, a fording place controlled by the Iberian tribe of the Ilerca-vones.[3] Hannibal would have had to either conquer or bribe this tribe to use its boats and other services to get an army over. Even in summer, the Ebro is at least a hundred yards wide at that point, while at its delta, the river broadens out even more through many meandering waterways.

It is the Ebro River that gave Spain its ancient name of Iberia, the land of the Ebro watershed. If the successful siege of Saguntum was not enough, Hannibal's crossing the Ebro was obvious provocation, demonstrating that he knew what he was doing by challenging Roman authority over such a clear demarcating line. It would have taken at least a day for the army to be ferried by the boats and manpower of local folk, requiring both constant logistical support for the scores of thousands of soldiers, pack animals, and elephants—and a well-trained wary eye for hostile local clans that could have objected that this was a major trespass into their territory. Hannibal knew his Ebro crossing would be perceived as a threat to many Iberians and a formal declaration of war to the Romans. It would further undermine Celtic confidence in Rome's power to stop Hannibal. But crossing the Ebro could also be a bottleneck that would further tempt Celtiberian resistance.

Hannibal now encountered considerable trouble from local Celtiberian and Iberian clans as he marched north beyond the Ebro during late spring and into the early summer. This resistance delayed him far more than he wished between May and early June. The hilly Catalonian area provided many hiding places for skirmishes and potential ambushes from Celtibe-rian tribes, which reduced Hannibal's pace northward.[4]

By the summer, Hannibal had endured an obvious lack of enthu-siasm from his erstwhile ally the Carpetani, a Celtiberian tribe that had provided soldiers only because it had little choice. They seem not to have been sympathetic to fighting their Iberian neighbors. Facing the Pyrenees Mountains—to them a daunting barrier they had never scaled and a point of no return—three thousand Carpetani infantry soldiers from the same tribe that had vigorously opposed Hannibal before being subdued quickly deserted, as Livy tells it.[5] This is not all that surprising, as they were now far from their home in central Spain and had been pressed into reluctant service after being conquered. Plus, there had been little shared loot to keep even their superficial loyalty.

Hannibal took stock and trimmed his force by dismissing another seven thousand Celtiberians, for a loss of about ten thousand soldiers before even leaving Spain. But he expected his Spanish allies to guard his flanks and keep intact his long communication and supply lines with Cartagena, paying bribes and leaving a sizable payment in silver to this end. To further ensure this lifeline and prevent reprisals from unhappy tribes, Hannibal also left behind in Spain another eleven thousand Carthaginians and Libyans along with twenty-one elephants and at least eighty-two ships under the command of his brother Hasdrubal.[6] This meant that his force was probably reduced to fewer than seventy thousand soldiers.

CROSSING THE PYRENEES

After about three months out of Cartagena, with his army traveling north through Catalonia, Hannibal's scouts would have determined the best route over the Pyrenees. Geography was always vital to any army's logistics, and Hannibal was a master at understanding advantages and disadvantages of terrain and geography, even unfamiliar new terrain. From reports via tenuous allies or conquests among the Iberian locals, Hannibal's scouts would have known the Catalonian coastal route was both difficult and long, complicated by steep cliffs plunging into the sea.

On the Spanish side, Hannibal's army would have continued along the Llobregat stream north up to its Pyrenees source through oak and scraggly pine forest flanking the Perthus Pass (El Pertus in Spanish; Le Perthus in French, or Col du Perthus), the lowest elevation in the region. The troops would have descended on the Celtic French side where the mountain stream tumbles north until meeting the Tech River, crossing at some point possibly just below Banyuls-dels-Aspres into fully Celtic territory of

Gaul. The Perthus Pass is thirty kilometers (eighteen miles) south of modern Perpignan in France. Hannibal's scouts would have heard from allied or conquered Celtiberians, Iberians, and Celts that this was the best route north directly into Gaul and thus the most logical crossing place through the Pyrenees. Even then, it seems to have taken Hannibal nearly a month to fight his way over the mountains.

In the late first century BCE, the practical Romans would build their Via Domitia road through this same low pass between Gaul (Gallia Narbonensis) and Hispania (modern-day Spain) for the same reasons that Hannibal chose the route: to avoid the coastal bays, cliffs, and marshes.

HANNIBAL'S PARLEY WITH THE CELTS

Polybius says that late that summer, Hannibal made promises to and received concessions from assembled Celts gathered from as far away as the Boii tribe of Italy about how together they would keep Rome from enlarging its territory in Gaul on both sides of the Alps.[7] Normally, competing Celts would not convene in such numbers, so Hannibal must have convinced them that he was only passing through their lands and forming an alliance against an expanding Rome that would not be content with Italy. No doubt Hannibal provided ample evidence from recent Roman expansion in central and northern Italy. Italian Celts like the Boii would have agreed from their own experiences with Roman expansion.

HANNIBAL'S TROOP STRENGTH FROM SPAIN TO GAUL

One question that ancient history always leaves open to modern debate is the reporting of numbers of combatants fielded by nations at war. The actual numbers of soldiers in Hannibal's army over the long journey from Spain to Gaul are difficult to confirm and even confusing or contradictory. It seems likely that his army was already reduced by nearly half before he even arrived in Gaul. The soldiers who stuck with Hannibal by late summertime in southern Gaul would have been mostly veteran, committed soldiers. It was certainly a typically wise strategy for Hannibal to keep some of his loyal North Africans (Carthaginians, Numidians, Libyans) in Spain to cover his back and send some questionably loyal Spanish allies over to North Africa—some as soldiers to guard Carthage and others as hostages.

HANNIBAL ARRIVES IN GAUL TO ROMAN SURPRISE

The surprised Romans heard from their Massilian allies that Hannibal had crossed the Pyrenees and was in Gaul. Some of the Celtic tribes, such as the Boii in the eastern Po Valley now rebelled en masse against the Romans in northern Italy, and the Boii brought the Insubres in the Piedmont region of the western Po Valley into their revolt with them,[8] driving the Romans eastward from around their outpost at Placentia (modern Piacenza) all the way back to their colony at Mutina (modern Modena). The Romans rapidly changed their own war plans. They had been too late to stop Hannibal at the Ebro. Now, hearing that he had already crossed the Pyrenees, Rome had to protect Italy against likely invasion, so it kept all these legions ready in Italy. Hannibal's relative speed through northern Spain and the Pyrenees— frustratingly slow by his standards—still eclipsed the Romans' marching pace.

Hannibal's next great challenge was to cross the wide Rhône River, which flowed from the Alps to the Mediterranean. Fortunately, he would be crossing at one of its lowest points. But after that would come the even greater challenge of traversing the Alps. Hannibal's allies in Gaul had informed him of the obstacles as well as the local routes taken by their people for centuries over the mountains. Hannibal had been advised by the Celts about the short montane summer at high altitude. He knew that the mountain passes would be covered in deep snow by autumn and that weather in the towering mountains was far from predictable. Having distributed silver to his Celtic allies, promising them much more loot, and gathering as much information as he could from scouts, spies, and allies, Hannibal began to move as quickly as possible toward the Rhône.

HANNIBAL'S USE OF SPIES AND
INTELLIGENCE GATHERING

While nearly all commentators praise or admire Hannibal's tactics of surprise, many fail to appreciate his superb use of intelligence gathering and espionage that helped secure his victories. In some ways, he set precedents in the ancient world.[9] Polybius says that Hannibal did not go uninformed over the Alps but carefully sought reliable information from Celts and other sources.[10] Hannibal employed many scouts and advance reconnaissance, as Polybius mentions frequently. Livy cites a Carthaginian spy who worked for two years in Rome itself before being caught. His punishment was to have his hands cut off.[11] Some of Hannibal's spies spoke Latin like natives, from long-term contact with Romans. He also used speakers of other languages, possibly Etruscans (from modern-day Tuscany and Umbria) and other Italians who were naturally wary of Rome. He must have employed local wagoners and carters, Etruscan metalworkers, craftsmen, and food suppliers, and possibly had more than a few moles among the Roman allies. He might even have had a bevy of camp followers—often foreign women—who used "pillow talk" to extract information from Romans. How information got back to Hannibal is impossible to say, since it was intended to be secretive, but it must have worked sufficiently well. And he was probably not squeamish about using some form of torture to extract information.

Both Polybius and Livy say that Hannibal often used disguises and wore different wigs and costumes for different occasions but mostly for concealment—so much that "even his familiars found difficulty in recognizing him."[12] Hannibal was so much like the "cunning" Odysseus, whom he certainly knew about. Some of Hannibal's deliberate models were readily found in Greek legend and literature. As long as he had the financial resources, Hannibal paid in silver, although he had to be careful that his Carthaginian money was not traceable to his enemies.

But now it was time to cross the Rhône.

Six

CROSSING THE RHÔNE

The most obvious reason Hannibal did not follow the Mediterranean coast to Italy is that the Alpes-Maritimes mountains stretch south almost to the modern Riviera, a route fully controlled by Rome. Here on the east mouth of the Rhône River lie Massilia (Marseilles) and Nicaea (Nice); Massilia commanded the only relatively flat ground to the west of the highland coast. The many towns and outposts loyal to Rome along the coast would have contested any passage through this territory. Hannibal certainly knew that taking this traditional route would have meant fighting all the way with fully engaged armies.

Hannibal skirted the marshy wetlands and salt lakes (*étangs*) on his right by staying close to the Rhône Valley's western low plateau, but he also veered away from any territory on the eastern Rhône mouth controlled by Massilia, hoping to stay clear of Massilian informants and spies who would report to Rome. He moved as quickly as possible by uneasy tribes such as the Volcae, which were on both sides of the Rhône River Valley. It was probably the end of August, and local crops would have been mostly harvested.

Despite the wide meanderings of this great river and intermittent Celtic farming on both sides above modern Fourques and the waterlogged Camargue, the vegetation changes from marsh to forest. At this time, deciduous trees such as poplars would have grown probably within a hundred meters of the riverbank at many places. If Hannibal's army had sought such forest cover while marching northeast, at the gain of disguising his movements, the risk was that it would have slowed him considerably.

Hannibal wasn't altogether successful in keeping his march secret, as word did make it to both Massilia and beyond to the Romans, but he still kept his enemies guessing due to his relative speed. It is likely that at about the same time that Hannibal arrived on the west bank of the Rhône, Cornelius Scipio's Roman fleet arrived at Massilia. The fleet had sailed for at least a week from Etruria and Liguria (the region around modern Genoa) with an army on board to try to stop Hannibal from traveling east along the Mediterranean coast, the usual route connecting Gaul and Italy.

The south-flowing Rhône made a major forking near a Celtic hamlet that would eventually become modern Arles (Roman Arelate), flooding into the swampy delta with western and eastern branches. As the army approached the river itself, Hannibal had to take decisive action, moving quickly because of some Celtic resistance and the likelihood that Rome would try to cut him off. At the same time, the swamplands near the mouth of the Rhône that separated Hannibal and Roman Massilia were so difficult to traverse and so sparsely populated that Hannibal could expect some lag time in his movements being relayed to the Romans. Cornelius Scipio consulted his tribunes (high military officers) after hearing that Hannibal was approaching the Rhône—unexpected since the Romans thought the enemy army would be literally bogged down by the marshy terrain and Celtic resistance—and decided to send out a cavalry group of three hundred to locate Hannibal as soon as possible. That maneuver, too, would also be difficult given the Camargue marshes.

Here Hannibal would need a major logistics breakthrough in crossing the Rhône. He would need not only a place to ford the river but also an area where he could muster enough boats and garner assistance from locals to bring the volume of soldiers and animals with as much speed and safety as possible, especially since his own spies were probably aware of the arrival of the Roman fleet at Massilia.

HANNIBAL READIES HIS CROSSING OF THE RHÔNE

Because it was late summer, the mostly shallow river was at its lowest ebb, but it was still likely several hundred yards across, with the strongest current in the center of the channel. Hannibal's army began massing on the west bank of the Rhône, most likely somewhere within a few miles of Avignon, where the river was a "single channel," as Polybius says, "four days march from the sea."[1] Hannibal used a combination of bribery and force to sequester existing boats and facilitate quick construction of new rafts needed to transport an army. While most of the hostile clans of the Volcae tribe—which generally profited from controlling river transport here— massed together on the eastern bank of the Rhône, enough of the tribes on the western bank accommodated Hannibal's army by selling their boats and canoes and aiding Hannibal's carpenters:

> Hannibal bought every one of their canoes and boats, amounting to a considerable number, since many of the people along the Rhône engage in water transport. He also acquired from them suitable volume of logs to construct more canoes so that in two days he had an almost countless quantity of ferrying craft, aided by the fact that as many as possible among his own forces worked without stopping to get across the river.[2]

Several motives underlie Hannibal's acquisition of all the Celtic boats and available timber. The obvious reason is that he would need this quantity to get his force across; the less obvious reason may be that he wished to leave none in the hands of the Volcae and other tribes should they turn against him, always a possibility once the local people had been bribed rather than cooperate freely.

But for whatever reason, the bulk of the Volcae Celts gathered on the opposite Rhône bank now tried to stop Hannibal's army from crossing the river. Hannibal considered all his options. Although he could not force a vulnerable crossing with a massed Celtic attack waiting, he decided he could not afford to wait. Rather than risk having more Volcae and other Celts gather on the eastern bank and perhaps even on both banks of the Rhône, he made a brilliant move.

HANNIBAL SENDS HANNO UPRIVER AND
ACROSS WITH SMOKE SIGNALS

On the third day beside the Rhône, Hannibal sent north a portion of his most mobile infantry and Numidian cavalry, with reliable Celts as guides. He dispatched all of them, most likely under cover of darkness, under the leadership of his relative Hanno, son of Bomilcar. They were to move quickly upriver on the western side and cross the Rhône at the shallowest fording place (probably at present-day Pont-St.-Esprit) with improvised boats—in this case, where the river is divided—and hide in a natural strong place for a day or two until the time was right. On the fifth night, they were to move stealthily south along the east bank, always just beyond the scouting range of the massed Volcae.

Hannibal was ready to cross but waited for a prearranged smoke signal from Hanno and his forces on the eastern bank when they were within quick striking distance of the Volcae at the river. It was not yet dawn, and Hannibal had the boats filled, starting with heaviest boats on the north wing and the lighter boats on the south wing. As soon as the sky lightened to the east, Hannibal coordinated his scouts to watch for the smoke signal to the north announcing that his ambush across the river was advancing. When the signal came, Hannibal timed his order that sounded out in relays along the bank. Boats set off at once into the weakest current along the bank, with the heavier craft upriver absorbing some of the force.

Voices of the opposing Volcae Celts could be heard across the river as they waited, brandishing their weapons, no doubt some of them howling their war cries that history has recorded as blood-curdling. Relishing the opportunity for what they thought would be fairly easy prey, working themselves up to their bravest raucousness, the Celts rushed to the river's edge. Their first barrage of spears would have sailed some fifty yards into the water, mostly as a warning of what would be coming as the boats approached. Their arrows carried farther, but the crossing army would have shields up to absorb or deflect missiles. Many of the boats were slowed by towing horses behind them, as three or even four cavalry steeds were bridled uncomfortably and roped to boats, half swimming but also caught in the river flow and no doubt frantic. Even one awkward crossing would have taken upward of twenty minutes in the current for the vulnerable army to be within distance of Celtic projectiles. The river-bound army would have tried as much as possible to stay together and land en masse to present a continuous battle front along the river. The cacophony on both sides of the river must have been striking as Carthaginians shouted encouragement, matched by Celtic fervor.

Hannibal's timing was apparently perfect. Just as the waiting Celts watched their expected prey, a sudden disarray erupted at the back of the Volcae force. Hanno's ambuscade had reached and set fire to their camp. Now the Celts realized that they were fighting the force coming from the river and another coming from behind, something they had not anticipated. This fearful discovery sent them into a panic.

HANNIBAL'S ARMY CROSSES THE RHÔNE

Hannibal must have crossed with the very first group of invaders because he immediately led his disciplined men with exhortations to meet the panicking Celts, many of whom were first looking forward and then looking backward. It was too much for the surprised Celts, who mostly turned and fled from Hannibal's tightly advancing veterans. Hannibal set himself to bring over the rest of his infantry and cavalry as soon as it was feasible, and within short order, this was accomplished with little resistance from the Volcae, who retreated far from his army. That night, Hannibal's army camped not far from the river on the east bank, with posted sentries watching for any Volcae who might sneak up on the camp and wreak havoc, although they did not bother him again.[3] Early the next morning, Hannibal confirmed the report that the Romans were at Massilia and dispatched five hundred cavalry to reconnoiter the situation from a safe distance.

THE ELEPHANTS CROSS THE RIVER

Hannibal apparently now had at least thirty-seven war elephants on the journey, brought all the way from Carthage when young and trained in Spain. In order to transport them, engineers had to create connected double rafts that looked almost like floating bridges. These constructions were secured by ropes tied to trees on both banks. Smaller rafts were lined up and linked by ropes and tow lines to the "bridge" until nearly the whole river width was covered except for the exact center, where the many small rafts would travel back and forth. The elephants were fairly manageable until on the small rafts, when the beasts perceived they were actually floating on an unstable water surface. Many elephants stampeded at this point, and their mahouts (trained men who rode or guided them) were thrown off and into the river, where a considerable number drowned in the melee. The elephants, however, did manage to put their feet down in the shallow places or even swam in a lumbering fashion. If the water was too deep for them, they held their trunks over the river surface while their heads were mostly underwater, and in this manner, many elephants "snorkeled" across the river. Not one elephant was reported lost, according to Polybius' text, which must have derived from an eyewitness account.[4]

MEETING CELTIC TRIBES FROM ITALY
AND ROMANS IN A GAUL SKIRMISH

Polybius reports two other important events about this time. The first is that the friendly Celts of Italy, led by Magilus (or Magol) of the Boii tribe (near Bologna), met on the Rhône's east bank with Hannibal and his officers, encouraging the army with their alliance and explaining what to expect from the more capricious Celts en route. Hannibal's army was particularly impressed and heartened by seeing Celts from distant lands who were on their side.[5] The second event was that Hannibal's scouting party of Numidian cavalry returned.[6] It happened that Cornelius Scipio had also sent out a reconnoitering force of cavalry to look for Hannibal's army, and the two enemy groups of horsemen actually ran into each other, either by accident or design. A deadly skirmish ensued, with the Carthaginians losing about 200 men, and the Romans and Massilians losing about 140. But this wetland clash slightly to the south in the Camargue had actually aided Hannibal's Rhône crossing by delaying the Roman contingent. By the time the Roman cavalry whirled back south to give an account to Scipio, Hannibal was already across the Rhône and marching north. Scipio gave chase with his army and found the abandoned camp, but the ashes of Carthaginian campfires were long cold.[7] To the Romans' great consternation, the first of many, Hannibal's army had disappeared completely.

The question is often asked why Hannibal avoided fighting the Romans here in Gaul. Hoyos suggests one reasonable answer: Hannibal was aiming to make as many allies of Celts as possible, whether disaffected with Rome or not. "Fighting the Romans in Gallic territory, even if he won the Gauls as allies or kept them neutral, was not a scheme likely to please people whose lands would bear the brunt."[8]

HANNIBAL'S ARMY MOVES NORTH

Moving north through upper Provence into the Drôme region, Hannibal could at times see the Alpes-Maritimes to the East. While the topography along the Rhône is mostly low here, Hannibal's scouts and his Celtic guides could ascertain the mountains' presence even when not visible by the cumulonimbus storm clouds that often rose above them. Cornelius Scipio did not rush off after Hannibal, of whose craftiness the Roman was now thoroughly persuaded.

Cornelius Scipio pondered the possibilities and deduced accurately that Hannibal was going north to avoid Massilia and the coastal route, attempting instead a most implausible ascent of the Alps. Hannibal would be trying to reach Italy by a route that not even a war veteran like Scipio would have predicted. Cornelius Scipio's Celtic allies affirmed that while such a tactic would be possible, it would be difficult this time of year, and neither he nor Hannibal should attempt it. Cornelius Scipio hastily sent his brother Gnaeus Scipio to Spain with half an army to disrupt the Carthaginian supply route and subdue Celtiberians or persuade them even by force to side with the Romans. Cornelius Scipio then wasted no time in setting sail back to Italy to meet Hannibal's army when and where it emerged from the fearsome Alps—if it emerged at all. We can wonder if, in addition to the Roman control of the coastal route, Hannibal was also predisposed to going over the Alps because his god—after whom he was named—was a god of mountains and storms.

Seven

GATEWAY TO THE ALPS

After turning north with his army column into the gradually narrowing Rhône Valley, Hannibal left behind sunny Provence. By the time the path through Gaul approached modern Montélimar on the Rhône, the distant jagged peaks of the Alps could be glimpsed from time to time eastward, especially up the Val Drôme where the Drôme River comes in. During the four-day march, Hannibal encountered little resistance from the Celts, but this does not mean that they were not watching his progress carefully. If anything, these Celts were not interested in delaying a hungry army that would overrun their farms, deplete their resources, or worse.[1] Hannibal may have purchased food provisions from time to time, distributing some Punic silver rather than risk a fight from bands of gathering Celtic warriors. He did not want anything to slow his progress by now.

September had come, and the leaves of deciduous trees that had been turning golden yellow were accompanied by increasingly cooler nights. Fall winds began to strip the trees, and more and more bare branches showed along the way. Stream waters to be crossed, however depleted by decreased runoff, were now considerably colder than when the army had started in Spain's summer.

The army paused in a low and fertile plain that formed a vast triangle where the fast Isère flows into the Rhône from the east.[2] This river junction was the traditional tribal boundary of the populous Allobroges for centuries[3] and in 125 BCE Romans would confront a combined army of Allobroges and Arveni from the Central Massif. Hannibal's army now encountered the Allobroges, the largest Celtic tribe yet, one whose territory stretched much of the way along the Rhône north of the Isère. One center of the Allobroges was near what would become Geneva, Switzerland; another was near modern Grenoble.[4] This part of Gaul between the Rhône and the Isère was most likely the delta region Polybius called "the Island."[5] Immediately to the east of the Rhône and south of the Isère, the Pre-Alps massifs begin to ascend to the northeast.[6] The Alpine pass route and the ultimate summit that follows—not the only reasonable possibility for the march—nonetheless aptly fit the difficult terrain and challenging high altitude for the conditions Hannibal's army encountered, according to Polybius.

HANNIBAL INTERCEDES IN A CHIEFLY DISPUTE

At this time, two chieftain brothers had a leadership dispute about which of them should be the king. Apparently only the eldest brother cautiously sent a peaceful delegation to meet Hannibal, making a personal overture to him to assist in placing him on the throne. Whether the younger brother also reached out is unknown, as Polybius does not say. But Hannibal agreed to this apparently sensible request: by a show of force, he drove away any supporters of the younger brother who were present.

In visible gratitude, the new chief of the Isère lowland plain supplied Hannibal's army with much-needed provisions of ample food, fresher weapons, and warmer clothing for the journey approaching colder weather, including thick leather shoes.[7] Hannibal's army was also grateful for an armed guard from the chief marching at its rear.

This eastward passage of the army along the Isère traversed some of the richest farm country in Gaul, with farms that were also plentiful in cattle. Harvests were stored in the Celts' wooden barns. Nearly all farming had stopped for the fall, as the last edible tubers and roots were dug out of the ground and stored carefully in cellars. Because this is fertile land, the elder brother could afford to sell to Hannibal or give him ample surplus agricultural bounty. Not so the brother to the east, whose territory lay within the mountain valleys, a far more rugged land.

On the south side of the Isère River, the brooding massifs approach closer and closer in the formidable, thickly wooded Vercors Pre-Alps that rise nearly vertical only a few miles from the river canyon. About this land, Polybius commented, "[H]ere the baseline is formed by a range of mountains difficult to climb and, one may say, almost inaccessible."[8] The impenetrability of the Vercor massifs was borne out during World War II, when the famously tenacious Vercor French Resistance proved impossible for the Germans and the Vichy government to root out. This was the mountain territory of the other Allobroges brother. Hannibal may have second-guessed his earlier decision, but it was too late if he wanted to advance eastward here.

GATEWAY TO THE ALPS

Just to the north, outside of modern Grenoble, are the twin bluffs of the towering "Gateway to the Alps," where the Isère River bursts through the mountains from narrow valleys upriver.[9] The Vercors Massif rises on the southwest, and the Chartreuse Massif rises on the northeast side of the narrow Isère. Rising abruptly on average more than two thousand spectacular feet from the river canyon that is just under six hundred feet in elevation, these massif ridges look literally like a huge broken wall. Here the Isère River pours out of the mountains.

This is the narrowest canyon of the lower Isère. The only easy passage is squeezed into an alluvial valley, full of sediment from floods, alongside the river: an opening no wider than three-quarters of a mile and shared by the river. Anyone would have sensed danger here—especially the acutely pragmatic Hannibal—and trouble was not long in coming. Unfortunately for the Carthaginians, their lowland Allobroges allies would go no farther and returned homeward.[10] They knew Hannibal's predicament and knew also how they themselves would be received here by their now-aggrieved kinsmen.

THE FIRST AMBUSH SITE

Control of this natural gateway lay completely in the hands of the mountain Allobroges, who may have had their fortress just above modern Voreppe, one plausible ambush place that fits what Polybius tells us. It had ample watch points along the ridge from which one could view any movement in all directions along the valley below.[11] The only feasible pathway lay imme-diately under their noses at the base of the bluff plateau on the north side of the Isère Valley. Hannibal's scouts reported back to him that this pathway was not only watched by armed men above but also that they made clear their intentions that they would oppose his army's passage.

However, Hannibal's Celtic guides also informed him that the Allo-broges had left their vantage posts and gone to their fort and nearby homes for the night, thinking Hannibal would not possibly advance after dark. A night sally by anyone, especially strangers unfamiliar with the steep terrain, would be completely unconventional. Hannibal, however, was always un-conventional, as the Romans would also discover to their misfortune. He carefully set his plan to foil the Allobroges at their own game of launching an ambush from higher ground. One wonders how much Hannibal had learned about raids and ambushes from the Celtiberians in Spain as well as in Gaul, where opportunistic Celtic raids were a common maneuver.[12] Hannibal would later employ similar raids and ambushes on the Romans with great success.

Hannibal left the bulk of his army camped below with their fires burn-ing as usual to lull the enemy and formed a contingent of his best men, which he led himself to climb up to the narrowest path and take over the Celts' watch posts by night. Leading the way always endeared him to his soldiers, who saw that he took the same risks they did. They recognized that he would not order anyone to do what he was unwilling to attempt himself. Hannibal's men took over every one of the Allobroges' watch points above the guarded road.

Daylight came, and the surprised Allobroges found that all of their control points were occupied by Hannibal's men. They probably would have given up had they not seen that Hannibal's long train of soldiers, who had to march in narrow file due to the terrain was accompanied by pack animals carrying the greatest amount of supplies they had ever imagined, laden and crawling slowly along the valley. This veritable cornucopia of an army's provisions overcame the Allobroges' initial hesitance over being outsmarted. They rushed en masse from their fortress—a typical Celtic battle maneuver of "all or nothing" in a headlong "frenzied assault" as Stephen Allen puts it[13]—to attack the long column exactly where the pack animals were thickest and least protected by soldiers. It was pandemonium for the narrowly constricted army, usually disciplined but nearly trapped here.

Even though Hannibal expected something like this, the ambush was horrible at first for his army, as many animals and men were casualties of both the Allobroges marauders and the steep path. Wounded army horses rushed pell-mell in both directions up and down the path and knocked many other pack animals off the route into the dense shrubbery on the steep hillside where the Celts stripped them of their goods and killed their drivers.

Alerted by the screams of men and animals, Hannibal realized that he could lose his entire provisions. He brought back all his men who had been guarding the route from higher ground above. Some were sent down into the Celts, many of whom scattered with their stolen goods, while other warriors were ordered to the head of his column, where the fighting was fiercest. Although he soon routed the Allobroges, his soldiers chasing them in all directions into the woods, it was at some material cost. Hannibal lost quite a few men and animals. A lot more pack animals laden with supplies were unaccounted for at first, having fled in terror. However, his men slowly collected them, and his army resumed its march over the most dangerous narrows until all emerged in the broader Isère river valley under the high ridges.

But Hannibal also took the nearly empty Celtic fort, since its Allobroges inhabitants had fled to the surrounding countryside, and here he not only recovered the remainder of his pack animals that had not been butchered in the battle but also took all the food supplies that the Allobroges had harvested for the coming winter. In addition, he took their abandoned cattle, which they normally kept within their walls when under siege or at war. The Celts' reports of Hannibal's success and the losses of the Allobroges were such an effective propaganda tool that none of the other tribes dared attack Hannibal's army as they wound their way up into the mountains.

MARCH TO THE MOUNTAINS

Hannibal seems to have turned away from the Isère and instead would have followed the ancient established Maurienne trade route of the Celts in the Arc River Valley—another demarcation point of different Celtic mountain tribes, as is true of so many Alps watersheds. His scouts must have informed him of this historic route. As the news about the Allobroges' losses spread to successive Celtic hamlets and towns, no one harassed the army for four days,[14] although these smaller tribes must have looked longingly at the uncountable wealth slowly passing by in both animals and the piled goods they carried.

The autumn weather in the mountains was turning increasingly cold. Darkening clouds now heavy with freezing rain, hail, and even sleet forced the army to slog over ground that was frost covered when they woke in the morning. It was now moving toward late October, and when the clouds lifted, the men crowded together around campfires could see that the mountain peaks above the tree lines were white with heavy snow. Every soldier and Hannibal himself must have wondered at night how much farther the army had to go and how high the army had to ascend to reach the frontier of Italy. But Hannibal quietly inspired his men by his own sacrifices. Instead of demanding special comforts befitting his rank as Carthaginian nobility and their general, Hannibal slept humbly on the hard ground just like his tough soldiers, wrapped only in a few heavy blankets. This fact—possibly intended to emulate a young Alexander the Great—would be remembered forever by his and other armies and later recorded by his duly impressed enemies. Everything Hannibal did had at least one strategic purpose and likely was layered with deeper intent to breed loyalty. But this quality would soon be tested in the high Alps towering just above the army.

Eight

THE SECOND AMBUSH

Hannibal was never a forgiving enemy. He hauled away more than a few Celts in chains as a harsh lesson, but his army did not stay long in the Allobroges area. Picking up the pace again after a day of counting forces, tending the wounded, reorganizing scattered supplies, and reconnoitering the way ahead, Hannibal relentlessly marched his army onward along the Arc River Valley for four consecutive days. At first, the going was relatively easy, as the wide valley was still sufficiently flat for a few ranks of soldiers and pack animals to walk side by side. The elephants still had plenty of fodder and enough plants alongside the river even in late autumn, but early winter would strain the fodder resource.

HANNIBAL'S PREPARATION FOR THE MOUNTAINS

Reflecting on what Hannibal knew in advance of his long, intrepid march to Italy and why he would attack it in the first place, Polybius makes it abundantly clear that Hannibal had long studied this problem while still in Spain, seeking added wise counsel of allied tribes such as the Boii in Italy:

"He had informed himself accurately about the fertility of the land at the foot of the Alps and near the river Po, the denseness of its population, the bravery of the men in war, and above all their hatred of Rome ever since that former war with the Romans."[1]

Polybius, too, scoffed at those who said Hannibal was unprepared for the daunting Alpine journey, saying that the general knew about earlier Alpine passages by Celtic armies and had good intelligence about possible routes.[2] Polybius also maintained that Hannibal knew it was "toilsome and difficult but not at all impossible."[3] Hannibal trusted the hatred of Rome by the Boii Celts and others like them on the other side of the Alps to make the mountain crossing worthwhile. He anticipated their assistance when he emerged from the mountains. It was the Romans who were surprised, partly because they were mainly flatlanders and a farming culture less inclined to mountains, hoping in vain that the Alps would shield them like a wall. But by now, the Romans knew Hannibal was coming and futilely tried to anticipate where he would exit from the Alps.

The Romans' general lack of knowledge of the Alps was exacerbated by the fact they had almost no discernible allies in the mountains who could report back to them. The Romans deployed mainly around Placentia in the Po Valley, far enough from the Alps to wait for Hannibal to reappear from the west.

Where exactly Hannibal crossed the Alps remains unknown in the absence of sufficient archaeological evidence.[4] Regardless of which pass Hannibal ultimately used on the alpine approach, the nights grew colder and colder for Hannibal's army as the valley narrowed and their gradient changed. The army had to cover itself with warmer clothes and leathers or skins of whatever they could find. Feet had to be wrapped in thicker skins to keep out the seeping frigid dampness of the ground.

The most likely Celtic tribes in the Arc River Valley area were the Medulli, a fiercely territorial people probably headquartered in the

Maurienne region near the modern town of St.-Jean-de-Maurienne, near where at least four vital montane passes debouched into the same Arc Valley.

As the tribal lands changed and became unfamiliar to Celts allied with Hannibal, the danger grew that he could be led into a trap. Here Hannibal exerted great discipline over his army and his scouts. He sent reconnoitering guides a day ahead in small groups, likely pairing Celts with his trusted scouts in order to verify information and topographic detail. If he suspected any danger or duplicity in their reports, he would grill the Celts face-to-face, closely watching their eyes and body language.

There is little doubt that Hannibal would have quickly punished false information with death, likely preceded by torture, both as a warning and to elicit further information that could be tested. An experienced military leader like Hannibal had little tolerance for anything but straightforward answers or honest uncertainty. Much has been made of Hannibal's psychological probity in reading people, especially enemies, and he certainly would have also relied on wise counsel as well as the most trusted translators in planning each day's journey in terms of where to stop at night, as well as allocating supplies and acquiring food for an army, always a demanding task, made even more complicated by voracious elephants.

THE LOGISTICAL PROBLEMS OF
AN ARMY'S FOOD SUPPLY

Unless quartermasters (supply officers) and pursers (accounts officers) are buying food from locals, and unless active hunters and foragers are constantly reserving food supplies and rations dispersal is well organized, an army on the move is a logistical supply nightmare. It can consume far more than the pack animals can carry from considerable distances. This is ultimately a daily battle of a totally different nature. That Hannibal faced this worrisome conundrum on a daily basis through the Alpine passage was compounded by the fact that winter was fast approaching and food sources were diminishing. Only the most farsighted leader can pull off what

Hannibal must have accomplished. And even then, his army suffered devastating losses that would be unacceptable in modern warfare.

Along the way upriver early on the fourth day since the first ambush, according to Polybius,[5] one group of treacherous mountain Celts pretended to bring Hannibal gifts and wreaths as a signal of peace. They claimed to know about the recent Allobroges humiliation. Their chiefs even offered cattle and hostages, but they may have been just as easily counting spears and mules and opportunities. Polybius says it was clearly a Celtic conspiracy but that Hannibal was also more than a little suspicious of their intentions. Ultimately, he trusted his honed military instincts and wasn't fooled by their sycophantic behavior. From years of experience in Spanish Celtiberian cultures, Hannibal knew that an attack could come during the day any time now. He set out his sentries and pickets at night, sure that the cover of darkness would nonetheless be too difficult even for the local Celts, who were almost certainly looking at the hundreds of campfires of the army as they waited for just the right place to attack.

If Hannibal's route was through the Arc Valley, he would have to cross the Arc River somewhere soon. Wary watchers and scouts in the hill forts of the Medulli above the valley had perfect views of the army now beginning to struggle much more slowly, as the ascent grew steep. It is likely that the army moved along the northern plateau along the valley toward Aussois,[6] which was the Celtic pathway and afforded a wider column until one had to descend to cross the Arc River at the shallowest fording. Celtic sentries would have seen the army coming, and there are several isolated rocky buttes that have yielded Iron Age finds, most likely from Medulli Celts.[7]

Even if substantial reports had reached the Medulli of how Hannibal had punished the Allobroges, the temptation of so many pack animals laden with food plodding along in single file must have promised easy pickings for these mountain Celts, whose own food resources and animals would be challenged by the coming winter.

Hannibal himself would not have missed seeing the occasional stubble of long-harvested fields in the narrow valleys as they passed a few rustic and small mountain hamlets. He would have seen occasional thin columns of smoke rising over the forest from cooking fires in higher hamlets. He knew there was a sizable highland population living here—large enough to amass a fierce battle force—and if few locals came out to greet him, Hannibal knew it was because of hostility among the mountain Celts.

Infrequent sounds of crashing branches at the margin of the forest heard by the passing army would have been animals such as foraging wild boars, not frightened Celts. Livy, more interested in color than Polybius, gives just the sort of expected cinematic embellishment to this part of the ascent from the point of view of the army: "The dreadful vision was now before their eyes: the towering peaks, the snowclad pinnacles soaring to the sky, the rude huts clinging to the rocks, the people with their wild and ragged hair, stiff with frost."[8]

Hannibal was duly apprehensive, according to Polybius, sensing the danger and the sudden absence of genuine friendly Celtic contact. He carefully separated his forces, especially placing his pack animal train and cavalry at the front of the long column and his heavy infantry at the rear. Polybius claims the army would have been destroyed completely if Hannibal had not done exactly as he did.

THE SECOND CELTIC AMBUSH IN THE MOUNTAINS

Two days later, the attack struck just as the army was preparing for the hardest ascent yet on the following day near the Arc River crossing. The army was slowly traversing the base of a steep, rocky canyon that Polybius calls *leukopetron*, or the "white rock place."[9] This stunning white gorge of the modern-day French village of Bramans stands out dramatically against the trees around it, its exfoliating dolomite and gypsum anticline (a geologic arch bending upward in mountains) a major landmark for thousands of years.[10] While "white rock" places above tree lines are too numerous in the Alps to count, this location commends itself highly because it is framed by dark forest and lies only one day from a summit connecting a major alpine route between Gaul and Italia.

Here at Bramans—if this is the right place—the knots of invisible Celts hidden just at the tree line suddenly unleashed their ambush from above, rolling boulders down or hurling rocks. Volleys of arrows rained down as well. Pandemonium took over amid the clamor from animals and shouts of Hannibal's army trying to bring order in this tight place where echoes magnified the din of screams and crashing rocks.

When the Celts, who knew this terrain well, assembled quickly from the nearby forest, attacking Hannibal's rear in a bristling wave of force, the trained heavy infantry placed there by Hannibal mostly met this immediate challenge. But nearest to the front, a majority of the pack animals and many men were crushed by rocks, and their mangled supplies were scattered or damaged. They became useless except to scavengers. Terrified horses reared and threw their riders as the rocks and boulders fell around them. The screams of maimed men and dying animals reverberated across the gorge. Perhaps only the elephants seemed relatively unscathed, as the Celts were afraid of these strange animals and may have stayed as far as possible from them.

With so many broken men dying, Hannibal's army appeared doomed. The Celts were sure they had bottled up the intruders when darkness fell and much of the battered army had to spend a most uncomfortable night in this gorge, the darkness punctuated by moans of wounded and dying men and animals. The rest of the army may have retreated back down the valley away from the gorge. Whether or not Hannibal was led into a trap here at Bramans by duplicitous guides is not known, and Polybius does not confirm it, but it is not unlikely. Livy claims that there was "deliberate deception" among some of the guides.[11]

But the Celts who staged the ambush, however fierce, were unaware of how quickly a trained army can respond. They made a grave mistake, similar to the Allobroges before them, completely underestimating this wily general with an uncanny ability to outsmart his enemies. Thinking Hannibal was trapped and immobilized in the gorge, the Celts apparently went home for the night to rest, relishing the fruit of their ambush waiting for daylight.

HANNIBAL ESCAPES THE GORGE

But the fast-thinking Hannibal had already planned his next move. The most likely scenario is that after sending trained stealthy assassins to circle around in the dark and slit the throats of the few guards left at the valley mouth, Hannibal waited only for the earliest light of dawn and moved his men as fast as possible over the rocks until they slipped away and the rest of the army rejoined him. If the ambush indeed took place at the Bramans Gorge, the most logical escape route would have been to ascend eastward out of the gorge rather than continuing north along the Arc Valley— occupied by the Celtic villagers, who could be mobilized to block an army's progress in such increasingly narrow places.

Imagine the shock of the Celts who returned excitedly early the next morning only to find the trapped army had escaped. They saw with acute disappointment the stripped bodies of the dead left behind along with the dead pack animals and useless food supplies scattered about the rocks and the streambed. The largest prize they had ever witnessed had slipped through their fingers, and they returned glumly to their villages after salvaging what they could of the supplies.

These Celts realized the element of surprise was gone and knew the rest of Hannibal's army had caught up. Hannibal was not yet out of danger, however, as he now had to confront the steepest part of the ascent. The spectacular alpine peaks towered above his men as they slowly climbed up a path alongside rushing streams and crashing waterfalls over huge rocks, and hemmed in by pine and larch trees. The newly wounded began to drop back behind the main body, gasping for breath as they climbed. Everyone in the shattered army could now see fresh snow on the heights above them, with huge expanses of ice on the highest peaks.

But the greatest burden Hannibal now faced was how to feed his army after having lost almost all his food train and with so few pack animals left. Many of the remaining animals would probably have to be slaughtered soon, since they now carried next to nothing except firewood picked up through the forest along the way. Even the three dozen or so lumbering elephants would have voiced their hunger; their occasional trumpeting echoing in the ascending valley when they couldn't find much grass between the rocks—what little that could grow in this cold place. Other historians have also posed the difficulty of elephants foraging in higher montane elevations, especially since they would need to consume a minimum of a hundred pounds per day to stay alive, a huge problem near an alpine summit if this sojourn took several days.[12]

BAD ADVICE TO HAUNT HANNIBAL

A gruesome tale fueled by some later Romans, although much debated and mostly dismissed, is that even before his alpine march, Hannibal was purportedly told to consider cannibalism of his soldiers who would die of starvation. This possibility was supposedly presented by a counselor named Hannibal Monomachos in the Carthaginian war council. The fact that Polybius discusses it[13] gave it added credibility, but it seems almost certain that Hannibal never actually resorted to it, because Polybius never comments on its implementation, instead stating that Hannibal could never persuade himself to practice cannibalism. Given the later exaggerated reputation of Hannibal for cruelty, such Roman propaganda is not surprising.[14]

Once Hannibal's army hit the wind-swept tree line, where only a few blizzard-blasted scrub trees clung to the rocks, only thin air and the jagged stone of surrounding cliffs met the eye. The cold valley trail wound higher and higher. The tiring army gasped for breath, and the elephants, surely, nervous at such a different, barren landscape, could be answered by a different chilling sound: gathering Alpine wolves howling to one another as they sensed death coming for some of the falling stragglers being left farther behind. Everyone would soon know deep and debilitating hunger. Aware that his battered army could not last long in these circumstances, Hannibal pushed onward at the front of the beleaguered army as fast as possible to the snow-whitened summit ahead.

Nine

SUMMIT OF THE ALPS

Ascending the high valley where jagged peaks loomed above, Hannibal and his exhausted men arrived at the summit of the Alps, where tough inclement weather is the norm and where there would be little fodder for animals.[1] Polybius said it was the highest pass of the Alps, which, of course, means the highest known to the Romans at the time, not the highest known today.[2] In early November Hannibal's army would have already crossed above that elevation where snow had covered the ground surface. Polybius writes:

"After an ascent of nine days, Hannibal reached the summit, and encamping there remained for two days to rest the survivors of his army and wait for stragglers . . . As it was now close on the setting of the Pleiades, snow had already gathered on the summit."[3]

In recording the time of year by the "setting of the *Pleiades*," a famous, highly visible cluster of seven stars marking the night calendar, Polybius refers to a time from late October though early November. In the deep shadow of overhanging peaks or facing north, where the sun barely reaches under high crags, the snow has already begun to drift and will often last year long above eight thousand feet. Streams shrunken by the gradual depletion of snowmelt at this time of year would have frozen over as water stopped flowing.

DEARTH OF MATERIAL ARTIFACTS ALONG HANNIBAL'S ALPINE ROUTE

One of the reasons that Hannibal's exact route is so contentious is the lack of artifacts. But this dearth can be explained. Anyone who died en route over the worst part of the Alpine ascent would be stripped almost immediately after he fell for the last time. It is conceivable that some of the fallen army hovering at consciousness would have found their approaching deaths accelerated by the knives of desperate comrades needing clothes. Anything of the remotest value whatsoever would be taken quickly.

Likewise, all coins, weapons, and traces of bronze or iron metal would have been taken from those too weak to defend themselves. There hardly would have been any attempt to bury the dead along these desolate paths, since the enormous effort required would have been too much in rocky, shallow soil. After Hannibal's army had descended, any Celtic marauders who braved the winter and scavenged the remains would have collected whatever little remained. Wolves would have disarticulated and carried away any bones for marrow.[4]

Even in remaining daylight, fires would be lit with the ever-present embers an army always carried in protected braziers, but at the altitude of probably no less than eight thousand feet,[5] the wood and tinder would take forever to light in the cold. Dampness made it worse, and if men's clothing were wet, the summit temperature that would now rarely rise above freezing could cloak their garments with ice even as they huddled in repeated paroxysms of chills around the many fires to survive. While moving, their metabolisms could stave off some of the cold, but when they finally arrived in the summit valley to camp, they would suddenly become painfully aware of the freezing temperature, most likely abysmally lower than many had ever faced.

According to Polybius, Hannibal's army camped at the summit under such trying conditions of cold, deprivation, and exhaustion that his men suffered severe depression. Polybius ascribes this collective state of mind and spirit to the enormous toll of the last two days following the second ambush, just as they were about to begin the final ascent at the most challenging part of the Alpine crossing.[6]

THE DEBATED VIEW FROM THE SUMMIT INTO ITALY

Hannibal made a concerted effort to raise the spirits of the army, leading his men to the dramatic precipice very close by at the edge of the summit camp possibly at the broad Clapier-Savine Coche saddle around 8,500 feet altitude with an immense vista when there are no clouds or fog to obscure the view. From this height, Italy opens up before the eyes of viewers, creating a spectacle of mountains dropping away in undulating waves to the plain of the Po Valley far below, especially from the south side of the Savine-Coche Valley, where humans have crossed since the Neolithic Age even with perennial snow traces here.

Livy gives us the extended text of a famous speech by Hannibal, but it is most likely an invention. Polybius on the other hand, gives us no such speech.[7] Livy even says that the hopelessness of utter exhaustion was written on the soldiers' faces, which was probably true, although Polybius doesn't record such an emotive detail. Polybius relates that Hannibal summoned his starving army to this meeting place at the summit in order to cheer them up. He showed them the plain of the Po below and reminded them of the friendly Celts who lived there, also pointing out the direction of Rome beyond the horizon. Polybius has Hannibal use a geographical simile, comparing a high acropolis fortress citadel (by the mountainous Alps) to a city on flatter ground below (Italy).[8] Polybius suggests this wise motivational moment worked partly, since the exhausted men could now clearly see exactly what he meant, and Hannibal's encouragement may have been reinforced by some of the Boii Celts who had been with them on the march since the Pyrenees so many months before.

THE DIFFICULT ALPINE DESCENT

Having waited three abysmal days to rest his fitful army in the freezing weather and to regather as many stragglers among men and animals that survived the ascent to the summit, Hannibal broke the Alpine camp and began the slow descent. Now he encountered a different challenge. As the steep eastern scarp into Italy is so vertical in many places, his army would have met with drop-offs and loose fallen rocks that were immensely dangerous, especially when covered by snow. Because a climber leans into an ascent but pitches forward in a descent, gravity can be an enemy going down, as force propels one too quickly. The Alps have a more severe slope on the eastern scarp into Italy.

Hannibal's army soon found itself stymied in one place by a fresh rock break-off and precipice, as mentioned in Polybius.[9] Footing was so much in jeopardy that Polybius says a time-consuming path had to be cleared.

LIVY'S FAMOUS BUT DUBIOUS VINEGAR ROCK-SPLITTING TALE

Livy adds here a very famous and fascinating but undocumented story, dismissed as fiction by most commentators. Trying to work through the fallen rock blocking the narrow path (Livy's later deviation from Polybius), the army engineers solved part of the problem with an "ingenious" method combining heat and liquid.[10] Cut timber was stacked against the impassable rock cliff and lit with difficulty at this altitude but aided by a strong wind. Then the heated rocks were soaked with "sour wine" (vinegar), a common army ration that rendered the rock more friable in combination with the heat. This method could work on some rocks, especially carbonate or similar rock if the natural fractures were thus expanded. As unusual as it seems, Livy's story is repeated after him by Ammianus Marcellinus and others, and has generated enormous speculation and comment for ages.[11]

Polybius does not mention this intriguing anecdote, stating only that after trying to detour around the break-off, the soldiers were set to work "to

build up a path along the cliff . . . a most toilsome task . . . so that [it took]
with great difficulty three days to get the elephants across but in a wretched
condition from hunger."[12] Livy states that large trees were felled—cut from
where?—while Polybius makes it clear they were still above the tree line: in
the Alps, generally just above 6,000 to 6,500 feet. Any trees growing at this
elevation would have been stunted.[13]

The terrible descent took three painful days[14] for the long army column
threading a narrow path, gradually leaving the boulder-strewn precipices
of the rockiest landscape and finally dropping into forest again and then
pasturage. The survivors likely couldn't move for days as they rested and
recouped strength from provisions in vegetation and hunted animals.

Polybius says that the descent was as costly in life as the ascent, and more
difficult.[15] It is likely that more lives were lost in the Alpine campaign to
natural dangers of mountainous precipices and slippery snow than to Celtic
attack or ambush. Accordingly, after starting out on the Alpine approach
with around thirty-eight thousand infantry and more than eight thousand
horses or cavalry, Hannibal lost almost half his army in the Alps. Such loss
of life would be unacceptable in modern warfare, seemingly so irresponsible
that any leader who did this would be sacked by his government.

But if Hannibal, far from any Carthaginian court of inquiry, was not
callous to such loss of provisions and men, he certainly was well aware of
what this meant in military terms. He knew that his task of attacking and
humbling the Romans was now all the more difficult. He would have to rely
heavily on allied Celts in Italy, a potential nightmare with their ever fickle
and ambiguous tribal loyalties. How much he communicated this to his
close circle of officers is unknown, but it is not unlikely this knowledge was
shared with his tired veterans who knew how many soldiers had perished
en route.

THE WRETCHED STATE OF HANNIBAL'S ARMY

Polybius also says gravely that at the end of their two weeks' time in the
Alps, these wretched human survivors of Hannibal's army were more like

animals than men in both appearance and condition, having been reduced to the bare minimum state of survival from starvation, frostbite, and utter exhaustion.[16] Here is where difficulties of food supply in winter could haunt an army most. Victualizing from spring to autumn was hard enough on the move, but in winter the risks are compounded.[17] Finally the army's near delirium from starvation and fear of imminent death was replaced with sleep and food, their troubled dreams giving way to glimmers of hope.

After restful days at the lower elevations, these soldiers would put their nightmare behind them as fast as they could. Now their feet were on soft flat turf again. Hannibal might have sacrificed in heartfelt thanks, possibly alone to his god Baal, the god of stormy mountains; perhaps even possibly wondering if the lives of his lost men were also sacrifices to this god who was as hard as the rock of his Alps.

Ten

TICINUS

After the fifteen days or so it took Hannibal and his army to cross the entire Alps from the foothills to the flat Po plain, time for much-needed recuperation was in order.[1] The soldiers must have understood that this journey was a one-way epic march. As commentators have shown, Hannibal's army would be unlikely ever to return. In Livy's words, Hannibal's speech to his men was blunt:

> "North and South, the sea hems you in. You have not a single ship even to escape in to save your lives. Facing you is the Po . . . Behind you is the Alpine barrier which even in the flower and freshness of your strength you almost failed to cross . . . You must conquer or die."[2]

Livy's words do not make Hannibal look hard-hearted but merely pragmatic. The inability to turn back was intended to make the army renew its will to fight harder. The only option was to win in its invasion of Italy because any other outcome was death. The soldiers had to take responsibility for their own survival, and the only way this could happen was to fight as a ruthless, organized battle unit that could not afford to be soft or merciful toward the Roman enemy.[3]

Polybius sums up the surviving forces after the Alps crossing as twelve thousand soldiers from Africa (Carthaginian, Libyan, Numidian, and so on) and eight thousand Spanish infantry along with six thousand cavalry, for a total of twenty-six thousand.[4] Historians have pointed out how pitifully small this invading force was, woefully inadequate to challenge Rome.[5] In order to bolster the size of his force, Hannibal would have to make a hugely favorable impression on the Celts, winning enough of them to confidently ally with him.

Now in his camp east of the Alps where the Po plains began, Hannibal could reassess his reunited and somewhat rested army. All the surviving stragglers were now caught up, and if Hannibal and his officers counted total losses, they must have been concerned about current troop strength.

Whether the survivors wondered about the fate of those who had dropped too far back—many falling victim to the skulking mountain Celts or the hungry wolves they had seen shadowing the gaunt stragglers—Hannibal's army repaired its equipment and stitched up its ragged clothes. If the route is deducible here, they would have most likely camped somewhere near Segusio (modern Susa, Italy) along the deep Dora Riparia River Valley, at this point still surrounded by mountains and not yet in the Po plain. They no doubt fed on game such as wild boar from the nearby forests, polished the rust off their weapons, and began to train again for the inevitable journey eastward down into Italy.

The Taurini tribe of Celts lived along the banks of the Po River on the edge of the plain in what is now Turin, which archaeology and textual history confirm.[6] Here where it is still easy to be in the shadow of the darkly visible Alps, Taurini tribal settlements and farming territories were spread along the western Po Valley. Livy too asserts that Hannibal came down among the Taurini.[7]

Hannibal's army now gathered out of the foothills. Their scouts and spies had reported that the Taurini were quarreling with an enemy tribe, the

Insubres, who apparently had sided with Hannibal. Just south of the confluence of the Dora Riparia and the Po was the heaviest concentration of their
farming tribe, the semiurban town of Taurasia, and west of here was where
the Taurini decided to oppose Hannibal.

Hannibal's envoys had sought an alliance with the Taurini—"making
overtures," as Polybius says,[8] and no doubt also playing up their anti-Roman
sentiments—but the xenophobic and overoptimistic Taurini rejected any
such friendship. Apparently no word had yet reached these Italian Celts
of what happened to the Allobroges, as distant over the Alps as if on the
far side of the moon. Hannibal now had to make a statement, a form of
"psychological warfare," as one historian notes.[9] Others affirm that despite
having granted relative clemency to captured enemies, Hannibal's "attitude
to those who resisted him was uncompromising."[10]

The Taurini were no match even for hardened soldiers who had recently endured so much and were still on the mend. Hannibal's army surrounded Taurasia[11] and in three days reduced it to a smoking ruin, as well as
massacred the Taurini. Suddenly unified by being attuned to their common
antagonist Rome, as Hannibal must have expressed to them, the western
Padana tribes rapidly turned their allegiance to Hannibal, as Polybius tells
us, well aware that resistance would yield the same result.[12]

But Publius Scipio had arrived, crossing the Po with his legions in the
center of the broad valley, effectively dividing the Padana Celts into two
groups and preventing them from unifying against Rome. This bold move
was successful initially. Even the Boii in the east were stymied. They had
recently embarrassed the Romans in an uprising that slaughtered many of
the regional Roman garrisons, and of course, had sent welcoming envoys to
Hannibal back in Spain the previous year.

A GRIM OBJECT LESSON

Now began a period when both Romans and Carthaginians bolstered their
troops along the Po Valley by various strategies. Publius Scipio had previously crossed the Po and was building a bridge across the Ticinus River,

which flowed into the Po from the north. He assembled his troops and emphasized to his men how the Carthaginians had fled in fear before them, choosing to cross the mountains rather than stand and fight.[13] He told them how weakened and depleted Hannibal's troops were now after their arduous Alps crossing and how Rome had an endless supply of recruits. They should now find it outrageous that the Carthaginians had invaded Italy and would now face them.

In stark contrast to the Romans, the meeting in Hannibal's camp also brings up a famous episode recorded by both Polybius and even more dramatically by Livy.[14] Some believe it shows the truer undercurrent of brutal cruelty in Hannibal's personality; others maintain it was merely a brilliant object lesson that Hannibal made unmistakably clear for his troops. One winter evening, likely lit by a bonfire, instead of first making any inspiring speech to his diverse army of hard veterans, Hannibal assembled his men and brought out enemy Celt captives in heavy chains, their bodies scarred from battle and emaciated from hunger. He gave those captives a stark opportunity: one that was later not lost on Romans such as Livy, who knew gladiatorial combat games to the death in arenas and amphitheaters. With his soldiers' eyes glued to the scene, Hannibal placed in front of these Celtic captives the most ostentatious and ornately decorated Celtic armor, rich weapons, and prize horses such as their greatest chiefs displayed before battle when they would go forward as single champions for their peoples. He offered whoever would fight to the death would win the glorious armor and rewards they coveted as well as freedom. The vanquished would die, and thus win another kind of freedom from their harsh slavery. In unison, each of the captive enemy Celts roared their willingness to fight one another, and two were chosen by lot. The other captive Celts all mourned they had no such opportunity for victorious freedom or the release of a quick death.

The Celtic warriors raised their arms and voices and prayed to their gods for victory and then began their furious battle against each other. Hannibal intended his troops to identify with both warriors, wanting them to feel pity for the vanquished as much as pride for the victor. When the dead man was dragged away, to the groans of his tautly attentive audience,

Hannibal stood and gave his short, blunt explanation already quoted above about conquering or dying. Hannibal wanted his men to see what they would suffer over the course of the long campaign. Victory was not a vanity of mere cloaks, loot, and horses but rather the envy of mankind. Even death on the battlefield was a kind of prize as well, a release from further suffering. Because of the long road they had traveled, the hostile numbers of enemies in between, and the wide rivers to cross, his men couldn't expect to reach home even if they escaped defeat by abandoning their dying companions or fleeing in retreat from a battle gone horribly awry. Instead, they must be single-mindedly hard and not let any Roman or anyone else take away their freedom, not suffer a lonely life of exile and slavery where they would never see friends or home country again. The Romans could always flee home; his army of Carthaginians, Libyans, Numidians, Spanish, and others could not.

One of Hannibal's concluding statements recorded for this event used an ironically nautical figure, perhaps like the inertia of a wave: "The courage of those who despair of safety will carry everything before it." Hannibal's lesson was received with sober reflection as intended, and his troops were not lulled by false promise but instead were made bolder with truth. Hannibal dismissed his army with praise for what they had done and endured so far, also commanding them to be ready to march again at daybreak.

Another account of one of Hannibal's dramatic abject lessons—compelling if also brutal—is his "sacrifice" before the Battle of Ticinus. In one hand, he took a young lamb and a stone in the other. He called on the gods, especially Baal, as witness that if he broke his word, may the gods do to him what he did: crushing the lamb's head with the stone and spraying animal brains on anyone close enough to witness this drama, which Livy says convinced his men that the "gods would guarantee their hopes."[15] Now each army was ready, Hannibal's possibly the more determined.

THE BATTLE OF THE TICINUS

The area of the Ticino River today is mixed farmland and poplar forest, but it is the flatness of the region around modern Vigevano (ancient

Victumulae) or Lomello that gave each general confidence in his cavalry, since the broad Padana plain, the Po River Valley, gives a great advantage to cavalry maneuvers. In any case, both armies were surprised to reach each other so quickly.[16]

The next day saw both Carthaginian and Roman troops advancing toward each other on the north bank of the Po, Publius Scipio having previously marched in advance of Hannibal to the Ticino River, where his bridge was now finished. Scipio marched west, and Hannibal east. The next day, after each army's scouts gauged the distance, they wheeled about, notifying each general of the other's position. The opposing armies camped and waited through the night, eager to engage. At daybreak, both armies advanced toward each other, intending to scope out relative strength, position, and which units were assembled. Publius Scipio brought his entire cavalry, as did Hannibal, and Scipio also brought his javeliners. When each leader saw the dust of his approaching enemy—which can only mean this was a drier part of the winter[17]—each general immediately gave the order for action. Scipio placed his javelins and Celtic cavalry at the middle of the front and his less mobile infantry behind. He must have hoped his heavy cavalry would mow down the core of Hannibal's infantry.

But this strategy could work only if Hannibal had no cavalry in front to counter the charge. Did Hannibal anticipate this? Both like and unlike the Romans, Hannibal also placed his heavy fighting units in the middle front—including his allied Spanish and Celtic cavalries and infantry. But he placed his highly mobile, light Numidian cavalry on the outer wings, hoping to outflank the Romans with speed.

With each general advancing eagerly and the heavy cavalries thundering toward each other, the battle engagement happened unusually fast. When the opposing heavy cavalries were about to meet head-on at full speed, the Roman javeliners (*jaculatores*) in the very front had no time to throw their projectiles.

At first, the battle was heaviest in the center and nearly equal. Roman infantry and their Celtic cavalry fought together, now with no room for the Celt allied cavalry to maneuver or charge due to the press of men and the lack of space, so the horses were essentially useless. This was apparently just what Hannibal had been hoping for, as his mobile Numidian light cavalry completely outflanked the clustered Roman army and now quickly whirled around to attack the compressed Romans from the rear, trampling and scattering the Roman javeliners who were retreating on foot, literally riding right over them.

Suddenly the battle turned when the core of Publius Scipio's Romans saw they were fighting both front and rear and that their rear guard was collapsing. The remounting Roman allied cavalry was now scattered in every direction, although a few actual Romans gathered around Publius Scipio, who had been severely wounded in the center of the fray. Livy makes a huge point of claiming that the soldiers who regrouped around Scipio and essentially saved his life were led by his young eighteen-year-old son, the younger Publius Cornelius Scipio[18] who would become a major figure in our story.

Much of the actual credit for saving the Roman commander may have belonged instead to a Ligurian slave.[19] Although the Romans had also inflicted casualties on Hannibal's army, their losses were now such that Scipio called a full retreat back to the Ticino. He realized that Hannibal's cavalry was vastly superior and hoped desperately to get his running legions across the Ticino Bridge before full disaster. Hannibal was hoping to engage more of the Roman infantry and gave chase, although not fast enough.

The bulk of the Romans made it across while attacked by Numidian horsemen on their sides. Placing an armed contingent of guards to face Hannibal, they destroyed as much of the Ticino Bridge as possible, reducing it to a skeleton of planks to stop Hannibal from following farther. Hannibal saw the bridge was useless, so he took the six hundred Roman men left to guard the bridge as prisoners, some of whom could have been army engineers dismantling the timbers.[20]

Publius Scipio, however, retreated back south to the new Roman colony town of Placentia over the earlier Po River Bridge the Romans had built, returning to seek needed medical help for his serious wounds. Placentia was a brand-new settlement of six thousand Romans, having just been established in early 218 from land taken from Anamares Celts, who lived in

the Po River Valley near the Trebia River.[21] Scipio's beleaguered men found
their spirits were as battered as their bodies, as they had not expected to lose
to the much-reduced Carthaginians. Hadn't their trusted veteran general
Publius Scipio said that Hannibal had fled before them near the Rhône?
And wasn't the remnant of his surviving soldiers still exhausted by its long
ordeal of crossing the mountains? How many Roman lives were lost is only
conjecture, but it was a clear defeat, and Hannibal captured at least the six
hundred Romans left at the Ticino Bridge. Livy noted that the brief Battle of
the Ticinus was also one of the first engagements demonstrating Hannibal's
advantage in cavalry.[22]

Hannibal marched back west for two days and had his own bridge constructed over the wide Po, commanding Hasdrubal to get the army across
after him, as he sped across first in order to meet envoys of Celts assembling
in peace. In the two days since the Romans had retreated, the word had
spread all over the Padana to the Celtic tribes, which already had either
resisted the Romans or had reluctantly been neutral. Now they came to
make alliances with Hannibal. The Celtic tribes in Northern Italy clearly
understood the intentions of the Romans to absorb what had traditionally
been Celtic tribal farmlands. No doubt the Insubres tribe, already having
at least a century of experience with the Romans' expansionist aims—and
now a tentative ally of Hannibal—helped to stir up antagonism against the
Romans. These Celts assembled at the Po now offered supplies and allied
warriors to Hannibal, who received their envoys and offers with dignity and
friendship.[23]

Now that his troops had successfully crossed to the south bank of the
Po, Hannibal marched them east again downriver in hope of encountering
any Roman soldiers in the vicinity, although they had all retreated to Placentia. So Hannibal marched his army to where the Romans could see him
in plain view, a clear challenge to fight. This may have been a safe bet on
Hannibal's part for several reasons, knowing it was the dead of winter and
that Scipio was in no shape to fight. It is even possible that he was posturing
for the sake of his new Celtic allies. But the recuperating Scipio wouldn't
budge, knowing his current position inside the walls was the most secure.

So Hannibal withdrew a little more than six miles west of Placentia and set up his camp there.

THE PROBLEM OF THE CELTS AND THEIR
TREACHERY AGAINST ROME

Seeing the bright prospect of Hannibal and the sudden reluctance of the Romans to fight, those Celts inside Placentia who had been Roman allies—possibly including many who were even forced to fight for Rome as conscripts—made a treacherous move. After waiting in their tents for the Romans to retire for the night, when all was still, they quietly rose up and quickly slaughtered any Romans sleeping nearby before fleeing the camp. With their typical[24] manner of decapitating enemies—"a more horrifying Celtic custom was that of the decapitation of foes"[25]—they took as many Roman heads as possible and fled.

All told, about two thousand Celts and two hundred Celtic cavalry quickly went over from Placentia to Hannibal's camp as dawn broke, greeting the general with their grisly trophy heads[26] as proof of their treachery. Hannibal welcomed them as allies and encouraged them but sent them back to their own tribes and villages with gifts or promises. He told them to tell their fellow tribesmen what they had accomplished in the middle of the Roman camp—a shrewd move for Hannibal because he knew they were proud and would find it more difficult to realign with Rome after going public. He also told them if they were now allies, they should urge their fellow tribes to join him against Rome, hoping that many Celts would be emboldened by the example of resistance to Rome.

Now the Boii (the region of Bologna, named after them) also came to Hannibal and brought with them in chains three captured Roman officials who had been delegated from Rome to divide up their tribal lands. They had taken them hostage by treachery and now offered them to Hannibal. Instead, Hannibal told them to keep them as bargaining power to force the Romans to return their Boii hostages, which had been the reason the Boii captured the officials in the first place.

This seemingly generous ploy—looking more like magnanimity than cruelty, but actually just pragmatism—shows that Hannibal not only had good military intelligence about the Boii but also understood how to negotiate with the Romans, who would be reluctant to abandon their officials as long as they knew they were alive. The Romans would be equally reluctant to kill the hostage Boii while they still had bargaining incentive. This was clear shrewdness in the game of war that Hannibal played so well.

In the meantime, Publius Scipio was devastated by the Celtic treachery in his Placentia camp and dreaded how much effect this would have on all the neighboring Celts. He knew this action would weaken whatever chance he had to regain the generally disaffected Celts who had been brewing trouble for some time. While Rome had some allied Celts in the region who had been loyal for years and were not changing sides to aid the Carthaginians, Publius Scipio knew the Celts in general were notoriously fickle— especially those who had only recently joined Hannibal—and could easily throw themselves to whomever they perceived had the current advantage. Publius Scipio hoped that the Celts would not be willing to fight outside their own territory for Hannibal's interests.[27]

But Scipio knew that his Roman troops had reinforcements coming soon in newly recruited legions marching west from Ariminum (modern Rimini) on the Adriatic coast under the command of consul Tiberius Sempronius Longus. He also knew they were green and mostly untrained, as was their consular commander. Scipio believed it would be best to train the new legions over the duration of the winter, and with his health at risk from healing wounds, he also knew he had to wait before engaging Hannibal again. He must have also worried because he rightly surmised that Sempronius would be eager to fight Hannibal for political gain in order to be renamed consul in the coming elections.

A FURTHER BLOW TO ROME: LOSS OF
CLASTIDIUM'S GRAIN DEPOT

An unexpected additional blow staggered the Romans and was particularly bitter to Publius Scipio. It was deep December. Despite provisioning by allied Celts, the Carthaginians were running low on food. A major fortified Roman storage grain depot at Clastidium (modern Casteggio) held a great quantity of grain. Clastidium was only six miles south of the Po River, but a few days west from where Hannibal's main army camped near the Trebia. Hannibal still had skirmishers and mobile units collecting food from wherever they could in the nearby Padana region, which included Clastidium and its fort, and Hannibal's men were probably about to attack the depot for this very reason. But then something no one expected happened.

The commander of Clastidium's garrison guarding the grain depot was not Roman but a Roman ally from Brundisium (modern Brindisi) named Dasius. His troops were also not Roman but allies from Messapia in Calabria. Not only were these cities south of the primary sphere of Roman influence in central Italy but they were also closer in culture, language, and southern outlook to the former Greek colonies of Magna Graecia than to Rome. Dasius essentially opened the gates to Hannibal's men and gave them all the stored Roman grain that had been harvested only a few months before, and which the Roman legions under Publius Scipio counted on as winter provisions. The Clastidium garrison of Messapian troops also defected to Hannibal, who welcomed them warmly.

The problem of the Celts would continue for both Hannibal, who needed their alliance, and for the Romans, whose occupation of their lands was greatly resented, particularly in North Italy. It also seems likely that the ease of acquiring the purloined Roman grain at Clastidium further opened Hannibal's eyes to how superficial Roman control was in the deep south of Italy where Dasius and the Messapians originated.

Eleven

TREBIA

Most historians, including Polybius, agree that the Roman and Punic forces had only a partial engagement at the Ticino, calling it more of a cavalry skirmish than a full battle.[1] Nevertheless, it was the first time Hannibal actually engaged an organized Roman force.

While it wasn't a decisive victory for either side, the Romans were demoralized and were likely the losers in many ways. First, the Romans had expected victory, and instead saw the end of the battle swing far more to the enemy's side. Second, Hannibal's cavalry proved more than a match for the Roman horsemen and legions, especially his mobile Numidian light cavalry, routing the Roman javeliners and attacking from the rear. Third, it was the Romans who retreated from the battlefield in disarray to escape back east across the Ticino Bridge. Fourth, Hannibal captured at least six hundred Romans, while no substantive Punic captives are mentioned in any battle texts. Fifth, and perhaps most important for what followed soon, Publius Scipio was severely wounded and could not fight again for some time. Last but not least, the fact that the Romans proved so vulnerable even

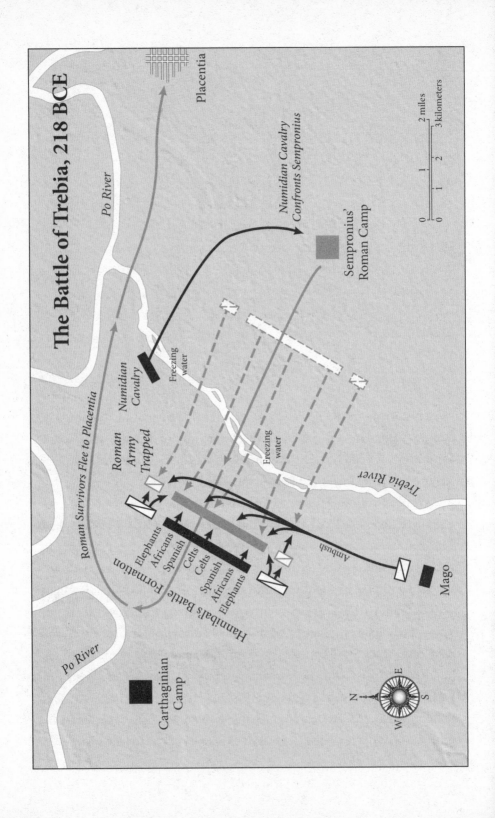

The Battle of Trebia, 218 BCE

Placentia

Po River

Numidian Cavalry Confronts Sempronius

Sempronius' Roman Camp

Freezing water

Freezing water

Trebia River

Numidian Cavalry

Roman Army Trapped

Roman Survivors Flee to Placentia

Po River

Elephants
Africans
Spanish
Celts
Celts
Spanish
Africans
Elephants

Hannibal's Battle Formation

Ambush

Mago

Carthaginian Camp

N
W E
S

0   1   2 miles
0   1   2   3 kilometers

under experienced leadership spoke volumes to the Padana Celts. Hannibal gained the alliance of the Celts at least for the duration of his sojourn in northern Italy.

Back in Rome, where the Ticino outcome took the city by surprise, rationalization suggested that the outcome was due not to Hannibal—his name did not yet strike such fear—or Roman overconfidence or negligence but mostly Celtic treachery. The Romans trusted greatly in their infantry, "still unimpaired"[2] after Ticino. When Tiberius Sempronius marched through Rome en route to meet up with Scipio, the premature consensus was that all Sempronius had to do was show up with his legions, and the outcome would be decided.

Ticino also appears to be the first time in any warfare engagement that Hannibal employed what would become his famous trademark maneuver: the double envelopment that compressed and crushed the Roman infantry.[3] Although Hannibal was always prone to tricks, feints, decoys, ambushes, and other stratagems, this incredibly effective use of his Numidian light cavalry was only offset perhaps by an overdependence on it at times. Regardless, however, of how many times he used it, it continued to flummox the Roman generals, whose own cavalry units were not as mobile.

DIFFERENT PLANS OF SCIPIO AND HANNIBAL

While Scipio holed up first in Placentia and then possibly at a new fortified camp south of Placentia after Ticino, hoping to wait out the worst of the winter, it appeared that Hannibal also wanted to delay further engagement in battle. On the other hand, it's entirely possible that Hannibal was waiting to pounce on Sempronius instead. Most historians have agreed for centuries that Hannibal had eyes and ears—most likely Celts—in the Roman camps reporting on the division between Scipio and Sempronius.[4] He may already have heard that the majority of Romans—excluding Scipio—were as overconfident as the impetuous Sempronius himself. Hannibal probably had spies in Rome providing him with this important information: Sempronius knew his consulship was running out by the next year, and any occasion to obtain glory must be taken quickly or not at all.[5] He would play right into Hannibal's hands.

By mid-December of 218, Tiberius Sempronius Longus and his two legions had arrived in the Padana. They had traveled more than a month from Lilybaeum (near modern Trapani on the west coast of Sicily) in a maneuver combining sea and land to Ariminum on the northern Adriatic coast of Italy, mostly by foot using the Via Flaminia north from Rome; exiting Rome by the Flaminian Gate, it was the most direct Roman road to the Po and the new Roman colonies there. Although Livy claims they sailed all the way from Sicily,[6] this is not likely given the lateness of year[7] and the fact that Polybius states that they marched through Rome. There are many places where the accounts of Polybius and Livy cannot be reconciled.[8] Polybius rarely errs on geography, partly because he traveled the routes himself, whereas Livy rarely did. Most historians prefer Polybius when differences occur unless there is a reason not to do so.[9]

TIBERIUS SEMPRONIUS LONGUS

After arriving in the Padana, Sempronius camped with his weary troops very close to Scipio's camp, with both camps possibly near the modern town of Rivergaro, just east of the Trebia River. It is doubtful that Scipio was all that happy to see Sempronius with his two legions: in some way, his being there was an implicit criticism. In the following days, Sempronius prepared plans to fight Hannibal following meetings with Scipio, who tried to dissuade him from expediting a battle.

Hannibal and Sempronius could hardly have been more different. Sempronius was mostly a politician bent on glory, while Hannibal was a soldier's soldier, a leader who sought not personal but national gain. Elected consul in 218 by the Senate along with Publius Cornelius Scipio, Tiberius Sempronius Longus (260–210 BCE) was supposed to pressure Carthage directly. He was first sent to Lilybaeum to muster and ready an invasion force to Africa. Livy says that Sempronius was outfitted with 2 legions of infantry and regular cavalry, totaling 14,000 allied infantry, and 1,600 horse.[10] He also originally had with him 160 quinquiremes for transport, although this may have been reduced to 60. Sempronius had been modestly successful in seizing the island of Malta from a Carthage that was preoccupied elsewhere. Scipio had been sent to Massilia in Gaul intending to reach Spain in order to head off Hannibal before he reached Gaul. Because he hadn't been successful, he had quickly turned back to North Italy to await Hannibal's exit from the Alps, leading to their encounter at Ticino.

With Scipio wounded and in retreat from Hannibal, the Senate quickly recalled Sempronius from Sicily with his new legions, dispatching him to Padana. Because of Scipio's near disaster at Ticino and Sempronius' overrated victory in Malta, Sempronius seemed to believe he was the more capable general and was impatient to prove it.

Livy suggests Hannibal had full knowledge of the impulsiveness of Sempronius, and Hannibal soon provided Sempronius with an opportunity he could not refuse. The Carthaginians had discovered that some of the local Celts were trying to play both sides, not surprising since the situation was still very fluid. To punish their duplicity and force them to choose, Hannibal sent out a raiding force of around 2,000 infantrymen and 1,000 Celtic and Numidian cavalry to ravage the local territory and take all surplus food from the duplicitous towns, evidently easy pickings. These towns now quickly showed their true colors and publicly went over to the joint Roman camps and requested justice against Hannibal.

At the news of Punic raids and a Celtic call for retribution, Sempronius practically leaped out of his headquarters. He sent out the bulk of his cavalry and 1,000 javeliners to find the small Carthaginian raiding force laden with booty. His Roman force took more than a few lives and most of the raided goods. The Carthaginians retreated toward the main camp. Hannibal sent out reinforcements to back up the raiding party, which was smaller than the number of troops Sempronius had in the field. In turn, Sempronius sent out the rest of his cavalry and javeliners to contest the Punic reinforcements, who, now fully outnumbered, retreated en masse back to the main camp. Hannibal now commanded this small part of his army to stop

its retreat and turn around to face Sempronius, but he forbade his men to
attack the Romans.

Hannibal knew he would lose psychological standing with his Celt allies if his men retreated back to camp without at least appearing to challenge the Romans to come any closer. Facing each other at a visible distance,
the two forces had a tense standoff, but when the Romans realized that
Hannibal would not fight, they turned and went back to their camp.

Sempronius believed that this had been a decisive test, especially since
more Carthaginians than Romans had died in this small skirmish. Sempronius was all the more fired up to have a full battle with Hannibal even
though Scipio had warned him to be cautious, claiming that his new recruits needed training and drills through the winter to be more prepared.
While Scipio also wanted to wait until he was fully recuperated, he also
argued reasonably that the Celts' loyalties were as liquid as water, and they
would not stay with Hannibal if they had to remain inactive for too long.
But his sound advice fell on deaf ears.

Sempronius urged his fellow consul and also, as Livy puts it, "passion-
ately harangued the officers." Livy says that Sempronius may have even
mocked Scipio's procrastination: "Were they waiting for a third consul and
another army?"[11] Sempronius may have hoped that without the still healing
Scipio, the glory of a Roman victory would be completely his!

Hannibal realized that the Celts were fickle and could easily drift away
given too much time or not enough victories to keep their morale high.
Worse, the Celts could defect to the Romans in enough numbers to reduce his
allied forces considerably, or they might pull out altogether, especially when
Celt tribes were fighting against Celt tribes in both armies. With his forces
trimmed drastically by the ordeal in the Alps, Hannibal needed the Celts
more than the Romans did. Hannibal also hoped to keep Scipio out of the
battle, preferring to prey on the untested Roman recruits led by Sempronius.

Thus, while Hannibal would have agreed with Scipio on several points
of strategy, he knew it was to his advantage to fight quickly in an enemy
land—moving as often as possible[12]—before Rome could field an even
larger army. He knew he needed rapidly but prudently to set up battle

conditions that would be favorable to him.[13] Hannibal wanted the fight on his terms, as would any general in enemy territory. He also wanted his allies confident of success—Polybius states exactly this.[14] He knew both his own resources and those of his enemy, thanks to his Celtic sources of intelligence in the Roman camp.

RECONNOITERING THE BATTLE SITE

In the near month he had been encamped in the Trebia River Valley, Hannibal had observed a flat, treeless plain on the west side of the river, roughly between the Punic and Roman camps, with an unobstructed view except at the river itself, where reeds and bushes provided good cover on the steep banks. Hannibal knew that he could hide ambush forces near the steep banks, stealth forces the Romans wouldn't notice because they would be beguiled by the wide-open spaces. He also knew that the wide, flat area would give his superior Numidian cavalry room to maneuver in battle.

Even now the Trebia River banks often reach a height of fifteen to twenty feet in many places, presumably a deeper river channel than in 218 after two millennia of erosion. But even if only half that height prior to modern farming in the region, many portions of Trebia brush-filled banks would have been sufficient to hide ambush forces.[15] Trees would not have been a factor because it was December, and the deciduous leaves would have been gone.

Hannibal devised a plan that would take advantage of this place and the Roman desire to fight on open plains. Hannibal then confided in his younger brother Mago, bringing him entirely into his devious strategy to trap the Romans. Together they chose two hundred of the toughest veteran leaders: a hundred cavalry and a hundred infantry who were to meet him that night in the camp.

When these veterans arrived to meet with him, Hannibal asked each to choose ten of the bravest soldiers he knew. When the force of two thousand was collected—a thousand cavalry and a thousand infantry—he sent them out secretly in the middle of the night to a protected ambush spot that

was concealed from the Romans. Hannibal may have already done reconnaissance on this very ambush place. No wonder he chose the hardiest and
bravest leaders and warriors, because they would have to sit out the cold
night outdoors! Hannibal also instructed Mago in the prearranged signals
for what to do the next day. If all went as planned, Hannibal could tell Mago
when to leave his ambush site; if not, Hannibal may have had scouts and bu-
glers hidden in the intermittent woods between his forces and the ambush
site to relay any messages or changes of plan. Timing was especially critical,
and Hannibal could not let poor communication ruin such careful planning.

BAITING THE ROMAN TRAP

The brilliance of Hannibal's strategy stands out. Hannibal made sure that
his army went to bed early and was thoroughly rested. They arose just before
dawn and ate well to strengthen themselves, also covering themselves with
grease and fat to insulate themselves from the cold because it was intermit-
tently raining and possibly sleeting. They may have also oiled or greased
their horses against the bitter cold. His primary plan was to draw out the
Romans, so after he explained his tactics and promised each man rewards,
he then sent his mobile Numidian cavalry across the Trebia at daybreak.
Their orders were to ride as quickly as possible to the Roman position and
shoot as many arrows as needed into the Roman camp, probably accompanied with taunts, hoping to draw out Sempronius and his army before they
had eaten. How Hannibal knew Sempronius would take the bait is astonishing. But what followed was even better planning on Hannibal's part.

Hannibal seemed to have chosen this day to engage in battle because he
knew that in the Roman system, generals alternated command every other
day. Hannibal must have known it was Sempronius' turn to lead. Scipio
may have warned him against fighting that day and that it was a bad idea,
especially with the foul weather all night that had made the ground either
wet or half frozen, but Sempronius didn't listen to Scipio, thinking only of
glory and vastly underestimating Hannibal. Sempronius foolishly did exactly what Hannibal wanted.

Having crossed the Trebia River, the nimble Numidians rushed the Roman camp with loud taunting as they wheeled their horses about. Sempronius gave the order for his several thousand heavy cavalry to engage these Numidians. Then he dispatched six thousand javeliners and followed them with mobilizing his whole army. He thought rashly that if the enemy cavalry merely saw his numerical superiority, the issue would be decided quickly by overwhelming force. But Sempronius ordered almost all his men to battle without breakfast and ill prepared for the bitter cold and now falling snow, just as Hannibal had hoped.

Driven by Sempronius' swaggering expectations, and confident in their heavy armor and numerical superiority, the Romans roared their approval as they poured out to battle. But the Roman heavy cavalry could not keep up with the fleet Numidian light cavalry that wheeled around them, trained for this purpose. Behind them, the Roman infantry could not keep up either, but the men could still hear the Numidians mocking them as they rode ever forward just out of range of weapons.

Consistently, the darting Numidians lured the Roman army north. The Romans were probably marching as fast and orderly as they could in the cold, bad weather in three columns,[16] at least three or so miles along the east Trebia bank. The Numidians knew exactly where to turn west to cross the river ahead of the slow Roman army. Ahead of the infantry, the Roman cavalry began to cross, and the mass of the Roman infantry maniples (subdivisions of sixty to a hundred soldiers) hit the river banks long after the Numidians had crossed. At first, the Numidians waited safely on the other side. As the Roman cavalry crossed, the Numidians darted to the sides, continuing their provocative taunting. The Roman army charged into the river by sheer momentum, fragmenting its organization in the surging water.

TREBIA RIVER AS A WEAPON

It is possible that after Hannibal's army had experienced the debilitating effects of the cold and snowy Alps, he realized the advantage he would gain by forcing a similar experience on the Romans. If weeks of bitter cold and gnawing hunger had reduced his troops to half strength, what could an icy winter day do to the Romans? At the same time, he probably told his men that they had already endured and survived far worse conditions, and this wintry battle would be mild in comparison.

Here is where the second phase of Hannibal's plan took force. Since it had rained and sleeted a lot the night before, the river was running higher than usual. When his Numidian cavalry had crossed the Trebia, its oiled horses bore the brunt of the freezing water; the horsemen rode higher, mostly out of the water. But the huge mass of Roman infantry of almost sixteen thousand soldiers and twenty thousand allies struggled up to their chests in the freezing water that surged around them. The Numidian cavalry took off with the heavier Roman cavalry in futile pursuit. The Roman infantry could hardly follow, sodden with cold water and probably freezing as they tried to move. The icing of their clothing slowed them down immensely and also began to rob them of body heat, but they couldn't stop now. Nor could they turn around to ford the freezing water a second time. After their officers reformed the ranks, the Roman army labored forward.

Everything was going exactly according to Hannibal's plans so far.

BATTLING MORE THAN MEN: WEATHER
AND HYPOTHERMIA TOO

Hannibal had been waiting and took action when he saw the entire Roman army, advancing "at a slow step," as Polybius notes,[17] up the slope of the plain. The Roman infantry was probably sluggish by now, having to march uphill as well. Hannibal first sent out his grease-protected pikemen and Balearic slingers—about eight thousand together, as they always worked jointly. Hannibal's army advanced about three-quarters of a mile. Then he ordered forward his heavy infantry, totaling twenty thousand allies from Spain, Africa, and Celtic lands in a single line. He put his cavalry on the flanks, about ten thousand, including Celtic allied horsemen, far more than the Romans had mustered because they relied so much on infantry.

Hannibal then placed his thirty-seven or so elephants—the strongest of these by now having mostly recovered after a month of rest—in front of his cavalry wings to provide additional protection.

Sempronius finally recalled his heavy cavalry when he realized that they could not keep pace with the Numidians. This was a fatal mistake because it left his flanks exposed. With his freezing ranks in some sort of order, Sempronius tried to march his legions forward slowly, hoping to terrorize the motley Punic forces merely by showing up. But it didn't work. The Roman army was exhausted from cold, heavy frozen clothes and famished with hunger even before the battle.

When the opposing lines met and combat started, many thousands in the Roman army hardly had sufficient battle strength left. The Roman javeliners had lost most of their projectiles against the elusive Numidians and were also affected by the persistent dampness. Sempronius seemed unaware of the doom awaiting his legions.

Hannibal's men were well fed and relatively warm, having moved only enough to stay warm while the Romans had been duped to travel in terrible circumstances. The larger Carthaginian cavalry moved on the Roman flanks and then turned inward, squeezing the sides of the massed Roman infantry, who were unprotected because their cavalry had fallen back. The Carthaginian pikemen joined by the Numidians crushed forward against the massed Roman infantry, who could go nowhere but forward.

MAGO'S AMBUSH SPRUNG

Suddenly Mago's combined forces of infantry and Numidian cavalry appeared from the rear, having left their ambush site. This caused great alarm and confusion among the Romans, but they mostly held their ground. Mago's smaller force mercilessly attacked the infantry rearguard, which turned to face it while being butchered.

Although the best Roman soldiers at the very front held out for a while because they could go only forward—some even breaking through the weaker line of usually disorderly Celts at the center[18] along with some

Africans—their flanks and rear were being demolished. But they knew they could not retreat back to their camp with the awful conditions and the superior Punic cavalry still attacking. This close-ordered Roman group of ten thousand soldiers at front (possibly the bulk of them Scipio's veterans) held their shields tightly together after they broke through Hannibal's thin line. They abandoned the battle site to flee north, protecting some officers, such as Sempronius, on horse. Retreating some thirteen miles all the way back to Placentia, the fugitives crossed the Trebia River by a bridge far to the north of the first battle. We cannot place Scipio during this battle and flight.

Most of the remaining Roman infantry at the battle site was pushed back and if the soldiers didn't surrender, they were slaughtered along the banks of the Trebia, trampled by Hannibal's elephants and heavy cavalry. Many of those who tried desperately to recross the freezing river must have died.

Some Carthaginians attempted to chase Sempronius and the Roman fugitives, but they gave up as the weather worsened. The horrible weather that day took a toll on the Punic army as well, mainly the Celtic allies, and the horses and elephants were also severely affected, possibly due to pneumonia. According to Polybius,[19] nearly all of Hannibal's elephants died within a short time of the Battle of Trebia.

AFTERMATH

It is estimated that some fifteen thousand Romans died at Trebia and many others—possibly thousands[20]—were taken captive along with an unknown number of Celt allies of Rome.[21] Regardless of the actual death toll, it was Hannibal's first real triumph against Rome and a foretaste of how he would fight in the future by exploiting Roman policy and environmental advantages.

Now most of the remaining Celts of North Italy swung to his side in alliance. Hannibal also did something very unusual, which before this time was only a Hellenistic Greek phenomenon. As Polybius records it,[22] he promised the Celts both liberation and friendship if they would accept his being there. He emphasized that his presence was intended only to defeat Rome. Unlike the Romans, who defeated the Celts, seized their land, and resettled them with Roman colonists, he offered freedom.

After Trebia, Hannibal pursued a policy of treating captive Romans fairly harshly—with minimal subsistence—while treating captive Celts kindly. On more than one occasion, Hannibal would release captive Celts to their tribes without any penalty or ransom so that when they returned home, they might recruit other Italian Celts to rebel against Rome. Hannibal knew the propaganda value of what he was doing.

Sempronius, more than reluctant to send the news of his horrible defeat back to Rome, suppressed all communication. Fearful of the political consequences for his future, he concealed the defeat from the Senate as long as possible. However, as Polybius relates,[23] he finally sent messengers to report that a terrible "storm had deprived him of victory."

The Roman Senate believed Sempronius at first, but from other sources the Senate learned that it was a horrible defeat. To its astonishment it found that not only had Hannibal not left the region, but that his army was mostly intact. Worse still, most of the Celts of the region had now defected to Hannibal.

At Trebia, Hannibal won his first decisive Italian victory by careful strategy and thoughtful preparation against a Roman army that outnumbered him. He exploited Roman weaknesses in leadership. He also exploited weakness in Roman tactics, especially the outmatched Roman cavalry and Roman overdependence on slow infantry, as well as the use of raw legions. Hannibal used nature fully to his advantage. Having found a way to defeat Rome, he would use all of these strategies again.

The only small consolation for the Romans from this disastrous loss was that there was now a winter reprieve from battle. The Romans also hoped that Hannibal would have to face rising Celtic resentment as his army occupied their territory without bringing them quick plunder and revenge against Rome.[24] But for now, the Celts swelled Hannibal's ranks and replaced a considerable portion of his severe losses in the Alps.

After his consulship ended in military disgrace, Tiberius Sempronius Longus returned to Rome to assist with the consular succession to Gaius Flaminius Nepos and fought other, less disastrous military actions against Carthage.[25] But Tiberius Sempronius Longus was only the first foolish Roman general to be outwitted by Hannibal.

Twelve

THE APENNINES AND THE ARNO MARSHES

Trebia was Hannibal's first strike against the Romans, and he learned much from it. He realized he could exploit Roman weaknesses with his strengths. He also knew he had to keep the pressure on and move closer to Rome itself. He understood how important his Celtic allies were but knew that their dependability was moot; if he didn't keep a fast enough pace, his Celtic allies would lose interest.

Even though Hannibal had forced Rome to acknowledge and respect his presence in northern Italy, the Celts were not willing to wait around, especially if the only action was in their own territory. One Celtic motivation was the prospect of booty seized from Romans, both rich territory and the goods that went with it—in some cases, what had even been Celtic lands a few generations earlier. Hannibal had to reckon on Celtic restlessness even in winter, and now that he had changed the terms of ancient battle by fighting in winter, he knew his allied Celts would expect him to maintain this invasion with lightning-strike quickness.

After Trebia, the Roman Senate levied massive conscriptions of plebeians and formed eleven new legions composed of a hundred thousand soldiers.[1] Hannibal needed badly to sack Roman allies or find non-Celtic provisions to lessen his dependence on his Celtic allies. It was one thing to be perceived as a liberator, another to be suspected as an occupying force.

Both Polybius and Livy share a bizarre story[2] about Hannibal's relationship to the Celts that modern scholarship has mostly discounted.[3] Supposedly worried about being assassinated by the fickle Celts, Hannibal is said to have donned different wigs to disguise himself in case of attempts on his life. But the suspicious incident does not ring true with Hannibal's position as one who had just beaten the Romans and given the Celtic tribes in North Italy new hope. As one historian sagely points out, Polybius visited a pacified northern Italy at least a generation after Hannibal and the end of the Punic War. Carthage was no longer a threat, having just been destroyed. Polybius would have seen only new Roman settlers felling trees and expanding farms, not a Celtic frontier. The militant Celtic residents had been deported or enslaved.[4] Regardless of whether the story about Hannibal is true or not, it speaks to a climate of mistrust between the new allies.

Cremona and Placentia, the two new colonies in the Padana, were Rome's outposts, vanguards of the inevitable. Rome had to expand by absorbing this region or never feel safe. Rome had felt safe until Trebia. Now it had to prepare for a war on its peninsula, and it made significant efforts to adjust.

Within a few months of Trebia, Sempronius and Scipio returned briefly to Rome, as their joint consulships were finished. Both faced criticism, and Sempronius was, to a degree, disgraced. Publius Scipio would soon reappear in Spain with his brother in ongoing battles with Carthage for the territory north of the Ebro River.[5] Hannibal expected a changing of the guard after making several Roman commanders look foolish, but he also knew that the consular rotation could favor him if the Romans continued pairing inexperienced consuls like Sempronius with battle veterans like Scipio. Therefore, he must have instructed his spies to gather as much information as possible about both new consuls.

After occupying Scipio's former camp east of Trebia for a few weeks—making a statement akin to triumph for the Celts, who could observe the camp vacated by the Romans now filled with their enemies— Hannibal may have paused to harass the area around Placentia.[6] But he would not have laid siege to the city, having found out the hard way at Saguntum how drawn out sieges could be.[7]

HANNIBAL WINTERS WITH THE BOII

Instead of staying near Placentia, Hannibal moved his army east all the way to the Boii tribal territory, the region of modern Bologna, for the next few months. The Boii had been his longest and most loyal allies. They may have been the earliest of the Celts who had sought his help against Rome when he was still in Spain. They were important in his parley with the Celts near the Pyrenees. The Boii had not only given counsel to Hannibal but also had been useful in persuading other tribes to join forces with him.

Finishing his winter with the Boii was not only a way to strengthen Hannibal's ties to this strong tribe but also a very pragmatic choice. The Boii lived halfway between the new but embattled colonies of Placentia and Cremona and the older established colony of Ariminum, between the mid-Padana and the Adriatic coast. Ariminum was a strong Roman city whose primary role was to guard the easier eastern coastal approach to Rome. Even more important, Hannibal knew from his spies that the Romans had mustered fresh legions under the new consuls and were moving toward him in two directions to attempt to corral him.

Once again Hannibal could count on the Roman system of pairing an experienced military consul with an inexperienced political consul. Gnaeus Servilius Geminus was the experienced one. He reassembled the remnant legions of Scipio and Sempronius at Ariminum. Servilius was tasked to stop Hannibal from marching east to the Adriatic coast. The second new consul, Gaius Flaminius Nepos, a novice at war, moved his two new legions and allies to Arretium (modern Arezzo), facing the southwest flank of the Apennine Mountains that run the spine of Italy, waiting for Hannibal if and when he crossed the Apennines into Etruria (modern Tuscany). Hannibal would not have crossed the Apennines in winter, despite Livy's account—contrary to Polybius'—that Hannibal made a dramatic but aborted attempt, failing, at great loss, to cross these mountains due to heavy snow and freezing conditions.[8]

After the winter snows began to melt, the long rains began to diminish, and Italy's land surface dried sufficiently for an army to move again without becoming mired, Hannibal formed a plan. The two Roman consuls were positioned against the probability of Hannibal moving out from the Boii, either east downriver along the Po to the Adriatic or south through the Apennines.[9] Servilius and Flaminius assumed wrongly that they had Hannibal contained.

DISTURBING OMENS FOR ROME

Yet Rome itself was troubled by fearful rumors and omens, and the transition of consuls had been marked by unusual events. Livy can be counted on to provide drama and color to what was happening in Rome, mentioning omens and prophecies that all seemed to imply chaotic events, many of which were somehow connected to Mars, god of war.[10] Roman citizens reported that several Roman soldiers' javelins had burst into flame, some had seen springs filled with blood, others said the sun appeared to be strangely locked in combat with the moon, or double moons rose in the east by some unnatural optical phenomenon that went against nature.[11] For the Romans, who were deeply influenced by divination and whose augurers were treated with great respect, these disturbing omens all suggested that the gods were warning them about chaotic and unusual circumstances, portents best interpreted by those long experienced with reading omens of war. Livy lays much of the blame for the uncertainty and bad omens on Flaminius as a scapegoat for the Roman disaster to come. Unlike Livy, a typical Roman steeped in divination, Polybius is silent about apprehensive omens causing consternation in Rome.

CROSSING THE APENNINES

The southerly direction in which Hannibal moved toward Etruria and Flaminius in Arretium may also have had something to do with Flaminius himself. Hannibal seems to have gathered damning evidence about Flaminius. Perhaps for this reason, he decided to march south to Etruria. In any case, a southerly march to Etruria might be more direct and quick if the right Apennine route could be chosen. One historian concludes that Hannibal set out from the Boii in early May.[12]

Carefully considering his choices, according to Polybius,[13] Hannibal led his army south of Bologna over the Apennines and then toward Arretium. The Romans were surprised that he did not take the expected major coastal route but instead chose an interior route to Etruria,[14] since the others were longer but obvious to any watchful Romans.

Many historians suggest that Hannibal followed the Reno River and crossed the Apennine Mountains by the low Collina Pass[15]—only 3,046 feet high (952 meters)—and came down near modern Pistoia, along the Arno River.[16] The word *Reno* derives from an old Celtic word—probably the same Celtic cognate as the *Rhine*—that means "flowing." This 130-mile-long river runs southwest almost the full width of the Apennines as it winds like a serpent from Bologna through the twisting valleys until it drops abruptly into the steeper Arno River Valley.

But instead of then heading south or west, Hannibal went east upriver along the Arno marshes, an unexpected transit because it was still flooded with spring runoff from both mountain snowmelt and prolonged rainfall. This may have been a slightly more direct route if dry, but with its waterlogged terrain, it was hazardous. Hannibal must have had Boii guides who knew this route. Believing the Arno route to be impassable at this time, the Romans (or at least Flaminius)[17] were unprepared for Hannibal to come toward them from the northwest.

NIGHTMARE OF CROSSING THE ARNO MARSHES

While not as famous as his Alpine march, Hannibal's four-day trek through the Arno marshes was perhaps equally terrible in other ways. Both Polybius and Livy recount the slow suffering of Hannibal's army on this long, unhealthy, and even life-threatening slog. Swamp conditions must have been much like those described in Dante's *Inferno* of the River Styx, sluggish with stinking mud and swarms of mosquitoes and other voraciously biting insects breeding in the stagnant water.

At first, Hannibal's army was unwilling to follow him into the Arno marshland. But he left no room for alternatives and placed his troops in a very deliberate order. In the front, he positioned his Spanish infantry and Africans, followed by his ally Celts in the middle, and his cavalry at the rear under the leadership of his brother Mago. He also distributed his pack animals in every location throughout the long train in order always to keep food at hand.

Hannibal sandwiched the Celts in between trustworthy troops because he could not trust the Celts to stay the course. If they thought they could melt away at night, Hannibal outwitted them. If the unruly Celts stopped or tried to turn back—they could hardly fan out sideways into the mired swamp—Mago's cavalry would block their escape and prod them forward—or threaten to ride roughshod over them. They had nowhere to go but forward.

These details in Polybius' history[18] suggesting previous Celtic intransigence must have happened enough times for the Punic veterans to force the Celts to stay mostly in line. But this strategy would have only increased Celtic sullenness and made many less likely to stay with Hannibal once the marsh was traversed. There must have been growing Celtic resentment against Hannibal because they always fared the worst of his army in every phase of his campaign. But no one could ever accuse the Celts of not being brave in battle. Their frenzied battle preparations bordered on a mix of hyperactivity and intense bravado.

On the other hand, Hannibal's placement of his troops also shows how much he respected his own well-disciplined men who had been with him since Cartagena and had already survived great hardships. It was increasingly obvious that because his supply lines back to Spain were gradually reduced and cut off by the Romans, Hannibal had to depend more and more on Celtic allies, which was not an ideal war plan. The Arno marshes would test the Celts' loyalty to the limit. At least one historian suggests this was deliberate on Hannibal's part to weed out the weakest Celts and harden the remaining ones.[19]

Even the usually terse Polybius describes graphically the harsh conditions in the marshes, as soldiers endured water up to their knees or higher, with sucking mud underneath.[20] It was impossible to set up camp[21] in the shallow water and mud, so the army struggled for four days essentially without sleep. The energy expended would have led to utter exhaustion, since so much effort was needed to make forward progress. The heavily laden pack animals fared horribly and died where they fell in the mire, probably in many cases unable to pluck their feet from the muck and unable to rise from the gluey mud. The pervasive wetness also soaked into and rotted their hooves. Expendable beasts of burden, the baggage animals mostly perished. Hannibal seemed not to mind the staggering loss of animals because he knew supplies would be plentiful when they reached rich Etruria. The variable quantity of Hannibal's pack animals over several decades, however, was an exigency of war in enemy territory that ultimately would prove insurmountable.[22]

Conditions were so bad in the marshes that the mired animal carcasses provided the only relative dry spots on the nearly continuous march. The men could pile whatever they could on the partly submerged dead animals and try to catch a few minutes of sleep whenever possible perched above the water. But even these would be only the shortest of intervals, never much more than nodding off and resting strained muscles when the bunched troops simply could not move forward and the long line temporarily came to a logjam standstill.

As usual, Livy adds extra color, saying that the Celts had to be guarded as they "lived up to national character" by their unwillingness to pass through the marshes except by the rear force of Numidian cavalry pushing them onward.[23] Describing the many deaths as miserable, Livy also claimed that the major contributing factor to the loss of life was lack of sleep for successive days, and he suggests the water level was up to the men's necks at times and that flood eddies near the Arno River also pulled men in and drowned them. Naturally, Hannibal would have kept as many men as possible in the shallower water.

At night, the marching conditions were even worse. And the smell of the stagnant water would also have been chokingly oppressive. Conditions were ripe for water-borne infections and septicity. Anyone already suffering from tuberculosis would have likely succumbed to the omnipresent seeping damp that penetrated infected lungs. The cold mud would only have gotten heavier, and the cold water would have dissipated body heat as well. Furthermore, the moans of animals dying prolonged deaths, and the coughing of sick or feverish men would have been a living hell, nightmarish especially in the dark. No fires could be lit other than torches to show the shadowy way. The soldiers would have even fouled their own passage, exacerbating the stench and unhealthiness. Cholera was an ever-present danger in such circumstances of compromised drinking water. Carrying an adequate supply of fresh water could only have become increasingly harder. Like Samuel Taylor Coleridge's *The Rime of the Ancient Mariner* ("Water, water, everywhere, and not a drop to drink"), dehydration from lack of potable water in the swamp only worsened the army's overall spirits.

This marsh passage would have haunted many who survived, and while Hannibal's iron will pushed them forward relentlessly, he too must have wondered if they were ever going to get out. No doubt he constantly grilled his Boii guides and forced himself to stay alert and set a good example, but Hannibal too would have been greatly fatigued because he could not relax his leadership while the army had such a difficult time making forward progress. Protracted sleep deprivation, exhaustion, and the endless damp all compounded to take their hellish toll not only on men and animals but also on their leader.

HANNIBAL'S LOSS OF AN EYE IN THE MARSHES

In the Arno marshes Hannibal contracted an eye disorder that caused ophthalmia, or inflammation of the eye or eyelid. In four days, before he emerged from the marsh, he lost the sight in one eye. Livy blames the eye problem on temperature fluctuations between heat and cold in the early spring variable weather.[24] While it is unknown what the agent of infection might have been, some logical guesses range from an aggressive conjunctivitis caused by detritus in the eye, to bacterial or viral infection from swamp microbes such as bacterial *Staphylococcus* or waterborne *Pseudomonas aeruginosa* and *Acanthamoeba*.[25] Medical treatment—for example, irrigating with clean water and an herbal poultice—was impossible given the surrounding swamp water and the length of this debilitating march. (A curious footnote to history is that the Romans seem fascinated with one-eyed enemy generals. Other warrior kings assembled against them were similarly afflicted.)[26]

Not only did Hannibal lose an eye in the Arno marshes—although some say he lost only partial sight[27]—but also his war elephants were reduced to the single elephant that he rode personally. According to Cato the Elder as recorded in Pliny,[28] this was likely an Asian elephant named Suros ("Syrian") that may have had one broken tusk.[29] One famous phrase that now identified Hannibal to not only his Carthaginians and allies but also to his enemies was "A one-eyed general riding on a huge Gaetulian bust [elephant]."[30]

Possibly emerging from the marshes east of Faesulae and modern Florence,[31] Hannibal's waterlogged army could stretch out at last on dry ground, camping for a few days to rest and then continuing unmolested in either a southerly or southeasterly direction.[32] Although he could still bypass Flaminius at Arretium, Hannibal could raid the rich farmland along the way and replace the dead pack animals and grain, some of which had spoiled with fungal molds in the Arno marsh.

The Celts were thrilled finally to pillage someone else's territory, as this had been nominally Roman since the late fourth to early third century BCE when Rome had broken the Etruscan and Samnite holds on the region.[33] One historian says that by marching into Etruria, Hannibal hoped to exploit Etruscan resentment against Rome, as he had with the Celts, in order to gain Etruscan support against their Roman overlords.[34] Hannibal's Celts now glutted themselves at last on Roman bounty, returning the favor on those Roman legions that had earlier stripped Cis-Alpine Gaul. Hannibal probably did little or nothing to curb the impetuousness of his Celts in their payback to Rome. At the same time, he replenished his supplies and pack animals, especially mules, with the provisions his army needed badly, all the while able to move successfully behind Flaminius' back.

Hannibal's swampy trek caused him considerable losses, a seemingly reckless choice of route, given the deaths of Celtic allies and most of his pack animals. The spring of 217 could have been a complete disaster for Hannibal. The element of surprise would work only if Hannibal retained enough of his army and Flaminius had no time to prepare for a showdown against Hannibal. Evidently, Hannibal had much better information and network of informants within the Roman army than Flaminius had of the Punic forces.

Hannibal had to have been doubly relieved. Not only had his army of disciplined veterans survived the Arno ordeal, but also the allied Celts could at last seize the booty he had promised to gain them as allies. Perhaps the best way to judge Hannibal's costly Arno marsh crossing is to note that he emerged where Flaminius wasn't looking for him. This part of his plan succeeded. Hannibal had now just turned thirty years of age, no longer young but a man nourished by war since childhood. His greatest battles were yet to come. Even in Livy's mostly unsympathetic eyes, Hannibal approached the Roman heartland as a heroic yet tragic figure.

Thirteen

TRASIMENE

Hannibal now capitalized on being where the Roman army expected him least. With renewed supplies and refreshed men, now also laden with whatever goods they had taken from the towns and farms of rich Tuscany and with a careful eye on any Roman troop movements or scouts, Hannibal took ample time and stayed as many miles as possible from Arretium (Arezzo) for as much as several weeks or possibly a month of plunder. If Flaminius had as good intelligence—from Celtic or other Italian spies—he might have been able to catch the Punic army emerging from the swamp and defeat them at their lowest point of exhaustion.[1] But he was either completely in the dark or inept with indecision if he actually knew where Hannibal was.

The Roman forces in Arretium knew by now that Hannibal was on the move in Etruria, announced by columns of smoke from burning villages and farms for several weeks, as Polybius records.[2] This destruction would be sure to draw the attention of Flaminius, who was known for championing small farmers, and the bulk of his army of conscripted farmers' sons would have deeply resented Hannibal's scorched-earth policy.[3]

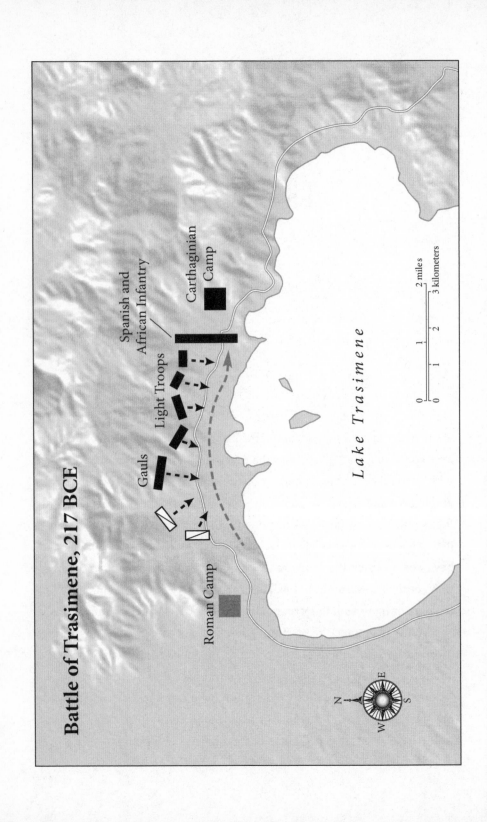

Battle of Trasimene, 217 BCE

Carthaginian Camp

Spanish and African Infantry

Light Troops

Gauls

Roman Camp

Lake Trasimene

0 1 2 miles
0 1 2 3 kilometers

N W E S

Hannibal moved very fast much of the time. Part of his speed of travel was necessary because he could ill afford to fight a larger enemy on its home ground too many times; battle attrition would become desperate with his relatively small army and dependence on Celts. His army had to hope to seize much of its supplies on the fly rather than have too long a train of slow pack animals, easily caught by the Romans.

Hannibal's decisions in Etruria and his prebattle moves were contingent on the character of Flaminius.[4] Whether Hannibal allowed little plundering through the Apennines and his first emerging into the Arno Valley—our sources are silent about it—such a decision would have been sensible because this kind of word spreads fast in relatively well-populated regions such as Etruria and would have revealed his movements en route to the Arno Valley. After the Arno marshes, however, Hannibal seems to have done little to keep his whereabouts secret. His actions may even have been provocative. Perhaps his plan was already laid to trap Flaminius in a place of his choosing. Moving south through the Val di Chiana in central Italy, Hannibal made it appear he was heading toward Rome.[5]

Surprising Flaminius, Hannibal continued quickly south beyond Arretium to the northern edge of Lake Trasimene and the hills above it. He had formed an audacious plan that would again require the help of nature as well as the impetuous Flaminius. It is vital to understand what Hannibal now knew about Flaminius.

THE CHARACTER AND CAREER OF
GAIUS FLAMINIUS NEPOS

Gaius Flaminius Nepos was already a man of contradictions and controversy before Trasimene, an arriviste with minimal history and a lot to prove, ready to risk everything to advance his career. The Romans call this kind of person with no patrician tradition and no family history in the Senate, a *novus homo*, "a new man."[6] Like other new men without noble ancestry, Flaminius was seemingly the first in his family to enter the ranks of the *cursus honorum*,[7] or the "course of offices," as a high elected official, leading ultimately to the Senate. Such advancement was rare at the time but possible, especially after 287 BCE, when the last patrician check on the Plebeian Council was lost, and the plebeians gained political equality.[8]

But in his case, Flaminius was entirely the beneficiary of the plebeian vote, not patrician backing. He had been a censor[9] and a tribune of the plebs and a plebeian consul just a few years before, in 223. His being a *novus homo* alone would immediately put him at odds with the majority of patricians in the Senate, but his flamboyant disregard for custom and his quarrelsome individuality were the deeper roots of his political problems. He regularly challenged the authority of the Senate, which naturally endeared him to the commoners.

While tribune of the plebs in 232, Flaminius helped pass a popular land reform that distributed recently conquered Etrurian land south of Ariminum to the poor, who had lost much during the war. Naturally, the Senate opposed this, but he did not consult them—a severe breach of custom and the Roman constitution. Flaminius had also greatly angered the patricians in the Senate in 218 by being the sole vote in support of the Lex Claudia law which was intended to stop senators from profiting from commerce abroad. He felt that they were already wealthy enough and believed this practice was a conflict of interest for those who govern. He overstepped his authority by trying to rein in the powerful Senate and was voted down vehemently.

During his censorship of 220 BCE, Flaminius had been responsible for creating and constructing a major trunk road north from Rome, through Umbria, to Ariminum. This was the famous Via Flaminia, one of the oldest Roman roads and duly named after him, crossing the Apennines considerably east of Arretium, a course of 210 miles (329 kilometers). Flaminius was very proud of this success, and to be fair, his leadership had some administrative and financial merit. But this is quite different from good military strategy.

As a patrician himself, Livy was scornful of Flaminius, deeming him unworthy of the office of consul for his multiple infractions. Just like a politician—exactly what Flaminius was—whose acute sensitivity to popular support made him often reactive rather than proactive, Flaminius sought every expedient opportunity, however ultimately foolish, to please his power base among the plebeians rather than appease the Senate. He knew he had no other means of support, unlike his wealthy patrician counterparts, who were landowners or had other commercial bases of power.

But as consul, he went quietly and directly to Arretium as a private citizen would, ignoring all the requirements incumbent on an office-holder before taking such action. This was outrageous to the Senate, and his colleagues promptly recalled him, to be dragged back if necessary. Flaminius ignored the Senate's messengers. This defiance was unprecedented. Livy says the Senate angrily proclaimed, " 'Flaminius'—such was the cry—'is now at war not only with the Senate, but with the gods.' "[10]

Flaminius had justified to himself that the patricians in the Senate would have delayed him, either to falsify the auspices or tie him up with petty duties that took too much of his time. We don't know whether the Senate fully understood his character, hastiness, and military inadequacy, but it is possible that they wanted to observe him and gauge his readiness, given the recent military setbacks at Ticino and Trebia. But Livy relates that an animal being sacrificed in the presence of Flaminius—presumably at Arretium—leapt from the altar, escaping before the deed was finished and spattering blood all over the bystanders. This was apparently interpreted universally as "an omen of coming disaster."[11] Livy may have been implying the coming defeat of Rome as a result of Flaminius' hubris and a divine act. He set up Flaminius against Hannibal: doomed before the battle began.

While not everyone blames Flaminius entirely,[12] Livy was not alone in his low opinion of the consul. Here's what Polybius says about Hannibal's discovery of Flaminius:

> He learned that Flaminius was a thorough mob-courtier and dema-
> gogue, with no talent for the practical conduct of war and exceedingly
> self-confident. Hannibal calculated that if he passed by the Roman
> army and advanced into the country in his front, the Consul [Flamin-
> ius] would on the one hand never look on while he [Hannibal] laid it
> waste for fear of being jeered at by his soldiery; and on the other hand

he would be so grieved he would follow anywhere, in his anxiety to gain the coming victory himself without waiting for the arrival of his colleague [Servilius Geminus]. From all this he concluded that Flaminius would give him plenty of opportunities of attacking him. And all this reasoning on his part was very wise and sound.[13]

The modern consensus is little different: Flaminius was rash and imprudent, and Hannibal had accurately assessed the man.[14]

LAYING THE TRAP FOR FLAMINIUS

Ever ready to cite divination as predicting human folly, Livy relates two more omens that spooked Flaminius' officers as he set out to chase Hannibal with his army. First his horse threw him, and then one of the legionary standards, a metal pole with an eagle and legion ID, was stuck in the ground. No matter how hard the standard-bearer tried, he could not budge it. Livy puts these words in Flaminius' mouth: "Tell them to dig it out if they are too weak with fright to pull it up." Flaminius' lack of humility stands out glaringly in this anecdote. He marched off without first sending his scouts to ascertain the situation. This must have agonized his officers, who knew better. Did Flaminius just rush out without giving his army adequate opportunity to verify where Hannibal was going?

By now it was mid-June. Making sure that Flaminius was following him and could see his movements, Hannibal turned east at the north end of the lake toward Perusia (modern Perugia) instead of south toward Rome. Timing it perfectly, when daylight was finally fading, the last of Hannibal's army disappeared into the very narrow Borghetto gap between the north end of Lake Trasimene and the steep hills of Cortona. The army of Flaminius had followed Hannibal from a modest distance, arriving at sunset, as Livy noted,[15] but the Roman army pulled up short as night began to fall. The soldiers could probably even see Hannibal set up camp at the far end of the lakeside valley. They would camp and pick up Hannibal's trail the next morning. Looking into the small valley through the Borghetto gap, one can still see at summer dusk—as I did—the last glow of sunset on the hills above even as the little valley is in the dark shadow of the high hills.

But that night, Hannibal shifted his men around to several locations. Under cover of darkness, portions of his army were split up and posted in several of the steep ravines whose streams fed the lake from the north. Had Flaminius' scouts reported anything, they would have seen only the red glare of the high number of army campfires clustered together in the distance.

The Romans apparently didn't notice the hidden movements of whole units of thousands of men and horses in the dark, most of them moving upward along the heights of the ravines above the small plain. Hannibal would have demanded stealth and quiet for this maneuver and few if any torches to show the way. Hannibal secreted his Numidian cavalry in the western hills nearest the Borghetto gap. He hid his light infantry of pikemen and Balearic slingers in the hills near modern Tuoro, above the lakeside route. Then just eastward, next to the light infantry, he hid his Celtic allies. Finally, his many units of Africans and Spanish heavy infantry stayed close to his camp in the east of the valley, the only ones who might have been visible the next morning. Polybius states that Hannibal's army units formed a continuous line under the hills,[16] albeit much hidden, so they would be roughly parallel to the lake's northern shore except at the very end of the lake.

That night, Flaminius' wary officers must have been telling him not to advance but to wait for Hannibal either to come out or for the army of the coconsul Servilius to arrive from Ariminum with an array of several legions he commanded, as he would have heard by now of Hannibal's movements in Etruria. But Flaminius overruled them.

THE BUGLES OF BATTLE, HORNS OF DEATH

When the next morning dawned, nature could not have been more accommodating for Hannibal's trap. Some ancient poetic sources such as Ovid (a Roman poet of the Augustan Age 43 BCE to 17 CE) say it was the summer solstice, June 21,[17] and Hannibal may have already seen in previous days a common local summer phenomenon when a warm air mass over land meets the much cooler air mass over a body of water: fog was thick along the north shore of Lake Trasimene, noticeably hemmed in by the steep hills. Whether or not Hannibal anticipated the early morning fog, he certainly used it to his advantage. Much of his army was invisible in either the foliated hilly ravines or the early-morning fog that hung thick in the valley.

Livy says that Flaminius sent no reconnaissance whatsoever ahead of him. Many have wondered why Flaminius did not send advance scouts into the narrow Tuoro plain before he raced his army through the narrow valley opening.[18] Was Flaminius that foolhardy in a makeshift battle plan?

If Hannibal on higher ground saw or heard Flaminius' vanguard pouring without hesitation into the gap at first light, he then knew his plan would work. He waited until the Roman army advanced in formation all the way to his front line of African and Spanish infantry. Then the war bugles gave the signals with their prepared sounds. The echoing call from all sides across the valley must have bewildered the Romans, surrounded as they were now in soupy fog.

Hannibal's cavalry descended downhill behind the Romans and cut off any escape by sealing off the Borghetto. Now the Romans were in a gauntlet: Hannibal's army attacked on three sides, with the lake to the south, likely in a line that stretched at least full four miles of the Roman column.[19] Here Hannibal used the marshy lake edge as part of his arsenal. Hannibal's separate forces seemed to have hit the entire Roman column simultaneously,[20] and the unready and totally surprised Romans had no time to change from marching formation to battle formation. A terrible onslaught came at them out of the fog with a roar—especially the Celts—and the thunder of horses. The Balearic slingshots pummeled the Romans, as did spears and other projectiles, appearing from nowhere, possibly before the Romans had their shields up.

The Romans fought bravely, and the fighting was fierce, but it was nearly a fait accompli. The sounds of battle came from everywhere in the fog, and the Romans would not have seen much of the enemy until it was upon them. No matter which way the Romans turned, death came from everywhere, and they were "cut down in their marching order," Polybius claims.[21]

Due to the fog, the sounds of battle—with thuds of blows, metal on metal, shouts, screams, and groans—would have been more apparent than visual evidence. This would have been part of the ethos of chaos intended by Hannibal and would have been much harder on the regularized formations of Romans than on Hannibal's army, especially his Celts, who championed individual hand-to-hand combat rather than close-knit organization. The fog hampered the efforts of Roman officers to turn rank and file into battle formation. It continued to stymie officers' commands to regroup if they could barely see one another, let alone the enemy. Many Romans must have fought valiantly, especially the veterans, who were trained to fight to the death. Their tragedy is due mostly to Flaminius' poor leadership, as Polybius says, "betrayed by their commander's lack of judgment."[22] Livy claims nobly that their one hope of life rested in their swords, ultimately dependent not on their officers but on their individual will to fight, however futile, but he may have been only putting a good face on one of the biggest ambushes in ancient history.[23]

If Hannibal's army had little visibility in the fog, at least it had the advantage of controlling the direction of the battle from the outset, whereas the Romans, individually and collectively, were caught in the vise of an attack that compressed them on all sides, with the only stationary force—the lake—being equally perilous. If the Romans backed too far into the water, some effects of hypothermia—such as the draining of body heat—would slow them down even more. Retreating up to their necks to escape, many Romans drowned in their heavy armor. Numidian cavalry were waiting wherever they might attempt to come ashore. Polybius says that many Romans surrendered in the lake, with only their heads above water, lifting their hands as they pitifully begged for mercy but were hacked down anyway.[24] The slaughter of Romans was everywhere: on the road, in the plain, and in the lake, whose lapping shallows were tinted with the blood of the Roman dead.

The battle lasted most of the morning—"three long bloody hours" as Livy puts it.[25] If there were an epicenter, it would have been around Flaminius. While Polybius denigrates Flaminius as being most dejected and filled with the "utmost dismay,"[26] and possibly dread at finally seeing his folly, Livy claims instead that he was moving about trying to help any Roman with a core group of his best men, who were "as determined to save him as the enemies were to kill him."[27]

But Flaminius was conspicuous in his ornate consular regalia and equipment, no doubt also surrounded by the glint and color of legionary standards, and this eventually was a magnet for enemy attention. At the heart of the battle, one Insubres Celt warrior on horseback, possibly a leader named Ducarius,[28] recognized Flaminius and spurred his horse forward into the thickest battle frenzy, crying that he would sacrifice the consul to the Celts whom Romans had turned into ghosts. This was a normal Celtic action, looking to be a champion with a glorious kill of an enemy commander. He rode with furious abandon over Flaminius' armor bearer and with great force impaled the consul with his lance, driving it through his body with his momentum. Flaminius dropped like a stone. His men surrounded him with shields to protect him as he lay dying, even as the Celtic lancer may have tried to take a trophy by stripping him of a piece of consular regalia such as his plumed helmet.

News of Flaminius' death spread faster than an official command and sent the surviving Roman army into final panic. Such an important death invigorates one side in battle just as it fills the other with dread, a now-headless army. The panic was probably exacerbated by the fact that, as one historian points out, many of these soldiers had already witnessed Hannibal's tactical surprise at the Trebia River in 218.[29] They had witnessed one impetuous general in Sempronius and now likewise in Flaminius.

One group of six thousand Romans at the front, however, had fought its way out, and when the soldiers could see nothing due to the fog, they climbed to a spur over the valley. But when the sun's heat on this June day finally dispersed the fog, it was clear that the valley was filled with Roman bodies piled everywhere. Hannibal's army was gathering groups of prisoners who had surrendered or were too wounded to fight. Reminders of the Roman bloodbath are still found today in relict names of local streams such as the Sanguineto (bloody place).

The isolated six thousand Roman soldiers who had escaped the slaughter were soon surrounded in a village where they had fled. Maharbal, Hannibal's Numidian cavalry commander, and Spanish infantry and pikemen had noticed them fleeing and soon found them. The Romans surrendered, thinking that if they abandoned their weapons their lives would be spared. But Hannibal freed only the Romans' Celtic allies, sending them to their homes with the astute propaganda of claiming their enemy was not him but Rome.

The number of Roman deaths at Trasimene is stated at 15,000, with an equal number of prisoners, including the wounded. This is as much as a 75 percent loss,[30] a staggering quantity for an ancient battle. An entire Roman army of at least around 40,000 men was reduced to only the 6,000 soldiers who escaped in disorder as the broken fragments of several legions. One of the ironies of this battle is that Flaminius had brought hundreds of manacles and chains[31] to carry off Hannibal's army as slaves to Rome. Now their own chains must have bound them as they were taken captive prisoners of Hannibal. Hannibal lost a tenth of the number of Roman deaths—about 1,500, according to Polybius—although Livy claims 2,500 enemy dead,[32] mostly the Celts who had been at the direct center of the Roman column that had fought first and probably last.[33]

The Romans protecting the body of Flaminius must have also soon perished because after the battle, Hannibal tried to give Flaminius a decent burial, but the body could not be identified on the battlefield. Flaminius' corpse had been likely stripped of armor and regalia and maybe decapitated in Celtic fashion. This possible decapitation was eerily symbolic of the now-headless Roman army at Trasimene.

The disaster of Trasimene was followed immediately by another awful setback. Up north, Servilius had by now heard that Hannibal was in Etruria and had sent four thousand cavalry from Ariminum to help Flaminius. He planned to follow soon with his full army, hoping to intercept Hannibal, possibly to march south along the Via Flaminia[34] so that he and Flaminius could bottle up Hannibal between them. Perhaps Servilius thought that together they could set up Hannibal in a trap, when it was the other way around.

Hannibal's informants who had been watching Ariminum told him of the cavalry force, and Hannibal immediately sent out Maharbal with some Numidian cavalry and pikemen. The more mobile Punic force caught the Roman reinforcements unprepared, slaughtered half, and took the remainder prisoner the next day. Three days after the battle at Trasimene, this action added another two thousand Roman deaths and an equal number of Roman prisoners carried away, an unheard-of catastrophe for a standing Roman army.[35]

The dire double news of the Trasimene defeat and of Servilius' reinforcements took Rome by utter surprise. The shock waves reverberated throughout Italy. According to Livy,[36] common citizens flocked en masse to the old Roman Forum, and the capital suddenly swelled with crowds who'd left their homes and gathered, filled with the dread of rumor. Wailing women waited at the city gates hoping to hear news of surviving loved ones. The crowds became so great that the Senate had to respond. The quaestor (a Roman magistrate, lower than praetor, involved in the treasury) Marcus Pomponius announced in the most laconic utterance, "We have been defeated in a great battle." Other praetors (an elected high Roman magistrate, sometimes legionary commanders of past armies) of the Senate forced the whole assembly to sit for days from dawn to dusk and debate who would succeed to restore leadership to the legions.[37] Trasimene was a true defeat, as the quaestor acknowledged before the assembled people of Rome; the most serious crisis possible.

Again, as at Trebia, Hannibal used nature—the lake and the fog—as a weapon of war, virtually as effective as a whole new army. Hannibal had achieved something unprecedented. He seems almost to have invented environmental warfare. Having incorporated it into his battle plan, he would be emboldened to use nature again.

Fourteen

FABIUS MAXIMUS AND ESCAPE

After the disaster of Trasimene, all of Rome was now wholly apprehensive, its confidence shattered. The Roman defeat with the death or capture of at least thirty thousand soldiers—adding in the defeat and capture of Servilius Geminus' four thousand cavalry en route from Ariminum—was a catastrophe that sent terror through Roman Italy. The paralyzed Romans were now unsure how to deal with Hannibal. First Ticino, then Trebia, and now Trasimene undermined their confidence in their vaunted military. Sharing leadership in the two-general system—a veteran officer and a political appointee—was now considered ill-advised.

After some worried dithering, Rome's primary response was to appoint a military dictator to coalesce military leadership. This decision was unusual because the last time a dictator had been appointed was in 249 during the First Punic War. While the surviving consul Servilius Geminus should have been involved in the appointment, he was still held up in Ariminum partly by wariness of Hannibal.

The Senate appointed the veteran Quintus Fabius Maximus as dictator to deal with Hannibal. This position consolidated power into one leader. His second in command, mainly over the Roman cavalry, was the younger Marcus Minucius Rufus, appointed *magister equitum*, or master of horse. Minucius had been a consul in 221,[1] and because Fabius could not choose his own cavalry officer, he had to accept Minucius, who was elected. Given their somewhat forced relationship and the complete contrasts between the two—Fabius being older, from a distinguished family, resolute and patient to a fault; Minucius being a proudly rising star, hyperactive and inclined to hot oratory—there was immediate friction between Fabius and Minucius.

QUINTUS FABIUS MAXIMUS

Hannibal had never encountered a Roman foe both so different from himself and other Roman generals and yet so cautious. Like the Scipios, Quintus Fabius Maximus (280–203 BCE) was a member of a prominent Roman military family, the Fabii. Fabius himself was a distinguished civil servant who had held the office of censor in 230 and was elected consul twice in 233 and 228 BCE, before his appointment as dictator. While everyone thought Fabius rigid, slow of mind, and inflexibly dull in his youth, Plutarch defended him as unwaveringly steadfast as an adult in military matters. Fabius was already much involved in this war because two years previously (219) he had been a member of the delegation that had gone to Carthage to complain about Saguntum, demand Hannibal's surrender, and ascertain Carthage's motives.

In the previous century, the family of Quintus Fabius had earned the right to style themselves Maximus as their final cognomen in the three-name system, identifying this branch of the Fabii as the "Greatest".[2] Fabius' new title of dictator (a temporary office of exceptional power, not a modern-day autocrat) for this severe military crisis allowed him enormous power, or imperium.[3] While he was old for this new office, around fifty-eight, Fabius was still the most respected survivor of the current Roman debacles, with considerable military experience.

Rome worried that Hannibal might be headed for the capital itself. Impromptu bulwarks of earthen berms were hastily reinforced, and farmers who feared Hannibal's advance quickly harvested their crops and fled to Rome. The few survivors of the encounters with Hannibal, possibly mostly deserters, improvised even more dramatic tales of this diabolic adversary and made themselves out as honorable veterans to detract from their shame.

Many superstitious Romans even fell back on religious fervor to curry favor with any god who might better protect them, including extra sacrifices to Mars, god of war. A special and serious banquet to which all the major twelve gods were invited—a *lectisternium*—was conducted after almost a two-century hiatus.[4] Added attention to omens was also important to make up for the apparent disregard of religion by Flaminius, who died at Trasimene, and Fabius made sure this neglect was corrected with massive public sacrifice and personal austerity.

After consolidating the city's defenses, especially strengthening walls, forging new weapons, and conscripting soldiers to man these walls, Fabius and Minucius raised about forty thousand men in replenished legions, half of whom were inexperienced recruits from burnt farms in the ravaged North. The new dictator assembled his two new legions of conscripts, gathered the remnants of Servilius' two legions, and then marched over the mountains east to Apulia to wait for Hannibal. Along the way, Fabius evacuated every town that he was glumly certain Hannibal would pillage. Fabius' grim determination was countered by Minucius' overambitious posturing—the master of horse convinced that Rome was superior.

Over the next few years, Fabius would ultimately earn, mostly posthumously, the famous—or infamous—epithet of *Cunctator*, "the Delayer," because of his cautious policies toward Hannibal, avoiding conflict wherever possible. As conservative as this strategy appeared, it was ultimately sound, given Hannibal's ability to destroy whatever Roman army he faced at this time. Fabius also rightly believed he could slowly restore Roman confidence with harassing tactics where he could pick off the enemy one by one in skirmishes against small raiding parties. He regarded such small successes as positive signs after battle debacles.[5] Whatever reservations might be held about Fabius relative to the more colorful Hannibal, it must be admitted that Fabius Maximus was the first to counter Hannibal's onslaught of favorable battle propaganda. He was the first Roman general who knew how to safely avoid Hannibal whenever possible.

HANNIBAL'S DEPLOYMENT AFTER TRASIMENE

After Trasimene, Hannibal had gone east through what is now Umbria over the Apennines to the region of Picenum and begun a slow march down the Adriatic coast. His troops were weary and their horses mangy. Hannibal's policy allowed as many foraging parties as necessary until the army regained strength, with seizure after seizure of autumn harvests. Once he learned how the Romans had filled the dearth of leadership after Trasimene, he used several ploys to sow Roman mistrust against their new dictator. He wanted to either provoke Fabius Maximus into a battle he could manipulate—as he had Sempronius and Flaminius, who were more experienced politically than militarily—or portray him as a weak coward.

Moving down the coast from Picenum to Apulia, Hannibal camped near the city of Arpi, where Fabius Maximus was camped nearby. Trying to draw out the Romans, Hannibal deployed his army for battle—but Fabius did not budge. Even though Roman officers such as Minucius were disgusted by Fabius' unwillingness to engage, Hannibal knew that caution was a virtue. Still, Hannibal now attempted to shame Fabius by open pillaging and amassing farm booty from territory that Rome had claimed from old Samnite holdings. Hannibal must have begun to appreciate that unlike prior Roman generals, Fabius was hard to provoke.

Wherever Hannibal went in a wake of destruction, a column of smoke marked his progress. Fabius followed at a reasonable distance, visible but sufficiently out of reach. Other than a few scouting skirmishes where he could take a few stray Carthaginian scouts, Fabius kept his mostly raw Roman soldiers out of harm's way, instead skillfully maneuvering to limit Hannibal from revictualizing his army by foraging. Fabius commanded Roman farms to destroy their farms and crops and evacuate them. The Roman dictator

harassed Hannibal's flanks with small skirmishes whenever possible to ex-
ecute without full engagement.[6] Fabius also kept to higher ground because
he recognized Hannibal's military superiority, especially in cavalry,[7] unlike
some of his fellow military officers, such as Minucius. Polybius makes it
clear that Fabius and the Romans had a distinct advantage over the invaders at this time: inexhaustible supplies of provisions and men.[8] Historians
have estimated the Roman free population at 300,000 adults from about 234
BCE, after the First Punic War, with Italian allies numbering about 600,000
and a slave population adding about another 2 million.[9] The same scholars also comment on Rome's extraordinary ability to levy resources for its
military mobilization in the Second Punic War. Even if this total is divided
in half to account for gender, there is no way Hannibal could compete for
soldiery and personnel for agricultural production even after heavy Roman
battle casualties. This may make his achievements with his veterans seem
even more remarkable.

With the Romans following behind and above on higher hill ground,
Hannibal marched west over the Apennines, through Benevento, and into
Campania, the richest and most fertile of all Roman lands—the *Ager Falernus*, because it was a volcanic region with the best soil. Campania was a
virtual cornucopia of Roman wealth. Hannibal had never seen such agricultural bounty, and he quickly acquired war booty, seemingly more than
his army could consume. The irony of sacking Campania's richest farmland
would not have been lost on Hannibal, because it was the rich Campanian
senators who had started the First Punic War when the Carthaginians had
threatened to overwhelm Sicily, which was close to their Roman villas in
Campania. One of Hannibal's camps for several weeks was close to Capua,
and the area was flooded with Hannibal's spoils and thousands of stolen
cattle.

Hannibal's Campanian sojourn was perfectly logical. First, as Polybius
stated,[10] this move would result in one of two Roman responses: either
the Romans would be forced to engage him in battle, or, by not engaging
him, they would concede he was the master of Italy. He in turn could then
persuade many more Italians to defect.[11] Second, because supplying and

feeding an army are such vital parts of warfare, having sufficient food for soldiers and fodder for animals can make or break a campaign. Tactics must adapt accordingly based on food availability. Living off the land, as Hannibal's invading army had to do—even more so than the Romans—meant that raiding farms and taking livestock were a necessity. In addition, what Hannibal seized deprived Rome of resources.[12]

Some historians have calculated the statistical needs of ancient armies and have compiled reasonable data to suggest that a consular army of several legions plus allies (around 20,000 men and 3,500 horses and pack animals) would consume around 35 tons of wheat and 25 tons of barley daily along with an optimum amount of 10,000 liters of wine and 2,000 liters of olive oil.[13] Daily grazing of animals during the right seasons was an absolute given, but winter added a huge strain on food supply. Armies would plan for whatever needs lay ahead from harvest time onward. So Hannibal felt justified in occupying Campania to acquire food for his army; whatever the risks Hannibal knew that this was his window of opportunity to acquire supplies.

According to Livy,[14] who rarely misses an opportunity to showcase Punic perfidy, Hannibal would soon devise a clever ploy to further undermine trust in Fabius. Like many Roman patricians, Fabius owned rich farmland in Campania, and Hannibal had learned the location from Roman deserters or locals. He then destroyed all the surrounding farms but left the land and vines of Fabius completely untouched. Livy says that Hannibal then spread rumors that Fabius was spared because he had made a secret deal with Hannibal. Fabius was mortified and delegated his son Quintus to sell the rich farm, using the proceeds to ransom Roman prisoners.[15]

Whether Livy's tale is true or not, Minucius was close to mutiny at Fabius' continuing reluctance to engage Hannibal. Even the Senate was beginning to doubt whether Fabius' caution was the right strategy as the profitable harvests of Campania were seized by Hannibal. Fabius *Cunctator*, the Delayer, was assailed by nearly everyone around him for his caution. This combination of rumor and scorn would have made many Roman patricians angry, but not Fabius, who had great patience and a thick skin.

HANNIBAL'S ESCAPE FROM THE AGER FALERNUS

Fabius determined in autumn that Hannibal was about to return east to Apulia for the coming winter, planning passage out of the *Ager Falernus* through the lower Apennines with his enormous column of spoils, including the thousands of head of cattle, many laden with harvested food supplies. Hoping to trap Hannibal in Campania, Fabius sent Minucius to block the Appian Way, the road south from Rome toward Capua, in the narrow coastal valley of Sinuessa. Meanwhile, he and his army occupied the heights of the Volturnus Valley at the gorge of Casilinum,[16] about three miles north of Capua—the only other way east out of Campania and where he expected Hannibal to cross. Fabius was right about Hannibal's route, and he was convinced he had Hannibal and his army boxed in. When Hannibal's scouts reported that the pass was blocked and guarded by Roman troops, Hannibal halted his army until nightfall in plain view of Fabius.

While Hannibal pondered the situation, Fabius sat tight, wondering what Hannibal would do. It certainly appeared that the Carthaginians were poised to break out the next day. Fabius knew that if Hannibal weighed the circumstances, he would see that only with great loss of life and a decimated army could he even reach the pass, since Fabius had four thousand Romans nearby to guard it and could easily defend the narrow route.[17] Believing the next morning would be one of destiny, Fabius retired after dark to sleep for the night, certain he had Hannibal contained and possibly could end Hannibal's campaign.[18]

But Hannibal hatched a clever scheme. At dusk he called a supply officer and told him to have his men collect and bundle as many dry sticks as possible from the surrounding valley floor and scrub. Since it was past harvest at the height of the year's dryness before the rains, this was accomplished easily, and the pile of dry tinder wood grew huge as Hannibal's men worked under the cover of dark and in silence.

By this time, the bulk of the Roman army had mostly gone to sleep, leaving only the Casilinum Pass itself guarded. Hannibal then had his men collect two thousand of the strongest cattle from the spoils and wait for his orders after their dinner meal. He pointed out a ridge above and not far from the Casilinum Pass but away from where he knew the bulk of Fabius' army to be camped and told them to mark it well because they would be furiously driving the cattle to that spot in the middle of the night. Hannibal's army rested for a few hours until around three o'clock in the morning when the Romans would be sleeping most deeply.

Awaking his army camp in whispered quiet, Hannibal ordered his men to tie the thick bundles of branches between the horns of the two thousand cattle and light them all together with fire as quickly as possible. The dry branches caught fire, and the cattle were prodded forward. It looked to anyone watching that a whole army was suddenly moving up the ridge through the low brush. The assembled bulk of Hannibal's full army with the rest of the spoils waited, hushed in great discipline below the Casilinum Pass under the noses of the unsuspecting Romans. The brilliant stratagem caught the Romans completely by surprise.

The frightened cattle with burning firebrands thundered up the ridge away from the pass, their fire-lit bundles looking just like thousands of torches carried by men; Livy says that the brands also scorched the hillside vegetation, causing even more fires that seemed to enlarge the enemy troops before the Roman eyes.[19] A group of Hannibal's chosen cattle drivers with pikemen herded the massed cattle from behind and on both sides, keeping them together, while others goaded them with weapons from the rear. The sleepy Roman guard units on watch noticed the moving fires and immediately jumped up, yelling and running toward the illuminated mass, thinking that Hannibal had sent his entire army that way because he was aware that the pass was guarded.

If the body of Fabius' main waking army also thought the same thing, and many of them tried to sleepily assemble and head off Hannibal's "army" of cattle ascending the ridge, the darkness covered the whole enterprise well. Meanwhile, Hannibal's army passed quietly en masse toward the now-unguarded Casilinum Pass and quickly and safely made it through. The Romans made so much noise in their haste that they were blind to anything but their mistaken quarry as they tried to cut off this escaping army of cattle.

Hannibal had anticipated this by choosing to run the cattle up the ridge in a direction away from both the Casilinum Pass and the main Roman army camp so that no Romans would cross his path as he took the pass.

When Fabius was wakened and told about the moving lights and noise, he refused to call out the rest of his army, thinking this was a trap.[20] Although there were a few fights between the pursuing bewildered Romans on the ridge and Hannibal's cattle-prodding skirmishers, even the Carthaginian pikemen and drivers quickly disappeared in the confusion. Some of the cattle escaped with them over the ridge and through the woods on the other side to catch up to the main Carthaginian force, the fires between their horns extinguished. Hannibal sent some of his armed Spaniards to fight any following Romans and accompany the last pikemen. About a thousand overzealous Roman soldiers were slaughtered as they tried to return to the Casilinum Pass.

The confused Roman army reassembled at dawn, and to Fabius' and the Romans' great disappointment and shamed befuddlement, morning light in the Volturnus Valley revealed that Hannibal's entire army had escaped Fabius' trap minus only a thousand or so cattle. This was the phantom army that had tricked the Romans in one of Hannibal's most famous maneuvers.[21] While Fabius had initially guessed right about Hannibal's route, his Carthaginian counterpart had more correctly gauged that the conservative Fabius would hold back his full army during the night, thinking rightly that there was a trick under way, as Polybius wrote.[22] Fabius waited out the night before fully assessing the situation.[23]

Hannibal's forces now moved quickly eastward, virtually unopposed, back to Apulia for their wintering. This was not only a return with rich rewards in booty from the very heart of Roman agricultural wealth in Campania—further demoralizing Rome—but also another psychological victory for Rome's enemies, rightly bolstering their confidence in Hannibal.

When word got to Rome, the humbled Fabius Maximus was criticized greatly for letting Hannibal escape—not least by his rival Minucius, who raged more at being absent during the maneuver than for hurt Roman pride. If overcautious Fabius *Cunctator* was personally prescient to delay meeting

Hannibal in battle, many Romans shuddered to think what might happen if their two armies actually met under the same leadership. Minucius lobbied everyone he could in Rome to replace Fabius as dictator. Fabius, unshakable although much maligned, was no fool and knew that the cleverest and most elusive commanders could reverse the tide by pretending to be the quarry when they were really the hunters.[24] Given the chance, he would still bide his time in the waiting game. For all the short-term perceptions of weakness in his "Fabian strategy," Fabius *Cunctator*'s decision to "not meet Hannibal in the open field unless Rome had the advantage" would turn out to be wise.[25]

Fifteen

CANNAE

Cannae still elicits a shudder from almost everyone after more than two thousand years. A considerable part of Hannibal's reputation as a military genius seems to rest on this half day in early August of 216 BCE, perhaps more than is justifiable.

Reconstructing the battle from sometimes confusing or even slightly contradictory sources is challenging, but enough consensus exists to provide a fairly reliable account. Even after winnowing out the hyperbole that accompanies such events, Cannae remains a singularly dramatic day. Standing on the hill above the valley where the Aufidus (now Ofanto) River winds to the coast, and walking back and forth on the narrow plain that is about a mile or so wide on an August day similar to that in the summer of 216, I was reminded that however peaceful and still it looked, the horrible fate of so many Romans in that battle had made Cannae infamous.

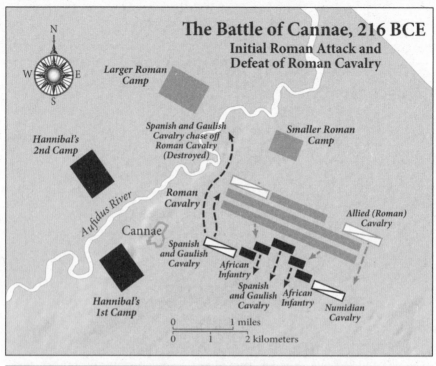

The Battle of Cannae, 216 BCE
Initial Roman Attack and Defeat of Roman Cavalry

N **W** **E** **S**

Larger Roman Camp

Hannibal's 2nd Camp

Spanish and Gaulish Cavalry chase off Roman Cavalry (Destroyed)

Smaller Roman Camp

Aufidus River

Roman Cavalry

Allied (Roman) Cavalry

Cannae

Spanish and Gaulish Cavalry

African Infantry

Spanish and Gaulish Cavalry

African Infantry

Numidian Cavalry

Hannibal's 1st Camp

0   1 miles

0   1   2 kilometers

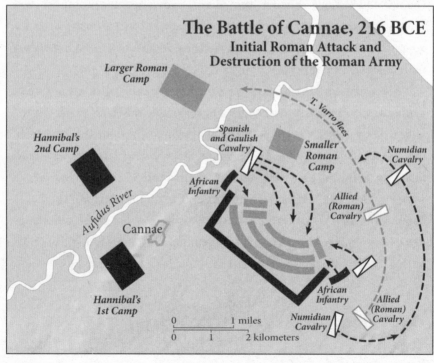

The Battle of Cannae, 216 BCE
Initial Roman Attack and Destruction of the Roman Army

Larger Roman Camp

Hannibal's 2nd Camp

Spanish and Gaulish Cavalry

Smaller Roman Camp

T. Varro flees

Numidian Cavalry

Aufidus River

African Infantry

Allied (Roman) Cavalry

Cannae

African Infantry

Allied (Roman) Cavalry

Hannibal's 1st Camp

Numidian Cavalry

0   1 miles

0   1   2 kilometers

THE HUMILIATION OF MINUCIUS

After Hannibal's brilliant but narrow escape at Volturnus, for most of 217 BCE, the armies primarily watched each other from a safe but wary distance. Whether encamped or moving, Fabius Maximus determined Roman policy despite his frustrated detractors in the field and back home in the Senate. Many skirmishes and raids took place between Campania and Apulia, not all of them in Hannibal's favor. But one skirmish—or little battle—stands out in 217 that reinforced the reputations of Hannibal and Fabius Maximus and showed the true colors of Marcus Minucius Rufus.

That summer, Fabius returned to Rome briefly to conduct obligatory religious rites, so the chafing Minucius as *magister equitum* finally had his chance to show his self-perceived valor and willingness to fight, in contrast to Fabius. Portions of Hannibal's army encamped at Geronium in Central Italy, 155 miles from Rome, had been sent out piecemeal to gather food supplies in raids in order to last the winter, and Minucius attacked a third of Hannibal's army that lacked the support of cavalry mobility. This action was counter to the strategy that Fabius had set in place in order to avoid direct engagement. While not entirely victorious in the skirmish—the Romans had five thousand casualties to the Carthaginians' six thousand—the rapturous accounts Minucius reported back to Rome made it sound like a major victory.

It seemed to many of Fabius' detractors that at last Rome had a champion ready to match Hannibal. In Rome, a senatorial decree made Minucius' office of *magister equitum* equal in authority to that of the dictator Fabius as army commander. That autumn, always looking for an opportunity to damage the Roman army, Hannibal discovered through his spies that an emboldened Minucius was chafing for action. Hannibal set a trap for him near Geronium.

Hannibal knew that a full Roman force would have been too large to take on at this time. But if he drew out one half of the divided Roman army under conditions he could control and inflicted great damage before the other half of the army joined, Hannibal could turn a numerical disadvantage into a temporary advantage. Plus, Hannibal understood Minucius' psychological disposition with his eager propensity to fight (now overconfident after the first summer skirmish) compared with Fabius' caution and unwillingness to fight. Hannibal believed he could thus exploit a divided army whose leadership was also divided. By night, under cover of darkness, Hannibal set up a force of at least five thousand soldiers hidden in many groups of two hundred to three hundred in hollows alongside and behind the main hill where he would lure Minucius.

In the morning Hannibal's army left the safety of Geronium and provoked Minucius with a visible force of light infantry. Minucius rashly engaged Hannibal with the half of the Roman forces under his command. Partly due to the hidden Carthaginians, who then rose up and attacked the Roman flanks that were fighting Hannibal, the skirmish turned into an ambush from behind and a rout of the Romans. A reluctant Fabius had to come to the rescue with the remaining Roman force. But after coming on the scene with his half army, Fabius disengaged without a full battle, instead committed warily to only a rescue and retreat. Likewise, Hannibal, having made his point and having destroyed many Romans, also withdrew his army rather than risk further attrition. Thus humiliated, Minucius was again reduced to being under the command of Fabius until Rome recalled both of them in December of 217, when Fabius' term of dictator expired. Hannibal had been bold when necessary and similarly held back as needed.

RAW ROMAN RECRUITS

One huge war factor almost always in Rome's favor was its seemingly endless supply of young recruits to form new legions of mostly citizen militia, whether fresh off the farms or from the cities. These soldiers would expect to return home to farms and cities when the war was over. By lowering the age of service to sixteen, Rome replenished the army from the attrition of Volturnus and Geronium as well as the legions lost by Sempronius at Trebia and Flaminius at Trasimene. These new legions would be added to the trained forces that Fabius and Minucius commanded while stalking

Hannibal. Rome's new army preparing that spring of 216 for a great battle in the summer was half made up of raw recruits who had hardly trained and had never faced a real enemy.

To deliver a knockout blow to Hannibal, Rome now put together a combined force of at least eighty thousand infantry of Romans and allies and six thousand cavalry—an astonishing eight legions[1]—but only four of them had any real battle experience. The discipline and battle order for which Rome would become legendary was not yet there, since molding recruits into a single fighting unit requires time for practice drills. Livy claims that almost two-thirds of the combined army were raw recruits,[2] thus relatively untrained. Some maintain the full army was together on the field only a few weeks before the great battle of Cannae, suggesting that so much time was spent in gathering recruits that the consuls joined in Apulia only a week prior to the battle.[3] If naïve Romans hoped that sheer numbers would be enough to overwhelm Hannibal's veterans desperate to survive in a hostile country, they were dangerously overoptimistic. On the other hand, if the Roman army was suspect, the leadership was somewhat impressive.

LUCIUS AEMILIUS PAULLUS

Lucius Aemilius Paullus was a member of one of the "first families" (likely the *gentes maiores*) of Rome, a famous patrician of the Aemilia family. As consul for the second time, he already had a distinguished career with a military triumph in Illyria in 219, having defeated Demetrius of Pharos, ruler of coastal Illyria—although with a dent to his reputation over unequal spoils of war.[4] As one of the consuls, he would share command of this army, the largest Rome had ever assembled for battle to date.[5] Rome was confident of his proven leadership abilities as one of the most respected generals from a prominent family steeped in the oldest traditions of Rome; a man who would bring time-honored values to the field of combat. The Aemilia clan was even said to trace its lineage back to Numa Pompilius, the second king of Rome as successor to Romulus, the orphaned mythical founder—with his twin, Remus—of Rome, and some legends even had it descended from

Ascanius, son of Aeneas. Although the Aemilia were most strongly associated with Sabine origins, the ethnic and cultured people east of early Rome, they were in any case one of Rome's vintage families.[6] Aemilius Paullus was at this time fairly old, possibly in his late fifties or even sixty, although this is uncertain, but he was undeniably one of the most senior Roman military commanders of this period. Aemilius Paullus as consul had not been in command very long—perhaps only weeks—and most of that time, he was on the march to Apulia. Polybius, generally reliable, wrote his history under Aemilian sponsorship, which influenced his account.

CAIUS TERENTIUS VARRO

On the other hand, Caius Terentius Varro was a plebeian, but he had risen in the Roman public ranks, having been a praetor in 218 and a popular speaker, often against the Senate. History has not treated Terentius Varro well, perhaps even more poorly than he deserves.[7] Certainly some of the shame of Rome's defeat at Cannae rests on his shoulders, yet perhaps too much relative to the fact that much of the newly composed army was inexperienced. Historians such as Livy, biased toward old patrician families, have also derogated him—contemptuous of his humble origins[8]—because Varro was another Roman "new man," first in his family elected to high office and not from one of the old patrician families like Aemilius Paullus, whose family could posthumously defend his name. While Varro was elected from the popular Plebeian Party, Livy calls Varro arrogant and impatient. He says that Fabius Maximus spoke words of counsel to Paullus in Rome before Cannae, warning him that his coconsul Varro was a demagogue, a reckless madman.[9] Fabius told Paullus he would be fighting two enemies; Carthaginian and Roman in Hannibal and Varro. Livy also claims the relationship between the two Roman consuls was more like competing gladiators than colleagues. Polybius is also unrestrained, although mostly omissive in his narrative about Varro, calling him inexperienced but also a disgrace.[10] How much of Livy's diatribe against Varro is true, we don't know, but Varro's battle actions around Cannae seem to have been more impulsive than those of Paullus.

TAKING THE FOOD DEPOT AT CANUSIUM

Summer was hot and dry in Apulia, leaving Hannibal somewhat desperate, with little possibility of foraging or raiding to feed his army. Knowing his supplies were on the verge of running out, Hannibal had moved his army south to Cannae to be closer to the rich farmland around Canusium. He captured the entire grain supply and other harvested food at this Roman depot, which may have even staved off a Carthaginian or allied rebellion.

Now in late July, the massive Roman army under its two commanders followed Hannibal through Apulia. By taking the food depot at Canusium, Hannibal even forced the Roman army to engage his army perhaps sooner than it would have liked, since the Romans too would have faced some of the same food and supply limitations.[11] Hannibal would also have known how many of the Roman army were recruits and would have preferred to face them before they were better trained, so the raid on Canusium could be construed as a brilliant tactic by Hannibal to get the Roman armies to fight prematurely.

PREPARING FOR BATTLE

Polybius says that like any good general before battle, when anticipation runs high but nervous fear can eat away at the very marrow of courage, Paullus gave a speech to encourage the huge assembled army, emphasizing their advantages. The Romans had an almost 2-to-1 numerical infantry superiority over Hannibal. Strengthening the resolve of the fresh recruits, Paullus told them they were fighting alongside two-year veterans who had fought under Fabius Maximus and knew Hannibal's tactics. He added that Hannibal's army was depleted—down to only a third of those who crossed the Ebro River in Spain—and was now far from home and deep in a hostile foreign land. Many of Hannibal's troops were mercenaries fighting only for pay. Boldly, Paullus reminded the Roman army that their forces were defending their homeland, fighting for their country, wives, and children, and that the unlucky circumstances of Trebia and Trasimene were now reversed in their favor. "Behave like men," he exhorted, "and there is no reason left why we should not be victorious."[12] It was mostly good advice, making some sense out of the previous reversals, but history would have it otherwise.

Plutarch tells the famous story of how some Carthaginians were in trepidation over the vast number of assembled Romans. A Carthaginian staff officer named Gisgo remarked how astonishing it was to see so many Roman soldiers, and, suggesting Hannibal overheard the comment, Plutarch places in his mouth the famous retort meant to ease fear: "Yes, but in all that sea of soldiers, not one of them is named Gisgo." The assembled officers laughed at Hannibal's wryness, and tension was broken as the ranks behind heard laughter and decided the situation must be favorable.[13]

THE BATTLE UNFOLDS

After replenishing his army's food with Canisium's supplies, Hannibal first set up his camp on the west bank of the Aufidus, facing north to the coming Roman army that his scouts had identified. This also gave him the benefit of not having the seasonal dust and sand-laden wind—the *libeccio*—blowing from Africa in his men's eyes but at their backs. The libeccio would limit Roman visibility just enough to be a factor in battle. Livy mentions this phenomenon most clearly,[14] and even Silius Italicus states it as a contributing factor in the battle.[15] Hannibal's decision to have the Romans face the wind must have been deliberate.[16]

The Romans—especially Paullus—were not happy with the flat ground Hannibal had chosen,[17] knowing that it would favor Hannibal's more numerous and more mobile cavalry. In fact, this large Roman army lacked full cavalry support, having only six thousand to Hannibal's ten thousand.[18] Several skirmishes took place over the next two days, with some of Hannibal's light infantry and cavalry harassing surprised Romans still on the march, although the Romans beat them back and inflicted some casualties before nightfall. The Romans divided into two camps on either side of the river, the larger on the southeast bank. But the following day, Hannibal moved his camp to the southeast bank, where his Numidian cavalry prevented many of the Romans dispatched to the Aufidus River from obtaining water, something that could prove disastrous in the heat of summer before a major battle. Again, this must have been a deliberate tactic. The Romans left one legion and allies to guard their camp, leaving about ten thousand out of the battle.

August 2, 216 BCE, was the fateful day for Rome. Polybius says that due to his inexperience and impatience,[19] the consul Varro was ready to fight on this terrain regardless of the disadvantage to heavy infantry, which needed more space. As the early morning sky lightened, Varro was in command, and at dawn the consular red flag could be seen from his tent, the sign of battle. The flag's red color would prove to be an eerie omen. The Roman army assembled slowly and joined forces. Although there has been some debate about the battle's exact location,[20] the larger force crossed the Aufidus River and met the smaller force already there. Together they massed to form a line of battle, with the right Roman flank by the river facing south and the left Roman flank on the plain. Both flanks were made up of cavalry, with the remaining allied cavalry on the right. The Roman center was the heavy infantry of the eight combined legions: at least fifty-five thousand soldiers with the support of the fifteen thousand *velites*, the light infantry armed with *hastae* javelins, Roman short thrusting spears. Unusual for battle and perhaps a factor in what would happen, the Roman infantry was packed much closer than normal,[21] probably because the river compressed its space. Not counting cavalry, the Roman line was likely a mile wide but much deeper, giving the combatants the confidence to press forward as needed, but unwise when they had little room to maneuver, retreat, or even flee as necessary because the plain was less than a mile and a half wide.[22] The Roman plan seems predicated at least in part on not being outflanked by the superior and more numerous Carthaginian cavalry. The proximity of the Aufidus River was meant to prevent this maneuver. The Romans trusted their heavy infantry to hold ground in the first clash of battle and then inexorably advance to break the less numerous Carthaginian line at its center with their superior numbers. It could work if the Roman legions moved as one well-trained and organized unit in battle and if their dual cavalry stood its ground and then broke the Carthaginian cavalry. But given the narrow plain, and because so many seasoned Roman troops had been decimated by the earlier debacles of Trebia and Trasimene, the heavy infantry was composed mostly of recruits without battle experience, commanded mostly by new officers who also had little real experience. This would prove to be disastrous. Varro headed the Roman allied cavalry on the right with some infantry, Paullus commanded the Roman cavalry on the left, and the proconsul, a governor of a province, below a consul, who could command an army, Servilius Geminus held the center of heavy infantry legions.

Hannibal was ready and immediately brought his entire forces to face the Romans, many of his troops having also been encamped across the Aufidus but now moving quickly and then swinging to face the Romans and lining up according to expected battle order. Hannibal first sent out his Balearic slingers and javelin force to cover his troop movement. With a total of about forty thousand infantry, Hannibal was outnumbered by at least twenty thousand additional Roman infantry.[23] His allied heavy cavalry of Spanish and Celtic horses was on the left under the command of Hasdrubal; on the right, Maharbal or Hanno commanded the Numidian cavalry.[24] Hannibal himself commanded the center, where he placed the allied Celt and Spanish infantry, possibly made up of twenty thousand Celts and four thousand Spanish, with the Libyans and other Africans divided on the two sides, possibly as many as ten thousand soldiers. The Africans were behind the line, where the Romans did not see them.[25] Hannibal's shallower line was stretched thinly to match the Roman battle width. When every unit was in place, Hannibal commanded the center to move forward in an outward bulge to face the Romans. His brother Mago was with him behind the lines to encourage the allied infantry. Hannibal must have realized this was where the full force of the Romans was going to be concentrated and knew his presence was most important here if he was to turn the enemy's own strength against itself, as planned.[26]

The spectacle of Cannae's massed armies just before full battle began must have been truly inspiring and at the same time frightening, especially to the Roman recruits. War trumpets and shouts of encouragement from officers would have been heard on the Roman side, along with prayers and the jostle of metal and leather as well as the stamping and whinnying of the horses. The early morning light would have reflected off the soldiers' new armor. From the Carthaginian side also would have come a wave of sound, especially the intense war cries and boastful bellows of the Celts, some of whom may have worn painted faces but not much more than that, as many Celts fought naked. The Celts whipped up themselves for combat holding up their long and heavy iron swords with vows of mayhem and maiming. More than a few of the soldiers of both armies would have been banging their swords on their shields, so the clamor must have been deafening for the moment. Hannibal's Spanish allies looked much like the Romans in their armor and shields confiscated from Trebia and Trasimene. They wore white tunics with proud purple stripes ("dazzling," says Livy[27]), but they carried different swords than the Romans— Spanish swords[28]—and they may have wielded the wicked, sharp *falcata*: cleaver and sword together, with a blade that was narrower near the hand but widened toward the front; its center of gravity was near its heavier front end, and it then narrowed again to its thrusting point. Polybius notes that the *falcatas* could "thrust with as deadly effect as they cut."[29]

Then the clear command for battle rang out across the plain on each side, and both armies surged forward with the growing thunder of cavalry. At first, the light infantry advance guards clashed—with the Balearic fighters doing damage with their slingshots, raining a barrage of missiles from a distance—until the bulge of Hannibal's center made contact with the deep Roman infantry pushing forward from behind. Because the space by the river was so narrow, the cavalries near the Aufidus collided quickly without the normal wheeling about in this constricted space. Dismounted hand-to-hand combat was fierce—even barbaric, according to Polybius.[30] Here, despite the bravery of the Roman cavalry, the superior experience, precise execution, and possibly greater numbers of the Carthaginians gradually gave them the upper hand. The Romans were driven along the river, where there was no escape, and slaughtered without mercy along the banks as they turned to retreat. However valiant they had been, this Roman cavalry unit was scattered and nearly destroyed by Hasdrubal's cavalry, which chased the survivors until they either dropped or were cut down. Aemilius Paullus had been wounded at the very beginning with a slingshot blow to the face—a Balearic slinger could hurl a projectile at 120 miles per hour and kill a man fifty steps away.[31] Although he no longer led the decimated cavalry, Paullus continued to rally the central mass of Roman infantry.

The Roman infantry legions pushed forward hard against the thinner line of enemy infantry at the center, massed in tight, traditional phalanxes, which was probably not the best formation under the circumstances because they were eventually so pressed together as a unit only the outer edges could actually wield weapons.[32] The opposing bulge of Celts and Spanish infantry resisted with fierce combat but was never as numerically deep as the Romans. The Carthaginian allies slowly began to crumple as they backed up before the line of almost endless Romans. The Romans must have sensed the enemy giving way. The advancing soldiers penetrated deeper and deeper into the shallower Carthaginian infantry, which had to yield, although Romans as well as Carthaginians fell in the heavy fighting.

None of the Roman leadership thought anything amiss or seems to have considered that this Celtic and Spanish infantry retreat could have been intentional. After all, relentless pressure from their men seemed to be the reason that the Carthaginian center buckled.

The wounded Paullus may have no longer been able to oversee the battle. Dismounted as he was, he probably could not see over the chaos from so many thousands on the battlefield plain. The Roman infantry was now committed to moving forward while still countless soldiers pushed from behind. Only the outermost edges of each row were actually engaged in fighting—the rest of the Roman infantry was squeezed too close together to use its weapons. This was ominous because as they had pushed forward, the Romans would be gradually surrounded on three sides by their enemies.

On the other side to the east, the superior Numidian cavalry facing the Romans likewise gradually routed the allied cavalry under Varro on the Roman left wing. This engagement had been a stalemate until Hasdrubal arrived at the rear of the Romans' left wing of allied cavalry after having destroyed the other Roman cavalry right wing by the river. This Roman cavalry on the left wing was now caught in a pincer between the Numidian light cavalry and Hasdrubal with the Celtic and Spanish heavy cavalry. The remaining Roman allied horsemen, still mobile enough to flee northward, did so with Varro, who abandoned the field of battle, the Numidians giving some chase. Instead of following them, an observant Hasdrubal turned his attention to the Roman infantry, as he was now behind it with his victorious force of Carthaginian heavy cavalry. The Roman cavalry had been taken out of battle and defeated, which would prove decisive.

This is the pivotal moment where history was made at Cannae. The savage intensity of the close fighting in the center of the battlefield now underlined the genius of Hannibal's shrewdness in turning a numerical disadvantage into an advantage. Until now, a Carthaginian victory was not predictable. But now the variables came into play. Much of the Roman infantry were over-committed to moving deep into the enemy line and were closely pressed be-cause of the terrain—which Hannibal had chosen—and falsely thought that their brute numerical strength would be decisive. The Carthaginian cavalry had defeated the Roman cavalry, which then could not come to the aid of the infantry. Paullus was wounded and unable to lead untested Roman recruits and their officers. Varro had fled the battle and abandoned his comrades in arms. There had been a lack of unity in Roman leadership that continued until the day of battle; now there was also thirst and dust, and finally the abyss of Roman terror and surprising despair that more than filled the void of inexperience. During the twenty-seven-year Peloponnesian War (431–404 BCE) between Athens and Sparta, the Greek historian Thucydides, who left an objective account of the Peloponnesian War in the late fifth century BCE, witnessed and recorded battlefield stress, noting that war was a "violent mas-ter teacher."[33] Surely the new Roman soldiers at Cannae suffered the classic symptoms of battle stress such as uncontrollable adrenaline flow causing a pounding heartbeat, a sinking feeling in the stomach, cold sweat, weakness, vomiting, involuntary urination and defecation, and other physical effects.[34] These signs of trauma so often trump bravery and valor, as we now know.

Because they had advanced far forward, thousands of Roman infantry were now trapped. Perhaps they had never seen the Libyan and African heavy infantry troops being revealed on either side of them, especially if, like the Spanish, some of the enemy was wearing Roman helmets or holding captured shields amid the vision-obscuring dust. While Hasdrubal closed in from the rear along with much of the returning Numidian cavalry, and the dismayed Romans in the rear turned to face them, the two contingents of Hannibal's Libyan and other African heavy infantry on the sides turned inward nearly simultaneously,[35] and the famous double envelopment began. Hannibal's central force stopped its retreat, whether genuine or false, and renewed the attack. The Romans were suddenly boxed in as Hannibal's army pressed even closer. Roman *gladius* short swords[36] were no match for Celtic long swords and the downward sweep of Libyan sabers and perhaps the deadly Spanish *falcatas* that could chop off arms and even legs.[37] The heavy weight of the Roman infantry arms—chain mail, helmets, shinguards, shields, and weapons—hampered full movement and now began to cause exhaustion.[38] Unable to even fully move their arms, the Romans were butchered. The plain began to fill with pools of Roman blood. There was no room to maneuver, let alone escape. This was the turning point at Cannae.

As Roman hopes evaporated amid an awareness of defeat, the army's strength was sapped. Meanwhile, Paullus bled profusely from his wounds while seated on the ground, too weak to remount a horse, surrounded by his few surviving cavalry guards. He was offered a horse to escape but refused, ordering his men to flee while they could in the precious minutes they had; to go and give word to defend Rome. Paullus was quickly surrounded and killed. The last thing he would have heard were the groans and screams of the dying men all around him as the pride of Rome was broken.

The awful sound of battle finally subsided as the dust settled. When it was over, Livy numbered fifty-five thousand Romans who died that day at Cannae; Polybius, seventy thousand. Carthaginian total dead numbered just under six thousand.[39] It was maybe six hours from oblique morning light to the intense sun of midafternoon. One full legion survived, including the ten thousand captured Romans who had been left at the camp and the few survivors of six thousand horsemen. Four tribunes, including Publius Scipio and the son of Fabius Maximus, went to Rome with Varro as quickly as possible. Livy says nineteen thousand Roman prisoners were taken at Cannae, which would amount to about two legions.[40] Historians estimate more dead soldiers at Cannae than in any other day of battle in Western History, and that 30,000 gallons of blood were spilled in that one day.[41]

Birds of prey descended quickly on the field as exhausted Carthaginians sat down to rest, while other, human scavengers, began collecting trophies. This went on for days. Hannibal must have joined the team of officers surveying and scouring the field where heaps of bodies lay, searching for his wounded and the dead Roman high command. Rome's military leadership was decimated. Not only had Aemilius Paullus perished, but other dead generals included Servilius Geminus and Marcus Minucius, the impetuous master of horse under Fabius Maximus. Twenty-nine out of forty-eight tribunes were killed,[42] and eighty senators or elected magistrates of senatorial rank perished, as did more than two hundred *eques*: Roman knights whose gold rings the victors collected on the field of death.

Terentius Varro was the most senior Roman leader who survived, because he fled. Why did Varro flee the battlefield so early? Was it merely self-preservation as a consul or was it the panic of an inexperienced war leader? While bravery can be foolish, we admire those whose bravery makes a positive difference just as we scorn those whose cowardice also makes a negative difference. On the other hand, was Varro's flight that significant? Was it the main contributing factor to Hannibal's cavalry completing the double envelopment at the rear and closing the box on Rome's massed infantry?

Some suggest that the great lengths that Polybius but especially Livy go to vilify Varro imply a deeper motive: namely, to deflect attention from the inconvenient truth that Paullus may have been actually the commanding consul that day.[43] If true, history has done Varro an injustice, but that still does not erase his flight from battle.

It has been often estimated that 20 percent of all Roman males between the ages of eighteen and fifty died that day at Cannae. Across its plain, the stench must have been terrible, as massing flies descended on the piles of bodies. The gravely wounded numbered in the thousands as well, some dying slowly, although many must have quickly succumbed to fever and septicemia. Livy describes in detail how some of the mortally wounded had dug their heads into the earth to smother themselves and end their suffering. He also relates in grisly fashion how one Roman, his useless arms unable to wield a weapon, in his dying rage bit off part of the face of a Numidian trapped beneath him.[44] Carthaginian medics dispatched those deemed too injured to be saved, both from Hannibal's army and the Romans. We don't know how many days it took to bury the thousands of dead.

AFTERMATH AND MAHARBAL'S RETORT

The Punic cavalry leader, Maharbal, urged Hannibal to march on Rome immediately—boasting he could feast atop the Capitolium, the main temple on Rome's most sacred hill, in five days—but Hannibal demurred. No doubt he was thinking back to how Saguntum had taken six months to fall even with siege weapons, and Rome was much vaster and better protected, with a large wall, a good water supply, and still a large population that could see to its defense. His army was exhausted, and the road would be very long—250 miles—for the hardened veterans, and longer yet for the wounded and sick they could not leave while still in enemy territory. Fresh cavalry could have barely made the trip in five days, let alone taken the city.[45] Maharbal is said to have retorted, "You know how to win but not how to take advantage of victory."[46]

Livy maintains that many believed this decision not to immediately move squandered an opportunity and saved Rome. This notion has been popular through history, some agreeing with Maharbal and Livy.[47] Whether taking Rome was truly attainable or too remote a goal we will never know for sure, although Hannibal was most likely wise in his assessment. It is certain that if Hannibal had been able to take the city of Rome, history would have been different but that looms as one of the largest "ifs" in military history. Hannibal had another plan and different ambitions.

When Hannibal began negotiations following his victory at Cannae, setting steep prices for ransom of the Roman prisoners but releasing the Celtic allies who had fought for Rome and sending them home, he told the Romans he was not waging a war to exterminate Rome but merely to recover the dignity and guarantee the survival of Carthage and its place in the Mediterranean. He wanted Rome to settle a peace that would reverse the humiliating losses of Sicily and Sardinia and the costly penalty of the war indemnity Hamilcar Barca had paid out from Spain; a peace that would return the status Carthage had before the Treaty of Lutatius of 241 that took away its sea trade.

Hannibal also predicted that the northern Celts who had rebelled against Rome following Ticino and Trebia, as well as Rome's mercurial allies in South Italy—including some of the Samnites and Greeks as well as Apulians, Lucanians, and Bruttians—would turn from Rome to him if he exerted enough pressure once they saw Rome's vulnerable position after such a resounding defeat. He was proven mostly correct for a few years. Livy claims that the upper classes in Campania generally preferred Rome, but the lower classes sided mostly with Hannibal.[48]

One Roman conclusion from Cannae must have been a concession that not only did their one "knockout blow to Hannibal" not work but also that one singular battle was unlikely. This would certainly justify Fabian caution.[49] Yet Hannibal seriously misjudged the Romans if he thought they would accept Cannae as a final defeat. Maybe earlier wars had offered sufficient outcomes for a thoroughly vanquished enemy to capitulate as he expected of Rome, but Rome was a new breed of people that would fully admit defeat only on its own terms. Too many Romans believed their destiny was to expand as an empire, not simply go back to being merely a regional power. Before Hannibal, Pyrrhus beat the Romans time and again, but the victories were costly, and Rome never gave up.[50] Nor would Rome relinquish its newfound sea rule. Cannae, terrible as it was, did not offer Rome enough of a reason to sue for peace because the city itself was untouched, however anguished it was over such a great loss. Polybius says the vanquished Romans died bravely,[51] but he omits this same eulogy of valor in the four thousand Carthaginian deaths. Despite Livy's popular tale about Maharbal belittling Hannibal, we can only wonder about Hannibal's exact thoughts and mood at the end of the battle and what he was calculating. His decision not to march on Rome after his overwhelming victory at Cannae would no doubt haunt Hannibal the rest of his life.

Sixteen

THE CAMPAIGN FOR SOUTH ITALY

When the unbelievable shock of Cannae reached Rome, the city was filled with the cries of loss and grief to the gods. When Varro arrived with his few stragglers, even this deserting general was welcomed merely because he had managed to survive for the sake of Rome when so many had perished. Fabius Maximus and his policy of not engaging Hannibal were vindicated, but he wouldn't have mourned any less than others over the disaster. Whether or not Fabius knew that his son and Cornelius Publius Scipio the younger had survived is mostly immaterial.

Now even the mention of Hannibal sent palpable waves of fear through the people. While the Senate tried its best to encourage the people and even strengthened city defenses, Rome was in a panic. A famous phrase, "*Hannibal ad portas*," "Hannibal at the Gates," became popular, although many people say that happened almost a decade later when Hannibal actually marched directly on Rome to draw a Roman army away from Capua. Would Hannibal now march on Rome? Would "Hannibal at the gates" suddenly be all too real? Polybius says that immediately after Cannae, Rome fully expected and watched for Hannibal to appear.[1]

Hannibal did not materialize at Rome, however. His attention turned elsewhere.[2] The mercurial erstwhile allies of Rome were his new targets, especially in South Italy, where Hannibal hoped to open resupply routes from Carthage. His fateful decision to move south instead of north to Rome itself would provide the battered city some badly needed breathing room. As Hannibal had hoped, the results of his victory at Cannae undermined the loyalty of many South Italians to Rome. He wanted to appear as the restorer of old Greek liberties through Carthaginian largesse.[3] Some South Italian cities surrendered fairly quickly and other city-states in Campania opened their gates to Hannibal, realizing it was better to be on the side of a victor. After Cannae, Hannibal had left Apulia, some of whose peoples now sided with him, and moved first into old Samnite territory south of Rome and eventually to the lands of Greek city-states.[4]

Many of the people who still resented Rome's expansions and who were only recent acquisitions or territories of Rome—forced by war or a superficial alliance, such as some of the Greeks of Magna Graecia—now backed away from Rome, as did Lucanians south of Campania. Along the Adriatic coast, the defections to Hannibal included many of the Italic peoples of Apulia and the Samnites of central Italy, who had been subjugated at the beginning of the century in the last Samnite War (298–290 BCE). But nowhere was realignment of non-Roman Italy toward Hannibal wholesale or quick. A portion of Lucanians remained loyal to Rome, but even the Lucanians who did align with him were more inclined to identify locally rather than regionally,[5] making it hard for Hannibal to bring a region into a relationship with him as a holistic identity.

Hannibal had sent many of Rome's captured Italian allies home, wanting to make a statement that his battle was with Rome, not Italy at large. Soon after Cannae, Hannibal sent Carthalo, one of his noble Carthaginian officers, with a small delegation of Roman prisoners to the capital to sound out Rome about conditions for peace and to demand ransom for thousands of Roman prisoners.[6] With both old and new leadership—Fabius Maximus was appointed consul for the third time, since his military strategy seemed to be the only one working—Rome refused to negotiate, rejecting ransom offers. Instead, the Senate levied new recruits for its depleted army, thus reconstituting four new legions that even included eight thousand slaves. Rome was sufficiently desperate to conscript paroled criminals, Romans nonetheless, who were promised freedom and annulment of former charges in exchange for enlistment.[7] In such an unconventional manner, Rome fairly quickly raised about twenty-five thousand army recruits regardless of public opinion. Making up for weapons lost to Hannibal, the Romans even took down trophy weapons—some possibly archaic—from temples.[8] Livy mentions the commission of six recruiting officers in order to inspect any able-bodied Roman male in every village for his fitness to bear arms.[9]

In a monetary crisis due partly to war, Rome increased taxes in order to rebuild the legions and even asked its upper classes to donate gold, silver, jewelry, and other capital assets. As a measure of its deep financial crisis, Rome secured a loan from old King Hieron in Siracusa in grain. The cost of war was heavy, since Rome even borrowed from the tax collectors, and the relationship between precious metals such as gold and silver was altered as money itself was devalued. Even large portions of the *ager publicus*—public land—were sold.[10]

While these Roman recruiting efforts mounted, Hannibal moved into Campania, aiming to take Neapolis (modern Naples) to acquire its excellent port. But a siege of Naples was very difficult due to its strong fortifications and excellent port, so Hannibal turned his attention to Capua instead as an easier campaign.[11] Capua was the major city of South Italy, north of Naples by about twenty-one miles. It also defected to Hannibal after debates and vacillations between the winter of 216 and the spring of 215, having seen enough of his marauding armies a year or so earlier when Fabius Maximus had tried to trap Hannibal within Campania. Capua's ruling elite still backed Rome to an extent, having made considerable alliances, including via marriage, but the bulk of the common population backed Hannibal. This was a decisive coup at the time for Hannibal.

However, one local setback south of Naples was that the elder Roman general Marcus Claudius Marcellus, a five-time consul who had conducted the successful Gallic War of 225 BCE, reinforced the city of Nola. His presence with an army of two legions in the newly refortified city turned away Hannibal's forces on several occasions.

The Italian territories newly backing Hannibal were by no means secure, and he would have to watch his back at all times. Hannibal sent his brother Mago south with half an army to secure as much allied territory and good will as possible, as well as local reinforcements for his army. In 215 the Bruttians in the extreme south also brought a force to fight with along with Hannibal's lieutenants Hanno and Himilco against mostly Greek city-states such as Rhegium, Locri, and Crotone that either still sided with Rome or withheld allegiance to Hannibal. Locri surrendered, and the Bruttian allies were disappointed they couldn't loot it because it became a Carthaginian holding. These city-states would become an Achilles' heel to Hannibal over the next decade because of stubborn fickleness and the South Italian patchwork of disorganized independence that allowed no one city-state dominance that would sway the others.

While quite a few Roman allies in South Italy were holdouts, including Brundisium and Barium (Bari),[12] much of Italy looked ambiguously upon the Carthaginians, with whom they shared little, including language and culture. They also had no common denominators among themselves when Rome was at its nadir. Instead, each city looked out for itself regardless of either a currently diminished Rome or a distant Carthage.

Hannibal purportedly set at least one bad example in Campania during 216 and 215, in a failure of diplomacy that would haunt him if true. When besieging Nuceria in the Sarno Valley about ten miles east of Pompeii, Hannibal promised the Nucerians they could surrender and leave the town with one or two garments, nothing else. Historians such as Valerius Maximus, Appian of Alexandria, and Dio Cassius, among others, said that when the city finally fell, Hannibal locked up the city elders in the civic baths and suffocated them; the rest of the people were forced to leave, allowed to depart to wherever, but he killed many on the way. Some of these late sources say he repeated this behavior at Acerra, also throwing its Senate into deep wells.[13] But the atrocity is not recorded by Livy, who rarely omits anything that would damage Hannibal. Instead, Livy repeats the story of the starved city and how its citizens were allowed to leave with one garment. Livy even adds that Hannibal promised rewards to anyone who joined his army, although all refused. Livy says the surface generosity was in keeping with Hannibal's policy "to maintain his character of mildness toward all Italians except Romans."[14] Some scholars are convinced that this Nucerian anecdote in Maximus, Appian, and Dio is fictitious.

Unfortunately, contiguous detailed narratives cease after Hannibal's victories at Ticino, Trebia, Trasimene, and Cannae. Even Polybius becomes spotty as a primary source. Although Livy provides continuing information, it is not necessarily reliable.[15] Polybius turns his attention away from Hannibal and Italy to the events of Greece and the East.[16] After Cannae, we greatly miss, as Richard Miles says, "the unfailingly critical eye of Polybius" for lengths of time in the Second Punic War.[17]

But Capua and other captured or aligned cities caused problems for Hannibal. Livy even claims that Capua greatly softened his veterans—suggesting it became "Hannibal's Cannae," winning his army's soul with the luxury of wine, women, and song.[18] This is an exaggeration, because his army was maintained over the next decade, but Capua would prove expensive to keep and eventually became a deadweight to protect. Needing quick sea links to Carthage,[19] Bruttium at the southern tip of Italy would be a promising staging area for Hannibal in the next few years, but ultimately it never fulfilled its promise, partly because its soldiers, like those of other locals in South Italy, were reluctant to campaign far afield of their home territory. Even under Carthaginian leadership, they did not fight as well against Roman forces as did Hannibal's veterans, who gradually diminished due to casualties.[20]

HANNIBAL AS RELUCTANT OCCUPIER?

After Cannae, Hannibal sent a victory delegation to Carthage. The delegation had mixed results. The spoils of battle were compelling, especially the two-hundred-plus gold rings of captured Roman *equites* magnified by the huge number of Roman deaths, but some in Carthage's Gerousia ruling council challenged how many Roman allies had defected as a result of Cannae. Hannibal's detractors back in Carthage, such as Hanno, also stated how costly "Hannibal's War" was in terms of lives lost and depleted resources, ignoring how little Hannibal had depended on Carthage for anything since 219. Plus, some of Hannibal's seasoned Celtic warrior allies now felt no longer needed for invasion and lacked the booty of new Roman loot to keep them in the far South. They chafed to return to their clans and were allowed to go home, which weakened Hannibal's military presence. The new South Italian soldiers from defecting cities were not their equal.

Mostly because the battles of Trebia, Trasimene, and Cannae had been lopsidedly decisive and Hannibal's envoys could make a summarily strong case for Rome's weakened military, some modest reinforcements joined Hannibal from Carthage in 215, first bringing 4,000 Numidian cavalry along with 40 elephants and some silver and provisions. That same year, Carthage planned to add reinforcements of 12,000 infantry, 1,500 cavalry, and 20 elephants, as well as a sea force of 60 warships. But Rome's new campaigns in Spain against Carthage diverted this promised aid. Carthage also hoped to win back Sardinia, so other Punic resources were diverted there too. Thus, Hannibal had to forego badly needed reinforcements that would have made his occupation much less of a burden and his Italian campaign against Rome much easier.[21] Only in 214 did Hannibal receive a few more reinforcements: troops, supplies, and war elephants landed at Locri from a Punic fleet under Bomilcar, whose naval role rarely did much good for Carthage in the extended war as Rome now controlled most of the western Mediterranean region.

From 216 to 206, Hannibal had to walk a fine line between forcing the South Italians to deploy against Rome and respecting their independence, since he had made a case for restoring the liberties Rome had taken. The South Italians did not respect a distant Rome, but neither did they fully trust Hannibal circling in their backyard for years. Ultimately, Hannibal's diplomatic policy did not work, especially backed by his nonindigenous occupation army, which could not forage and loot these mercurial quasi-allies. Hannibal had met his objectives for wreaking havoc on Rome's military, expecting a conventional surrender that never came.[22] Was he prepared to consolidate his allies with an army of occupation? Following the Fabian policy of nonengagement, the Romans waited to nip at his heels wherever he marched because he could not be putting out fires everywhere at once. Italy would soon become what one historian has aptly named Hannibal's "shrinking prison of success."[23]

Cannae was Hannibal's pinnacle but, as Mark Healy notes, "paradoxically, the very success of Cannae was in some way his long and slow undoing"[24] because the Romans finally learned the lesson of Fabius Maximus: do not fight Hannibal directly but let the circumstances of occupation wear him down. This may not yet have been obvious when Hannibal sat encamped on Mount Tifata overlooking Campania, just as the Samnites had done many years before. Hannibal knew he was being observed warily by three Roman forces that kept their distance: one southward at Suessula above Nola, where Claudius Marcellus guarded the access area east of Naples and possibly Naples as well[25], another force on the northern edge of Campania at Teanum (Teano), led by none other than Fabius Maximus as consul, watching over approaches to the Via Appia and protecting the northern interior access route to Rome too; and the last, near Casilinum (modern Capua) on the Voltumus River, led by Tiberius Gracchus, only a few miles northwest of ancient Capua. A fourth Roman force would soon be stationed east in Apulia near Brundisium, under Marcus Valerius Messalla, to guard the loyal Roman allies there.[26] Most of these troops had the dual purpose of keeping an eye on rebel Capua and containing Hannibal, keeping him from a possible march north toward Rome.

How long could Hannibal afford to sit it out? In Greece, having heard of Rome's defeat at Cannae, King Philip V of Macedon agreed to an alliance with Carthage, and Hannibal had received his emissaries in his Mount Tifata camp. This was a positive development. Partly because of new high taxes demanded by Rome, Sardinia also revolted against it, a move bolstered by Carthage, and this made Hannibal look good as well. In the North, the

Celtic Boii tribe would soon crush a Roman force under Postumus Albinus at Modena in early 215, reasserting its independence. This too was good news. When Hieron II died at ninety years old in 215, after he had aided Rome for decades, his grandson and successor, Hieronymus, led the city of Siracusa in Sicily away from Rome, temporarily undermining the Roman hold on the Mediterranean between Carthage and Italy.[27]

These events could have lulled Hannibal to ignore diplomacy as a tool, less familiar to him than the battle strategy he used so masterfully as a weapon. Although he was a superb commander of disparate peoples and as charismatic a leader as any general in history, Hannibal's strong suit was not negotiation. The profound difference between the harshness of an aggressive war in an often-hostile battle environment and the need for more open communication and protracted negotiation with potential allies cannot be overstated.

Campania was hardly Rome, but it was a ripe Roman plum and close enough to Rome for Hannibal to savor, especially for its agricultural bounty from rich volcanic soils. A general who had faced challenges of feeding his invading army would look favorably on maintaining sway over Campania for as long as possible. But the tide would soon be turning and the successes short lived. The Romans cannily began to perceive that Hannibal could not easily conquer walled towns by siege, having no equipment to do so, and any fortified city allied with Rome possessing adequate freshwater access and a good hoard of food or located on a coast and supplied by sea was practically invulnerable. Even the small Greek city of Petelia on the Gulf of Taranto held out against a siege for eight months in 215. Although he tried three times, Hannibal was unsuccessful in taking Naples, which easily received goods by its excellent port, while the patrolling Roman fleet and Greek allies in Italy such as Rhegium controlled the Strait of Messina between Sicily and mainland Italy. The Carthaginian fleet under Hasdrubal the Bald meant to reinforce the Sardinian revolt was driven by storm into the Balearic Islands, and the old Roman veteran Titus Manlius Torquatus crushed the Sardinian rebellion against Rome in 215 for a second time. He had already originally subdued it in 235 in between the First and Second

Punic Wars. In addition, a Roman naval fleet of fifty ships under Marcus Valerius Laevinus at Brundisium in 215 discouraged any real Macedonian alliance in Italy with Hannibal.

SUCCESSES OF FABIAN STRATEGY, AVOIDING HANNIBAL IN DIRECT BATTLE

The wise delaying tactics of Fabius Maximus were working and beginning to wear down Hannibal's veterans and allies. Did Hannibal wonder how and why the Romans had changed the rules of war—defeated decisively in the First Punic War until their surprise victory at the very end in 241 BCE, and then defeated decisively again between 218 and 216 at Trebia, Trasimene, and Cannae but still resistant? Did the superb tactician sense that the wheel of fortune that had stopped with him on top was now beginning its descent?

How much of Hannibal's tactical experience would be wasted if no Roman would throw down the gauntlet of battle challenge or if Rome engaged in battle only with the armies of his Italian allies? Both Hannibal and the Romans ravaged South Italy as the theater of a strange war where the armies circled but hardly fought. Each side inflicted a scorched-earth policy on the neutral territories or punished the allies of the other, devastating the small farms and savaging the local agrarian economies as they seized the crops to feed their armies. If Hannibal ravaged farmlands allied with Rome, or if the Romans ravaged regions allied with Hannibal, this competition for basic food needs often sent the residents fleeing and left rich farm areas empty—a bleak situation from which an independent agricultural South Italy may have never quite recovered.[28] Historians have estimated basic rations of Hannibal's army during winter alone to be about six hundred grams of grain per day for each soldier.[29] This bare minimum would contribute to long-term malnutrition if the army could not acquire more food. Long after the fact, the Roman statesman and writer Marcus Tullius Cicero relates an odd dream of Hannibal in his philosophical treatise De Divinatione that he says originated from Coelius, a student of Hannibal who had carefully read the contemporary Greek account of Silenos, Hannibal's Greek "recorder."

In the dream that reputedly came to him after Saguntum, Hannibal was ordered by Jupiter to bring the war into Italy but given a divine guide who warned him not to look back. In the dream, he couldn't resist looking back and saw a horrible, monstrous apparition, covered with snakes, following him into and through Italy with immense devastation as it overthrew every house and tree. But his divine dream counsel was not to look back wherever he marched, only to continue onward.[30] It is not without irony that the dream imagery seems to resemble a trampling elephant shaking its trunk in its ravaging charge.

HANNIBAL'S SACRIFICE AT AVERNUS AND SOJOURN AT SALAPIA

Since Cannae, Rome had raised a total of eighteen legions and had a hundred thousand soldiers in the field, even excluding allies. Hannibal moved troops back and forth from his camp at Mount Tifata in Campania to his camp at Arpi on the other side of the Apennines, a maneuver he would repeat several times with the change of seasons.

Two unrelated events from 214 show a different side of the previously successful general, who may have begun to wonder about the future. The first happened on his march to the town of Cumae, which was the location of the oracle of the Sibyl of Cumae. According to legend, Hannibal made sacrifices and inquired about the future from the oracle of the Cumaean Sibyl at this time. If true, it gives insight into a man of the highest military ingenuity whose confidence may have been eroding.

The second brief narrative that surfaces among so much military history is Hannibal's winter at Salapia, situated between Arpi and Cannae, where he is reported to have shared his bed with a local prostitute of note (or she shared hers with him). Both Pliny and Appian relate the story[31] almost as a consoling event during his frustrated occupation. This tryst seems to have lasted all winter, and some have concluded that Hannibal fell in love with the prostitute. Because it is one of the rare texts about Hannibal having anything to do with a woman other than his wife, Imilce, back in

Spain—whom he hadn't seen for more than a decade—there are historians who have suggested that Hannibal was not given to womanizing but that instead the general's appetites were moderate and under the same discipline as the rest of his nature.[32]

THE TAKING OF TARENTUM

Although fewer military opportunities came his way with the Romans' Fabian strategy of avoiding confrontation, Hannibal showed that he could profit by other means beyond the devious and flexible battle strategy he had mastered. The main southern port city of Tarentum fell to Hannibal by intrigue beginning in the winter of 213.[33] Facing west on the great arch of the instep of Italy's "foot" on the Gulf of Taranto. Tarentum was originally a well-placed Greek colony from Sparta established in the late eighth century BCE, named Taras after a myth hero. The original colony was very wealthy. Its prized location gave it an exceptional inner harbor inside a protected bay, one of the reasons Hannibal badly wanted it as a potential resupplying base for Carthaginian reinforcement.

By 264 BCE,[34] the Romans had renamed this old colony Tarentum as a station along the Via Appia en route to Brundisium. With an island (Isola San Pietro) protecting its outer bay, Mare Grande, its old city and acropolis were on a peninsula guarding only one entry into the large inner bay harbor, the Mare Piccolo. All of this made it an exceptional catch for Hannibal if it could be turned away from Rome. The ancient walled city of Tarentum—which had also sided with Pyrrhus against Rome at the beginning of the century—was thus protected by water except for a fortified narrow isthmus. A frustrated Hannibal would have been unsuccessful in taking it by force.

Hannibal also needed Tarentum because Fabius and Rome had captured his eastern Apulian redoubt of Arpi. This limited the maneuverability Hannibal needed badly in the large peninsula of South Italy, since Brundisium to the east and Rhegium in the west remained stoutly Roman ports. Hannibal also hoped to join forces with Philip V of Macedon and needed a port to do so. Rome considered the Tarentines soft and ill-suited to military endeavors, partly because their climate was mild and their fishing culture relaxed. The marine ambience and hot sun reflecting off miles of sea seemingly combined to make everything happen slowly, giving them an appearance of indolence that contrasted with northern vigor in the eyes of Rome's citizen militia farmers.

Rome had long suspected Tarentum of not being trustworthy and had demanded hostages in the capital; some had escaped and been cavalierly executed by a stern Rome as examples of perfidy, which turned Tarentine sentiment further against Rome. When Hannibal was back in the South and looking for ways to take the Roman-garrisoned city, thirteen young Tarentine aristocrats took matters into their own hands. Led by a young man named Philemenus, they pretended to go out on a hunt and left through a Roman-guarded city postern gate right before nightfall. When they neared Hannibal's camp, his sentries caught them and brought them to Hannibal. Having complained about their treatment under Rome, including the execution of hostages, their story seems plausible. These young Tarentines would betray their city to Hannibal to be better treated. The stratagem appealed to Hannibal's wiliness. Hannibal promised these Tarentines several vital concessions: his army would not set up a garrison inside the city, and he would not ask for any tribute from its citizens. Furthermore, there would be no looting by his army when Tarentum fell. Only the Romans in the city would be plundered or forced to pay tribute. But the real question Hannibal and the Tarentines faced was how to get Carthaginian forces past Roman guards.

As ringleader of the plot, Philemenus was also known in Tarentum to be a good hunter, so when he returned to the city early the next day after having spent much of the night in Hannibal's camp, he took with him animals that Hannibal had given him to make his hunting foray appear successful. Philemenus arrived at the same postern gate from which he'd left, and the Roman sentries who knew him by sight from frequent passages thought nothing unusual.

The next phase of this stratagem required Hannibal to appear sick and laid up to the Romans, unable to go out from his camp for a while. But as the plan matured with details, Philemenus left Tarentum by the same postern gate on multiple occasions overnight and met secretly with Hannibal, returning each time with animals or meat that he appeared to have hunted. This mollified the Roman sentries, with whom he often shared the meat. Finally, when the pattern was so well established that the Roman sentries opened the postern gate upon hearing him whistle his return, the plot was set. By night, Hannibal stealthily moved ten thousand infantry, including two thousand Celts and a cavalry force, on a fast march about ten miles outside Tarentum. But he apparently split the force into two groups, approaching the small, fortified peninsula from opposite sides. A Numidian cavalry contingent of eighty horsemen was to scout out the intervening distance, pretending to be on a foraging raid if the Romans noticed them. But their orders were also to kill anyone who might have observed the troop movements.

Another Tarentine conspirator, Nico, waited by the city's larger Teminitis gate. A fire signal announced the quiet approach of Hannibal's two forces in the dead of the night near the wall, since timing was critical. As soon as Hannibal's signal fires flared and were observed inside the city, Nico at his gate gave the same flare signal, as did Philemenus near his usual gate. The flares inside and outside the city were just as quickly extinguished before anyone else noticed. Nico's small group of Tarentines suddenly forced its way into the eastern gate's Teminitis barracks, killing all the sentries and opening this gate. Half of Hannibal's designated troops quietly entered the city in organized haste, with Hannibal himself in the column. Then Philemenus arrived at his postern gate with about four men, likely a little earlier than usual before it started to become light. But his familiar voice and whistle told the Roman sentries all was well, and they opened the gate. Two of his companions carried an enormous boar. He must have dawdled a bit at the open gate, displaying the boar to the admiring sentry. As Livy recounts,[35] while one Roman looked at his trophy boar, from the blind side, Philemenus skewered this sentry just as Hannibal's other force of a thousand Africans arrived at the now-unguarded gate. His men killed any other sentries as the Carthaginians poured into the city from two sides. The Celts were split into three groups of about seven hundred men and reconnoitered the city with two Tarentine guides each, being ordered to secure the main streets and slay any Romans recognized by the guides, who also informed any Tarentine citizens awakened in the uproar and warned them to be co-operative and quiet.

The noise of combat in the city roused many, but confusion reigned. A Roman trumpet pealed in the theater, having been stolen by the con-spirators and calling any Roman soldiers who rallied there into an ambush. The Roman commander escaped in a small rowboat to the well-fortified citadel guarding the water channel at the end of the peninsula between the large and small bays, locking himself in with the remaining few thousand soldiers who managed to escape the wholesale slaughter of Romans. When dawn arrived, the citizens saw slain Romans in the streets and Carthagin-ian and Celtic warriors and realized that Hannibal had taken the city. They quickly acquiesced except for any Roman allies, who were either impris-oned or slain or also escaped to the citadel.

That day when civic order was restored after the fighting ceased, Hanni-bal gathered together all the citizens and promised in amicable words that no harm would come to them. He also asked them to go home and inscribe the word "Tarentine" on their doors so that his men would instead plunder only Romans or their sympathizers. In this way, his men were released into the city and acquired significant Roman booty, while the Tarentines were spared as promised. Hannibal kept his word, and the transition was mostly peaceful.

One immediate drawback was that the Romans controlled the citadel, meaning they could be resupplied from the open sea by a relieving Roman fleet. Hannibal tried to attack the citadel but found it was nearly impreg-nable, somewhat isolated by a partial channel. Worse, the Tarentine fleet that he'd hoped to employ was also trapped inside the inner bay. In usual manner, Hannibal devised a way to get the ships out of the inner harbor without going by the threat of the Roman citadel. He had the citizens drag their ships overland on the isthmus by wheels or rollers attached to their undersides on vehicle yokes and brought them safely out to sea, where the outer harbor was accessible and now usable for Hannibal.[36] He also had a channel dug deeper to fully isolate the citadel and reinforced it with a stockade to keep the Romans locked in. He also hoped to use the Tarentine fleet to blockade fresh supplies delivered to the citadel.[37] By this clever ruse, Hannibal took a wealthy and great city with a good harbor and coastal access. Nonetheless, although Metapontum and a few other cities were soon taken by Hannibal, strengthening his position in South Italy, he had not succeeded in completely dislodging the Romans from Tarentum. They kept the citadel until the city was retaken by Rome in 209, again by betrayal.

Seventeen

THE MARCH ON ROME

Two cities were now allied against Rome: Capua in Campania and Siracusa in Sicily. But Carthage was not able to reinforce and protect its allies in Italy or Sicily, both by lack of commitment and foresight but also because it no longer controlled the seas. Rome was stung by Capua's defection to Hannibal after Cannae, but Capua was close enough for Rome to mobilize multiple armies against it until Rome finally recaptured it after a siege. Siracusa held out longer than expected in part because of the ingenuity of one man: Archimedes.

SIRACUSA AND ARCHIMEDES

After Hieron of Siracusa died, his successor Hieronymus struck a deal with Hannibal to realign with Carthage if in return Siracusa could be strengthened to dominate eastern Sicily; the Romans kept a watchful eye on developments there. In 214 the Senate realized that Sicily could be key to the prospects of Carthage and Hannibal, so it turned some of its attention back to Siracusa.

The city was one of the richest in the Greek world. Siracusa could host Carthaginian and Macedonian fleets, both enemies of Rome, in its great natural harbor, so the Senate decided to act to prevent a new Punic supply base from strengthening Hannibal and his allies. Rome sent Claudius Marcellus to Sicily for his third consulship. Marcellus was a good commander, loved by his troops for his dedication as well as his toughness. Plutarch says that in his opposition to Hannibal, Marcellus was Rome's sword to Fabius as Rome's shield.[1] Plutarch says some of the Roman soldiers under Marcellus had survived the infamy of Cannae. They were desperate to prove their worth again, and his was a redemptive leadership for them.[2]

A Roman fleet and army under Marcellus sought to blockade Siracusa and wear it down by sea and land until it could be conquered. Carthage sent Himilco with twenty-five thousand infantry, three thousand cavalry, and a dozen elephants. After landing near Heraclea Minoa, they captured Agrigento (Akragas) on the south coast of Sicily. These Punic reinforcements would soon suffer from fever in the marshy Anapus River just to the west—thousands of Carthaginian soldiers and two generals died—and with decimated ranks became unable to assist Siracusa.

Laying siege to Siracusa from the autumn of 214 onward, Marcellus was up against not only the walled city but also one of the greatest engineers and mathematicians in history: the polymath Archimedes, whose military inventions kept the Romans at bay for almost two years. This defense amazed the Romans, especially the naval forces, which were unable to approach too close due to the mysterious arsenal Archimedes invented. Among these weapons were a fusillade of rapid-fire mechanical projectiles, known as fire ballistae; perhaps also a mysterious parabolic mirror that could burn ships from a distance[3]—not at all unlikely, given he had authored treatises on parabolas; or "the Claw," which could plummet into a Roman ship and catch it with a grappling hook, lift one end high, and then release it with a violent capsizing drop (described by Polybius[4]). Archimedes earned the respect of the Roman besiegers.

The inner harbor was guarded by the fortified insular peninsula of Ortygia, with its freshwater spring, Arethusa. From the raised citadel of

Ortygia, originally named for the quails that nested on the island, Archimedes could protect both the seaward outer harbor and the great inner harbor with his machines. Legend even credits him with early biological warfare by dropping baskets of venomous snakes into Roman ships. Clearly, this time Rome was up against a different kind of genius than Hannibal.

Marcellus finally had an opportunity to take the city with a land force on the north side in 212. When the Siracusans celebrated a nocturnal feast of Artemis, the Greek goddess of nature, wild animals, and childbirth with more relaxation and wine than was wise, Marcellus had his men successfully attack a weakly fortified northern gate at the Galeagris Tower, far from the populated town center. The Roman troops quickly descended into the surprised city and slaughtered Siracusans on all sides. Marcellus commanded his army to spare the life of Archimedes, possibly hoping to employ his military genius against Hannibal. Plutarch quotes Marcellus as jokingly even calling Archimedes a "geometrical Briareus," the mythical giant son of Uranus, who had a hundred arms and fifty heads and who could hardly be defeated.[5] Archimedes was apparently not celebrating like most of the city but instead pondering calculations traced in the sand when a Roman soldier entered his house and commanded him to stop. Legend says the annoyed mathematician replied, "Do not disturb my circles." The Roman soldier ran him through with a sword or spear. Livy says the soldier did not know the man was Archimedes and that his death distressed Marcellus.[6]

The Carthaginian fleet escaped from the inner harbor. The admiral, Bomilcar, had been mostly ineffective in aiding Siracusa and had escaped any major conflict, as was his pattern.[7]

After the Siracusan citadel at Ortygia was taken—betrayed by a deserting Spanish officer—the Romans were astonished at the city's wealth, but history suggests that Siracusa's greatest treasure was Archimedes himself.

With Siracusa taken, Hannibal lost not only an ally but also his best hope for resupplying his Italian campaign from Carthage. Without Siracusa, there would be little opportunity to profit from Tarentum or to chase the Romans from the Strait of Messina. Agrigento would also fall in 210, ending forever any chance of a Punic Sicily.

THE FRUSTRATIONS OF CAPUA

Once it had turned against Rome in 215, Capua was too rich and large for Hannibal to abandon easily. He hoped great things for populous Capua as a capital city of his war against Rome, likely believing that other cities would rally around it as a power base. But this did not happen in a fractious region where no city reigned over the others, a legacy of the old Greek city-states and their colonies. The ancient Capuans were also seemingly notorious for indolence and luxury and were now mostly paralyzed due to their dependence on Hannibal to defend them.

Fairly soon after Capua went over to Hannibal, Roman forces began to assemble armies against it, partly because it was one of the largest cities in Italy after Rome and, as such, a potential threat to Roman dominance. In 214 a force of four armies comprising six legions set out to blockade Capua. This action required Hannibal to protect Capua's citizens and infrastructure. The Roman troops surrounded Capua with berms and palisades (staked wooden walls). Not only were the Capuans trapped inside their walls, no one could easily come to their aid. The ensuing sallies and retreats between Hannibalic and Roman forces resembled a chess match, with no clear victor yet in sight. Hannibal, who was far to the southeast near Tarentum, sent his lieutenant Hanno from Bruttium to Benevento. Hanno eluded two Roman forces under the consuls Gaius Claudius Nero and Tiberius Gracchus, and set up a fortified grain depot not too far from Capua. He requested that the Capuans send wagons, hauling oxen, and whatever other animals they could muster to collect the grain they needed to withstand a protracted Roman siege. At first, the Capuans could find only four hundred wagons, and Hanno is supposed to have remarked, "The Capuans cannot even be stirred by hunger, to which dumb beasts respond better." He ordered more transport for the grain, but the Capuans were slow, and the Romans found out by the time they had finally managed 2,000 wagons. In Hanno's absence, the Romans attacked his grain supply camp and carried away all the grain along with the wagons and whatever was in the camp. Hanno escaped the debacle and returned back to Bruttium in disgust at the Capuan inertia. Hannibal then dispatched 2,000 Numidian cavalry to help Capua. Their successful stealth avoided the Roman noose around Capua; after getting inside the city at night, the Numidians were joined in a sortie to leave the city in the morning and attack the unwatchful Romans, who were trying to gather up the grain and supplies without concern for a Carthaginian counterattack.

The surprised Romans suffered 1,500 casualties and retreated back to their own siege fortifications outside Capua. They suffered another blow when Tiberius Gracchus was ambushed and killed while advancing from the east to assist the blockade of Capua. Hannibal gave him a proper burial as a worthy adversary. The Romans did not engage Hannibal when he returned to Capua faster than they thought possible, pulling back before him in Fabian fashion. But Hannibal soon departed the city, which still lacked sufficient supplies to house his army. He followed the army of Appius Claudius Caudex moving in a southeasterly direction. It must have appeared either to Hannibal or his scouts that Claudius planned to attack toward Lucania. Hannibal's withdrawal eastward from Capua allowed the Roman force that had moved north under the command of Quintus Fulvius Flaccus to return to Capua and renew the siege. Claudius' move was only a feint because somewhere in Campania's eastern hills and valleys, he eluded Hannibal and returned to Capua. This was an outcome of Fabian strategy—a game of cat and mouse that the Romans soon mastered, avoiding direct open-field combat with Hannibal out of respect for his genius at battle but attempting to divide and draw his energy and resources elsewhere whenever possible. A Capua under perpetual Roman siege would require an investment that Hannibal could ill afford.

The year 212 was a watershed year for Rome: somehow, despite scarcity of resources, it was able to put two hundred thousand soldiers in the field and seventy thousand sailors on ships, amounting to almost 10 percent of the available population,[8] something mercantile Carthage could never mobilize. Capua may have seemed so promising when it defected to Hannibal, but it was ultimately a double-edged sword. The city hoped for its own hegemony in the region, thus discouraging further defections that Hannibal needed because other South Italian city-states feared its expansion.[9]

HANNIBAL'S MARCH ON ROME

In the prolonged siege of Capua from 212 to 211, Hannibal tried to trick the Romans in a match of wits. Attempting to draw the besieging Roman armies away from Capua, he suddenly marched north toward Rome itself. Livy says this diversion was on impulse and a possible dream of accomplishing what he had not done after Cannae.[10] Word of Hannibal's progress northward—with raids, seizures, killing fugitives, and devastating farmland, according to Livy—reached Rome. A furious Senate debate ensued between Publius Cornelius Asina, who recommended that all Roman soldiers leave Capua and come to the aid of the capital, and the ever skeptical Fabius Maximus, who said astutely that Hannibal's intent was not Rome itself but the relief of Capua. Valerius Flaccus suggested a compromise, and so a Roman force of fifteen thousand soldiers and a thousand cavalry under Fulvius Flaccus left Capua and quickly marched north a day behind Hannibal along the mostly coastal Via Appia. Their crossing of the Volturnus River was delayed because Hannibal had burned a bridge made up of floating boats lashed together with planks crossing them. Fulvius, however, may have possessed two advantages Hannibal did not: the Via Appia was shorter than Hannibal's route, and he did not have local opposition as he raced to Rome.

Although it is difficult to establish Hannibal's route, he left his fires burning near Capua to give the appearance of still being there. He arrived east of Rome along the Anio River. His route is uncertain, but we do know that Fulvius arrived in Rome ahead of Hannibal. He entered a panic-stricken city via the Porta Capena. To expedite matters, the Senate had granted Fulvius authority equal to the consuls so that he could enter the city with his army but without the usual loss of imperium when a commander entered Rome with forces.[11] His forces camped between the gates of the Porta Esquilina and the Porta Collina, perhaps on the Viminal, while the troops of the city praetor, C. Calpurnius Piso, camped near the Capitolium and the Arx citadel on the west side of the city. Other troops under consuls camped near the Porta Esquilina and Porta Collina, where Hannibal was expected. According to Livy, the whole of Rome was full of fear, packed with peasant farmers who had fled into the city, along with their livestock, at the news of Hannibal's approach. The Senate sat in session around the clock to be available for advice. Guards bristling with weapons were posted in the heights of the city and along the city wall to watch.[12]

Being close enough to be observed by Romans stationed on the walls, his combined forces of Carthaginian, Numidian, and other African troops alongside the wild-looking Celts, now accompanied by Bruttians, were closely watched. The Romans were no doubt trying to count the assembled forces of their worst enemy.

Hannibal then marched from the Anio to the Porta Collina at the northern edge of the city. He inspected its gate with two thousand cavalry and conducted a reconnaissance of a section along the city's walls. This must have been unnerving to many raw Roman recruits watching a living legend before their eyes.

For Hannibal too, this moment must have been exciting. He knew from long and often bitter experience—from Saguntum, to Naples, to Brundisium, to Rhegium—that fortified cities were impossible to take without siege equipment. He also knew that Rome's high perimeter walls were fortified for their length of fifty miles and his troops were far too few to break through even one gate like the Porta Collina before him. Further complicating a possible siege of Rome was the necessity of supplying his army with food while surrounded by hostile territory, with other Roman armies in the field away in Italy capable of mobilizing back to Rome. Roman armies did not need food raids and broad scavenging forays as his had to do. Says one scholar, "Rather than showing the shortcomings of Hannibal, his avoidance of a siege shows that Hannibal was a sufficiently great general not to try and undertake the impossible."[13] Although Rome had more armies in the field in 212, Hannibal could now see for himself that his decision not to march on Rome after Cannae was the right decision. Was this ephemeral moment at the gates of Rome Hannibal's greatest, or was it the beginning of a long sigh of resignation?

Hannibal had little time to appreciate his proximity under Rome's walls because Fulvius quickly sent out a large body of Roman cavalry—likely from another gate such as the Esquiline, where no Carthaginians lurked. A group of 1,200 Numidian horsemen who had deserted to Rome at Nola descended through the city from the Aventine Hill of Rome to join the Roman cavalry. Livy says the sight of them caused added panic in Rome, as it was thought by some that Hannibal's forces had breached the city.[14] The skirmish between Hannibal's small force and the Romans was mostly a standoff, and both enemies soon went back to their positions inside the city or on the Anio. Hannibal then plundered the countryside and drove a large number of animals into his camp.

Twice in the next several days, Hannibal's army and the Romans squared off for full battle, but each time, a fierce torrent of heavy hail prevented it. Was this spring storm from Jupiter or Baal? Both of these gods were storm deities, but it was possibly a worse omen for the invaders. Centuries later, St. Augustine even claimed that it was the gods themselves who terrified Hannibal with lightning and tempest.[15] The hailstorm may have shaken Hannibal's resolve, although he knew this city could not be taken even if he slaughtered the army facing him. Hannibal turned around with his troops and headed south again. Livy claims that Hannibal was acting on irrational emotions. Polybius says Hannibal had amassed sufficient plunder on the march and felt he had achieved his objective. He thought he had forced the siege of Capua to be lifted as the collected Roman armies, including that of Appius Claudius, had to come to the aid of their capital.[16]

But this was one of Hannibal's few haunting miscalculations. The fall of Capua came soon after in 211. Not only had the Romans under Publius Claudius Pulcher not lifted the siege—only Quintus Fulvius Flaccus had come from Capua to Rome's assistance—but the fickle people of Capua thought Hannibal had abandoned them, and they quickly surrendered, opening their gates to the Roman army, hoping for mercy. Instead Rome was brutal, inflicting a heavy lesson for Capuan infidelity. Many of the town leaders were beaten severely with rods and then beheaded. The bulk of the population was sold into slavery along with adjacent towns that had resisted. While the town's structures were left intact, the city lost its independence and became the property of Rome. By the time Hannibal arrived back in the region, the people of South Italy were reeling from the treatment of Capua, thinking their fate would be similar: that Hannibal would ultimately desert them, and they would pay harshly to Rome. This was just what Rome intended. Hannibal marched back south to Bruttium, and, like dominos, the towns of southern Italy submitted to Rome.

Tarentum, too, soon fell back to Rome, betrayed yet again in 209. Deploying his army as bait, the Roman general Marcellus had drawn Hannibal away from Tarentum. Plus, Hannibal had needed to round up eight thousand marauders let loose by Rome—mainly Bruttian deserters and Sicilian criminals, to do damage around Caulonia[17]—and Fabius Maximus had moved in with an army. As before, the city gates were opened by a traitor, and Carthalo the Carthaginian officer and his men were slain along with many Bruttians and Tarentines, including the original conspirators Philemenus and Nico. Livy says Fabius Maximus wanted to give the impression that the city had been taken by Roman force, not Tarentine treachery.[18] Tarentum was utterly plundered, and thirty thousand Tarentines were sold into slavery to underscore the ultimate unprofitability of joining Hannibal. Rome captured the Tarentine fleet that Hannibal had hoped would help to resupply him from Carthage and also secure a landing for Philip V of Macedon. Where Hannibal had treated Tarentum fairly, the Romans dealt in swift reprisal with the harshest blow. Although not all was lost, Hannibal must have realized that the tide had turned against him.

THE LOSS OF TWO ROMAN CONSULS IN ITALY

In 208, after losing Tarentum in 209, Hannibal caught by surprise a legion that had marched from Tarentum toward Locri, a city allied with Hannibal. The Romans were hoping to join a siege force. Unknown to Rome, Hannibal had gone to relieve Locri but was still far in advance of any Roman troops he knew were coming, so he concealed his men beneath the hill of Petelia on either side of the road. The unsuspecting Romans thought he was up north and blundered right into the trap, enveloped on two sides. Some 2,000 Romans were slaughtered and another 1,500 were captured, with the rest fleeing back to the safety of Tarentum. Such successes were now rare for Hannibal, but an even greater victory beckoned. Hannibal moved back toward Venusia, where a larger Roman army under Marcellus was camped.

The beloved Claudius Marcellus had been elected consul for the fifth time and was now about sixty years old. The other consul general was his lieutenant from Siracusa, Titus Quinctius Crispinus. Between them, they had four legions. Although Hannibal was outnumbered, he camped close enough for the Romans to know he had arrived and was waiting for battle. A wooded hill lay between the two camps, and Hannibal saw that it wasn't large enough to set up another camp but could be used to spy on the Romans if they hadn't already set up scouts there, which they should have done. Hannibal then concealed several Numidian cavalry detachments on the hill overnight. Deciding too late that they should occupy the hill, Marcellus and Crispinus went up the hill to reconnoiter it with hardly any backup: fewer than 220 men. They would scout out the hill themselves and then bring up a sufficient force to take it, thus gaining an advantage over Hannibal. This reconnaissance in woods where the neutral territory was not open to distant view should not have been undertaken by such senior commanders.[19] The action reveals a weakness in Rome's armies: a lack of junior officers who could make responsible field decisions.

One can only imagine the elation of the hidden, disciplined Numidians to see the highest Roman officers coming uphill toward the dark wood, their polished armor gleaming under their scarlet cloaks. In the shadows, the Numidians had probably separated a distance from their horses to not give themselves away. Seizing the unprecedented opportunity, they waited until the entire small Roman force was within their grasp and attacked from all sides with war cries, also blocking retreat from the rear. Likely focusing their attention on the two consuls, the Numidians aimed to do the utmost damage. Totally surprised, Marcellus fell at once from his horse with a lance running through him and took his last breath. Crispinus too was struck and wounded mortally by multiple javelins, losing blood but managing to escape on horse along with the son of Marcellus, also wounded. At least forty-three soldiers were killed either in the ambush or trying to escape.

The shouts and screams alerted both camps. Livy not only wonders at the consuls' surprising lack of caution but also blames the Etruscan guards, who fled without trying to help.

Hannibal, who had been not far off, was apprised immediately and came to the bloody scene. He took away the body of Marcellus for respectful cremation. He also took Marcellus' consular signet ring, hoping to use it for a further ruse. He honorably sent back Marcellus' ashes to the Romans and to his son, since he had respected Marcellus like few other Romans. Crispinus, having retreated to the mountains, although now dying, realized Hannibal must have the signet ring and, before he succumbed to his grave wounds, arranged to alert the surrounding allied cities to be vigilant of any trickery. Roman signet rings conveyed authority and were used for wax seals and on important documents.

Rome was greatly discouraged by the needless deaths of their two consuls, especially the heroic Marcellus, who had been so successful in the war. After their wise general's refusal to engage directly with Hannibal after Cannae,[20] hadn't the Romans learned never to underestimate Hannibal? Using the signet ring Hannibal sent men dressed as Roman soldiers to the city of Salapia, which was allied with the Romans. But the Romans in Salapia had been warned. They let in only the advance party before they sealed the gates and killed the messengers inside the city. Hannibal had been waiting not far off but left as soon as he found that his subterfuge had been discovered.

Hannibal's few minor victories after Cannae continued to show his dominance in the battlefield when any Roman army was foolish enough to meet him head-on. Although Hannibal would move around Bruttium and Calabria mostly at will but as a virtual prisoner of this extreme southern territory, his stalemate with the Roman armies ensued. Hannibal's South Italian allies fell one at a time, while Carthage's assets in Spain also began to crumble. The old campaigns to hold Spain would eventually prove too costly for Carthage. For all Hannibal's audacity and leadership ability, his protracted diplomatic negotiations with South Italians—always sensitive—were never equal to his military brilliance against Roman armies.[21] Such diplomacy needed time and a skill set that, even after so many years, Hannibal never mastered.

Eighteen

WAR IN SPAIN

While Hannibal's invasion slowed down and eventually mired in South Italy for nearly a decade after Cannae, with no major battles—which would have allowed him to further undermine Rome's hold over the rest of Italy— between 216 and 208 nothing stood still elsewhere in the war. Events in Spain, especially during the better part of that decade, would bring the invasion little relief. In order to catch up to what was happening in Italy and in some way shaping it, the focus shifts west to Spain and other Punic and Roman engagements there.

Rome's overall situation continued to improve the longer the war dragged on. The Romans added more legions in the field as the number of Hannibal's trained soldiers dropped. His troops who had crossed the Alps and his older Celtic veterans were much depleted after Trebia, Trasimene, Volturnus, Cannae, and countless skirmishes since. Support for his Italian campaigns also diminished precipitously after the fall of Capua in 211, Salapia in 210, and Tarentum in 209, especially when South Italians saw what harsh punishment befell cities that had befriended Hannibal if Rome won them back. Recruits from Italy made up the bulk of his rag-tag army, but their incentives after 209 were hardly as promising as the mercenary promise of Roman booty that had brought his original army into Italy in 218. Hannibal now faced up to a hundred thousand Romans in increasingly better-led armies than his approximately fifty thousand men, most of them inferior South Italian allies.[1]

It should not be forgotten that when new taxes and forced tribute had been burdensome to Italy between 216 and 213, a great strain was placed on Rome's resources. Many cities complained that their resources had been so depleted by the war effort, they had nothing more to give. Rome had also been able to augment its needed war chest through its victories in Siracusa and Tarentum, whose enormous wealth booty provided needed tax relief, but twelve out of thirty Roman colonies in Italy revolted against further taxation and levies. The Senate even taxed itself to bring in family jewels and private wealth to continue. On the other hand, the Roman leadership knew that Hannibal could not be everywhere at once. Along with a Fabian strategy of nonengagement, which took away any possibility of Hannibal's best policy of quick and decisive victories,[2] the Romans now had another masterful tactic working well to keep him running to put out fires among his shrinking allies. Having to protect so many South Italian allies who seemed incapable of defending themselves taxed his resources in ways hard to measure,[3] but it was a drain he could not afford as he became cut off more and more from Carthage and Spain. No Spanish silver for mercenaries and little to no troop reinforcements from Africa would be disastrous for augmenting the fractious Bruttians and Lucanians, who were just as ready to attack anyone other than Rome and to loot neighboring cities that Hannibal was trying to amalgamate under his alliance against Rome.

Hannibal had tried to lure Fabius Maximus out of Tarentum shortly after Fabius had taken it by betrayal when Hannibal was away chasing Marcellus north to Venusia. Hannibal set up an excellent prospective ambush near Metapontum, west of Tarentum. He enlisted the help of its leading citizens who came to Fabius and promised they would betray their city if

he would come. It could have worked had Fabius not been true to character. Conservative through and through, in religion as well as character, the
cautious Fabius took omens. They were probably not auspicious for a sally
out of Tarentum, so he dragged his feet, probably pondering that Metapontum, up to this point, had supported Hannibal for quite a while. Maybe he
also wondered where Hannibal was. His delays forced the Metapontines to
return and inquire why he had not entered their city, raising just enough
suspicion that it was a trap. All surprise was lost, and Hannibal, realizing
Fabius was not going to budge, gave up the ambush idea.

As long as Hannibal could be kept at arm's length and relegated to the
southernmost region of Italy, Rome believed it was much safer with its combined forces greatly outnumbering Hannibal's. That didn't mean Rome ignored him: consular armies continued to avoid open battle and nipped at
his heels, often forcing him to be on the move from spring to fall from 211
onward. Philip V of Macedon was now also thoroughly engaged in western
Greece against the Aetolians north of the Gulf of Corinth, whom Rome
supported in order to keep him occupied: Philip V was no longer a threat
to sail to Italy and join forces with Hannibal as long as he was engaged at
home. Spain would prove to be costly for Carthage if it could not resupply
Hannibal in Italy.

THE EVOLVING CONFLICT BETWEEN
CARTHAGE AND ROME IN SPAIN

After Hannibal had left Spain a decade earlier, much transpired between
Roman aims for expansion and Punic aims for trying to maintain some
control south beyond the Ebro River[4]—the provisional territorial boundary initially claimed by Rome in 219. Roman fleets kept Carthage at bay,
especially since Gnaeus Servilius had chased a Punic fleet back to Carthage
in 217 and had also retaken the island of Kossyra (Pantelleria) halfway between Carthage and Sicily, demonstrating full Roman naval superiority.[5]
The Romans now concentrated on keeping any further reinforcements
from reaching Hannibal via Spain and aimed to break the supply chain

from Spain to Italy, as Polybius asserts.[6] Publius Cornelius Scipio had recuperated from his severe wounds received in the Battle of the Ticinus against Hannibal, having also witnessed the Roman disaster at Trebia, both in 218. Because he still had full support, in 217 the Senate gave him a proconsulship, and he sailed a Roman armada to Tarraco (Tarragona) on the Spanish coast, about fifty miles north of the Ebro. He brought with him a force of eight thousand Roman soldiers and joined up with his brother Gnaeus Cornelius Scipio Calvus. Keeping tradition, their father, L. Cornelius Scipio, had been a consul in 259 during the First Punic War and a censor in 258. They commanded the first Roman force ever to cross the Ebro and negotiated hostages from Saguntum before wintering back at Tarraco. From 217 onward, the two Scipio brothers began to effectively cut off Hannibal's resupply from Spain around the Ebro River. Carthage had commanded Hasdrubal to join his brother Hannibal in Italy but the Romans under the two Scipios managed to keep Hasdrubal Barca occupied in Spain instead. Several battles demonstrated and reinforced Roman strategy under the Scipios.

First, the Battle of the Ebro River took place in 217. There the Roman fleet of thirty-five quinqueremes under Gnaeus Scipio Calvus were reinforced by twenty Massilian allied ships, and the ensuing surprise naval and land battle overwhelmed the combined and slightly outnumbered Carthaginian forces of Hasdrubal on land and the admiral Himilco's forty-two ships on sea. The Romans and Massilians were better trained, whereas this Punic navy had 25 percent new crews, many of them Iberian. The Punic ships had anchored near the estuary, and their unprovisioned crews were searching for sufficient food onshore; the Roman fleet arrived in a surprise and many of the newly assembled and not fully trained Punic crews were disorganized as they quickly tried to reboard and disembark. The smaller Punic fleet was caught unprepared and not even fully manned as it tried to escape the estuary. The Roman ships lined up in an arc, with the Massilian ships behind them, and the Roman quinqueremes rammed the first Punic ships, sinking four and then capturing two more. Gnaeus Scipio's Roman legionaries on board the Roman fleet also overran Punic ships when they grappled together. The rest of the Punic navy abandoned its ships and tried to row back to safety to join Hasdrubal on land. The Romans quickly captured twenty-three deserted Punic ships. Hasdrubal retreated back to Cartagena to levy more troops against increasing Roman incursions into Spain, as the two Scipio brothers led many raids across the Ebro to harass Carthaginian interests in Iberia while Hasdrubal worked hard to subdue the rebellious Turdetani tribe in 216.

Second, the Ebro River again proved to be an important front line dividing Punic and Roman control of Spain. On the south bank of the Ebro, the Battle of Dertosa followed in 215 and was another decisive Roman victory. Hasdrubal had marched north again to the Ebro with an army of 25,000 infantry, 4,000 cavalry, and 20 elephants, meeting the Roman forces again led by Publius and Gnaeus Scipio, who commanded 30,000 infantry and 2,500 cavalry. Although Hasdrubal's army outnumbered the Romans, his troops included more allied Iberians in both infantry and cavalry alongside Libyan and mercenary infantry and Numidian horsemen, whereas the Roman forces consisted mainly of Italian soldiers.

Even with numerical superiority, the Carthaginian cavalries on the flanks were unable to displace the Roman cavalry from the battlefield. The Libyan infantry was actually pushing the Romans back and had gained an advantage. But while the Iberian infantry in the Punic center pulled back similarly to Hannibal's Celtic infantry at Cannae (more likely one of Hannibal's strategies), the Iberian front collapsed and then fled in retreat, which completely changed the momentum. Unable to outflank through their skirmishes and seeing their own infantry center break, the Carthaginian cavalry then also turned and retreated, leaving now-isolated Libyan infantry surrounded.

Although the Libyans fought hard as long as possible and caused significant Roman losses, combined Roman infantry and cavalry overwhelmed them. Hasdrubal had been forced to retreat with his Iberians in full flight and made it to safety, as did his cavalry and most of the elephants, but his Libyan infantry was decimated. The two Scipio brothers overran the Punic camp but did not pursue Hasdrubal. A disturbing trend for Carthage was that war elephants were becoming useless as the Romans learned how to neutralize them, avoiding their charges or using fire arrows to alarm them.

Hasdrubal retreated all the way back to Cartagena and did not venture to the Ebro again, needing to replenish his troops by levying new armies in the south of Spain. Roman recruitment of Celtiberians now began in earnest, as Rome owned the Ebro, and many of the tribes that had supported the Punic side now gave Rome more respect after the two victories at the Ebro and Dertosa near its delta. Barcid control of Spain ended as Hasdrubal was forced to accept coleadership in Spain with Hasdrubal Gisco, who now commanded his own army.

Although they maintained their year-round base at Tarraco, Publius and Gnaeus Scipio continued many raiding sorties and encroachments south of the Ebro to Saguntum and inland for several years. The net result for Carthage from the losses at the Ebro and Dertosa—one mostly naval and the other on land—was that any new armies raised that had been meant to reinforce Hannibal in Italy at a crucial moment when momentum had swung his way after Cannae were unable to reach him. Instead of going to Italy, now full armies were needed to keep Spain under as much Punic control as possible south of the Ebro after 215, as the Scipio brothers increased their successes in enlisting Celtiberian mercenaries to fight Carthage because Rome looked like it was growing stronger.

Hasdrubal Barca's brother Mago now also commanded a third Punic army in Spain—which would have been better deployed in Italy had Hasdrubal not lost at both the Ebro and Dertosa—but this did not turn out to offer any advantage for long. With trouble brewing near home, stirred up by Rome to also relieve pressure in Italy from Hannibal, Hasdrubal was recalled from Spain to North Africa. His mission was to bring relief in 213 when Syphax, king of the Massaesyli western Numidians in what is now Algeria, fulfilled a bribe to support Rome made in 218. After Roman military advisors trained his forces, he brought an army east and attacked eastern Numidian allies of Carthage, especially the Massylians under their King Gala.

Hasdrubal Barca and his army in North Africa successfully fought

Syphax, killing thirty thousand western Numidians and forcing the king to flee back to his territory in the west. Brought up in Carthage as a glorified hostage, Massinissa, son of eastern Numidian King Gala, brought an army of three thousand cavalry to assist against Syphax—when he was under twenty-five years old[7]—and then before 212 returned with Hasdrubal to Spain with Numidian cavalry fighting against the Roman forces of the Scipio brothers.

Between 213 and 211, Hasdrubal Barca continued his battles with the Scipio Brothers all over Spain as he ventured out from Cartagena and they set forth from Tarraco. Both the Romans and the Carthaginians worked to bring as many Celtiberians to fight with them against the other. Hasdrubal's access to the silver of Cartagena gave him some advantage in bribes, but the Romans were formidable in their tenacity, and each Roman victory, however small, persuaded more Celtiberians to either declare sides with Rome or switch allegiance from Carthage to Rome.

THE DEATH OF TWO ELDER SCIPIOS IN SPAIN

A rare positive note for Carthage also sounded from Spain in 212. As the Romans worked their way deeper into Spain from their base in Tarraco, the Carthaginian forces, rather than confront the Romans, attempted to keep their Celtiberian allies under control because many had rebelled after the Ebro Battle debacle. Two successive battles followed where the brothers Publius Cornelius Scipio and Gnaeus Scipio Calvus had separated their armies to pursue the different Punic forces. The two Scipio brothers thought that because the Carthaginians were divided into different forces, this was a weakness they could exploit.

Having spent seven years keeping Hasdrubal Barca and other Punic forces from leaving Spain to relieve Hannibal in Italy, the Scipio brothers were far south of their usual exploits, penetrating all the way to Andalusia in clear Carthaginian territory inland and southwest of Cartagena. They had hired 20,000 Celtiberian mercenaries to augment their armies of 30,000 Romans. The Campaign of the Upper Baetis (Guadalquivir River), encompassing both the Battle of Castulo and the Battle of Ilorca, was the place of double entanglement where the Scipio brothers met their fate. Splitting their armies, Publius decided to attack Mago Barca's army of 10,000 near Castulo with his 20,000 Roman and added Celtiberians. The Numidian prince Massinissa harried Publius from the front with his cavalry near Castulo, and then the Spanish chieftain Indibilis blocked his rear with 7,500 Iberians. Publius Scipio left 2,000 soldiers in his camp and, after a night march, surprised the 7,500 Iberians with his 18,000 soldiers at dawn. But although at first it looked like it would be a quick Roman victory, the Iberians fought well and long enough for Massinissa to arrive with his cavalry of 3,000 Numidians in relief on the flanks. This dual battle occupied Scipio's Romans until, to his alarm, the combined armies of Mago and Hasdrubal Gisco also arrived and began to butcher the outnumbered Romans. The Battle of Castulo ended with some Romans fleeing, including those guarding the Roman camp, but the majority of Romans lay dead—with Publius Cornelius Scipio among them. The Battle of the Upper Baetis (Guadalquivir River) in 212 was the last major Carthaginian victory in Spain.

Gnaeus Scipio had moved with his army, including many Celtiberians, to attack an encamped Hasdrubal Barca and was unaware of his brother's fate. Hasdrubal made no move to engage and stayed in his secure encampment with his army. But then after annihilating Publius Scipio's Roman army, the combined army of Mago and Hasdrubal Gisco turned north to track down Gnaeus Scipio. When he heard of the Punic forces coming— possibly also fearing his brother's death by now—he faced another grim fact in the desertion of his Celtiberian mercenaries near Ilorca. Scipio knew he would have a grave disadvantage far outnumbered by two experienced generals in their own territory. Gnaeus Scipio retreated north hastily, aiming to make it back to the Ebro, but Mago and Hasdrubal Gisco caught up with the Romans later at Ilorca. Hasdrubal Barca now also arrived with his army, and the Roman situation was desperate: facing three Carthaginian armies. The Romans tried to fortify a rocky hilltop in short time but were unsuccessful in digging into the stony soil or making an earthwork berm.

Like Castulo, the Battle of Ilorca was a hopeless defeat for the Romans, as the three combined Punic armies overwhelmed their hastily assembled barricade of baggage and saddles from all sides and slaughtered the Romans and their general, Gnaeus Scipio. In this dual battle in the campaign of the Upper Baetis River, at Castulo and Ilorca, the Romans lost not only their two generals but also around twenty-two thousand soldiers. Looking for blame, Livy claims the Scipios were overreliant on their Celtiberian mercenaries, who deserted because Hasdrubal had bribed them with silver.[8] When word eventually made its way to Rome from the fugitive Romans who had escaped back to Tarraco, numbering about eight thousand, Rome was devastated. Roman interests in Spain were also in shock and the loss was mourned as a national disaster in Rome.[9] Perhaps worse, the defeats and deaths of the Scipio brothers was a disaster that lost for Rome all of Spain south of the Ebro River, presumably also Saguntum, and even put Tarraco under risk of Punic attack again.[10]

After Capua had fallen back to Rome within the next year, the Senate sent the praetor Claudius Nero with an army of ten thousand, leaving with a fleet from Puteoli in 211 and arriving near Tarraco to bolster the area north of the Ebro. Having destroyed the armies of the Scipio brothers and feeling some relief, Hasdrubal Barca ventured north beyond the Ebro. But Claudius Nero trapped Hasdrubal unusually far north among the Ausetani tribe in a gorge called "Black Stones" in the foothills of the Pyrenees in Catalonia, where he was likely stirring up trouble against Rome on Ausetani turf. Hasdrubal engaged in some diplomatic sleight of hand by calling on Claudius Nero's patrician largesse, promising he would leave Spain altogether with his army if let go. Did Nero know this was the son of Hamilcar? Claudius Nero was left with egg on his face in the ensuing space of several nights when Hasdrubal sent a flurry of messengers with different proposals before he would enter formal negotiation; in reality, he was quietly evacuating his men under cover of darkness, slipping soldiers and even elephants away little by little. Requesting a last day of postponement with time for a private religious ceremony, Hasdrubal used a thick fog to hide his remaining troop movements that night. Finally, morning dawned clear, and Claudius Nero's men saw a deserted Carthaginian camp. The Romans gave chase, but Hasdrubal faced only hasty skirmishes as he escaped,[11] moving his forces back south of the Ebro all the way to central Spain, effectively out of reach.

Nineteen

SCIPIO CAPTURES CARTAGENA

After his father's death in Spain, the young Publius Cornelius Scipio (later Africanus,[1] whom I will call Scipio from now on), had been only about twenty years old as a likely survivor at Cannae and was now about twenty-six in 210. Normally that was too young to command, and although a patrician from one of the best Roman families serving in the military, the Cornelii Scipiones, he had not climbed enough ranks of the *cursus honorum* with the necessary time in grade in the offices. Polybius asserts that Scipio helped save his wounded father's life at the Battle of Ticinus in 218,[2] when he would have been about seventeen or eighteen, and Livy likewise relates a now-famous romantic story about young Scipio surviving Cannae as a young officer and, at Canusium, taking a vow with bared sword in front of other survivors to never desert Rome.[3] Others have suggested the romantic story of the vow is a late embellishment, probably by Livy, since Polybius makes no mention of it, but that Scipio likely was at Cannae—possibly even a very young military tribune under Aemilius Paullus.[4]

Now since Spain required new leadership to fill the gap created by the deaths of his father and uncle, the consuls Cnaeus Fulvius Centimalus and Publius Sulpicius Galba called the Senate's electoral *comitia centuriata*—an assembly that elected annual consuls, praetors, and censors—to convene and choose in a special election a leader who would measure up to the challenges of Spain. Scipio had been a military tribune[5] and had only been a *curule aedile* (a magistrate supervising markets) a few years before in 213, but he certainly had not yet been a praetor or consul with authority to lead an army.

Derived mostly from Livy's hagiography but also from Polybius, who compares Scipio to the Spartan lawgiver Lycurgus,[6] many historians[7] have commented on how young Scipio sat in temples—ostensibly meditating and communicating with the gods of Rome—and related "dreams" where the gods intervened on his behalf. If Scipio was prepossessed with his possible future role, he was certainly also planning it well, making every effort to influence public opinion on his behalf by allowing people to draw favorable conclusions about him—neither denying nor confirming supposed marvels at his birth that recalled Alexander[8]—and his hinting at every opportunity of his divine mission. One military historian makes it clear that Polybius is to be read that one "acting on dreams and omens alone would not have won such an empire," rather to not underestimate Scipio's exceptional mind.[9] Scipio was no doubt subtler and more psychologically complicated than even the normally religiously skeptical but admiring Polybius understood, along with modern commentators who may see his publicly "religious" side as persuasively manipulative rather than brilliant and insightful. Even Livy says he "prepared men's minds"—planting ideas that he most likely carefully constructed for a considerable time—and Polybius accepts that Scipio calculatingly "instilled into men the belief his projects were divinely inspired" without criticizing him for it.[10] Scipio is one of the best examples in history of a leader who planned carefully, not only for his battles but also how to bend people to his will. Scipio knew that many people are persuaded more by religion than by reason, and that power of devotion often trumps power of deduction; no doubt a Machiavelli could later paraphrase this.

Whether or not Scipio was the sole candidate for leading Rome's forces in Spain, he was the primary adult heir of the Scipio clan—seemingly paterfamilias—but a *privatus*, or private citizen, rather than a ranking officer. Spain, after all, was not an easy place for a Roman general with inadequate supplies battling vast Punic assets. He did have military experience from the Battles of Ticinus and Cannae, but his appointment was about as extraordinary as he was. In some sense, it shows some desperation brought on Rome by the dire loss of his father and uncle, but other factors were also invested in his choice, such as the patrician families ruling the Senate. The *comitia centuriata* could not actually elect him, but its formal vote possibly legitimized an already-made decision as one historian notes, adding that part of the mystery of the choice of Scipio may have been name recognition in Spain. His father and uncle had already courted Celtiberian tribes, and continuity could be an asset.[11] Named commander of Spain—actually proconsul—Scipio was given ten thousand infantry to add to the eighteen thousand in Tarraco and north of the Ebro, and he left the Roman port of Ostia with thirty ships and landed at Emporion (Empúries, Catalonia) in late 210.

SCIPIO CAPTURES CARTAGENA

Yet a sure sign of the future was the bold and brilliant taking of Cartagena (Punic *Qart Hadasht*) in 209 by young Scipio, almost in the mold of Hannibal. The great personal loss of his father and uncle in 212 seemed to have increased his motivation to give Rome greater success, and he certainly needed to balance the miasma of his family tragedy, one that had the superstitious apparition in Rome of misfortune, which could taint a family if the gods were perceived as averse. Scipio certainly knew that during the winter of 210 in Spain, the three Carthaginian armies were widely separated over a considerable distance of hundreds of miles, with at least one in the south near Gades under Hasdrubal Gisgo; another to the west of Cartagena near Castulo under Mago; and another under Hasdrubal Barca, most likely also in the west among the Carpetani tribe at the headwaters of the Tagus

River near Toledo in central Spain, southwest of the Ebro but northwest of Cartagena.[12]

Because the road to Cartagena was thus open, unprotected by Carthaginian forces and only a ten days' march away at a distance of 280 miles, this fact encouraged Scipio to plan a move as daring as any. It was a great risk but also a great undertaking if planned carefully, something Polybius says was his hallmark.[13] Cartagena—*Carthago Nova* (New Carthage) is the Latin translation of *Qart Hadasht*[14]—had the best harbor in Spain and was enormously wealthy. Perhaps Cartagena stored more bullion than Carthage kept at home, since the Spanish silver mines a few miles away around La Unión to the east and other mines north of that between Murcia and the red-hued Los Victorias hills—many less than a day's journey away on foot—were so rich. Polybius points out how much Carthage itself depended on Cartagena, offering such great service to the Punic enemy that funded damage to Rome.[15] This prize, seemingly so far away but casually defended, was an irresistible lure that would help realize Scipio's vast political ambitions if only he could take it, thereby also cutting off any hope Hannibal had of resupply from Spain either of silver or Iberian allies.[16] Without waiting for any permission from Rome, Scipio shared his plan with only Gaius Laelius, a Roman admiral and friend, to prevent word getting to the far-off Carthaginian armies who thought Cartagena was both a safe distance from any Romans and also nearly invincible in its maritime setting. At the outset, Scipio would be outnumbered by about three to one, given that his total force was, as Goldsworthy says, only "barely equal" to one of the three Punic armies in the field.[17]

After setting up 3,000 infantry and 500 cavalry under Marcus Junius Silanus to guard the Ebro, Scipio assembled the fleet under Laelius at the mouth of the Ebro then near Dertosa and took off quickly with 25,000 troops and 2,500 cavalry on the march, with the fleet likely shadowing their journey offshore. While Polybius and Livy say the journey took a week, the length of the march is better understood as a week plus a few days,[18] and although his army marched very fast and mostly by stealth—his advance scouts probably killed any hostile observers who could have sent messengers to Cartagena and possibly even to the Carthaginian armies in the field to the west and the south—Scipio arrived and quickly set up his army camp east of the walled city of Cartagena. At that time, Cartagena was on a peninsula flaring east from a narrower isthmus where the deep Gulf of Cartagena gave sea access from the south and a lagoon protected the city from the north. From the extant Roman theater, one can easily still see the remnant five hills of the ancient city, once covered with sacred areas and the Carthaginian citadel. The walls of the city only enclosed a circumference of twenty stades, or about 4,500 yards, according to Polybius.[19] Mostly surprising the Carthaginians, the Roman fleet first rounded Cape de Palos from the north, sailed west, and entered the gulf harbor from the south under oar to ready the assault by sea facing the south-facing walls: Scipio's army would attack by land on the isthmus mostly from the east.

Famous stories about Scipio telling his army of his dream of Neptune coming to his aid are great fodder for Scipio's propaganda mill and enhanced his own carefully constructed legend by playing on Roman superstition, love of dreams, and attention to omens. But even if the stories are exaggerated, there are feasible interpretations of what local fishermen may have related about the extremely shallow water of the lagoon and daily wind-aided lowering of the lagoon surface and its ebbing.[20]

This battle underscores one of the worst issues in Carthaginian policy in Spain, a fault due either to Cartagena's distance from Carthage or the lack of clear leadership in Spain in terms of chain of command—three disputing generals—or some other lacuna: Why were so few defenders in the city? Did they really think the city was invulnerable, or did they assume Roman power concentrated at Tarraco and the Ebro was too remote a threat? Polybius says the Carthaginians didn't dream of anyone assaulting the city, when they controlled almost the whole of Spain.[21] The city first tried to fend off seaward assault of Laelius that encircled the walls accessible on the gulf, putting the more trained Carthaginian forces there—up to a thousand men at hand—and leaving up to two thousand townsmen along the landward isthmus walls.

Scipio's landward assault of the city walls on the east was not fully successful. He was beaten back at first. Normal assaults would, as Polybius suggests, wait a day or so to renew strength. One of Scipio's multiple intentions in attacking both from the isthmus and by sea may have also been to divert attention away from the lagoon. But when Scipio saw the water indeed begin ebbing out of the northern lagoon channel in the afternoon, as described by fishermen in Tarraco, he gave the order for enough unnoticed Romans—five hundred men carrying ladders—to scale the walls after wading the shallow water. This new small force found the walls there unguarded, climbed over, and quickly entered the city. Here is a curious event, almost a paradox or at least ironic for a culture that once was so careful about its relationship to marine contexts. The general consensus must be that Cartagena's lagoon provided only an illusion of water depth, since it is very difficult to gauge water depth from a distance.

More than a few have wrestled with this text of "Neptune's aid" as related somewhat differently by both Polybius and Livy.[22] While recent commentators have discussed the phenomenon, the best analysis to date suggests variables of tides and shallow salt flats mixed with offshore wind.[23] The deep water of the Cartagena Gulf harbor toward the sea was possibly a better defense, although Roman ships could also approach here without hulling, so, in summary, Cartagena's perceived impregnability was most likely an illusion.

Scipio's canny invocation of Neptune from his dream enhanced his standing among Rome's Spanish forces, perceived as a leader with divine blessing when his soldiers crossed the lagoon. In any event, one historian makes a good case for interpreting Polybius as "attributing Scipio's success to his own forethought rather than the fortuitous aid of Neptune" in listening to the account of the fishermen of Tarraco who knew the phenomenon of the lagoon's variable depth.[24] This is also firm evidence for Scipio's capable use of military intelligence long before an established imperial Roman spy-craft service, documenting that Scipio was disposed to and had learned from Hannibal's example of how to gather intelligence and was also fully able on his own to carefully consider source information and plan accordingly.[25]

Scaling the undefended walls along the lagoon, the Romans moved rapidly east and killed anyone resisting, also helping to open the isthmus gates that Scipio had placed under renewed assault—his men hacking at the gates with axes but covered by testudo shields (large curved shields that covered at 1 to 2 soldiers when held overhead)—so that the landward forces met about the same time as the seaward forces also scaled the underdefended walls on the south. The Roman forces swept through the city to the citadel, where the remaining Carthaginians had retreated, and soon its surrender was accelerated by the obvious sight of marauding Roman soldiers filling the city, a custom of killing all who stood in their way, as Polybius noted, without looting, to inspire terror in a mayhem that did not even spare animals.[26]

Not even counting the Carthaginian treasury of silver, the collected booty from Cartagena was indeed huge, brought into the city square and guarded before some of it was distributed among Scipio's forces. Gold, silver, and military equipment such as catapults are just a few of the materials taken as part of the Roman prize. Some of the silver and bullion from Cartagena may have been claimed as personal fortune by the Barcids themselves and held in reserve there, but now all of this was gone too. Scipio took the Carthaginian commander named Mago and several high-ranking members of Carthage's Gerousia Council and its Senate as prisoners to be guarded by Gaius Laelius.[27] Spanish hostages numbering about three hundred were freed and released back to their tribal homes with gifts on condition of promising to guarantee their tribes would ally with Rome. Many of the city's slaves were promised freedom after the war if they served Rome; then Scipio allocated them for rowing the eighteen captured Carthaginian ships or to reinforce the Roman rowers of Laelius. This use of slaves as rowers, whether in crisis or not—and to be freed after war service to Rome— may not be at all unique.[28]

In astute magnanimity he could usually fan into legend, Scipio not only was said to have kept the hostage women from being raped but also turned down one offer the hostages made of a beautiful Spanish maiden, releasing her back to her father and her fiancée, who had hoped to ransom her.[29] Livy likely embellishes the story that Scipio gave back the gold for her ransom as a wedding present to the young Spanish chieftain in order to better recruit from his tribe. That Scipio took Cartagena in one day confirms not only that it was inadequately defended—only a thousand Carthaginians and townspeople were pressed into defense—but also that Carthage made a grave error in thinking it was invulnerable with its walls and surrounding water, since the shallow lagoon provided only an illusion of safety.[30] Scipio's strategy was fast coming into parity with that of Hannibal, from whom he had learned well (if unintentionally on Hannibal's part).

The continuing importance of Cartagena to the Romans—as Carthago Nova—would be evidenced in its strategic venue as a depot for metal production since its Punic establishment, as well as the fact that it became one of three Roman military command centers in eastern Spain, along with their previous base at Tarraco and the other established at Emporion.[31]

BATTLE OF BAECULA

After Cartagena, Scipio had one decisive battle where he defeated Hasdrubal Barca at Baecula (Baelen) in 208, his first victory in Spain. Now controlling vast reaches of Spain south of the Ebro and Cartagena, this last battle was also in the upper Baetis (Guadalquivir River) region, not far from the disasters that had wiped out his father and uncle. Scipio had an army of about thirty-five thousand soldiers compared with Hasdrubal's twenty-five-thousand-plus Iberians. This time the Carthaginians and Iberians were trapped in a steep valley when Scipio closed both the road to Baecula and the valley entrance. Hasdrubal moved his army to the heights, but after a few days, he was surprised when attacked on three sides by so many Romans climbing up the ridge. Scipio had pretended it was only a feint or a skirmish of a few troops, and yet Hasdrubal, abandoning his camp, managed to retreat with most of his men. Hasdrubal lost the battle along with many of his Iberian mercenaries and light troops, as well as his baggage and supplies when his camp was overrun by the Romans.

Hasdrubal's losses were possibly about six thousand dead and up to ten thousand captured, while Scipio lost fewer than two thousand at the Battle of Baecula. Scipio did not pursue the retreating Hasdrubal Barca, who moved west with his remaining army, although Hasdrubal still had a large reserve of precious metal, including gold and silver, to pay his mercenaries. The news of this last defeat reached Carthage, which now knew Spain was lost. Carthage then ordered Hasdrubal to go to Italy and assist Hannibal. Hasdrubal avoided Roman territory and moved as far west and north as possible in late 208, to Galicia near the Atlantic, passing over the western Pyrenees to Gaul. He was also ordered to take his remaining money with him to hire as many Celt mercenaries as he could. Scipio now controlled the Cartagena silver mines and their prolific production, and without Cartagena and the mines, there would be no more revenue from most of Spain, severely diminishing Punic revenue.[32]

Hannibal still reigned in direct combat on the open battlefield and was capable of similar ambushes that took out senior Roman leadership such as Marcellus and Crispinus or Roman troops daring to confront him. The death of the Scipio brothers in Spain was another Roman tragedy impacting Spain in the short run, but it may have motivated young Scipio, quickly leading to the conquest of Cartagena and Carthaginian control in Spain.

The loss of Cartagena—Carthage's precious metal depot—and subsequently the loss of all Spain soon after Gades surrendered in 206[33] was almost incalculable, with both its wealth in gold and silver as well as its supply of allied Iberian soldiery gone forever. Hannibal would be forced to survive on his own. His presence in Italy would now be a burden on a region severely strained by war. No new numismatic Barcid or Punic presence in coin finds in South Italy after 207 is evidence to some extent of this loss of Spain.[34] How much Spanish silver came to Hannibal before 211 is hard to quantify, but some estimates suggest as much as 135 kilograms a day came to him from Spanish mines like the mine at Baebulo alone.[35] Spain's rich precious metal was now forever lost to Carthage.[36] What little silver would trickle indirectly from Carthage itself would be inconsequential in comparison.[37]

After Punic loss of Spain, Hannibal knew his options against Rome were shrinking like his power base at the foot of Italy. He had no ports, no new silver, and was becoming more and more dependent on less-committed Bruttians and Lucanians instead of his veterans, who were old, tired, and dangerously diminished. Yet while his brother Hasdrubal had a fresh army to bring to Italy from Spain, there was still hope.

Had Hamilcar Barca lived to see two of his three "lion cub" sons on Italian soil, one in the South and one in the North, it surely would have made him proud. It might have even given him some vindication over the bitter outcome of the First Punic War, when he knew as a warrior that his merchant-dominated Carthage had capitulated too quickly.

Twenty

METAURUS

After his defeat by Scipio in Spain at Baecula in the spring of 208, yet with much of his army intact, Hasdrubal Barca was again commanded from Carthage to join his brother Hannibal in Italy. This time he made the decision to abandon Spain, since Rome was now establishing its own dominance there. It must have been with some regret that Hasdrubal obeyed, knowing that the wealth of Spain's silver mines and rich iron was something Carthage could ill afford to lose. Hasdrubal had eluded the army of Scipio in the late fall of 208 by passing with his mixed Carthaginian and Celtiberian force over the low Cantabrian Mountains in the extreme west near a Galician source of the Ebro River. One of several clear differences between Hasdrubal's and Hannibal's armies is that Hasdrubal lacked the advantage of the sizable force of Numidian cavalry that his brother had used so well as a tactical weapon in his considerable arsenal.[1] The debated original number of soldiers with him may have been fifteen thousand soldiers and fifteen elephants.[2]

Moving east through Southern Gaul, Hasdrubal wintered there, picking up many Celtic recruits along the way. Because he had started from

Spain so late in the year, this was not the best plan of action to spend so much time on his route wintering with an army west of Italy, because it gave the alarmed Romans ample time to prepare for him, as their allies the people of Massilia (modern Marseilles) warned them of Hasdrubal's coming. Hasdrubal crossed the Alps in the spring of 207. Polybius says Hasdrubal's arrival in Italy was much easier and quicker than Hannibal's.[3] Appian (ca. 95–165 CE) says that Hasdrubal crossed the Alps using the "same pass" as his brother did almost a decade earlier.[4] This is not impossible but unlikely for several reasons, including the ease of marching without resistance from either difficult route or enemies such as the still hostile Allobroges. It is more likely that Hasdrubal used a much lower pass such as the Montgenerve, with much easier conditions, avoiding mountain Allobroges.

HASDRUBAL IN THE PO RIVER VALLEY

After leaving the Alps, Hasdrubal moved east in the Padana but was delayed at fortified Placentia, the same fairly recent (218 BCE) Roman outpost that Publius Scipio and the remaining Roman soldiers had retreated to after both Ticinus and Trebia. At Placentia Hasdrubal attempted to lay siege to the Roman colony, hoping to starve it out. While he waited, he likely thought a victory there might win over more Celts in the region to his new invasion. As the first Roman colony among the Celts of the Padana or Po Valley of what would later be Gallia Cisalpina, or Gaul on this side of the Alps, Placentia's fortified position was often precarious, sacked multiple times by Celts and Ligurians.[5] The Insubres tribe on the west and the Boii tribe on the east were constant threats to Placentia that Hasdrubal hoped to tightly amalgamate under him along with other tribes.

But Hasdrubal's Placentia encirclement was fruitless, possibly because the Romans had learned to stay put in a siege as long as possible, and as his own resources were being wasted to no effect, he lifted the siege and abandoned hope of taking Placentia. He may have been joined by eight thousand Ligurians around the time he left the area.[6]

Hannibal certainly thought considerably about his brother's forces in North Italy in the spring of 207 and hoped to trap Rome between their two armies, but he may have been surprised by how quickly Hasdrubal had crossed the Alps and then possibly assumed Hasdrubal's siege would last longer, so his timing was thrown off. Added to this, Hannibal was under repeated rear attacks by a Roman army at Grumentum (near Grumento Nova)[7] in Lucania as he moved south toward Bruttium along the upper Agri River; he couldn't free his army from the dogged Romans under Gaius Claudius Nero at his heels, and he was bleeding men and resources from so many skirmishes meant to keep him in the deep south.

The Romans were also well aware that much of Italy lay between the armies of two Barcid brother generals, both of whom had been successful against Roman armies in Italy and Spain, respectively. Livy even later raises the specter of Hamilcar Barca, their father, who had been so difficult to dislodge in Sicily during the First Punic War, no doubt on the minds of Rome itself.[8] The Romans had not yet fully mobilized, but a large part of their plan was indeed to keep Hannibal from getting anywhere near his brother's approach into the heart of Italy or to keep both of them away from Rome itself. As long as Hasdrubal was far north in the Padana and Hannibal down in Lucania or Bruttium, the prospect was less dire, but if somehow the unforeseen tactical pincer movement came, the possibility of another debacle like Cannae would be dreadful. No doubt this was also what Hannibal, Hasdrubal, and even Carthage aimed to make happen.

After Placentia, Hasdrubal sent six messengers on horseback—two Numidians and four Celts—with a sealed letter on the long journey south toward where he expected Hannibal to be, requesting him to meet him halfway down Italy, seemingly "in Umbria." But Hasdrubal made at least one very foolish mistake. Unfamiliar with the territory and unaware that Hannibal was on the move constantly putting out fires or coming to the aid of his allies, the messengers made it almost all the way to the farthest southern coast of Italy along the Gulf of Taranto but got lost down by Tarentum. The messengers had planned to find Hannibal somewhere around Metapontum, since they apparently knew that Tarentum had been retaken by

Rome in 209, but they were discovered and captured by a Roman patrol much more familiar with the region. The first error of getting lost and being captured was greatly compounded by the fact that when their letter was found on the messengers, Hasdrubal had also made everything plain in the sealed letter, which could have also provided sufficient details of his route. Worse yet, the communiqué was possibly also written in Punic, easily translated by Roman military interpreters, instead of being written in a cipher, or perhaps best transmitted only in verbal form. Whether or not the messengers' interrogation included torture, the damage was irrevocable once the Romans read and acted on the contents of the letter. Moving up the chain of command, the letter came to Claudius Nero. He immediately dispatched the letter to Rome, where he recommended decisive action.

Never having received the letter—maybe not even knowing one had been sent—Hannibal only knew his brother was somewhere in the north of Italy but had no way of connecting without specific details. Part of the irony of this dilemma tells how very different Hannibal's overall position was in 207 relative to 218 to 216. Before, he had ample military intelligence with a network of spies everywhere, many of them bilingual or trilingual Celts or disaffected local mercenary Italians who could melt into different communities, including those that must have provisioned Roman armies. Hannibal's line of communication was now far more haphazard, fragile, and easily disturbed.[9] His resources were also much more limited—with apparently less silver to bribe for vital information—and his live assets for ground intelligence seemingly greatly reduced.[10]

One bold move by a united Rome was almost all that was needed. An army under the consul Marcus Livius Salinator now marched north to meet Hasdrubal if he chose the coastal route. It would eventually be reinforced by either two legions from near Ariminum under Porcius Licinius or by another army coming from Etruria if Hasdrubal came via the Apennines. This last force was under previously disgraced Gaius Terentius Varro, who had disastrously abandoned Cannae but still had plebeian electoral popularity. Thus the separate Roman armies hoped to contain Hasdrubal on one or the other side of the Apennines and force him to choose a route—either west of the mountains or along the Adriatic coast—and guard both of these options.[11] Now with a force numbering around thirty thousand, Hasdrubal followed the Po River Valley all the way east, possibly on the Via Aemilia, which took him along the Adriatic coast route south past Ariminum.[12] There the combined Roman armies of the consul Livius Salinator and the praetor Licinius assembled to stop him. The Senate was also concerned that Hasdrubal would rouse the rebellious Etruscans of Etruria, a region "ripe" for rebellion.[13]

More dramatic and consequential was that after having followed Hannibal south to Grumentum in the late spring of 207, the other consul, Gaius Claudius Nero, had moved his army about a hundred miles north to Canusium (modern Canosa di Puglia)—very near Hannibal's great victory at Cannae—when he received the intercepted message about Hasdrubal's movement around mid-May. Such was the seesaw movements of cat and mouse between the Romans and Hannibal that after Grumentum, Hannibal had also turned around northward to follow the Romans back toward Canusium. Claudius Nero quickly persuaded a divided Senate in late May to let him quickly take a secret force to meet Hasdrubal and to keep Hannibal completely in the dark, thinking he and his army were still nearby. This Roman deception would not have worked either between 218 and 216, but it seemed to take a page from Hannibal's own tactics.

GAIUS CLAUDIUS NERO

Gaius Claudius Nero was a member of one of the most ancient and venerable patrician families, the gens Claudia, and also one of Rome's increasingly more qualified generals as the Second Punic War dragged on. Claudius Nero had been a staff member under heroic consul and kinsman Claudius Marcellus at Nola in 214 during Hannibal's effort to secure Campania, which was excellent training for a rising officer. Later, holding the military office of praetor and civilian office of propraetor[14] in the *cursus honorum*, Rome's expected sequence of offices for its elite, Claudius Nero took part in the siege of Capua in 212 and 211.[15] Perhaps Claudius Nero was even one of the Roman officers present under Marcellus when the Romans repelled one of the armies of Hannibal at Nola in 214, as discussed in the previous chapter, and who learned then that Hannibal, however brilliant, was not invincible.[16] Showing he was a teachable Roman military leader, Claudius Nero had even been wisely using some of Hannibal's own tactics against him at Grumentum by concealing some of his soldiers and coming at Hannibal from both directions—a successful strategy that Livy said was "taking a page from his enemy's book." Although not a very Roman tactic, it resulted in difficult attrition for Hannibal's troops.[17]

Whatever his ambitions, Claudius Nero managed to overcome the fears of the Senate that to leave Hannibal and go north to Hasdrubal could be disastrous if Hannibal knew and followed. Out of his army, he chose six thousand of the best soldiers—the cream of veteran Roman soldiers with great stamina and strength—and a thousand cavalry of the same caliber. He left behind the rest to guard Hannibal, leaving on a secret night march in the deepest quiet but with the greatest haste.

FROM VENUSIA TO METAURUS

In order to cover the distance of more than three hundred miles between Venusia (Venosa) and the Metaurus River at an almost unheard-of pace, most likely traveling not far inland along the Adriatic coast but certainly east of the Apennines, Claudius Nero's small army marched day and night.[18] Because the troops traveled extremely light for speed, much of their provisions came from the local people who watched them march by the rich farmland, apparently in generosity for protection. Some of the food came from the Piceni,[19] the local Adriatic population, which had never sided with Hannibal. The Roman soldiers had brought little more than their weapons and ate along the way only what they needed. The pace was such that while we do not know how long the march took, it must have been at least seven or more days. It would have been extremely unlikely to make more than thirty miles a day on foot even in fairly open farm country from Apulia northward past Ancona, the chief city of Picenum, originally a Greek colony from

Siracusa in the early fourth century. The countryside between Apulia and Ancona itself consists of many rolling hills above a shallow coastal plain, and whether Claudius Nero's army kept fairly along the hilltop ridges or marched on the coastal plain, his journey was so fast that Hannibal's scouts had possibly been unaware of his nocturnal exit. If Hannibal even noted the prolonged absence of seven thousand soldiers, he may have been stymied because there was still a substantial Roman army camped at Venusia under the legate (a high officer of the Roman army from the patrician or senatorial class) Quintus Catius and possibly one under the proconsul Fulvius Flaccus in the area of Canusium. Hannibal may have been unable to follow even if he did know, since the "curtain wall" of Roman forces numbered about thirty thousand between Venusia and Canusium.[20]

From the outset, Claudius Nero had first sent an envoy on horseback ahead to his senior coconsul, Livius Salinator, now camped near Hasdrubal, who had also arrived south of Ariminum close to Sena near the Metaurus River and not far from the Via Flaminia.[21] Sena, or Senagallia (also Sena Gallica),[22] was a Roman colony on the coast in the territory of the former Senones tribe along the Misa River near Ancona. The present Senigallia town is about ten miles south of where the Metaurus River flows into the Adriatic. Hasdrubal was evidently well aware of the presence of the combined Roman army under Livius Salinator and Licinius.

When Claudius Nero's army arrived as quietly as possible by night, although their direction had been from the south, his scouts had no doubt apprised him of the least likely angle of approach to be discovered by any Carthaginians, who were likely coming directly up the coast now and entering from the east. To complete the deception, Livius Salinator's army shared its tents with the new soldiers so that the Roman army camp looked exactly as before: no new tents, no visible expansion of space or spreading of quarters that Punic spies would notice by daylight.[23] The Romans were cramped and uncomfortable, but the Hannibal-like ruse worked almost perfectly. Against the protests of Livius Salinator, whose day it must have been to order time and place of battle in the shared leadership pattern, Claudius Nero advocated immediate battle the next day despite how tired his men were.

Not wanting to lose the element of surprise, before Hasdrubal discovered he was now facing a much larger army, worsening his chances considerably, Claudius Nero won the argument against his senior colleague. Claudius Nero's speech before the battle and the *oratio recta* (straight talk) have been noted in Livy's narrative of a general's harangue before battle with rhetorical similarity to Thucydides, suggesting a deliberate literary narrative following precedents.[24] Claudius Nero had encouraged his men before they left Venusia to think of themselves as the small weight added to the scale to tip it to victory; even an incremental change such as theirs would be decisive. In addition to the initial element of surprise, their presence alone would soon unsettle Hasdrubal. On the night before battle, Claudius Nero emphasized that maintaining a brisk marching pace—in this case more than halfway up Italy—would make their strategy successful; any delay would reduce it to a reckless adventure. Ignorance worked in their favor as long as Hannibal down south thought nothing amiss. Delaying battle against Hasdrubal would give more time to both the Barcid brothers, eliminating their dual advantage: it would betray the Roman camp down south to Hannibal as having fewer troops on hand and take away any surprise benefit of larger troops assembled here against Hasdrubal.

Morning broke with the Roman army mobilizing a short distance away. Hasdrubal's camp was possibly only seven hundred meters from the Roman camp. In a famous story related by Livy,[25] Hasdrubal, with a small cavalry escort, cannily observed some old shields facing him along with some emaciated horses. Both seemed unusual to him, and he had not seen them before. Wondering if the army facing him had been reinforced, a canny deduction, he sent out his scouts to reconnoiter a long way around the Roman camp. But they reported back that the camp was the same size, with no new tents. Uneasy at the mixed report of what seemed possibly contradictory, the experienced general looked for other evidence as he had his men pull back from their camp, calling off the immediate battle. Hasdrubal soon found his answer when a report told what the Roman trumpets blared: one trumpet sounded in the praetor Licinius' camp but *two* trumpets sounded in what was supposed to be only the consul Livius Salinator's camp. The trumpet peals must have been different to distinguish a praetor from a consul, and Hasdrubal was seasoned enough to know the difference. This revealed what he possibly suspected: that two consuls were now present, where only one had been the day before. Many have said this kind of detail is too clear to be fiction, but Hasdrubal now had a conundrum to unravel with multiple possible bad implications. Could he fight a battle facing a now-compounded Roman force, leaving him even more outnumbered? Had the new consular army facing him won against his brother Hannibal? Was that why they could mobilize to meet him? Had he come to Italy too late? Had his message to his brother been intercepted? Whatever the answer, it wasn't good and wasn't in his favor. Hasdrubal avoided battle that day and began to retreat to the southwest, quickly making distance away from Sena until he could come up with the best strategy. Some commentators think that Hasdrubal's quick retreat to the Metaurus panicked his army and turned their resolve to fight into fear, the worst possible scenario for planning a battle.[26] Everything fell apart from that point on.

Hasdrubal had by now hired or acquired some local guides to help him avoid the coastal route he had taken to Senal and began to march mostly west that day. Maps of the region, including satellite maps, show many twisting oxbows of the Metaurus River about ten miles upstream from the coast. And, at that time, it was heavily wooded in many places. Beginning above present-day Calcinelli on the north bank of the Metaurus, many of these old oxbows are steeply sided and joined on both sides by many stream gullies off the surrounding plateau.[27] The guides were not exactly trustworthy, however, and if they had promised to lead him to safety or over the river at a major fording place, they did not keep their word. It is even possible they had some allegiance to Rome and were hoping to lead Hasdrubal into a tight spot before disappearing.

The Romans were in hot pursuit, and night brought the darkness Hasdrubal hoped would cover his next move. It might have given him an option to escape into the forested hills, where he could hide, or he might have intended to follow the general course of the Metaurus deep into its Apennine source where he could cross the mountains, but we cannot easily reconstruct his reasons.[28] In any case, the Romans were too close for Hannibal's brother to escape without detection.

Hasdrubal was possibly unnerved by the prospects of what had happened to his brother Hannibal, who had not met up with him while an enemy army had met him instead. His army was in flight mode, and this signaled a bad portent to his allied Celts and his guides. The retreat backfired when his two guides disappeared during the night, likely not wanting to be caught with his army. Hasdrubal was now forced to follow the river course with its channel cut into the plateau, his only topographical clue of direction in the dark. Caught in the bends of the river valley, Hasdrubal may have been looking for a fording place in the river[29] where he could cross with his army to relative safety at some point, but without the guides, his army became lost in the steep bends, enabling the Romans to catch up easily by morning. Livy notes the "twists and turns of the tortuous river,"[30] suggesting that Hasdrubal's retreat was now deep into the old Metaurus oxbows. Many of his Celts had also either scattered, abandoning the rest of the marching army somewhere along the way, or had made camp where Hasdrubal had initially planned to rest until he found his army too closely pursued. The Celts may have stopped to sleep, aligned in their tribal groups—reverting to old loyalties when Hasdrubal's infrastructure began collapsing—although they had also consumed enough wine to be in a stupor.[31] Many knots of Celts possibly slept along high gullies or up streams they had followed. Hasdrubal forged on in the dark with the rest of his army. The Romans intercepted Hasdrubal partly because their scouts were following an army rather than a river, and the Romans could have avoided the oxbows by traveling above along the plateau away from the bends, knowing where the oxbows would come back if they had proper local guides. Many of the Roman troops could have come straight across from Sena, halving the distance once advance scouts who observed from safe distances signaled Hasdrubal's troop movement directions.

That next morning—ironically, about the midsummer solstice, possibly even the same day Hannibal had won at Trasimene a decade earlier—a weary Hasdrubal heard and saw he was trapped. He had to face a Roman army bristling and ready for battle. He may or may not have made his way out of all the oxbows, but his back was to the steep hillside in the Metaurus River Valley. He had no choice but to do battle. He tried to assemble his army in order in the tight space, setting his Spanish forces on his right behind his fifteen elephants at the far edge, with his remaining Celts on his left but uphill.

Hasdrubal knew the Romans would find it difficult fighting uphill and that his doughty Spanish forces on lower ground would face the brunt of the battle. Livius Salinator's army faced Hasdrubal's Spanish, who fought bravely and gave no quarter, although outnumbered. Porcius Licinius faced Hasdrubal's center with his army. At first, the battle was fairly even because Hasdrubal used his remaining Celts in the steep terrain to his advantage to attempt offsetting the numerical discrepancy—an echo of his brother's tactics. But having no time to escape, Hasdrubal also had no hidden ambushes for the Romans as Hannibal had often set up.

The Punic war elephants were mostly useless and unmanageable, charging pell-mell into the tight space, causing as much havoc to Carthaginians as Romans. Six elephants were killed outright—some slain in battle with their drivers or miserably by their drivers, who pounded spikes with mallets into the base of their skulls when they attacked their own forces—and at least four elephants crashed right through all the Roman lines, wandering aimlessly in the countryside until captured later. The elephants were either abandoned by their drivers or some drivers were picked off along the way through the Roman lines.[32] War elephants needed open ground to build up any momentum in charging and were not at all effective in a steep river valley.

Claudius Nero soon realized he would not prevail uphill against the Celts and could not come around their flank on the right because of the steep topography, so he changed his tactics by improvising brilliantly. He pulled back a considerable number of his rear troops, leaving the rest engaged against the Celts, and moved the smaller force around behind Livius Salinator's fighting line all the way to the far left, where the ground was flatter and more open. Now Hasdrubal's veteran Spanish troops were exposed in a dual attack on their rear from Claudius Nero while still fighting Livius Salinator's army on their front. Claudius Nero's maneuver proved to be the deciding factor at Metaurus, as the Spaniards, however resolute, along with Hasdrubal himself, were mowed down from both sides—"cut to pieces," as Polybius says.[33] The Celts gave way to the relentless onslaught once the Spanish were decimated, or even before, when they saw the battle turning, some fleeing. Hasdrubal now knew the battle was lost and threw himself courageously and somewhat suicidally into the thickest fighting where he fell, choosing to die honorably rather than be taken prisoner and paraded through Rome in shackles.

The Romans ransacked the Carthaginian camp, killing the sleeping Celts, who could barely move. Gathering up loot and as many of the captured enemy who had survived or surrendered, the Romans were elated at their success—perhaps the first major victory in Italy. Hasdrubal, a once mighty but now slain Barcid, was likely soon decapitated to relieve years of Roman frustration. Once the knowledge of victory soaked into the minds and emotions of the resting Roman soldiers, the news bolted like lightning to Rome along the Via Flaminia. Although some rumor possibly trickled in an advance wave, the city quickly knew by the sight of the joy and confidence on the faces and demeanor of the victory envoy of cavalry officers riding thunderously into the city and straight to the Senate. Rome declared the victory of Metaurus a temporary national holiday, and rejoicing was heard everywhere by an astonished people rushing along the streets to the heart of the city to celebrate ridding themselves of one of the shadows looming over their shoulders. Although the long war was far from over, the sun must have seemed to shine brighter that day than most could remember in Rome.

For his part, Claudius Nero turned quickly southward with his tired army back to Venusia, marching as fast as possible—it all happened in about two weeks—before Hannibal had any news of the defeat and death of his brother. Unless the military intelligence in the ancient world had a superb chain of human links and spies on horseback, two weeks would be a fair time for word to travel on foot three hundred miles, especially if the Romans were attempting to keep the news from Hannibal. Perhaps it is not odd given the patrician politics of Rome that the bold consul Claudius Nero was not given the victory he mostly earned; instead, the credit went to his coconsul Livius Salinator, who had commanded a larger force. At this time, the Claudii were greatly overshadowed by the Aemilii, Fabii, Cornelii, and other families. If Claudius Nero felt robbed, we will likely never know, although he served out the war honorably but quietly mostly in the backwaters.[34] On the other hand, because he did his duty by returning quickly to the field in Lucania, he apparently did not accompany Livius Salinator back to Rome, where the senior consul received the hero's welcome.

More dramatic, the number of Carthaginian dead at Metaurus is likely best summed up by Polybius as only ten thousand Carthaginians and Celts (in contrast to Livy),[35] although the "Carthaginians" included Spanish as well as African troops.[36] Some important captured Carthaginian officers who had survived were held for ransom. After this defeat, the Celts were almost done as an ally of Carthage. The Romans lost only two thousand in the battle, and Metaurus was the most lopsided battle since Cannae but with a dramatic reversal of fortune. Metaurus became the turning point of the war both in confidence for war-hardened Rome and in undermining whatever success Hannibal had achieved in his string of incredible victories. This was a squandering of capital that Hannibal had accumulated as a fearsome juggernaut. The double threat Barcid invasion of Italy feared for so long was finally answered.

Partly because he was still hemmed in by Roman armies and because his own intelligence network had failed for resources and dwindling revenue, Hannibal found out after Rome did about the Carthaginian disaster at the Metaurus. But Claudius Nero had a trophy Livius Salinator did not, even though his colleague had the victory. If the story is true, Hannibal was in his tent in his camp, possibly wondering where his brother was, when a hard-riding Roman cavalry envoy was allowed under diplomatic truce into the camp. The Roman horseman flung a sack into his tent, and the startled Hannibal peered inside to see his brother's gory head. Hannibal responded: "There lies the fate of Carthage."

Twenty-one

ROMAN TRIUMPH, ITALY TO SPAIN

After Metaurus, Rome breathed a considerable sigh of relief, and the Senate decreed three days of grateful prayer. From a distance at Venusia, Claudius Nero had shown Hannibal some of his captured African soldiers now in chains. If the sight shocked him, Hannibal would not have given the Romans any satisfaction. Hannibal soon left for Bruttium, where no Roman armies went after him, but armies on several sides mostly penned him in. For the moment, Hannibal had only two small ports left: Croton in the west side of the Gulf of Taranto (he evacuated his garrison from Metapontum), on the "ball of the instep foot" of Italy; and Locri on the Ionian coast farther south across the mountains on the opposite side of Rhegium, practically at Italy's "toe." But Hannibal would lose Locri to Scipio with help from the city of Rhegium in 205, when Scipio crossed over from Sicily. So Hannibal's territory and influence continued to wane as Roman fortunes waxed. As one scholar observes: "Ultimately the Romans prevailed on the battlefield because, however incompetent and divided the leadership was at times, military service formed a part of every aspiring citizen's upbringing."[1]

HANNIBAL AT LACINIUM AND HIS BRONZE PLAQUE

Around this time that Rome left Hannibal alone at the foot of Italy during 206–205, and he entered a lull without fighting anywhere—there were few territories and allies to defend anyway—he must have had enough time on his hands to be somewhat reflective. Since no armies came after him, maintaining their distance, did Hannibal wonder if Rome now chose to consider him little of a threat?

Apparently for the first time, Hannibal did something difficult to read as having any tactical or strategic value. He erected a bronze plaque in the Temple of Juno at Cape Lacinium, now long since gone along with most of this temple at what is now called Capo delle Colonna but witnessed by Polybius and others. As the earlier hybrid Phoenician-Etruscan gold tablets of Pyrgi indicate,[2] Hannibal's Phoenician ancestors had considered Juno (or Uni) to be an Italian version of their goddess Astarte—hence some of the myth symbolism of the Roman poet Virgil for the reciprocal relationship between Juno and Queen Dido in the *Aeneid*—so this was an apropos dedication from a Carthaginian in a Juno temple.[3] The full bilingual Punic and Greek text of Hannibal's plaque is unknown, but if Livy is right, it recorded some of Hannibal's achievements as his self-reflexive *res gestae*, or "things accomplished."[4] Polybius, who saw it, has quoted only the numerical troop strengths listed there by Hannibal,[5] including from his long march of 218.

Several have called the bronze tablet a memorial to a huge ambition[6] that, in retrospect, went mostly unfulfilled. Others wisely noted Livy's text deliberately culminating his book 28 about this bronze tablet as a literary bridge that "indicates the end of Hannibal's successes in Italy, separating the past, which belonged to Hannibal, from the future, which will be Scipio's."[7] Regardless of Livy's rhetorical intent in his narrative, he must not be far off if Hannibal is now sufficiently contemplative about his Italian sojourn of fifteen years, wanting to leave some document of his impact in a mostly hostile land that would love to erase all traces. If this is an accurate assessment of Hannibal, he must have been pensive after Hasdrubal's recent defeat and death and his own confinement to Bruttium, knowing that Carthage was unable and unlikely to send him any more significant help.

THE BATTLE OF ILIPA AND CARTHAGE ABANDONS SPAIN

Spain remained a war theater into 206, as Carthage empowered Mago Barca, Hannibal's youngest brother general, and Hasdrubal Gisco to fight on in the South, west of Cartagena. Near present-day Seville on the Guadalquivir River, about 275 miles due west of Cartagena in southern Spain and only sixty miles from the southern coast of Spain, lay the Roman town of Ilipa, showing how deeply Romans had penetrated into what was only recently the stronghold of a thoroughly Punic Spain.

Scipio set up camp only to be attacked by dual cavalry forces commanded by Mago and Massinissa the Numidian prince. Scipio had been prepared for this and had massed his own cavalry behind a hill from where they swooped in and put the Punic cavalry to flight. The Roman and Carthaginian armies—about 50,000 infantry and 4,500 cavalry for the Carthaginians, if Livy is right,[8] nearly equal in infantry at 45,000 and equal in cavalry, according to Polybius[9]—soon gathered in force and lined up for battle without full engagement, only to do reconnaissance of each other with a few preliminary skirmishes of light infantry and cavalry for sensing strengths and weaknesses for several days. Hasdrubal Gisco commanded the Carthaginians, and Scipio observed his deployment tactics, including that the Carthaginians were slow to assemble for potential battle in the mornings. He had also observed that Hasdrubal placed his heavy Libyan infantry in the center of his battle formation, with his elephants on the two flanks. Scipio now put in place a devious plan that would have impressed even Hannibal.[10]

Scipio assembled his prebattle line mimicking the Carthaginians, arriving even later than Hasdrubal's army to provide a cover illusion of indolence. He also placed his heavy Roman infantry in his center and his Spanish troops on the flanks. This went on for several days to establish in the enemy's mind that this would be the order of battle.[11] Scipio might have deduced from the deaths of his father and uncle, attributed to their Iberians abandoning them possibly after being bribed, that he should not put too much confidence in Iberians,[12] but he did not yet want the Carthaginians to guess his true intentions.

Scipio now sprang his trap. On the day he calculated best for battle, he began before dawn, making sure his army rose early and had food. Then he sent his light infantry *velites* (light infantry and skirmishers) to harass Carthaginian positions and arrived ready for battle. This early start took the Carthaginians by surprise, rising without eating and hastily assembling for battle in some disarray, having been lulled by Scipio's prior turgid pace that any battle would take place late in the day. But Scipio had disguised his line—mostly unobserved, as dawn had hidden his changes, and he reversed his first deployments—as Polybius says, in a "precisely opposite manner."[13] Polybius is a reliable source on Scipio's tactics here because he was keenly interested in military strategy, having also apparently written a lost study on tactics.[14] To the surprise of the Carthaginians, Scipio's Iberians were now at the center instead of his heavy Roman infantry to face Hasdrubal's core of African infantry, and there was nothing the Punic commander could do about it because Scipio had caught him off guard in the first place by being so early to battle, and he had no time to change his formations. When Scipio's advancing army was only five hundred or so feet from the Punic force, not only did he place his best heavy Roman infantry on the flanks, with cavalry and *velites* behind them, but he also executed an unorthodox maneuver that required great discipline from his troops.

His next order was perfectly executed. Scipio's line was suddenly very broad when the Roman heavy infantry spread out behind and around his Iberians, possibly almost doubling their original width, and certainly wider than the Punic line as they met. On a command that required perfect timing, both flanks of Roman infantry having quickly marched forward were ordered simultaneously to turn inward at 90 degrees. The left infantry rank, led by Scipio, turned right, and the right infantry rank, led by Junius Silanus and Marcus Septimus, turned left. The Carthaginians were thus caught in a pincer movement that echoed Cannae—although none of them had witnessed it—this time, however, initiated by the Romans.

Hasdrubal's Iberians, who faced Rome's disciplined legions on both flanks, were quickly overwhelmed in the double jaws of heavy Roman infantry and routed. Hasdrubal's center was rendered mostly useless because Scipio's Iberians blocked his experienced African infantry. These Iberian allies had nowhere to go and, more importantly, refused to fight, merely staying behind their shields.[15] Their presence in the battle now seemed to be more window dressing to occupy the Carthaginian center. At the same time, this Carthaginian core began to face battle on its sides. The remaining exhausted Punic forces—including their commanders Hasdrubal and Mago, and possibly Massinissa—began to retreat slowly, but as entropy and collapse took over from every direction but behind them, their pace increased rapidly to remove them as much as possible from calamity.

The Battle of Ilipa would have been even more disastrous for Carthage had a violent storm not suddenly stopped the pursuing Romans. The surviving Punic Iberian allies pulled out when what was left of Hasdrubal's army retreated into the hills above the Guadalquivir River. The Carthaginians fortified their new camp with rocks, but after their Iberian allies left during the night, Hasdrubal Gisco and Mago went separate ways south to the coast to Gades, the major port and one of the last Punic bases in Spain. Gisco and his fleet sailed off to Africa, while Mago remained. As one historian notes, Scipio had learned from observing Hannibal how deceptive appearances can be, and how to match not his strength to an enemy's strength but his strength to an enemy's *weakness*.[16] Scipio went back to Tarraco slowly on a diplomatic junket of several months, visiting Iberian allies and showering them with gifts, as a way of ensuring a modicum of allegiance in easing the transition of power from Carthage to Rome.

The concentrated battle at Ilipa was the last major engagement between Rome and Carthage in Spain and proved Scipio as a formidable strategist. It is historically ironic that while Livy consistently castigates Hannibal for duplicity and deceit in employing strategy, he praises Scipio for brilliance using the same practices. But overall, Livy is cautious about stratagems, implying that they are somehow "un-Roman." Romans are supposedly open and manly in their directness in war. Naturally, Livy's positions mainly reflect his bias against Hannibal and almost all things Punic.

Mago Barca tried to re-establish a Carthaginian toehold in Gades, but the Battle of Ilipa had convinced Gaditans that Carthage was finished in Spain. They told Mago it was time to go. A few resisting towns such as Castulo capitulated under siege, but it was denouement for Punic presence in Spain after hundreds of years of influence and outright dominance by Carthage. Scipio left lieutenants such as Silanus to hold key towns in Spain. There would be a few mutinies and rebellions in Spain,[17] as well as a diplomatic side trip to Africa to cultivate his coming master plan for Africa. Scipio made increasingly promising plans to return to Rome in triumph.

A SPY MISSION TO AFRICA AND
NUMIDIAN MUSICAL CHAIRS

Scipio's clear vision was to take the war beyond Italy to Carthage, but he knew he had to tread carefully because of opposition, especially from the conservative Fabian Party in the Senate, whom he knew to be territorially myopic and Italocentric. At first, only the glimmers of Scipio's grand scheme were revealed on the periphery because now with so many threats neutralized, Rome could afford to dabble more openly in North Africa. Rome had obviously penned up Hannibal in Bruttium, and no other Carthaginian army would dare march to Italy after Hasdrubal Barca at Metaurus. What's more, Spain was now under control and getting stronger by the month.

Earlier, to prevent new allies coming to Hannibal from the east, Rome had succeeded in distracting Philip of Macedon with the Aetolians in Greece. Likewise in North Africa, they had stirred up a bit of trouble for Carthage using Syphax, king of the Massaseylian western Numidians, until Hasdrubal Barca had repelled Syphax. According to Livy, Scipio understood that the Numidians were unreliable, although it is more likely they had no real permanent investment in Carthage if their own interests did not intersect. With typical literary flair Livy writes almost sarcastically that Romans such as Scipio expected "barbarians" like the Numidians to be fickle:

"expecting treaties have no more weight or sanctity than agreements ever do with barbarians."[18]

Since Spain was no longer a war theater, if the expanding periphery was to exercise new Roman muscle across the Mediterranean in Africa and extend the war to that turf, it would have been suicidal unless Rome had serious allies on the Continent. Some Romans, like Scipio, thought that the Numidians were the best candidates for forging alliances that would help them secure a foothold in Africa and also undermine Carthage.

About this time, Syphax decided to test the water again in Numidia. He had bided his time after being chased out of eastern Numidia by Hasdrubal Barca. Plus, he was not alone in Numidian vacillation. Massinissa too saw the fate of Punic Spain after the Battle of Ilipa, and, seeing which way the wind was blowing in Spain, covertly decided to switch sides, setting up clandestine meetings with Scipio himself in 206 in Gades.[19]

Back in North Africa, Syphax had attracted attention again from Rome after a lull. Whether he made overtures to Roman ears or Rome took the initiative, it was Scipio who was now finely tuned to all things North African. Scipio first sent his friend Laelius to Syphax, who received him politely but with reserve. He was adamant that he would negotiate only with a commanding general—and rightly so, as he wanted to be honored as a king by being taken seriously.

So Scipio had to come almost by himself—the equivalent of a Roman spy—to North Africa in a quick but risky mission; an envoy to the land of the enemy without full diplomatic immunity. He was greatly outnumbered by hostiles or by hordes uncommitted to either side. No doubt with some trepidation mixed with excitement at his dangerous task, Scipio came with a very small and mostly invisible accompaniment of only two quinqueremes. They were soon swallowed up in the vast North African horizon en route to a harbor somewhere in present-day Algeria. Scipio's thoughts and emotions seeing North Africa come into view for the first time must have been tumultuous—especially when to his and others' surprise, the sails of a small Punic fleet was spotted right behind them. Scipio might have wondered if it had all been a ruse and a trap, as Hasdrubal Gisco arrived at nearly the same time, but despite the shouts and calls to arms, there was no engagement as they berthed. It turned out that Scipio and Gisco were not expecting each other, and both were coming to woo Syphax and his considerable Numidians. We can assume that at their meeting, Hasdrubal recalled past Numidian and Carthaginian camaraderie to Syphax, but Livy was not reluctant to natter about the expensive gifts Scipio brought that greatly pleased the Numidian king.

Scipio seemed to brilliantly pull off this tough diplomatic assignment on enemy turf. He was so compellingly charismatic at Syphax's table that even Hasdrubal Gisco was disconcertingly charmed. This was the same Roman Scipio whose family Hasdrubal Barca had slaughtered in Spain and then the same stern but clever Roman who had bested him in battle at Ilipa. If Livy is not exaggerating, the archenemies who had decimated armies of Rome and Carthage between them now shared not only the same table but also perhaps even the same couch like bosom buddies.[20] But Scipio's own personal talents included personal warmth, natural courtesy, and tact with a pronounced ability to relax both his enemy and his host. Syphax was delighted, his Numidian royal pride massaged by having the commanders of two powerful nations vying for his allegiance at his table. Underscoring Scipio's magnetism, Livy purportedly quotes Hasdrubal as saying of Scipio, "Carthage should not so much attempt to understand how we lost Spain but how we will now keep Africa."[21] Although he was too experienced a Punic leader to be naïve, Hasdrubal Gisco may have nonetheless left Syphax wishing Scipio was a better candidate for friendship than for war, but the Carthaginian probably had few illusions about this. On the other hand, Scipio may have thought that Syphax had been more flexible than reality soon showed. Syphax did not sever his old ties to Carthage.

Hasdrubal Gisco was not done either, however, as he soon played a card that Scipio would be unable to trump easily. Knowing Syphax's interest was already building, Hasdrubal fanned the smoldering embers by offering his nubile and accomplished daughter, Sophonisba, to the king for continuing loyalty in keeping his people's old faith with Carthage. Sophonisba was hardly a pawn but a beautiful woman with intellectual energy and reasons of her own, playing Syphax for all she could muster—and not necessarily just for gods and country but also for her new queenship. With Sophonisba at stake, Hasdrubal compelled Syphax to warn Scipio against coming to Africa. Whether or not Carthage had been behind the whole scheme from the start, it also perceived it was a good alliance for Sophonisba to marry a friendly king who would rule a large tribe on their borders. The Sophonisba story would take another turn, however, as Massinissa later reentered the picture to claim Sophonisba with the help of Rome. Massinissa's father, King Gala, had died and having left Spain to assume his kingship, his rule was postponed a bit while he waited for Roman help because Syphax had attacked his country on behalf of Carthage. For now, old king Syphax had a young trophy wife to fan both his ardor and his Punic alliance.

SCIPIO LEAVES SPAIN IN TRIUMPH

Scipio's long planning for this day was paying off, and if he was impatient to leave Spain, he seemed not to show it. All Rome was abuzz about his accomplishments in Spain, and he knew it because he had made sure it was well publicized. Carthage had been beaten and its armies chased out, many forced to go home or wherever else they could find a base of operations. After Carthage conceded Spain, Mago Barca was ordered to go to Hannibal's aid in Italy. He left Gades for the island of Minorca and then sailed to the Ligurians of Genoa, where he tried to raise new troops for several years.

When Scipio finally left Tarraco in late 206 with a fleet of ten ships to return to Rome, he brought with him a staggering sum of silver treasure from Spain, mainly confiscated from Punic treasures such as Cartagena's, or from abandoned army camps, or from Spanish mining operations now under Roman control.

The Senate met with Scipio outside the walls of Rome, near the Field of Mars at the Temple of Bellona, because, as stated earlier, a commanding general was not allowed into the city with arms or soldiers and had to relinquish imperium.[22] The Senate gave Scipio an august audience to personally recount all of his Spanish campaign successes over his five years whittling away at Carthage's power until it was reduced to nothing. According to Livy, Scipio reminded the Senate that when he'd arrived in Spain, he faced four successful Carthaginian commanders and four victorious Carthaginian armies, but he left not a single Carthaginian soldier there.[23] His service record was nothing short of magnificent—better than any Roman general had accomplished in several generations—and the Senate could not fault or deny anything Scipio related. Scipio probably spoke firmly but humbly as possible to mitigate envy or fears that he was reaching beyond his station. He could hope but not ask to march triumphantly through the streets of Rome with his booty, yet he would have to hide any disappointment.

Because he was a commanding general but not a consul, no triumph would be allowed by custom. Leaving his horse outside the walls, Scipio walked through the streets of Rome. Before him rolled his open slow carts, bringing to the public treasury his enormous gift that he deposited as the spoils of war from Spain: 14,342 pounds of silver ingots and a great quantity of silver coins, as Livy relates. This is estimated to be the equivalent of almost 1 million denarii (around 58 million dollars).[24] How do we know the exact amount? If Scipio looked on at the counting, he was making sure that not an ounce was untallied, because this would not only be important to have on record but also to be talked about through Rome. Although this deposit was by no means a bribe in exchange for public adulation, and Scipio tried to make it look altruistic, no one would be naïve enough to assume there was no underlying motive for such public largesse. Polybius had already noted his earlier *megalodoros*—munificence—as programmatic while in Spain.[25] While there were no stated strings attached, Scipio knew what he was doing and expected something in return, as Livy describes what quickly followed officially after the roar of unofficial public approval from the people of Rome.

He soon received a different kind of triumph, won in the overall public adulation that had not only welcomed Scipio as a hero but also visible in now thousands of people lining the streets of Rome clamoring to glimpse this man whom the gods had earlier chosen when he was elected consul for 205. He sacrificed a hundred oxen to Jupiter, as he had promised in Spain, and throngs massed to see him. Scipio could not have asked for a better public relations campaign in advance of going as consul to Sicily, his stepping stone to Africa, although he still had formidable opposition from the Senate and the party of Fabius Maximus, who may have been envious and suspicious of Scipio. Perhaps Rome didn't permit electoral bribery (*ambitus*), but is the related word *ambitio* (ambition) applicable?[26] No doubt the Senate and Fabius in particular wondered if Scipio would try to circumvent their power by appealing directly to the people, as he seemed to threaten. If so, they would have to preempt him by giving him carte blanche for Africa in order to make it look like they were in control. Scipio was now justly renowned, and the powers of Rome knew it.

SIBYLLINE BOOKS AND ORACLES CALLING AN ORIENTAL DEITY TO ROME

While in general Livy loves to relate a litany of omens, other than to comment that 204 BCE was a year of raining stones more often than usual and that a wave of superstition swept over Rome, he is fairly restrained about the omens and readings from the consulted prophetic Sibylline Books that called for hauling the Eastern cult of the goddess Cybele from her shrine at Anatolian Pessinus near the ancient Greek kingdom of Pergamum to Rome.[27] The Sibylline Books said Cybele's presence was necessary in order to drive out an unspecified enemy foreign invader from Italy, but obviously it was interpreted as referring to Hannibal.[28]

Livy is also strangely tight-lipped about all this being so superficially un-Roman, although in reality it was uber-Roman. Partly because she was worshipped in Asia as the Great Idaean Mother of the Gods, the Magna Mater (or Mater Deum Magna Idaea), the event is almost a foil to Hannibal's plaque event dedicated at the temple of Juno in Lacinium. More important, Cybele also antedated history in Rome's mythical Trojan origins. After stopping in Delphi, where the oracle also predicted success, the envoy accompanied by five quinqueremes found the Attalids in Pergamum were friendly to Rome. According to Livy, the royal party of the client king of Pergamum,

Attalus, even accompanied them to Pessinus, where they obtained Cybele's sacred stone that was possibly meteoric, being "from heaven." The sacred stone was to be received in Rome by the worthiest Roman citizen, the *optimus vir.*

The Sibylline-Cybele story is famous from multiple sources, including Ovid and Appian,[29] alongside Livy. Livy also states the Senate chose the son of Gnaeus Scipio (Calvo) who died in Spain, and Juvenal confirms him as the worthiest Roman who received the statue in Ostia, her "unimpeachable host." This was the cousin of Scipio[30] and it was a great Scipio family honor. Renaissance artist Andrea Mantegna tells the story in his grisaille painting gem from 1505–1506, *The Introduction of the Cult of Cybele into Rome*, with the patrician matron Claudia leading the entourage, because in Appian's version, she was a virtuous woman, who almost single-handedly pulled the boat carrying the cult statue with her girdle tied to it when the boat was stuck in the mud.

What is also telling in the majority of historical and literary narratives about the 204 introduction of Cybele is that Scipio's family was chosen as the most worthy for Rome to receive and revive the Cybele's Idaean Mother Goddess link to Troy. In concert with his carefully cultivated public image of religious devotion and connections to the gods, Scipio himself would not have denied his family to be perceived as connected to a divine agent of salvation in Cybele's cult coming to Rome. This divine association would enlarge his own persona to undertake bringing the war to Africa, which he could work into being part of prophetic fulfillment to rid Italy of Hannibal.

Like Hannibal, whom he seemed to emulate more and more, Scipio's ability to read people was unusually adept from youth onward. But while Hannibal brooded in Bruttium with no battles to fight, his influence waned in the war by much the same degree as Scipio's waxed. Even if details are tailored slightly by Polybius—and considerably by Livy—after the fact, only a few glimpses of Scipio's tactical genius at Cartagena and the Battle of Ilipa and his diplomatic ease with old allies of Carthage such as Massinissa in Spain and Syphax in North Africa are enough to warrant respect for his constructed persona. Whether he cleverly manipulated his own people's perceptions and superstitions is immaterial; his intellectual probity to plan for years ahead through complicated maneuvers, where the external circumstances were often beyond his control, evidences great intelligence and unusually deep confidence combined with the subtlest political shrewdness. As one military historian suggests, each time Scipio had a different opponent, "Scipio's military motto would seem to have been, 'every time a new stratagem'" as an artist of war,[31] although many of his precedents were from Hannibal as a master teacher. Scipio had his focus fixed on Carthage and would not be turned away from Africa for long. He had the strongest conviction that the surest way to rid Italy of Hannibal was to take the war to Carthage. Hannibal may have been a caged lion, safe only from a distance, but he was still a lion.

Twenty-two

ZAMA

Now that Spain was no longer important in the war theater for Carthage, mostly removed from the picture and providing no silver for its war efforts, and because Italy had so far survived two invasions from sons of Hamilcar, Rome concentrated in keeping Hannibal isolated in Bruttium during 205 and 204. There was growing perception, no doubt encouraged by Scipio, that Rome had survived the Carthaginian threat and should turn its eyes toward Africa, where Carthage's original Numidian allies were fractious and less likely to support their old masters.

So much had changed in the landscape of war with increased Roman successes, the Romans could make some compelling arguments to divide the Numidians still further in questioning Carthage's ongoing ability to wage war if it was so dependent on allies such as the Numidians and mercenaries. The Celts in the north of Italy—who had been Hannibal's allies while the booty flowed and Rome was backing up—were now also wary because Hannibal's old gains had been reduced to only a foothold in Italy, and his promises of returning their hegemony had turned sour.

SCIPIO FORCES THE SENATE TO BRING
THE WAR TO CARTHAGE

With less threat than ever in the war from Punic armies or their allied forces, Scipio was eventually persuasive in 205 in making his case to the Senate that the war could be taken to Africa and thus force Carthage to recall Hannibal. This seemed reasonable to many Romans, but his overtures were not met without resistance and argument from some, including from the faction of Fabius Maximus, whether from some hidden jealousy at Scipio's success or prudent fear of leaving Hannibal untended in Bruttium, or both. Scipio argued that there was a huge contrast between ruining an enemy land, as Hannibal had been aggressively doing, than seeing one's own land ravaged by fire and sword. Italy had been devastated for almost two decades. Give it some rest and now let Africa be the theater of war; let Carthage see from its gates what Romans had witnessed for too long.[1]

Some in the Senate, such as Quintus Fulvius Flaccus, voiced that Scipio was merely sounding them out about his plans and would put his bill before the people, who were thought to be firmly under his spell. In order not to be circumvented in its authority and made to look weak, the Senate confirmed Scipio not only in his consulship with power over Sicily but also with the provision that he could go to Africa if needed. Scipio always seemed to carry himself with sufficient moral rectitude—living publicly with abstemious behavior and delaying most of his personal gratifications[2]—that the Senate found little ammunition to pillory or undermine his stated intentions.

WAR PREPARATIONS IN SICILY

Locri had been one of the last cities left to Hannibal in Italy but was betrayed to the Romans in late 205. Hannibal lost a valuable outpost and Ionian port—also famous for its Temple of Proserpina and its zephyrs—but a city that the Carthaginians had not found easy to rule, with customs that Polybius also came to know well later.[3] Scipio sent a Roman force of three thousand to take it under tribunes and his legate Pleminius, who was ultimately so heavy-handed that many complaints of mistreatment—some confirmed by quaestor Marcus Porcius Cato—went to the Senate in 204, where Fabius Maximus was still seeking restraints on Scipio and looking for any ammunition to limit his power. When the Senate's investigators came to Sicily, Scipio was busy preparing for his invasion of Africa. His camps and military exercises and training drills were so impressive, he was able to escape censure.

Scipio's provisioning for Africa was well planned, properly inventoried, and commissioned on an expected two-year campaign for as many as twenty-five thousand to thirty thousand men, although the actual number is debated.[4] One nerve center of Scipio's Roman forces was a core of retrained survivors from Cannae eager to prove their worth by erasing the shame of that defeat as O'Connell has so ably argued. The invasion of Africa would be done with forty transport ships carrying soldiers, arms, siege machinery,[5] and rations. Almost two months' worth of fresh water and food were packed, some bread even already baked. Safe passage across from Sicily to Africa was invoked by requisite sacrifices at sea by the general himself, and although it was somewhat risky to invade across more than 120 miles of water, during the actual voyage there was no Carthaginian naval resistance, either due to lack of Carthage's resources, depleted Carthaginian naval power, lack of preparation in Carthage, or some other unknown reason.

SCIPIO LANDS IN AFRICA

Although the Roman fleet may have intended to land at Cape Bon on the east wing of the Gulf of Tunis, it veered west and landed instead at Cape Farina, not far from the city of Utica, either delayed by seasonal fog or possibly by intent if trying to surprise Carthage. Sextus Julius Frontinus, a highly respected Roman senator and author of a first-century CE book of war stratagems, tells the anecdotal story, true or not, about Scipio's adept use of omens and transforming negative into positive: "Scipio, having transported his army from Italy to Africa, stumbled as he was disembarking. When he saw the soldiers struck aghast at this, by his steadiness and loftiness of spirit he converted their cause of concern into one of encouragement, by saying: 'Congratulate me, my men! I have hit Africa hard.'"[6] While this tale of Frontinus is almost certainly spurious, it nonetheless conforms to Scipio's recorded keen skills in manipulating perceptions.

SCIPIO LAYS SIEGE TO UTICA

Soon after the Roman fleet landed, the immediate coast cleared as local people fled to nearby Utica or even farther south to Carthage. The city-state sealed its gates perhaps for the first time in decades, considering this huge turn of events as a perceptibly great threat for the first time in this war. While Scipio set up camp on land a brief distance from Utica, the Roman fleet soon moved to blockade Utica from the sea where it anchored.

The fact that Utica—actually an older Phoenician colony than Carthage[7]—was well fortified thwarted Scipio's hope of a quick victory to establish a more secure African base as the days wore on. Assault barrages from his siege towers (fortified wooden towers that were filled with soldiers to attack city walls) were unable to make much headway from land, and attacks from the seaward side also proved ineffective against Utica. After forty-five days, another circumstance turned his attention elsewhere. A joint Carthaginian army of infantry and cavalry assembled by Hasdrubal Gisgo and the Numidian Syphax—larger than the invading Roman force—arrived to relieve Utica, and Scipio was forced to withdraw his army to a nearby walled camp for wintering on the headland.

Scipio now mulled a different approach: How could he disentangle Syphax from Carthage despite the king's marriage to Sophonisba, his Carthaginian wife? Syphax was lured into private negotiations. For his part, Syphax demanded both a Roman exit from Africa to coincide with Hannibal's exit from Italy. Typical for heated Numidian rivalries, Syphax seemingly wanted this so that he could try to get rid of his rival Massinissa himself and keep Rome out of Africa—better for his Numidians with a weakened Carthage than a surging Rome. Scipio knew this.

He was content to keep Syphax dangling, lulling the Numidian with a noncommittal exchange of envoys while playing his waiting game. Scipio sent trained officers as military spies under the guise of being lackeys or slaves to keenly observe the Numidian camp and the adjoining Carthaginian one. Scipio's garnering intelligence assets was similar to what Hannibal had accomplished years before when he had resources among disaffected locals and Celts throughout Roman army camps in Italy.

The intelligence results Scipio learned in this way were useful in early 203: the enemy armies had an overly relaxed attitude, and morale was low, with both Carthage and Numidians eager for a treaty. Scipio concluded correctly that the enemy was ill-prepared for battle. Plus, the Carthaginian army was housed in wood huts, and the Numidians in reed shelters not always within the army camp stockade. Now Scipio acted far more like devious Hannibal than a methodical Roman, cleverly dissembling by pretending to reopen his siege of Utica with a renewed blockade and war engines. Since the enemy camps were made of highly flammable dry wood and reed, Scipio's plan was to set fire to the two enemy camps simultaneously if needed and take advantage of the pandemonium to mow down the sleepy soldiers who fled their burning shelters. The enemy troops seven miles away went to bed thinking they were safely distant when Scipio sent a stealthy night force down to his enemies' camps after the Roman night trumpets had sounded a pretend tattoo for bed in case any foe could hear.[8]

On arriving in the middle of the night under cover of darkness, Scipio quietly divided his forces, sending his adjutant Laelius with Massinissa to Syphax's Numidian camp while he went to Hasdrubal Gisgo's camp. Laelius and Massinissa with cavalry were easily able to quickly enter the camp of Syphax and his sleeping Numidians because much of it was outside the stockade; they set fire to it, and it was soon engulfed in flames as the Roman and allied forces rode through, cutting down any who stumbled around suddenly awake. Scipio in the same way took out the Carthaginian camp's fighters when they were distracted by the neighboring conflagration. The outcome was that although their leaders Syphax and Gisgo escaped in time, the disastrous loss of both enemies, Numidian and Carthaginian, was almost complete, with many thousands dead or captured. If this act seemed treacherous on the part of Scipio—contra Livy, who repeatedly mentions "*Punica fides*" as the only fitting description of untrustworthy Carthaginians[9]— when Syphax and even Gisgo had expected peace as hinted, it was also brilliantly ruthless. A relentless Scipio pursued his enemies, who paid severely for their negligence as he mercilessly drove them away in slaughter before they had time to arm themselves. After his victory, Scipio swept through the region mopping up in North African towns before finally returning to Utica to renew his siege. But the inaction was temporary, as neither Scipio nor Carthage could afford to let an invasion simmer.

ANOTHER CARTHAGINIAN DISASTER AT
THE BATTLE OF THE GREAT PLAIN

Carthage, with its still-deep pockets, quickly raised another mercenary army of thirty thousand within a few months, a portion of them reinforcements comprising the last four thousand mercenary Celtiberians from the south of Spain—those few remaining who still opposed Rome. This time the new Carthaginian army assembled on the Bagradas (Medjerda[10]) River southwest of Utica at a flat area called the Great Plain, again with King Syphax and whatever Numidians Hasdrubal could muster.

With Massinissa's cavalry as his most mobile wing, Scipio formed three other Roman lines of battle: the faster light infantry (*hastati*) as the front line; the intermediate, better-protected infantry (*principes*) forming the second line; and his heavy infantry (*triarii*) as his rear line. Scipio sent Massinissa and his cavalry into a furious charge driving forcefully into the Carthaginian line—almost like the flying wedge Alexander had used successfully against the Persians of King Darius III—which buckled the Carthaginian line. Most of the Carthaginian infantry fled in scattered retreat along with the modest Carthaginian cavalry, and the Numidians of Scipio chased most of the Carthaginians from the battle. This left only the veteran Spanish mercenary infantry fighting fiercely to hold the line against Scipio's light infantry *hastati*, whose number they equaled. Scipio then sent in his second and third lines of heavier infantry from behind to move right and left along both flanks—the old Hannibal tactic of envelopment—and the Celtiberians were surrounded by battle on three sides with great loss. Only a few Celtiberian mercenaries escaped along with scattered troops led by Hasdrubal and Syphax, who again were able to flee. Hasdrubal fled back to Carthage and Syphax trying to reach the Numidian city of Cirta. As soon as Carthage found out it was such a clear victory for Scipio, the Carthaginian elders met in council to decide the safest salvage plan.

THE TRAGEDY OF SOPHONISBA

Massinissa and Laelius maneuvered southwest to Numidia, where Massinissa aimed to recapture Cirta, which had once belonged to his tribe before Syphax usurped it. Massinissa also hoped to take the king's beautiful wife captive because Sophonisba had once been promised to him. This kind of "wife stealing" was not unprecedented in the ways the hotheaded Numidians conducted romance, given how history has portrayed Numidians—however barbaric in Roman eyes.[11] The complete defeat of Syphax—thrown from his horse—was a coup for Massinissa and Laelius, who captured him alive en route to Cirta. Massinissa asked Laelius to let him go to Cirta without any accompanying Romans, where he was also temporarily successful in claiming Sophonisba, making her his wife in a hasty ceremony to keep her from Roman hands.

But this proud Carthaginian woman knew her fate—even begging for death as she clung to his knees—when Scipio instead demanded her as part of the Roman spoils, not for himself but for Rome. Regardless of Massinissa's hopes that she would accept both marriage and captivity, she refused as a Carthaginian to go to Rome as a spectacle of triumph and committed suicide by taking poison. Apparently the poison had been provided by Massinissa, according to Appian[12] (a variant on the idea that if he couldn't have her, nobody could). As historical tragedy, her story has been adapted to many artistic genres more than a few times by sympathetic masters such as Petrarch and Voltaire in epic poetry or drama, Mantegna and Rembrandt in painting, and Henry Purcell and Christoph Gluck in opera. Although he had lost Sophonisba, Massinissa quickly took over the Numidian kingdom of the humbled Syphax, who would soon go as a prisoner to Rome, unlike his lost wife. Despite the mercurial way the besotted Numidian victor had tried to save Sophonisba but also allowed her poison, Scipio saluted Massinissa with the scepter of Numidian kingship, and Carthage had almost no remaining Numidian allies.

After this disaster of two Carthaginian forces defeated at the hands of Scipio and his Numidian allies close to home, a worried Carthage sued for terms of peace. This was most likely in part a delaying tactic while it also played the one card it had left: recall Hannibal from Italy to save Africa. Although cooped up in Bruttium with his military intelligence resources now far less extensive, Hannibal could have even guessed this last-gasp gambit if he had been following the events unfolding in Africa. Certainly the war that Hannibal's original strategy must have envisioned and hoped would be short[13]—for the sake of his invasion and resources—had dragged on interminably and drained his military campaign coffers as well as Carthage's patience—however stingy the homeland had been.

HANNIBAL'S RECALL TO CARTHAGE

Hannibal would now have to abandon the extensive field of his many victories—where he had first roamed almost at will—but which had now shrunk to a mere wild peninsula at the extreme southwestern end of Italy. He first had to make sure to send home all his useless Italian allied forces; those unable to be counted on away from Italy and their own homes. Then Hannibal had to do something that must have been even more difficult: he was forced to slaughter all the horses he could not transport[14] so that the Romans would not capture them and use them against Carthage. It must have been awful for a general to destroy such valuable assets, and if the screams of horses dying not in battle but in useless death were not utterly heart-wrenching to anyone who heard—despite the assertions of Diodorus Siculus and Appian, even one as tough as Hannibal would probably not want to be around for the destruction—the report of this slaughter does underscore the brutality of war and how ruthless a hardened general like Hannibal could be.

THE DEATH OF MAGO

In Bruttium, Hannibal had doubted that his brother Mago would reach him from Genoa in Liguria for several reasons, one of them being his own isolation and another the increased power of Rome to mobilize. Hannibal's doubts were soon confirmed. After Scipio had already taken the theater of war to Africa, the Romans blocked Mago Barca in Italy with four legions distributed from Ariminum to Arezzo. In 203 Mago tried to fight this combined Roman army of four legions near Milan with his Ligurians and remnant Carthaginians, even fielding war elephants, but, early in the battle, he was wounded in the leg and fell off his horse, likely then sustaining added injury. The battle quickly turned, and without his leadership, his army was defeated. Mago escaped to his ships at Genoa, but died at sea from his wounds. When Hannibal found out later, he mourned his second brother's death. Two Barcid lions were down, and only the one—fiercest of all three—remained.

HANNIBAL LEAVES ITALY

Carthage managed to get sufficient transport fleet protection to Italy and bring Hannibal home. Embarking from the Ionian coast, what Hannibal must have felt and contemplated looking back at the receding shore of Italy and his sixteen years there will always be a tantalizing prospect for historians. Livy concludes that Hannibal left Italy with bitterness and regrets, and while this may be true, it is also typical of Livy to negativize Hannibal whenever possible.[15] However, Hannibal may have indeed felt as Livy wrote: that it wasn't Rome undermining or conquering him but his own people and foes in Carthage, and that his Punic enemy Hanno could only bring down the Barcids by ruining Carthage.

In reflection, more than a third of Hannibal's life had been spent on Italian soil. The first three years of lightning success had been so rewarding and full of promise as he brought Rome to her knees. But the last thirteen had been an endless, slow series of frustrating circles, at times one step forward and maybe more than one step back at other times. He had lost two brothers in or around Roman lands and waters, and had not accomplished his ultimate goal of forcing Rome to give way to Carthaginian sovereignty. And while he never backed down from his vow to his father of eternal enmity toward Rome, now he faced a greater obstacle. Rome had reversed the table on him, also slowly at first but unmistakable now with Scipio in Africa threatening the very survival of Carthage.

As his fleet neared Africa, it is equally fascinating to consider what Hannibal felt having been away from his homeland and his childhood city of Carthage for most of his life. Did he feel a deep, inherent loyalty to a place he hadn't seen for so many decades? Did he feel betrayed, as his father had, by the decisions of weak leadership in Carthage? Hannibal could certainly sum up all the circumstances in which Carthage had taken the expedient and conservative but not so bold policy route, perhaps as could be expected for a commercial rather than military power. While it had tried to reinforce his campaigns, mostly with his brothers' forces, Hannibal knew that Carthage could and would blame him for the largest share of responsibility of failure if Scipio could not be stopped, but it is likely Hannibal would not have necessarily shared that shouldering of ultimate responsibility as his forces landed and he touched the soil of Africa once again.

In the autumn of 203, Hannibal landed considerably to the south of Carthage—a cautious hundred miles away—at Leptis Minor (modern Lemta)[16] in Tunisia. He brought with him possibly fifteen thousand to twenty thousand of his remaining veterans: Balearians, Libyans, Carthaginians, Spanish, and Celts, as well as the best of the Bruttians. How few of his original veterans remained from crossing the Alps is unknown—certainly not many—but if Hannibal had any left, most of them would have been in their thirties[17] or, like him, in their midforties. This would make them at least a decade older than the average age of troops in general. These veterans may have been experienced and wily, but likely no longer strong enough to last through a full day of battle. If Hannibal cursed the gods and men, as Livy says, he was too smart to let his men know how low his spirits must have been at this irrevocable turn of his fortune.

HANNIBAL ASSEMBLES AN ARMY TO MEET SCIPIO

Hannibal managed to secure a bit of time through the autumn and early winter before Scipio would march to meet him or he would confront Scipio, despite Carthage's missals to defend its lands. In addition to his veterans from Italy, he was able to secure another twenty-five thousand soldiers— including Balearic islanders, Ligurians recruited by his brother Mago, and other African mercenaries—but could muster only three thousand to four thousand cavalry of mostly new Numidian allies. Hannibal had already long culled out the useless men in his forces while back in Italy. In addition there were those who probably refused to go to Africa,[18] those his practiced eye knew could not fight a prolonged battle because they were now too old, those who would not be able to leave Italy, or those who had vacillating priorities (fear rather than loyalty, according to Livy[19]) and therefore weak ties to his war effort. Thus Hannibal had probably reduced his standing army to half its size. He knew he was deficient in cavalry, and while he also pulled together eighty war elephants, these were young beasts and not battle trained; hardly a surrogate for the mobile Numidian cavalry that had been so decisive in his best battles. He thus assembled an army of about forty thousand foot soldiers,[20] likely around half of them totally inexperienced relative to about a third who were veterans.

When Carthage had called him to defend the city, Hannibal had de-layed in bringing his forces to battle, knowing they were unready and that he was outmatched by Scipio's trained army. But when he understood at last the danger of Massinissa's Numidian cavalry joining with Scipio's forces, he marched quickly and tried to intercept Scipio before Massinissa reached him. Hannibal failed to reach Scipio in time, since Scipio was already far to the west on the edge of Numidia, and Hannibal had to march from the

Gulf of Sidra to the southeast of Carthage in short order, likely a distance of several hundred miles.

Scipio already had around twenty-eight thousand well-trained infantry, including some veterans of Cannae who had been exiled in Sicily and were now resolute in their new zeal and strength to acquit themselves honorably because Scipio had redeemed them.[21] He also had two thousand cavalry ready for battle before Massinissa's reinforcements. Hannibal may not have known the full state of Scipio's cavalry, but he was highly aware of what Numidians could do in battle. Massinissa met Scipio with six thousand Numidian infantry and four thousand cavalry. Hannibal sent spies to assess the Roman army, but Scipio intercepted them. Rather than kill or torture them, the Roman general instead sent them around his camp with a Roman tribune to tour all of his preparations and gauge his strength so that they could go back to Hannibal with a full report. Perhaps this happened after Massinissa's arrival, which would have given Hannibal an even more discouraging assessment.[22] This subtle but daring move on the part of Scipio had the desired effect on Hannibal's army: it was apparent that Scipio was so unafraid in the knowledge of his strength that he seemed already confident of the outcome. It was a page right out of Hannibal's tactics copied by the master's best student: getting inside the minds of the enemy. Hannibal, too, was canny enough to sense the outcome before the battle began.

HANNIBAL AND SCIPIO MEET ON THE EVE OF BATTLE

Both brilliant generals had a strong sense of the outcome beforehand, a rare event in history. Too often the brutal psychology of war is reduced to mere statistics. Stripping the physical horrors and mental devastation from one side and the exhausted elation on the other makes warfare seem like a sporting event with only win and loss columns. But it is equally naïve to ignore the calculation and planning for supply lines and the jockeying to intimidate and outwit the opponent.

Some extrapolate from Polybius the idea that Rome's aim for universal dominion came via Scipio just before his victory at the Battle of Zama.[23]

Perhaps one of the best war planners in history, Scipio marshaled every known possibility to his advantage before taking the field at Zama, and Hannibal was no less aware of this than Scipio. Before, Hannibal's best ploys had always been to quickly analyze his immediate options and his enemy's weaknesses and then to seize the day by springing the element of surprise and undermining his enemy's confidence as part of his battle plan.[24] Hannibal usually had been able to use stratagems and ambushes to strike terror into his enemies, but here at last in Scipio was a formidable enemy who would not be swayed—a master of manipulation himself.

At Zama, Hannibal knew he had no surprise to unfold. Carthage had given him little that he could play into a winning hand. The environment and terrain yielded no advantage for him on the large plain, which the greater Roman cavalry could exploit, having chosen the battlefield. Weaknesses that had precipitated previous Roman failures—insufficient training and overwhelmingly raw recruits and lack of mobility in cavalry—were now Hannibal's. Whether through bribery or Scipio's diplomacy, the Numidians who had been a considerable part of Hannibal's previous strength and success were now mostly on the Roman side. Hannibal may not have been afraid, but it is certain that his new army assembled at Zama would have been. "The profoundest truth of war is that the issue of battle is usually decided in the minds of the opposing commanders, not in the bodies of their men."[25] This sentiment of military historian B. H. Lidell Hart was epitomized by the speech Livy puts into the mouth of Scipio right after the battle of Cannae, when he berates Lucius Caecilius Metellus and his fellow surviving Romans for their flight and possible treason. Referring to the fear and defeatist thoughts of the Roman stragglers from Cannae, Scipio reputedly says, "The enemy's camp is nowhere more truly than in the place where such thoughts can arise."[26] The perception of despair would haunt the combatants in war, first the Romans between 218 and 216 and now Carthage, especially from 205 to 202. In the time leading up to Zama, Carthage's armies were already "defeated in spirit" after the failure at Utica, as Polybius assesses accurately.[27]

After his spies were sent back—graciously—with a full report of Roman readiness, Hannibal gauged Scipio's confidence from a distance and perceived it was not the overconfidence displayed by prior Roman generals. The report of Scipio's surprising treatment of the spies must have spread like wildfire in the Carthaginian camp and added to its trepidation. Knowing the effect Scipio was having on his army, Hannibal admired Scipio's courage and apparent magnanimity. Hannibal asked Scipio to meet him, hoping to avert disaster but also wanting to see his new worthiest foe face-to-face and make his own judgment, after having learned—as Scipio might have even wanted—that Massinissa's Numidian cavalry force had joined the Romans.

The famous story of the momentous meeting between Hannibal and Scipio and a few of their aides before battle reveals much about both commanders. Although it is likely both spoke each other's language, they appear to have used translators for effect: neither would want to appear the least bit inarticulate or be judged by their accents. Livy says Hannibal and Scipio were struck dumb at first in each other's presence out of respect, but Hannibal broke the silence. He is supposed to have said, "What I was at Trasimene and Cannae, you are today."[28] But Polybius emphasizes as always the fickleness of fortune in Hannibal's words to Scipio about his own reversals.[29] Hannibal would have been about twelve years older than Scipio and likely tried to exploit the age and experience differences by expecting the younger man to defer to his fame—looking for a psychological advantage.

But knowing how difficult a victory would be for Carthage this time, especially given Roman cavalry superiority with Numidian allies, Hannibal asked for the previous terms of settlement offered before Carthage had broken the truce. To maintain Carthaginian freedom, Hannibal offered that Carthage would give up all claims to Spain, Sicily, Sardinia, and all islands between Italy and Africa—a hollow concession, since Rome now controlled them anyway—and that Scipio could make this settlement for Rome without any risk of battle. These terms were less onerous than Rome's demands after Carthage had attacked the envoy. Scipio essentially said, "No deal," noting that Hannibal fully understood the Romans had the advantage. Scipio demanded instead that Carthage place itself under the authority of Rome with respect to the broken truce or fight this decisive battle to determine it by a military outcome. Livy's reconstructed long speech has Scipio finishing with these words to Hannibal: "Prepare to fight because evidently you have found peace intolerable."[30] Of course, peace is what Hannibal requested; it was the Roman terms for peace that Hannibal found intolerable. Scipio offered to renegotiate if Carthage offered compensation for the Roman cargoes taken and the violence suffered by the envoys, but neither Hannibal nor Scipio would concede anything.[31] They returned to their respective camps—possibly even both of which were visible from the meeting place—knowing that battle was imminent.

THE BATTLE OF ZAMA

The two generals' speeches to their men, as Polybius records them before battle, employed different psychological ploys. Scipio exhorted his men to remember their recent victories rather than their past defeats. He left them no choice but to conquer or die, warning that any outcome other than victory or death would end in dire captivity for surviving Romans, as there could be no safe place to hide in Africa in defeat, and they were far inside Punic territory, where little relief would come to them from the distant Mediterranean if they lost.[32] Scipio said men who enter the field with steady resolve to conquer or die have the advantage of no other choice for living. Hannibal, on the other hand, reminded his men of the long string of past victories in Italy, not their recent trials in Spain, south Italy, and Africa, suggesting that the Romans facing them had the tainted memory of defeat, a weakening factor. Hannibal additionally had his squadron commanders speak to his multicultural forces in their own languages. Using fear as motivation, they specifically singled out Carthaginians to consider what would happen to their wives and children if they lost. The whole army was further encouraged to maintain its reputation for invincibility under Hannibal's leadership at Trebia, Trasimene, and Cannae.[33]

The battle that would end the Second Punic War commenced the day after the two great generals met. It was probably around mid-October during a dry spell, which would be optimum for troop and animal movements.

It took place somewhere at or around Zama, about eighty-five miles and a five-day march to the southwest of Carthage, on the often vague frontier between Carthage and Numidia, within modern Tunisia. It seems to have been a wide place on the plain now loosely called Zama Regia (Djama), between two modern *wadis* (creekbeds that are dry much of the time), Tessa and Siliana, and somewhere around the modern villages of Maktar, Sebaa Biar, and Lemsa.[34] Scipio's position seems to have been nearer a spring than Hannibal's. Better water access could easily affect battle outcomes.

Hannibal may have had a numerical advantage with perhaps as many as forty thousand infantry in his army, but many of the soldiers fighting for Carthage would have been fairly raw recruits or recently acquired mercenaries. Hannibal's cavalry included in the above total would have been barely four thousand after his force had been doubled earlier when joined by a minor Numidian prince named Tychaeus. Hannibal also had eighty war elephants, but these were mostly young and untrained. The makeup of the Carthaginian army was extremely diverse, with Carthaginians. Libyans, Balearics, Celts, Ligurians (from Mago), and Spanish added to Hannibal's troops from Italy, which would include Bruttians and Lucanians as well as his old veterans.[35] Hannibal knew that Scipio now had an advantage of 50 percent more cavalry than he could muster for Carthage, and Hannibal also knew from experience that the Romans' Numidian cavalry were skilled.

Even given the disadvantages he faced, the outcome of the battle was not inevitable. Hannibal arranged his battle formation to suit what strengths he had. Starting at the break of day, the battle would favor Carthage, since the Romans would have faced east into the sun about the time the war elephants would be charging. But if the battle lasted long into the day with growing heat, the Carthaginians would be fighting with the sun glaring in their eyes.

Thinking hard about his position and possible outcomes, Hannibal placed his eighty war elephants in the front with some of his light infantry skirmishers, hoping the beasts would cause fear and confusion and break up the Roman center with their charge. Next he placed his first line of twelve thousand mercenaries, possibly quite a few of whom were trained in some form of warfare. Behind them he assembled his Libyan and Carthaginian levies and recruits numbering at least eight thousand to ten thousand, although because many of these would have been young and undertrained, they would be fighting for their homeland as a primary incentive, a mindset different from the mercenaries'. Finally, Hannibal placed his old veterans from Italy several hundred meters behind the other lines. Possibly numbering up to fifteen thousand, Hannibal's Italian veterans would have been the least mobile and needed to reserve their strength, as they were likely the oldest men on the field except for the Bruttians among them. On his flanks, Hannibal placed his four thousand cavalry, with his Numidian allies at his left making one half, and the other half being Carthaginian horsemen at his right.

In his troop placements, Hannibal seems to have predicted correctly that Scipio would try an enveloping tactic with his superior cavalry, but he hoped his cavalry would draw Scipio's off the field of play.[36] Hannibal was asking his own cavalry to bear a hard burden, which could have worked if their smaller numbers had been able to keep the larger Roman cavalry occupied long enough for Hannibal's numerical advantage in infantry to bear fruit. Given the choice between having more cavalry or elephants, Hannibal would surely have chosen cavalry, but he didn't have that choice. Both Hannibal and Scipio knew that the elephants could be frightened.

Scipio also planned well for possible outcomes and especially designed a way to neutralize the war elephants.[37] He also divided his Roman army into the similar three lines he had used at the Battle of Ilipa in Spain in 206 and the Battle of the Great Plains west of Utica in 203. His *hastati* or lightest infantry made up the front line, his heavier *principes* were the second line, immediately behind the *hastati*, and his *triarii* were the heaviest infantry, his third line, deployed close behind the *principes* to prevent the war elephants from getting between the lines. Massinissa's Numidian cavalry flanked the infantry on the right, and Laelius commanded his Italian cavalry on the left. Scipio, by this time, expected Laelius to almost fight as an extension of himself. The two generals, Hannibal and Scipio, appeared to be mostly imitating each other's placements at this point, and there was nothing immediately deceptive or daring about their battle tactics as re-corded.[38]

Scipio introduced a unique strategy aimed at the elephants. From his experience with Carthaginian battles in Spain, he knew that the beasts were often unmanageable.[39] But Scipio took Hannibal's elephants into account with more deliberation than he had Hasdrubal's elephants at Ilipa.[40] He now divided his Romans into distinct groups of small mobile maniples, units of sixty to one hundred soldiers, that would separate to each side when the war elephants charged straight ahead, drawing them through the empty corridors.[41] This would have been frightening for the soldiers unless they were highly trained to block with their shields together almost in unison. Scipio may have practiced these tactics if he could have done it without prying eyes. The elephants could be disposed of behind the army lines if they charged straight through the lanes made for them. Scipio placed his very mobile light *velites* skirmishers either between the maniples to hide the slight maniple breaks in his ranks or in small groups barely in front and between the maniples. When the elephants came, these light *velites* would run back through the gaps as fast as possible.

This canny maneuver depended greatly on the trained maniples and their commanders knowing when and how to move to the side and how far. The tactic may suggest that the Roman maniples left more space between the ranks of soldiers than usual, and that the three lines were so close behind one another to keep elephants from moving left or right through the line gaps. The assembly of the army on the field had to be extremely well executed, but the broad Zama plain made this new maneuver possible, as Scipio planned, unlike the much narrower field at Cannae, where the compression of Roman forces had been fatal.[42] No doubt Scipio was aware that no matter how much he prepared in advance, he was dealing with a brilliant adversary who could improvise on the spot in the heat of battle.

The war trumpets sounded, and the first phase of battle began. Romans beat on their shields and gave their war cry while the shouts of the assembled Carthaginian army must have been a cacophony of languages. Livy says the Romans were louder, but this is dubious, since they were fewer, although contrasting vocables uttered in so many languages would have just added to the confused din. Livy, however, implies the opposite, that war cries made a slight difference in the spirits of the soldiers: Hannibal's forces made a discordant noise, no doubt loud but possibly canceling any desired effect because there was no discernible meaning; whereas the Roman war cry was in unison and thus all the more terrifying.[43]

Hannibal's elephants and skirmishers charged forward, kicking up clouds of dust, and aimed straight ahead to make breaches in the Roman line. But many elephants, always hard to control when their vision was relatively suspect, veered away to the right; many of those who did charge were channeled forward as the Roman maniples opened up as planned. Some elephants did inflict damage on the Roman front lines. If the Roman army faced eastern sun, the low morning light reflected off metal traces may have even disconcerted some young elephants, who were also unused to the din of horns and trumpets, as Polybius notes.[44] Some mostly untrained elephants who veered right never encountered Romans and instead ran amok into Carthaginian lines, wreaking great damage and confusion there as they stampeded their own forces. Most of Hannibal's war elephants were ineffective, spoiling his desired aim of sowing great confusion among the Roman ranks. So the first phase of battle did not go Hannibal's way.

About the same time, the superior cavalry forces under Massinissa and Laelius overwhelmed the Carthaginians and their allied cavalry units, driving them back, especially on the Carthaginian right cavalry flank, where Laelius and his Roman horsemen attacked after elephants had broken up that side of the infantry. Livy says that the rogue elephants caused Carthaginian cavalry to flee away from battle rather than charge the Roman cavalry.[45] Hannibal had hoped that if his inferior cavalry retreated on his flanks and the Romans chased them, then the Roman cavalry would be drawn off the battlefield and could not outflank Hannibal's infantry. This worked as long as the Carthaginian cavalry could engage the enemy cavalry, but soon the cavalry engagement ended.

The initial infantry phase of battle also disappointed Hannibal. Even though the Romans were outnumbered, the surge of Hannibal's front line of allied mercenaries did not penetrate the disciplined Roman line. Instead it gave way to Scipio's deeply massed front of trained *hastati*, *principes*, and *triarii*. Hannibal's first line of mercenaries then retreated into his untested second line of Carthaginian and Libyan levied recruits, causing disarray as they backed into their own army. Now the mercenaries, who had never fought under Hannibal, were more than matched by the advancing Romans, who had formed into a cohesive army since Sicily and had yet to be defeated under Scipio's bold leadership. The mercenaries tried to turn away from the Romans but had nowhere to escape, blocked by their allied second line of Carthaginian recruits and levies. Instead, in pandemonium, to preserve their lives, the feckless mercenaries began to attack their own Carthaginian allies of the second line to get away from the Romans.

Because the number of Roman infantry was now mostly equal to the combined first and second lines under Hannibal, the Roman advantage began to show, as it was also the better trained fighting force. The esprit de corps of the untrained and confused Carthaginians in the second line turned to panic as they were pressed between their first and third lines, the mercenaries forcing them toward the third line of Italian veterans, who refused to move back. Because Hannibal had kept his old veterans in the rear as needed reserve, the empty space he had left between his first two lines and his third line quickly disappeared as the Romans continued to move forward fighting as a tight-knit block now that the elephants were no longer a threat.

Now many of the desperate Carthaginians and mercenaries fell victim to their own army, mostly unknown to one another and having no loyalty to the oversight of their general, fighting internally in great disarray as well as falling to the more disciplined Romans. To arrest the retreat, Hannibal's Italian veterans of the third line put their wall of spears facing forward, not allowing the Carthaginian and mercenary lines to back up any farther. The veterans finally forced their allies instead to run to the right and left, at first filling up the flanks left by the evacuated cavalry and then many fleeing the battlefield altogether. But somehow Hannibal masterfully pulled his disorganized army back together, mostly stopping the hemorrhage of flight.

In this second battle phase, Hannibal's army coalesced into one line as Scipio advanced his army, keeping his *hastati* in the center and spreading out his other two lines of *principes* and *triarii* to right and left on his own flanks to also make one line so that Hannibal could not outflank him. The difference was that Scipio's infantry strength was now on his two sides, whereas Hannibal's Italian veterans created the strong center of his line. Both armies were now fighting in full engagement, and Hannibal's wily veterans in the middle—his original third line—could have turned the day in his favor, since they were mostly fresh and were facing the weaker Roman center of light infantry. The courage of Hannibal's Italian veterans may have temporarily rallied their remaining mercenary infantry and Carthaginian companions, even though these were hard pressed by the Roman heavy infantry fighting on the flanks. Both master strategists, Scipio and Hannibal had balanced their strengths against the enemy's weakness. The battle seemed to become a stalemate for a while.

But in the third phase, the tide turned after the superior Roman and Numidian cavalry had routed the smaller Carthaginian and allied cavalry. The Romans and Numidians on horseback now returned to the battle from the rear, and as they were far more mobile on horseback and had suffered few casualties, they began to systematically slaughter Hannibal's army from behind. Once again this became a battle where superior cavalry seemed to have the ultimate role in victory. It was an enveloping outcome eerily similar to Cannae but where the victim was the teacher and the victor his student.

At Zama, the death toll for Hannibal's army mounted to twenty thousand, with another twenty thousand captured, as Polybius maintains,[46] whereas Scipio's losses were possibly only about two thousand men.[47] Whether the western sun was glaring in the Carthaginians' eyes and whether the accessibility to fresh water in the spring—here controlled by Scipio, who had arrived first at Zama—were factors in battle, we will likely never know, but these were in any case certainly minimal to Carthage's defeat. Zama was Hannibal's Waterloo, and like Napoléon, it was his last battle against his arch foe.

At the end of his Zama disaster, Hannibal escaped with a small detach-ment of cavalry that had either stayed with him or returned before the final outcome, making his way east not to Carthage, where he would have faced only enemies among his countrymen, but the farther distance to his old family estates in Hadrumetum, now Sousse, Tunisia, 120 miles to the east.[48] Scipio then plundered the Carthaginian camp and soon returned to Utica with his prisoners and great booty as a Roman victor before sending his fleet toward Carthage to present Rome's demands.

When Hannibal finally returned to Carthage weeks later to give his report—his first visit in thirty-six years—he told the tribunal of Carthage he had lost both the battle and the war. He told the elders their only recourse was to seek peace with Rome and pay whatever indemnity was imposed. Scipio's ships were thus met with a vessel out of Carthage laden with olive branches and herald's devices—which protected the occupants as messen-gers, not soldiers—suing for peace. Its humbled ambassadors were to see firsthand what Scipio's victory now meant. As in the First Punic War a half century earlier, one decisive battle determined Carthage's fate. But unlike the prior campaigns, this defeat took place in their homeland rather than on the sea. It must have been perceived as far more disastrous. Hamilcar had contested the first war and the indemnity of 241, but his son made no such protest after Zama.

At Zama, Scipio had figured out how to render war elephants useless or more dangerous to their own ranks, somehow observing from military intelligence or Numidian complicity that these difficult animals could be Carthage's first attack force. The inequity in cavalry was also a major factor and had probably been uppermost in Scipio's mind for some time, whether that meant bribing the Numidians or creating compelling circumstances such as Massinissa's passion for Sophonisba and desire for revenge against Syphax.

Conversely, Hannibal, having just returned from Italy, did not have such opportunity to assemble sufficient Numidian cavalry or train his new army as a unit between the late autumn of 203 and the autumn of 202 lead-ing up to Zama. The better training of Scipio's army was also very much a factor, since he planned and trained his men for almost two years and had fought with at least some of them since Spain. The slight advantage in number of Hannibal's army was not a factor when so many of his forces had not fought together like Scipio's army had.

Polybius says Hannibal had done all he could at Zama as a good and experienced general. He had tried by interview with Scipio before battle to secure a diplomatic resolution, knowing the odds were against him. Even though he had a long history of victory, he understood the many possibilities and unexpected contingencies of war. Thus, he had accepted battle when he had no other choice, and planned as best he could for it both before and during battle. Hannibal likely understood that the outcome would be universal dominion for Rome.[49] Zama made Carthage despair in similar terms as Rome had despaired after Cannae, but Zama was the beginning of the end for Carthage, whereas Cannae proved to have been only a setback for Rome.[50] Few would disagree with a bluntly honest Hannibal that his loss determined the course of history. As one historian has said, Zama was "one of the most crucial [battles] in the history of Europe."[51]

THE AFTERMATH OF ZAMA

At Tunis, where Scipio met the ten humbled ambassadors from Carthage in the late fall of 202, Scipio's authority imposed a far heavier penalty than in 241. Carthage could continue as a sovereign state for now without a military occupation by Rome, but it would exist with severely limited scope. It had already lost all claim to Spain, Sicily, and the islands, but now it also had to accept that its fleet was reduced to ten triremes, its elephants must all be handed over to Rome, it was expressly forbidden to wage war outside Africa, and it must seek Rome's permission to exercise any war in Africa.

Whereas the Treaty of Lutatius in 241 exacted 2,200 talents of silver, the new indemnity for defeat was 10,000 talents of silver to be paid out in installments for fifty years. Carthage must also submit 100 hostages chosen by Rome between the ages of fourteen and thirty,[52] and therefore in their prime, who could be rotated or replaced. Carthage must also release any Roman prisoners, amounting to 4,000 Roman slaves released from Carthaginian captivity—some of them patricians such as Terentius Culleo, who walked behind Scipio in his now triumphal return. Some have calculated the value of the indemnity, in the most current estimate, this 572,000 pounds of silver would be worth over $183 million.[53] This would not bankrupt Carthage as a state, but it did penalize the people with added taxes rather than coming from the official treasury, which Hannibal later on protested to the Council of Elders.[54] Interestingly many modern war reparations assigning responsibility for war are derived partly from at least the spirit if not the letter of this Carthaginian precedent.[55]

Many of the Carthaginians wept as their ships were burned in the gulf in plain sight of the city, with the whole populace watching the primary means of their trading wealth go up in flames, possibly in the presence of Scipio and his army. If Hannibal were also there witnessing the conflagration, he surely suffered as a defeated general at home rather than as a victorious commander who had made Rome tremble for years. For the first time in his adult life, Hannibal had no army.[56]

Scipio's victory at Zama worried some in the Senate that he might covet the tyranny of an old-style *rex* (king).[57] Livy even mentions the words *regius* ("royal" or "regal") and *regnum* ("rule" or "realm") as allegation by Scipio's critics.[58] But Scipio was content to bring Carthage and its territory to defeat.

The Senate ratified Scipio's terms by early 201. Confirmed in his proconsulship over Africa, Scipio remained there until 201, arriving at Lilybaeum in Sicily and then marching through Italy in triumph until he arrived in his chariot in Rome as the conqueror of Africa. He would thereafter be known as Scipio Africanus, the conqueror of Africa.[59]

Hannibal was not forced to march alongside Scipio as his defeated enemy. Perhaps Scipio understood that the very sight of Hannibal in Rome might have been unnerving to Romans and would even detract from Scipio's own persona of victory. Plus, he might have concluded that taking such a dangerous person as Hannibal to Rome might not be wise, since Scipio gauged Hannibal to be as crafty as himself. Possibly also out of respect for his adversary's reputation, Scipio allowed Hannibal to remain in his homeland. He may have considered Hannibal the only person strong enough to keep Carthage on the stable path of honoring its financial payments as they came due.

Immediately after Zama in 202, when negotiations were brokered over the treaty with Rome, while voting, Carthage's Council of Elders had a sole elder opposing the treaty—likely named Gisco—and an angry Hannibal is reported to have seized this dissenter and thrown him from the speaker's platform. When Hannibal's indignant fellow Carthaginians objected to his physical aggression, his verbal response was both an apology for being away so many years and for behaving more as a military leader before the council than as a legislator. But he also offered a compelling argument that Rome could have acted much more severely against Carthage. Livy recorded this event, so word got back to Scipio and to Rome.[60]

When the first indemnity installment of silver came due for Carthage to send to Rome, Livy says in a singular anecdote[61] that many Carthaginians wept in shame but that Hannibal laughed a bitter laugh, possibly revealing contempt for the mercantile powers of Carthage that had never fully supported him and must now pay up in consequence. The prolonged conflict had been called "Hannibal's War," since Carthage had disavowed him more than once.[62] Hannibal also knew that the charge of this being his war was in many ways an accurate assessment.

Livy put a retort in Hannibal's mouth that seemed prescient: he was not laughing except at misfortune. He who had long been the beneficiary of Fortuna, the Roman goddess of luck, as Polybius reminded, now mistrusted her.[63] Hannibal now warned that Carthage would find out all too soon that this war indemnity was the least of its troubles to come.

Twenty-three

EXILE

Zama shattered Hannibal's long-held dreams of putting Rome back in its place on mainland Italy and restoring Carthage to power in the Mediterranean. He never fought directly against Rome again; he never won another major battle and never commanded another army. In fact, his greatest battles over the remaining third of his life were reduced to the survival of Carthage and to merely stay alive himself. Now in his midforties, he no longer had the energy, strength, and stamina of youth or the yearning hope and positivism of a young man as he had been at the summit of the Alps looking into Italy and forward to many years ahead. His future looked bleak even in Carthage.

If the Battle of Zama's outcome made Rome the undisputed most powerful nation of the world at the time, whose unquestioned supremacy now also was its springboard to dominating the Mediterranean, the year 202 was also a natural conclusion as one of the turning points in ancient world history.[1] Carthage did not lose its considerable wealth, in fact, even with the war indemnity and much-diminished navies after 201. Its established

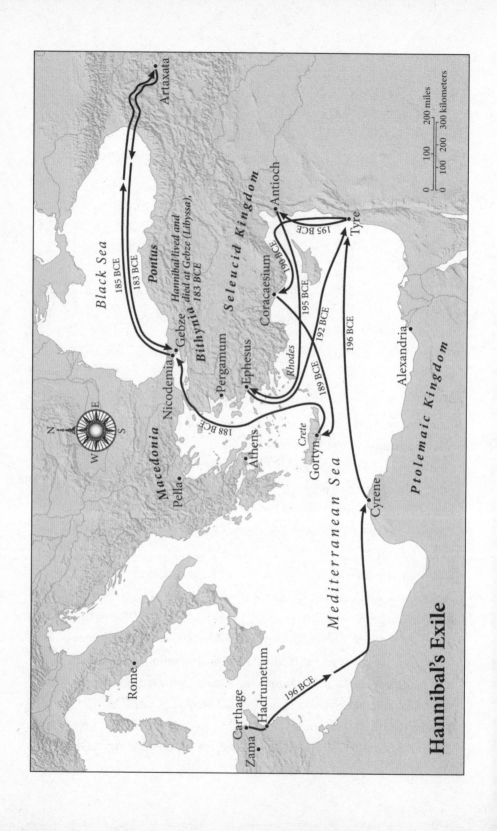

Hannibal's Exile

trading networks continued to ply goods along the southern Mediterranean coasts between North Africa and the Levant, the eastern coast of the Mediterranean Sea, where Rome had little footing. The burning of the majority of Carthage's fleet was certainly beyond symbolic punishment, but there would have been more than a few commercial ships belonging to Carthage that were not in their home port when this punitive conflagration happened. Given how duplicitous Carthage's leadership could be, this sparing of some ships was likely a deliberate ploy warning just enough sea captains to stay put abroad and not return home during this mandated destruction by a Roman conqueror.

No doubt Rome kept a watchful eye on Carthage after 201. Treating Italians who had fought for Hannibal very harshly—those "traitors" from the Latin allies were beheaded, while Roman deserters were crucified—the Senate in Rome and even Scipio's foes there allowed Hannibal to survive with Scipio's approval and likely more than tacit permission, not only because Scipio was still basking in victory but also because he could argue as compellingly for peace as for war.

Hannibal may have at first taken some time to stay out of the public eye of Carthage while repairing to his old family estates at Hadrumetum. Here Hannibal possibly even employed some former soldiers or mercenaries to plant vast swaths of olive trees adjacent to what is now Sousse,[2] and the adjacent region around El Djem (ancient Thysdrus) about forty miles to the south later became famous for extensive Roman olive oil production,[3] partly because it was close to shipping lanes. If this late source (fourth century CE) for Hannibal's olive planting is true, he may have tried to prevent similar unemployment woes of soldiery that disturbed Carthage after the First Punic War and led to mercenary troubles.[4]

What happened to Hannibal during the years after Zama is often difficult to elaborate fully because the volume of press devoted to him thins out considerably. Though he was no longer a visible military foe, Roman spies would still have watched him fairly carefully at home, but this is not always so obvious, since Rome's historians treated him as less of a threat after 201. A living legend perhaps, but Hannibal was still capable of stirring up more trouble for Rome, especially if he could avoid detection. When he was allowed any added role, Carthage's leadership was more than apprehensive about Hannibal, particularly if his integrity and incorruptibility seemed to threaten its interests.

For the first few years after Zama, Hannibal's role in Carthage was a curious one of contradiction. No longer at arm's length away across the sea, he became instead a familiar figure to his own people at home, necessarily visible in the affairs of state where the people were concerned rather than the oligarchy. While he toed the line with Rome's economic sanctions and made sure the indemnity was paid as a populist who tried to reform Carthage, beneath the surface Hannibal likely upheld his vow to his father. Like Dido's invisible wound to her soul smoldering beneath her breast in Virgil's epic poem the *Aeneid*,[5] an omen of her suicidal pyre, Hannibal's concealed undying enmity to Rome still fueled enough of his life even if few glimpsed it because he was clever enough to keep it hidden.

There is little question that Hannibal was now a marked man: a larger-than-life personality walking around Carthage with some kind of target on his back. He knew that sooner or later, his luck could run out if he were perceived as Rome's greatest enemy, however seemingly neutralized in defeat. Hannibal knew that he was now unprotected by an army around him; a Roman assassin or even angry Carthaginians could quickly finish him in broad daylight or in stealth, given his notoriety to both his enemies in Rome and at home.

HANNIBAL THE SUFFETE OF CARTHAGE

Although understanding his motivation after Zama is almost impossible, Hannibal had several methods to transform his persona away from his formidable immediate past as Rome's greatest living enemy. Did he plan on becoming valuable as a statesman for Carthage and in Rome's eyes in various capacities as a way to garner some hope of diplomatic immunity? This would certainly be walking a tightrope. The best avenue to do this would not be through the mostly antagonistic Council of Elders but instead to obtain a popular people's office like that of *suffete*, a public chief magistrate acting in some way as a judge, a Phoenician and Punic office with arbitration powers.[6] *Suffete* was a related Semitic cognate word to the biblical *shophet* in the book of Judges, recalling the reach and power of a biblical judge.[7] The word *judge* is used for Moses, Samuel, and Samson, among others who led the people of Israel before the monarchy.[8] Around the Mediterranean, the idea of the office of *suffete* was even borrowed into forms of Greek magistracy as in Sparta.[9]

Well attested in 196, Hannibal took this pathway as *suffete* elected by the people's assembly,[10] an office that usually lasted only a year[11] unless reelected, and it appears that his election by the people of Carthage ran counter to the more aristocratic, merchant- and landowner-dominated Council of Elders, which had long resented popular Barcid leadership since Hamilcar. But an added benefit to being *suffete* was that Hannibal cultivated the public persona of one who talked sense into Carthaginian politics and on public record of not acting averse to Rome's interests. As long as he played the part of an honorably vanquished war leader who helped Carthage keep up its indemnity payments, on the visible surface Hannibal could be safer from harm than if he continued to be perceived as a threat to Rome.

It is difficult to assess how much of Hannibal's new role may have been partly a smokescreen, as some suggest, but it appears that he took the office seriously with industry and integrity. The Romans may have not been completely lulled—not even the pragmatic Scipio—but how much should one beware the lion who no longer roars? As usual from modern military historian Dexter B. Hoyos, one of the clearest analysts of Hannibal on record, Rome was generally ambiguous about this man who was both a fearsome enemy and a resourceful leader to be admired.[12] But Scipio, holding Senate offices of censor in 199 and *princeps senatus* (leader of the Senate) in 198, was the voice of reason before the Senate in trying to keep Carthage stable.

Several recorded events illustrate Hannibal's new strategy, no longer as military commander seeking Rome's recognition of Carthage's ancient territorial claims over sea and trading monopolies but now as a statesman working tirelessly for what remained of Carthaginian sovereignty.

While Hannibal was *suffete*, he summoned another Carthaginian official—a despotic judge elected for a life term (not a *suffete*)—who ignored the order to appear before the people's assembly. Because this judge belonged to the anti-Barcid party and had previously acted cavalierly against the people in financial matters, Hannibal then had him arrested. The official was brought before the popular assembly, not the Council of Elders, which would have exonerated him. Instead, Hannibal denounced him publicly and quickly sponsored a new law in the people's assembly that made it impossible for anyone to hold the office of judge more than two successive years.[13]

Rome's somewhat lenient stance through Scipio in indemnity rather than full conquest, maintaining Carthaginian sovereignty for the time being, was partly because so many Romans among the plebeians wanted peace and trusted Scipio's judgment.[14] They hoped for a resolution that would promise some economic relief and draw down military occupation in North Africa. The heavy indemnity Carthage was made to pay would be better than continuing austerity when they had been living in penury for decades while fresh legions and taxes were levied.

In 196–195 an event drew the final wrath of the anti-Barcid faction. It happened over state embezzlement by powerful oligarchs within the Council of Elders. As *suffete*, Hannibal kept an eye on financial accounts, including land and sea taxes, and he noted that some wealthy ruling members of the council were avoiding taxes or had illegal loopholes while also misappropriating public funds entrusted to them, thereby putting the burden of taxation and the Roman indemnity on the people while they personally profited. In the people's assembly, Hannibal made it publicly known that if the state were repaid, there would be sufficient funds to meet the indemnity to Rome without having to further burden private citizens with higher taxes. Promising justice, Hannibal kept his word and prosecuted several wealthy offenders before the people's assembly.

Some guilty rulers in the Council of Elders were not only furious that their private pilfering was discovered and that restitution was demanded but also that a Barcid was challenging their oligarchy. They denounced

Hannibal in multiple letters to the Roman Senate, claiming he promoted resistance to Rome through secret negotiations with Antiochus III, the Seleucid king who opposed Roman interests. The Council of Elders also accused Hannibal of being in league with Antiochus in plotting war with Rome. Scipio Africanus was evidently among a minority who did not believe the accusations, but eventually others in Rome who were against Scipio triumphed and sent a delegation to Carthage demanding an account of Hannibal and to bring him before the Council of Elders for censure and possibly worse treatment. It is less likely that Carthage's Council of Elders was seriously afraid he would lead the country back into war and more likely the members were afraid of his power and his leadership. The Roman biographer Cornelius Nepos also maintains that Hannibal expected this Roman delegation would seize him and bring him back to Rome,[15] not an unlikely apprehension.

This reprehensible action of Carthage's rulers against their own countryman—their sole champion for decades—shows how accurate Hannibal's assessments of his country's leadership were throughout the war, depriving him of assets when needed in Italy. It may also hint that their support of Hannibal immediately before Zama is also suspect and raises questions of what more Hannibal could have done if he had had Carthage fully on his side throughout the Second Punic War. Carthage may have also expected Hannibal to create more of his own resources through conquest and personal profiteering,[16] but such a policy would have been unrealistic and unlike the austere Hannibal.

The Roman Senate's delegation to Carthage investigating Hannibal included several enemies of Hannibal and perhaps Scipio, especially Gnaeus Servilius Caepio and Marcus Claudius Marcellus, son of the great Roman general Hannibal had killed in an ambush in Italy in 208. Livy makes it clear—possibly sympathetic for once to Hannibal—that "whatever popularity, however, Hannibal gained amongst the people by his action was counterbalanced by the offence given to a large number of the aristocracy."[17] Livy is typically willing to believe, however, that Hannibal was also secretly working against Rome. What is more likely is that now that Hannibal had new resources in Carthage from his suffeteship, he also had renewed intelligence-gathering abilities to gauge what other Mediterranean entities thought about Rome's growing powerbase beyond Italy. Whether or not Hannibal's new reach was a web of intrigue is unknowable. But Hannibal certainly understood a relentless Rome would not stop at Zama and would never leave Carthage to itself in North Africa.

This Roman delegation to Carthage in the summer of 195 pretended it was sent there by the Senate to pursue difficulties between the Numidians of Massinissa and Carthage, but Hannibal knew better. With his public official resources as *suffete* giving him an ear to the ground and full awareness that those who led the delegation were not supporters of Scipio, Hannibal knew his life was in danger in Carthage—both from his own countrymen and from Marcellus, a Roman patrician possibly intent on revenge against his famous father's ignoble death in ambush. About the only possible truth to any later charges against Hannibal was that he was prepared to flee on a moment's notice, but this was less the sign of a guilty fugitive than one who knew the cards had long been stacked against him.

HANNIBAL'S FLIGHT FROM CARTHAGE

On a summer day in 195, Hannibal made sure he was seen by day and waited for nightfall. He did not go home as usual but went instead to a Carthage city gate where house servants met him with horses. Leaving Carthage forever, Hannibal rode off into the night and, after changing horses, made it overnight all the way—about a hundred miles—to a seaside estate he owned at the edge of the Gulf of Sidra near modern Chebba on the small headland of Ras Kaboudia. A ship was waiting secretly, ready to cast off, no doubt part of his advance plan. The ship took Hannibal to Cercina Island just offshore from Sfax, where Hannibal was recognized by ships of Phoenician traders and had to improvise a plausible reason for being there. He put out verbal notice that he was on an embassy to Tyre, which was a half truth, since he was indeed heading there for safety. Back in Carthage, his house was searched, but Hannibal was nowhere to be found.

At the Cercina harbor, Hannibal duped the traders and their crews by staging a sacrifice and an elaborate party where everyone else not privy to his escape became drunk with the profuse wine flowing at Hannibal's expense. Since it was full summer, Hannibal requested from the other sea traders that they loan their sails to cover all the partying crews and captains from the hot sun. Lasting into the night, when the dock was filled with the distraction of noisy celebration and all the others too inebriated to notice, under cover of darkness, Hannibal had the one ship with full sail ready and embarked quietly into the night, sailing straight to Tyre in a matter of a week and leaving any possible pursuit immobilized for lack of ready sails. One historian comments ironically that Hannibal, "Carthage's greatest son," finds refuge in Dido's Phoenician mother city"[18] from which legend said she left more than six hundred years earlier.

EXILE IN TYRE

If Cornelius Nepos can be trusted for this detail, the Council of Elders in Carthage likely took added malicious action against Hannibal immediately after his flight to Tyre. Not only was his property confiscated but also his house was razed, and he was declared an outlaw. Carthage possibly sent two ships after him to overtake and seize him.[19] Even if Nepos is not entirely factual here, some punitive action would be plausible. Hannibal was wise to vanish from Carthage. It is most likely that he had long been quietly mobilizing the bulk of his private fortune to safety outside of Carthage, possibly even beyond Hadrumetum and partly overseas. Some of this fortune—with whatever possibly remained of Spanish silver Hannibal had retained as his personal war chest and any liquid capital from his family estates in North Africa—must have been put on the ship to Tyre, ready to go at a moment's notice. As for his family, we have no knowledge of any members escaping with Hannibal.

Hannibal knew that Rome had been deeply concerned about the ongoing problems posed by King Philip V of Macedon. Rome's alliance with the Aetolian League, the loose confederation of Greek city-states, in 211 had stymied Philip until his final defeat in 197 at the Battle of Cynoscephalae at the hands of Rome under Titus Quinctius Flamininus. Rome was also vigilant and exercised by the ambiguous aims in Syria of Antiochus, who played his own enemies against Rome while not making his own allegiances clear. Antiochus had tried to expand farther into Greece from his territory in Thrace after Philip's defeat. Closer to home, the old cities of Asia Minor, especially Smyrna in Ionia and Lampsacus in the Troad (the area centered around Troy), had appealed to Rome to protect them. Antiochus diplomatically resisted any Roman intrusion into Asia and in 196 had told surprised Roman envoys that he was consolidating with Ptolemaic Egypt (the Greek kingdom of Alexander the Great's successors centered at Alexandria) by marrying his daughter to young Ptolemy V—the king of Rosetta Stone fame[20]—and basically worked to keep Rome guessing while he considered his political and military options.

In contrast to his departure from Carthage, Hannibal was apparently not given a cold reception at Tyre or perceived as an enemy of the state; how much this had to do with Antiochus is unknown.[21] What Hannibal did at Tyre is mostly left to guesswork. Phoenician Tyre was the mother city of Carthage, its early colony. The trade wealth of Tyre has long been immortalized in the biblical passage of Ezekiel 27 and abbreviated in verses 9 and 33: "All the ships of the sea and their sailors came alongside to trade for your wares . . . When your merchandise went out on the seas, you satisfied many nations; with your great wealth and your wares you enriched the kings of the earth."[22] No doubt Hannibal wondered if Carthage too was beyond hope and would soon follow Tyre "as prey of the nations" as recorded in the verse of Ezekiel 26:5. Even though now much reduced, Tyre had been so long prominent in the purple dye industry from the murex shell, and its legendary wealth from this and other far-flung trading had caused it to colonize Carthage, that it was famous in poetic memory as well as accepted fact.[23] Even though Tyre was under Seleucid dominance as a vassal city of Antiochus, ruler of the Seleucid kingdom around Syria, it still maintained a degree of its legendary trading prominence; part of this trade was directed to its daughter city Carthage and another part oriented to its Levantine supply routes.[24]

It seems mostly ignored that this long-standing trade between Tyre and Carthage would have been squarely within Hannibal's focus during his magistracy as *suffete* while trying to maintain Carthage's economic health, so while the Council of Elders impugned him at Rome for stirring up trouble with Antiochus, some negotiation could have been necessary for Hannibal. While in Tyre, Hannibal would likely have planned to visit Antiochus as soon as possible, but after a short visit to meet the king's son in Syria, he finally left Tyre and formally met with Antiochus in Ephesus, the famous city on the Aegean coast of what is now Turkey near Selçuk, in the fall of 195.

MERCENARY REBEL IN SELEUCID ASIA

Antiochus had something of a dilemma regarding Hannibal right from the beginning in 195. On the one hand, he wasn't ready to engage the full might of Rome extending ever eastward, nor did he want to provoke a war and bring Rome on either his hereditary or claimed turf. But on the other hand, Antiochus might keep the Romans at bay if they knew Hannibal was his military advisor—a peerless trump card at his side.[25] But Hannibal's motives were to stymie Rome's expansion in the Eastern Mediterranean. So the king's ultimate relationship with Hannibal for several years was mostly at arm's length, and his own military hierarchy surely resented Hannibal's reputation and counsel both as a foreigner and as a daunting figure of legendary prowess who had commanded large multicultural armies for decades. Antiochus must have even wondered how content Hannibal would be in the limited role of an advisor. Possibly Antiochus himself was threatened by such an experienced general.

When asked by Antiochus about his Seleucid army's large and proudly outfitted soldiery, glittering with costly ornaments, a force that even outnumbered Rome's, Hannibal seems to have also replied sarcastically, "Yes, it will suffice for the Romans, greedy as they are," because he saw it as worthless and inefficient, and more as booty for the Romans than as an intimidating force.[26] If true, such scorn was unlikely to endear him to Antiochus. Even his brief leadership moments were usually limited to naval battles against the more experienced navy of the island of Rhodes who were extremely adept at sea. Hannibal was often outmaneuvered, being out of his element as a land commander. He would have also been more easily exhausted by stressful battle conditions, as he was now almost sixty years old, an age when most experienced soldiers had retired or gone home to nurse their wounds in peace and quiet if possible.[27] Hannibal's time of glory had long passed, and he must have often wondered how badly Rome still wanted her old enemy out of the picture.

When in 192 Antiochus had himself declared as the "true champion of Greek liberty" and the best mediator between Rome and the Aetolian league, Rome was incensed, "never accepting outside arbitrators" in its interstate disputes.[28] Rome's interpretation of the forces of Antiochus gathering in Greece and his intentions meant that war was inevitable. Decisive battles at sea—where Hannibal may have commanded a small fleet that was repelled—and on land culminated in 190–189 as overwhelming Roman victories. The terms of defeat were heavy against Antiochus: not only had he been forced to give up all claims to Greece but also to all of Asia Minor north and west of the Taurus Mountains. His indemnity was fifteen thousand Euboean silver talents, and he had to pay the war costs, but most germane here, he must turn over Hannibal to Rome as an enemy of the state. Antiochus was compelled to agree to the punitive terms.[29]

Hannibal and Scipio met again briefly at some point in the Eastern Mediterranean, generally said to be Ephesus, although both time and venue are debated. Scipio was in Magnesia, a city on the Meander river near Ephesus in Ionia (now Turkey), in 190 with his brother Lucius and in the Roman war against Antiochus, but the time of the meeting between the two great warrior generals is often thought to be slightly earlier—at least around 192. The respect each had for the other did not stop Hannibal from denying Scipio what he sought as they discussed the greatest commanders of all time, a conversation repeated in different ancient sources.[30]

Because both of them were steeped in the literature, Hannibal and Scipio knew the battle accounts well from the prior annals of war. When asked by a pensive Scipio to reflect, Hannibal said that Alexander was the greatest and Pyrrhus second, but Hannibal claimed the third spot for himself. Scipio asked, apparently gracefully, "What would you have said if I had not conquered you?" "In that case," Hannibal replied, "I would not have ranked myself third but first." Even then, Hannibal denied Scipio his place, but while it was a proud answer, it may have also had some element of jest. We hear of no further enmity between them at this time or ever again.

Hannibal knew he had to flee again from the grasp of Rome's lengthening reach after Rome humbled Antiochus.

AN ANECDOTE ABOUT HANNIBAL TRICKERY IN CRETE

There is a story repeated enough in antiquity to have some credibility that Hannibal fled from Syria to Crete after Rome demanded Hannibal from Antiochus. Several ancient sources record the event,[31] and some historians regard most of the story as true.[32] If so, Hannibal resided in some anonymity in lawless Crete, an island full of pirates and brigands and mostly out of reach of Rome at the time. Living in the Gortyna Valley in central Crete but not trusting the loose mores of locals, he made a show of depositing large clay jars for safekeeping in the Temple of Artemis. This was not an unusual practice, since many Hellenistic temples had a thesaurus ("treasury") guarded by priests and their staff and protected somewhat modestly by a healthy respect for divine wrath and retribution. Such donations functioned mainly as semipermanent votives for celebrating the deity but could have other purposes, possibly including forms of collateral in private arrangement with the temple.[33]

But here Hannibal showed his typical craftiness, if the story is true. His large clay jars—likely the common *pithoi* of Crete, which were very large storage vessels of fired clay capable of holding an adult human in size, but holding liquid or solid volume—were actually filled with scrap metal, possibly mostly lead, and only the top layer up to several hands' depth, in case anyone searched, had mixed gold and silver, jewelry, ingots or coins, and the like. Instead, he placed his actual silver inside bronze sculptures at the house he rented. Since the ancient lost wax method ensured that such bronze statues were hollow, with heads seamed at the neck and arms fixed to shoulders where lead joints were painted with dark copper sulfide,[34] no Cretans seemed to have guessed the trickery. Because his wealth could have put him in danger to the Cretans, one wonders if Hannibal, who was versed in Greek culture, knew Odysseus' beguiling ancient Trojan Horse stratagem of Greeks bearing gifts and gifts bearing Greeks.

When a Roman fleet eventually came under Quintus Fabius Labeo in 189, whether to impose law on Crete or looking for him, Hannibal disappeared again and took with him the bronze statues holding his secret treasure. If any of the possibly many dishonest Cretans had heard of Hannibal's departure while leaving his wealth in the not-so-safe temple treasury and hoped to purloin some of it, they would surely have been surprised when the heavy clay pots were turned over to spill their disappointing lead contents. Even if the story might be a fiction, it is mostly in character with Hannibal's cunning.

MILITARY ADVISOR TO BITHYNIA'S KING

Although it is uncertain exactly where and when he went after leaving Crete, Hannibal soon went east again, possibly again via Tyre. Since Antiochus was diminished and the Pergamenes were allies of Rome, Hannibal went much farther east and visited distant Armenia, where Rome's sway was barely recognized. If the Greek historian and geographer Plutarch and the Greek historian Strabo are correct—Strabo describes a mountainous land so deep in violent snow that people had long poles that were also breathing tubes ready for avalanches—Hannibal seems to have been at the court of King Artaxias of Armenia, where he might have aided in planning a royal capital at the more salubrious Artaxata on a plain whose river surrounds and protects the city.[35] Hannibal certainly would have been an expert in fortification and natural defenses.

But whether the story of King Artaxias is true or not, we do know that by 186, Hannibal had become a military advisor to King Prusias of Bithynia in his ultimately unsuccessful bid of holding out against Rome's ally Eumenes II of Pergamum. Prusias had even been courted by Rome, but the sticking point was a claim by both Pergamum and Bithynia to the territory of Mysia. Hannibal encouraged Bithynia's resistance and reputedly even helped Prusias plan and build a new capital at hilly Prusa (Roman Brusa, modern Bursa) on the Sea of Marmara, as Pliny claims, with Hannibal administering the construction—more evidence of his expertise at organization and supervising defensive fortification.[36]

HANNIBAL'S BIOLOGICAL WARFARE

Another Hannibal anecdote repeated by a few late ancient sources[37] is likewise worthy of mention, whether accurate or not. While Hannibal was working on behalf of the embattled Prusias, King Eumenes II of Pergamum put a navy to sea that Hannibal was compelled to fight in the Sea of Marmara, although the Pergamum force was larger than his own fleet. The story relates that because Hannibal knew he was at a numerical disadvantage in ships, he devised a stratagem that worked marvelously—if also diabolically—and is often quoted, true or not, in modern thought to be one of the first recorded examples of biological warfare.[38] Before the naval battle, Hannibal had his forces gather up as many vipers as they could find, loading them into baskets with loose cords that would release if dumped. Then when this superior fleet of Eumenes came alongside Hannibal's ships to engage, all the baskets were thrown into the Pergamene ships—especially into the ranks of oarsmen.

If they mocked at first what kind of weapons basketry made, the Pergamenes soon realized to their horror what had escaped and was slithering inside their boats. Abandoning any battle plan, some Pergamenes dove into the sea, and the rest tried to get to shore as quickly as possible to empty the vessels. Because the alarmed Pergamene navy fled in chaos and fear with Hannibal's fleet in pursuit at the "double peril" (Justinus' words) of venomous snakes plus armed enemies at sea, this gave Hannibal a brief moment of naval victory alongside a possible place in the early historic records of biological warfare. Nonetheless, even if this event did not happen as told with Hannibal as perpetrator, the testimony of antiquity confirms that this rain of serpents into ships was not only plausible but must have happened somewhere in the distant past, so why is it not possible given Hannibal's ingenuity for military stratagems?

FINAL BETRAYAL AT BITHYNIA

While Hannibal worked for Bithynia's king, he was certainly aware of Rome's ever-encroaching moves toward dominating the East, readily apparent after Antiochus was forced to cede territory in Asia Minor. He also knew that while King Prusias could hold out against Pergamum by itself, Bithynia was no match for Pergamum plus Rome. Even though he had a role in making the new capital of Prusa safer against invasion, Hannibal understood that Prusias had no real loyalty to him as an exile, however gifted.

By 183, Rome had persuaded King Prusias to give up his war with Pergamum and accept Roman hegemony. The Senate sent as its ambassador Titus Quinctius Flamininus. He was the same general who had defeated Philip V of Macedon: a Roman who was adept at handling Greeks and intrigue in the East; a rising star who was both ambitious and quick to climb the *cursus honorum*.[39] But was this envoy really en route to capture Hannibal? King Prusias had been triply suspect in Rome's eyes because he was married into the family of Philip V of Macedon,[40] had fought Rome's ally Pergamum, and because he had given refuge to Hannibal.

Hannibal was alert to the great risk of this Roman visit under whatever guise of diplomatic subtlety. Being an exile for twenty years had raised and fine-tuned his antennae for such a threat. Prusias betrayed Hannibal, whether because Flamininus persuaded Prusias—angrily, according to Plutarch—that Hannibal was the "most dangerous of all living men to Rome" or because Prusias tried to curry favor with Rome by taking Hannibal into custody in a preemptive strike.[41] Regardless of which incentive is true or even some possible combination of both, Prusias decided to turn Hannibal over to Rome.

HANNIBAL'S DEATH

Hannibal's servant reported that Bithynian soldiers were stationed at the main entrances to Hannibal's stronghold in the town of Libyssa (near modern Gebze) on the Bithynian peninsula. Hannibal had every secret exit and bolt-hole checked: an armed soldier was indeed waiting at every exit. Hannibal refused to be taken alive. Because he was prepared as always, he took the fatal poison he always had on his person and ended his own life, denying Flamininus what even Scipio had not demanded. At least one late Roman writer claimed Hannibal had a ring he always wore, and that under its gem he had poison stored for just this moment when it finally arrived as he long expected.[42] A few centuries later, Pliny claimed that nothing was left of Libyssa in his day except Hannibal's tomb,[43] but it is conjectural whether there ever was an actual monument there.

For once, Livy offers—in concert with Plutarch—a sad semblance of dignity to the last moments of Hannibal, claiming a breach of faith by King Prusias, an ironic inversion of the *"fides Punica"* (Punic trust, i.e., treachery) against Rome in his dying breath.[44] Even most Roman writers praise Scipio for restraint the ambitious Flamininus lacked; that Scipio's clemency and magnanimity contrasted with Flamininus' vindictiveness. Cornelius Nepos said that Hannibal's death was the end of the bravest of men.[45] Hannibal was around sixty-four years old in 183 when he took the poison. Rome's greatest enemy and her greatest fear was no more.

Twenty-four

HANNIBAL'S LEGACY

Not all Romans were like Livy in trying to undermine Hannibal's achievements, especially those who saw Rome's last days of fading glory, when its territories were shrinking. Possibly because of Rome's wane, the late Roman author P. Flavius Vegetius (circa 400–450 CE) looked back on Roman military history with an apparent modicum of humility. He singled out military discipline as explaining Rome's eventual greatness, an outcome not guaranteed in the initial contests with their neighbors:

> Victory in war does not depend entirely upon numbers or mere courage; only skill and discipline will insure it. We find that the Romans owed the conquest of the world to no other cause than continual military training, exact observance of discipline in their camps, and unwearied cultivation of the other arts of war. Without these, what chance would the inconsiderable numbers of the Roman armies have had against the multitudes of the Gauls? Or with what success would their small size have been opposed to the prodigious stature of the

Germans? The Spaniards surpassed us not only in numbers, but also in physical strength. We were always inferior to the Africans in wealth and unequal to them in deception and stratagem.[1]

Careful not to mention him, Vegetius is clearly referencing Hannibal in his description of African deception and stratagem, both of which practices in war were so often shunned in writing (especially Livy) as unmanly or un-Roman. This denial continued even when brilliant generals such as Scipio and Caesar excelled at tricks and traps, both following Hannibal as the master tactical teacher of such devices that our militaries now embrace as necessary psy-ops.

SCIPIO'S PARALLEL EXILE

Some of the greatest ironies surrounding Hannibal's last years and his growing legacy were not lost on his contemporaries, especially how he was as feared by enemies in his own motherland who knew his leadership could challenge theirs and effect change that would not be in their interests. Even Scipio experienced exile after not being fully appreciated by Rome. After rumors of embezzlement and false charges of bribery in the East, he retired to his estate above Naples at Liternum near Cumae in Campania, long before he should have been forced out of Rome's circles of power in the Senate. Scipio died in exile the same year as Hannibal, in 183, and Valerius Maximus much later gives this as his putative bitter epitaph: "Ungrateful fatherland, you will not even possess my bones."[2] The striking parallel to Hannibal in Rome's cavalier treatment of its best general reminds how threatened lesser minds too often deal with originality and brilliance not so easily controlled or subverted.

OTHER ROMAN VOICES ON HANNIBAL

Livy is the most virulent voice against Hannibal, especially accusing him of almost criminal cruelty, among other vices. But Livy was not alone in demonizing Hannibal. Seneca too makes Hannibal the paragon of cruelty and inhumanity (Latin *crudelitas*), delighting in bloodshed as he supposedly exclaimed, "What a beautiful spectacle" when seeing a vast ditch full of blood.[3] Horace and Juvenal[4] used "dire" (Latin *dirus*) as a stock adjective meaning "dreadful, terrifying, abominable" to describe Hannibal. Ovid also uses multiple examples of Perfidious Phoenicia in reference to Rome's often repeated refrain of alluding Hannibal's "untrustworthiness"[5] in treaties as well as serving up judgment on how many tricks he used in tactics. As one scholar points out, the "whole question of *fides* (faithlessness) was a Roman obsession here imposed on the Carthaginians."[6]

In his life of Flamininus, Plutarch too uses the epithet of "terrifying," one who caused great fear (*phoberòn* in Greek) to describe Hannibal and one not easily deceived in his life of Fabius and inversely full of ambushes and stratagems himself in his life of Marcellus.[7] Diodorus Siculus paints the "savage cruelty" of Hannibal in his telling of how he pitted captive family members against one another in single combat fights to the death and how cavalierly he slaughtered twenty thousand men who did not want to accompany him back to Africa, along with three thousand horses and countless pack animals he did not want to fall into Roman hands and in an "excess of anger" also slaughtered four thousand Numidian cavalry who deserted.[8] Dio Cassius details how Hannibal deliberately plowed Cannae to stir up dust for the wind to blow in the Roman army's faces and threw slain Roman scouting parties into the Aufidus stream to spoil Roman drinking water.[9] Even Polybius mentions the awful suggestion of H. Monomachos, a counselor in Hannibal's circle, that he teach his troops to employ cannibalism of their dead comrades to avoid starvation, as mentioned here in the chapters on his Alpine passage, although Polybius asserts that Hannibal rejected such an atrocity as bad advice.[10] Overall, how many of these accumulated stories are true or embellished from primary sources such as Polybius is difficult to gauge, but historian Brizzi suggests the many corroborating Roman accounts of Hannibal's atrocities lead to a sufficient truth,[11] that where there is smoke there is fire.

In the *Aeneid*, Virgil tells of Dido's curse against Aeneas and his Roman descendants. Here Dido prophetically demands her Tyrian brood to "persecute the stock and hate the future race," echoing Hamilcar's vow exacted from his son. In the *Aeneid*, Dido calls from her "ashes" an "unknown avenger." The idea of rising from ashes or bones suggests a wordplay on the mythical *Phoenix*, a *Phoenician* in the wordplay. All have recognized Hannibal as this unnamed avenger, a descendant "to harass [Rome] with fire and sword" exactly as the Second Punic War accomplished.[12]

Valerius Maximus praises Hannibal's acts of honorable mercy, although he called him Rome's "bitterest enemy." In the anecdotes of Valerius Maximus, Hannibal searched for the body of Aemilius Paullus and did not let it go unburied on Cannae's battlefield. Likewise, he gave back to Rome the body and bones of the elder Tiberius Gracchus, slain by Lucanians, and sumptuously buried Marcus Marcellus in Bruttia with a pyre, a Punic cloak, and a golden wreath.[13]

When ruses and tricks were no longer despised as un-Roman, Sextus Julius Frontinus recorded Hannibal's deeds many times in his *Strategemata*, a book on historic military stratagems, as good war maneuvers.[14] Valerius Maximus said Hannibal "entangled the Roman people with many nooses of cunning."[15] Valerius Maximus also relates the story of King Prusias of Bithynia, who would rather follow the omens of entrails than Hannibal's advice, and Hannibal's exclamation, "'Would you rather trust a lump of calf flesh than a veteran general?' . . . He did not brook calmly that his glory attested in long trial should yield to the liver of a single victim." Valerius Maximus added to this anecdote:

"And in truth, if it came to exploring war's stratagems and estimating military leadership, Hannibal's brain would have outweighed all the braziers and all the altars of Bithynia, let Mars himself be judge."[16]

Hannibal's immediate legacy on Rome—examined countless times from Rome's own historians—can be measured in part by how much changed in Roman war policy and operations between 218 and 202 and afterward. It is perhaps easy to agree that Hannibal has been called "one of Rome's best military instructors."[17] His general strategy of surprise has been discussed for centuries, but perhaps can never be overestimated. As one historian said, "In war, it is the unexpected which triumphs. And in preparing for war the unexpected is never given its proper weight."[18]

The power of plebeian consuls elected by popular vote to lead armies was diminished after Sempronius at Trebia, Flaminius at Trasimene, and Varro at Cannae were each provoked by a Hannibal who understood their fundamental weaknesses. Second and related to the first, even though the underlying aim of checks and balances between military and political leadership may have been essentially a good idea, Hannibal proved that alternating the battle authority from one strong general on one day to another weak general on the next day was disastrous at these three iconic battles.

After Hannibal showed them to be useful battle ploys, contemporary Romans such as Claudius Nero and Scipio successfully adopted deceit and stratagems in Italy, Spain, and North Africa. As Frontinus noted, Claudius Nero deceived possibly both Hannibal and Hasdrubal: the first by lighting enough night fires in his camp in South Italy so that Hannibal would not know he had departed with thousands of men; the second by arriving quietly at night to the Roman camp of Livius Salinator near Metaurus without first alerting Hasdrubal.[19] Scipio also appreciated the great potential of psy-ops, especially when the enemy expected something else, and yet Livy's disdain for trickery does not in any way poison his praise for Scipio. In a somewhat similar vein to disinformation, Hannibal undermined his enemy by trying to make the Roman Senate suspect the integrity of Fabius Maximus over real estate in Campania that Hannibal captured but left immune from ransacking.[20]

Professional Roman armies—similar in a way to Hannibal's trained and battle-hardened mercenaries—would ultimately fill the legions previously levied by Roman citizen militias whose military discipline and training was often suspect, although their loyalty to homeland was guaranteed. Of all the transformations of Roman war policy, one of the most dramatic and important Hannibal-inspired changes was this gradual transition to a more professional army rather than mere conscription or levies from citizen-farmer militias and levies of Latin allies. By forcing Rome to dig deep to find soldiers—even enlisting boys and debtors and exonerating criminals to fill new legions[21]—Hannibal paved the way for the later change under the Roman general Gaius Marius that even abandoned the property requirement for service "and the idea that possessions guaranteed a man's loyalty to the state."[22]

Polybius had noted after Cannae the battle advantages Numidian cavalry gave Hannibal: "it demonstrated to posterity that in times of war, it is better to give battle with half as many infantry as the enemy and an overwhelming cavalry than to be in all respects his equal."[23] In 218 Hannibal started out from Cartagena in Spain with an enormous advantage cavalry relative to Roman standards, and by the time of crossing the Rhône, he still had nine thousand horsemen, mostly Numidian, an unheard-of quantity of other cavalry.[24]

Learning from Hannibal, Scipio implemented an enhanced role for mobile cavalry, especially Numidian, the most feared of Hannibal's cavalry. Scipio derived battle advantages from using them wisely at Zama, where he outnumbered Hannibal in cavalry for the first time: As Hyland notes, "Scipio Africanus was quick to take advantage of Numidian cavalry when he turned the tables on Hannibal at Zama."[25] Successive Roman armies adopted Scipio's cavalry model that was based on Hannibal's.[26]

Hannibal's peerless tactics of using topography, fighting in winter, night fighting, depriving enemies of water sources, and other environmental factors as a secret weapon eventually became part of the Roman arsenal, beginning with some in the Second Punic War, such as Scipio. Hannibal had made the Romans cross the icy Trebia River in high winter, which froze the legionaries and also deprived them of strength, especially since they had not had any morning meal. He used fog at Trasimene as a weapon.[27] Hannibal employed the swampy ground as well as the night cover of darkness at Volturnus and used cattle with lit burning brands to confuse the Romans, as well as making them face the sun and dust at Cannae.[28] He likely prevented Romans from watering at the Aufidus River, possibly even tainting the Roman water supply.[29] Scipio employed similar tactics when he knew that the shallow "tidal" water at Cartagena could be crossed but attributed the crossing to divine assistance.[30] Imitating Hannibal, Scipio exploited the cover of darkness and chaos in his night attack in burning the camps of Syphax and Hasdrubal Gisco near Utica. He commandeered the water sources around Zama before battle there. Demonstrating a new Roman willingness to mirror Hannibal's tactics, Cornelius Nero in South Italy left camp quietly under cover of darkness,[31] taking a page out of Hannibal's night maneuver book.[32]

Hannibal made copious use of military intelligence, gathering hard intelligence on the ground by employing Celts from Italy as scouts and informants, and continuing with spies who dressed like Romans and spoke Latin in Roman territory and behind the Roman lines.[33] Few understood the need for reliable information better than Hannibal when he had the monetary resources in Spanish silver to acquire it.[34] Hannibal's precedents in gathering military intelligence seemed not to be followed by Romans prior to Scipio.

Not all the changes in Roman policy in the third century BCE and beyond were due to Hannibal, and some of Rome's changes affected him greatly in ways he could not understand until after Zama. A huge difference in the rules of engagement that Rome followed in the First and Second Punic Wars signaled an evolving outcome: Rome would not quit because she suffered losses. Hannibal had to be one of the first enemies to realize that Rome would never consider itself defeated. Hannibal would also be one of the first commanders to witness Rome's plans to conquer lands beyond Italian soil: Spain, North Africa, Celtic lands, Greece, and Asia were all part of Rome's vision of increasing territorial expansion. Rome used Carthage after its conquest as a source of food (and slaves) and a fortress boundary in North Africa on the perimeter of the known world.[35]

One of the unintended consequences of Hannibal's invasion of Italy, where he found on arrival a "collection of fiercely independent and competitive polities bound under Roman hegemony" under bilateral alliance he hoped to disrupt, was that by the end of the Second Punic War, these same communities suffered Roman reconquest under terms that ultimately made them Roman and no longer independent.[36] Hannibal's South Italian allies paid a price when Rome brutally punished and then absorbed them.

Ultimately, Hannibal taught a reluctant Rome how to conduct war. Satirist Juvenal's ambiguous poetic nod to Hannibal is telling: "Put Hannibal in the scales; how many pounds will that peerless general mark up today? . . . No sword, or stone, or javelin makes an end of a life that once troubled humanity."[37] But he was not without his flaws. D. B. Hoyos is right that Hannibal made "geostrategic, diplomatic, and military miscalculations that are too often underestimated," even though he is generally regarded as one of ancient history's three greatest generals alongside Alexander and Julius Caesar.[38] Because modern scholarship with full access to sources often considers Hannibal with deeper scrutiny than in the past, one cannot easily judge him in terms of overall greatness as a strategist, however much his tactical genius and historical influence are acknowledged.

Perhaps the leading modern authority on Hannibal, Dexter B. Hoyos, points out how risky Hannibal's invasion of Italy was, how he mistakenly thought the Romans would give up after his decisive victories, and that no real evidence remains that a hostile Carthage sabotaged Hannibal's enterprise. Hoyos observes that after both Capua and Siracusa fell, Hannibal was holding a wolf by the ear. He could not let go, nor could he achieve much more. Overall, Hoyos concludes Hannibal had genius and was great, but not quite great enough. Hoyos maintains that Hannibal's most important decision was not marching on Rome after his victory at Trasimene, a judgment that other scholars share.

Could Hannibal have taken Rome? Could he have won at Zama or victoriously concluded the Second Punic War[39]? That his was a gifted military mind is not usually one of the lingering questions. If too much ambition destroyed Caesar, perhaps not enough stopped Hannibal.

While it is often popular to attempt to negate his genius, citing the downfall of Carthage at Zama and eventually its fiery end in 146, which he neither precipitated nor hastened, Hannibal's legacy remains intact: he still inspires immense curiosity after two millennia, demanding scrutiny with his intrepid behavior, and he always will. Hannibal knew that one man alone could not beat Rome, yet perhaps history has unfairly held him accountable for not having the confidence to do so even when it looked unreasonable to him or for lacking the will to try after Trasimene and Cannae. His humanity is not always obvious, and much about him remains a riddle. At times he carefully cultivated the appearance of being terrifying and pitiless to his enemies while staying unflinchingly commanding to his men. This is the Hannibal history preserves.

ACKNOWLEDGMENTS

So many people and institutions have been instrumental in the research and writing of this book that it is impossible to name and credit all of them. I am also indebted to visionary institutions whose leadership encouraged the fieldwork that enabled much of my research, including National Geographic Expeditions Council and Stanford University. These institutions helped me assemble and direct excellent teams through departmental student grants and other research grants over several decades, officially between 1994 and 2012 and unofficially to this day. The Archaeological Institute of America has also sponsored my lectures as a National AIA Lecturer to many academic institutions since 2009, where I have been able to learn much through collegial dialogue at universities and museums. I am also grateful to the Liechtensteinisches Landesmuseum (Liechtenstein National Museum) for opportunities to share research via lecture and to multiple Swiss cantons for different phases of fieldwork, including Valais, St. Gallen, and Graubunden, as well as the Soprintendenza Archeologica del Piemonte and the Soprintendenza per i Beni e le Attività Culturali del Valle d'Aosta, both in Italy, and the Commune of Bramans in Savoie, France, among others. National Geographic Learning and its partner Cengage have also been generous in publishing aspects of our fieldwork as well as providing lecture opportunities to share research. The United States Naval War College in Newport, Rhode Island, has also been generous in inviting me to lecture on several occasions to military historian colleagues and graduate students there; its *Naval War College Review* has also published some of my reviews. Both the Society of Military History (of which I am a member and occasional publication reviewer in its journal) and the Royal Geographical Society (where I am an elected Fellow) have encouraged geographical studies related to topography and war. Wiley's *Encyclopaedia of Ancient History* and *Encyclopaedia Britannica* have also provided me a forum for concise written scholarship on ancient history, especially the latter for Hannibal-related entries.

Individuals at Stanford University who have been tremendous personal resources for my Hannibal research include Vice Provost Dr. Charles Junkerman and Associate Dean Dr. Dan Colman (both for postgraduate teaching opportunities), Professor Susan Treggiari (Classics, on Roman life), Emeritus Professor Antony Raubitschek (Classics, on Greek epigraphy), Professor Josh Ober (Classics, on Political Theory and Hannibal), Professor Michael Wigodsky (Classics, on Polybian Greek), Professor Richard Martin (Classics, on the Greeks), Professor Walter Scheidel (Classics, on ancient economy and slavery), Professor Ian Morris (Classics, on war), Dr. Adrienne Mayor (Classics), and Dean and Professor Richard Saller (Classics, on Rome). All have been inspirational. Professor Victor Davis Hanson (Hoover Institution at Stanford) has also been greatly helpful on ancient warfare. Elsewhere, I am indebted to Professor Roger Wilson at the University of British Columbia (for Roman history); Professor Edward Lipiński at Katholieke Universiteit, Leuven (for Phoenician studies); the late Professor Frank W. Walbank, Emeritus at Liverpool University and Fellow of Peterhouse, Cambridge (for Polybian studies); and Professor Andrew Wilson, Oxford University (for archaeological science). Professors Timothy Demy, Michael Pavković, Yvonne Masakowski, and Jeffrey Shaw, all at the United States Naval War College, have also been enormously helpful in providing military history insights. Among my own teachers, I must also thank Professor Anthony Snodgrass of Cambridge University; while he was Sather Professor and briefly teaching the Sather Graduate Seminar at University of California, Berkeley, his knowledge of Greek warfare inspired much of my thinking on ancient war. Along the way, I met and conversed with Professor Frank Walbank, as mentioned, at British Museum colloquia, where I was invited to speak in 1996, and when I was a doctoral student at the Institute of Archaeology, University College London, I met Professor Lawrence Keppie, University of Glasgow, and learned from his Roman military expertise. I was also fortunate to participate in events during Sir John Boardman's distinguished Eitner Lectureship at Stanford, including hosting him for dinners and related conversations.

Other colleagues and collaborators who have been most helpful for many years include Dr. François Wiblé, Office of Archaeological Research, Canton of Valais, Martigny, Switzerland, and John Hoyte and Sir Richard Jolly—friends, fellow authors, and fellow mountaineers over Alpine passes who brought an elephant over the Alps in 1959 and with whom I've had many relevant conversations while we hiked—as well as archaeologists and friends Dr. Irving Finkel (Department of Middle East), Dr. Ian Jenkins (Department of Greek and Roman Antiquities), and Dr. Jonathan Tubb (Keeper, Department of Middle East) at the British Museum in London. I am also grateful to Dr. Jean-Pascal Jospin, Directeur du Musée archéologique de Grenoble and at the Musée Dauphinois in Grenoble, whose work on the Allobroges Celts has been greatly useful; archaeologist Dr. Paolo Visonà on Punic numismatics; Sir John Boardman of Oxford on Roman history, as mentioned; Professor Lionel Casson at New York University on ancient seafaring and travel; Professor Dr. Rainer Vollkommer, Director of the Liechtenstein National Museum; Dr. Thomas Reitmaier, Archäologischer Dienst Graubünden, Canton of Graubunden, Switzerland; Dr. Martin Schindler, Archäologischer Dienst St. Gallen, Canton of St. Gallen, Switzerland; archaeologist Davide Casagrande of Vercelli on Piemontese archaeology; archaeological scientist Dr. Lorenzo Appolonia of the Soprintendenza of the Valle d'Aosta; historian Geoffroy de Galbert, whose books and hypotheses on Hannibal are important resources; and officers of the Voreppe Historical Society in France, as well as Dr. Samuel Wolff and Professor Lawrence Stager while both were affiliated with the Harvard Semitic Museum and after their Carthage Tophet excavations. Other fellow Hannibal authors whom I know and respect include the insightful Andreas Kluth; John Prevas, a brilliant writer and friend; and Emeritus Professor William Mahaney, indefatigable scientist. Even though we may not agree on minutiae, these individuals have shared a common passion for Hannibal studies. Conversations with Adrian Goldsworthy have always been enormously profitable.

Scholars whose Hannibal work I know and respect greatly have also been enormous assets even though I do not know them personally. These include Dexter Hoyos, Nigel Bagnall, Giovanni Brizzi, Barry Strauss, Richard Miles, Robert Garland, Richard Gabriel, Robert O'Connell, Michael Fronda, Everett Wheeler, Paul Erdcamp, Nic Fields, Eve MacDonald, Peter van Dommelen, and Mark Healy. I also learned from military historians such as John Lazenby, H. H. Scullard,

Basil Liddell Hart, and Serge Lancel. All of these authors have made valuable and permanent contributions even while embracing different viewpoints. If I have overlooked or forgotten debts, it is not intentional. And although they are relatively distant, I acknowledge that Napoléon and Carl von Clausewitz were also instrumental in my own Hannibal quests; both were intrigued by his tactics, and Napoléon even attempted to follow Hannibal in multiple Alps crossings—hedging his bets—plus also copying aspects of his marches and maneuvers.

Finally, last but not least, I can never thank enough my most patient editor at Simon & Schuster, Bob Bender, Vice President and Executive Editor, who endured my absences over a decade of archaeological field seasons as this book evolved and whose encouragement has sustained years of research and writing. I also thank Johanna Li, Associate Editor, always efficient but also amazingly sensitive to nuance; Phil Metcalf, Associate Director of Copyediting and a most careful proofreader; and their publishing team. All errors in this book that have escaped attention are my own; if they are interpretive only, perhaps time will settle some debates even as it may leave others unsolved. My family has been most supportive even during fieldwork absences and late nights poring over details, especially my wife, Pamela, whose gentle exhortations will never be repaid or forgotten. To all these, my many debts are obvious while they have enriched my life in uncountable ways.

Stanford, 2017

NOTES

ONE: THE VOW

1. We do not know if this story about Hannibal under his father's chair is true. Our best source is Valerius Maximus (first century CE), in his *Factorum ac dictorum memorabilium (Memorable Deeds and Words)*, bk. 9, 3.2. Here Valerius mentions four sons of Hamilcar, but most historians acknowledge only three: Hannibal, Hasdrubal, and Mago. In any case, Hannibal appears to be the eldest male sibling.
2. Patrick Hunt, "The Locus of Carthage: Compounding Geographical Logic," *African Archaeology Review* 26, no. 2 (2009): 137–54.
3. Commentaries on the *Aeneid* by Virgil (Publius Vergilius Maro) tell a different story about the founding of Carthage. Romans tell of a family feud in which one brother king of Tyre was murdered by another brother. The widow queen, known as Elissa or Dido, fled with her loyal Tyrians and founded Carthage. The grudging local African chiefs gave nominal permission to the Phoenician exiles, telling them they could have as much land as a *bursa*, or "ox hide," could measure. Dido's clever counselors capitalized on this stingy land permit by "treacherously" cutting the hide into one long strip, enough to

measure out the territory for a whole citadel. It is more historically likely that the original seafaring Phoenicians found this location with its deep bay and a potential ideal harbor to be the perfect stepping-stone from Africa across to Italy by way of Sicily, opening new trading colonies and markets beyond.

4. Dexter Hoyos. *Hannibal's Dynasty: Power and Politics in the Western Mediterranean, 247–183 BC* (London: Routledge, 2003), 21.

5. The Atlas Mountains were then fairly heavily forested (note Virgil, *Aeneid*, bk. 4, 248–49, "pine-wreathed head" *Atlantis, cinctum . . . piniferum caput*), but they have been much deforested since the late Roman Empire. Whole cities such as Hippo, Hadrametum, Sabratha, and Leptis Magna were later gradually abandoned as alluvial silt from the deforested Atlas slopes clogged the rivers. The waterways eventually stopped flowing when rainfall mostly ceased in the long subsequent Saharization of North Africa; most likely partly anthropogenic, or human influenced, by a combination of overpopulation and deforestation. Again see Hunt, "Locus of Carthage," 137–54, esp. 142 and the following pages (ff.).

6. Raymond Chevallier, review of *Hannibal*, by G.C. Picard, *L'Antiquité Classique* 36, no. 2 (1967): 730–33, esp. 730.

7. M. E. Aubet, *The Phoenicians and the West: Politics, Colonies and Trade*, 2nd ed. (Cambridge: Cambridge University Press, 1991), 1–5, 6–11ff.

8. Serge Lancel, *Hannibal*, trans. Antonia Nevill (Malden, MA: Blackwell, 1998), 23.

9. Polybius, *The Histories*, trans. W. R. Paton, bk. 3, 10.4.

10. Aaron Brody, "From the Hills of Adonis Through the Pillars of Hercules: Recent Advances in the Archaeology of Canaan and Phoenicia," *Near Eastern Archaeology* 65, no. 1 (2002): 69–80, esp. 76.

11. This needs further study. See F. Brown, S. F. Driver, and C. A. Briggs, *A Hebrew and English Lexicon of the Old Testament* (Oxford: Clarendon Press, 1951), 1075; H. G. Liddell and R. Scott, *Greek-English Lexicon* (Oxford: Clarendon Press, 1996), 1761.

12. Phoenician and Punic religions are very complicated. Interpretations are contentious regarding what happened in normative Phoenician and Punic sacrifice. See Richard Clifford, "Phoenician Religion," *Bulletin of the American Society of Oriental Religion* 279 (1990): 55–64. On the *tophet* at Carthage, see Lawrence E. Stager, "The Rite of Child Sacrifice at Carthage," in *New Light on Ancient Carthage*, ed. John Griffiths Pedley (Ann Arbor:

University of Michigan Press, 1980), 1–11; Stager, "A View from the Tophet," in *Phönizier im Westen*, ed. H. G. Niemeyer (Mainz, Ger.: Philip von Zabern, 1982), 155–66; Lawrence E. Stager and Samuel R. Wolff, "Child Sacrifice at Carthage: Religious Rite or Population Control?," *Biblical Archaeology Review* 10 (1984): 30–51; Patricia Smith and Gal Avishai, "The Use of Dental Criteria for Estimating Postnatal Survival in Skeletal Remains of Infants," *Journal of Archaeological Science* 32, no. 1 (2005): 83–89.

Diodorus Siculus (first century BC) also wrote in his *Library of History* (*Bibliotheca Historia*), bk. 20, 6–7, a contentious passage about human sacrifice that has usually been deemed Roman propaganda but seems credible nonetheless. On the other side, among those who argue against Lawrence Stager and Joseph Greene and the interpretation of Carthaginian child sacrifice are credible Italian and Tunisian archaeologists and historians such as Sabatino Moscati, M'hamed-Hassine Fantar, and Piero Bartoloni, and most recently Jeffrey Schwartz. It is understandable that Tunisians and Italians who might consider their ancestry to be of mixed Punic descent would challenge any idea that such sacrifice was normative or even occasionally casual. Instead, the counterargument maintains that these child bones are merely a children's cemetery and may reflect high infant mortality or disease. With almost seven centuries of accumulated stratigraphic evidence piled up layer after layer, and more than three thousand votive urns (that is, offered with vows) containing infant and animal human remains excavated in 10 percent of the total possible *tophet* in Carthage, Stager's premise that it was infant human sacrifice is bolstered by the presence of animal remains mixed in some urns and votive inscriptions to deities such as Tanit and Baal. Furthermore, Carthage is not the sole location of a *tophet*; other Punic *tophets* can be found at Motya in Sicily as well as Sousse in Tunisia, and Tharros, Sulcis, and Monte Sirai in Sardinia. One primary question is whether this was a normative practice or merely occasional; perhaps the even more important question is whether this was truly sacrificial or merely a sacral deposit of stillborn at the earliest age or already dead children at a more advanced age.

13. Polybius, *Histories*, bk. 3, 11.5–8; repeated in Livy, *The History of Rome*, and Valerius, *Factorum ac dictorum memorabilium*, among others.

14. Polybius, *Histories*, bk. 2, 1.6.

TWO: YOUNG HANNIBAL

1. Polybius, *Histories*, bk. 3, 9.6, specifically the "wrath" (*thumós*) of Hamilcar.

2. Giovanni Brizzi, "L'armée et la guerre," in *La civilization phénicienne et punique: Manuel de recherche*, ed. V. Krings, Handbuch der Orientalistik, sec. 1: Near and Middle East, vol. 20 (Leiden, Neth.: E. J. Brill, 1995), 303–15, esp. 303 and 304–6.

3. J. S. Richardson, "The Spanish Mines and the Development of Provincial Taxation in the Second Century BC," *Journal of Roman Studies* 66 (1976): 139–52.

4. Livy, *History of Rome*, bk. 21, *From Saguntum to the Trebia*, trans. Aubrey de Selincourt, 10.

5. Cassius Dio, fragment 46. This story is not attested anywhere else and seems dubious.

6. Diodorus, *Library of History*, bk. 25, 10.3–4; Polybius, *Histories*, bk. 2, 1.8; Cornelius Nepos, *Hamilcar* 4.2; Lancel, Hannibal, 37, dismisses the tale of Appian of Alexandria (*Roman History: Iberia* 5) as too fantastic a death, where circling wagons were set afire by Celtiberians, and Hamilcar perished inside the flaming circle.

THREE: SPAIN

1. Brizzi, "L'armée et la guerre," 303–4ff.

2. Polybius, *Histories*, bk. 3, 8.1–9.5.

3. Livy, *History of Rome*, bk. 24, 41.7.

4. Ibid., bk. 21, 4 (translation mine).

5. Richard Miles, *Carthage Must Be Destroyed: The Rise and Fall of an Ancient Civilization* (New York: Viking, 2011), 263–64.

6. Polybius, *Histories*, bk. 1, 68.6; Lancel, *Hannibal*, 12–19.

7. Ora Negbi, "Early Phoenician Presence in the Mediterranean Islands: A Reappraisal," *American Journal of Archaeology* 96, no. 4 (October 1992): 601.

8. Roger Collins, *Spain: Oxford Archaeological Guide* (New York: Oxford University Press), 1998, 13, 100, 104–6.

9. R. F. Glover, "The Tactical Handling of the Elephant," *Greece & Rome* 17, no. 49 (1948): 1–11; F. E. Adcock, *The Greek and Macedonian Art of War*, Sather Classical Lectures (Berkeley: University of California Press, 1957, esp. chap. 4, "Cavalary, Elephants, and Siegecraft"), 47–63.

10. Vicki Constantine Croke, *Elephant Company* (New York: Random House, 2014, chap. 26, "The Elephant Stairway"), 269–77. Regarding elephants and

mountains, here is excellent corroboration about how Asian elephants can climb very narrow paths on steep cliffs in mountains step by step, recounted from a trek experience in World War II in Burma, while noting Hannibal's difficult mountain experience as precedent.

FOUR: SAGUNTUM

1. Polybius, *Histories*, bk. 3, 30.1.
2. Brian Caven, *The Punic Wars* (London: Weidenfeld and Nicolson, 1980), 88–99; Adrian Goldsworthy, *The Punic Wars* (London: Cassell, 2000), 144, notes that Saguntum should have been included or mentioned in the Ebro declaration if the link was strong at that time (226 BCE).
3. Ernle Bradford, *Hannibal*, reprint (repr.) (London: Folio Society, 1998), 26.
4. Lancel, *Hannibal*, 47.
5. Polybius, *Histories*, bk. 3, 17.5–7.
6. John F. Lazenby, *Hannibal's War: A Military History of the Second Punic War* (Warminster, UK: Aris and Phillips, 1978), 25.
7. Polybius, *Histories*, bk. 3, 30.4.
8. Paul Erdkamp. "Polybius, the Ebro Treaty and the Gallic Invasion of 225 BCE," *Classical Philology* 104 (2009): 495–510, esp. 508.
9. Thomas F. Madden, *Empires of Trust: How Rome Built—and America Is Building—a New World* (New York: Penguin, 2008). In pers. comm. (2008), this author has corresponded with Madden about this as he raises this issue from his thesis onward: that Rome's late republic and eventual empire were built on trust, and Saguntum was the first breach of trust that needed such a huge repair as to forever become policy.
10. Silius Italicus, *Punica*, bk. 1, 350–64.
11. Polybius, *Histories*, bk. 3, 30.3.
12. Klaus Zimmerman, "Roman Strategy and Aims in the Second Punic War," chap. 16 in *A Companion to the Punic Wars*, ed. Dexter Hoyos (Malden, MA: Wiley-Blackwell, 2011), 280–98, esp. 281–82.
13. Lancel, *Hannibal*, 54.

FIVE: OVER THE PYRENEES

1. For his invasion of Greece in 480 BCE, Xerxes had an army that Herodotus claims was over 2 million people, which is most unlikely, regardless of how many were mercenaries or even slaves pressed into battle. For the Battle of Issus in 333 BCE, Arrian claims 600,000 soldiers in the Persian army, which

is generally considered implausible, and even his 10,000 Greek mercenaries seems small. Diodorus Siculus claims 400,000 soldiers for Darius III, and Quintus Curtius Rufus claims 250,000 soldiers for Darius III. See, by way of comparison, Donald Engels, *Alexander the Great and the Logistics of the Macedonian Army* (Berkeley: University of California Press, 1978); Peter Green. *Alexander of Macedon, 356–323 B.C,* repr., *A Historical Biography* (Berkeley: University of California Press, 1992; John Warry. *Warfare in the Classical World: An Illustrated Encyclopedia of Weapons, Warriors, and Warfare in the Ancient Civilisations of Greece and Rome* (Norman: University of Oklahoma Press), 1995.

2. Polybius, *Histories,* bk. 3, 40.2.

3. Patrick Hunt. "Ebro River," in *The Encyclopedia of Ancient History,* ed. Roger S. Bagnall et al. (Malden, MA: Wiley-Blackwell, 2012), 2259–60.

4. Polybius, *Histories,* bk. 3, 35.2.

5. Livy, *History of Rome,* bk. 21, 23.4–6.

6. Polybius, *Histories,* bk. 3, 43.14–16.

7. Ibid., 44.4–9.

8. Ibid., 40.7–8.

9. Francis Dvornik, *Origins of Intelligence Services: The Ancient Near East, Persia, Greece, Rome, Byzantium, the Arab Muslim Empires, the Mongol Empire, China, Muscovy* (New Brunswick, NJ: Rutgers University Press, 1974), esp. chaps. 3–5 on the ancient classical world. Dvornik relates some of the Greek and Roman types of spycraft; also see Chester G. Starr, "Political Intelligence in Classical Greece," supplement (supp.) 31, *Mnemosyne: A Journal of Classical Studies* (1974); N. J. E. Austin and N. B. Rankov, *Exploration: Military and Political Intelligence in the Roman World from the Second Punic War to the Battle of Adrianople* (London: Routledge, 1995), esp. 10, 13, 35, 53, 60, 63, 90–91.

10. Polybius, *Histories,* bk. 3, 34.2 and 48.1–4.

11. Livy, *History of Rome,* bk. 22, *The Disaster of Cannae,* 33.1. Note the recommendation that spies live in dense urban environments where they can mingle in crowds undetected. *Anon. Strat.* 42.7 quoted in J. A. Richmond, "Spies in Ancient Greece," *Greece & Rome* 45, no. 1 (April 1998): 6.

12. Livy, *History of Rome,* bk. 22.1; Richard Gabriel, *Hannibal: The Military Biography of Rome's Greatest Enemy* (Washington, DC: Potomac Books, 2011), 239n36.

SIX: CROSSING THE RHÔNE

1. Polybius, *Histories*, bk. 3, 42.1.

2. Ibid., 42.2–4.

3. Dexter Hoyos, *Hannibal: Rome's Greatest Enemy* (Liverpool: Liverpool University Press, 2008), 109, makes the relevant point that the Volcae were aware of the advancing Roman army and left the field to allow the two intruder armies to fight it out to the reduction of both without any further loss to themselves.

4. S. O'Bryhim, "Hannibal's Elephants and the Crossing of the Rhone," *Classical Quarterly* 41, no. 1 (1991): 121–25.

5. Polybius, *Histories*, bk. 3, 44.5.

6. Ibid., 45.1–4.

7. Ibid., 49.1.

8. Hoyos, *Hannibal: Rome's Greatest Enemy*, 109.

SEVEN: GATEWAY TO THE ALPS

1. Livy, *History of Rome*, 21, 31.9. Most reputable and serious philologists competent in Greek and Latin (Walbank) and philologists-archaeologists (Lancel) dispute Livy on this matter regarding Hannibal's route. Livy, in obvious confusion—"veered now to the left (*ad laevam*)," as if he now turned west—and then has Hannibal return to the Durance River watershed through other montane passes to the southeast after traveling north. Walbank, as the preeminent modern Polybius historian, and Lancel, as a classical archaeologist of the first order—who was also more familiar because he lived long term in this region—refute Gavin de Beer's arguments on this geography. See Lancel, *Hannibal*, 74–76, and Walbank, "Hannibal's Pass," 37–45, and *Polybius, Rome and the Hellenistic World: Essays and Reflections* (Cambridge: Cambridge University Press, 2002), which maintain that de Beer was utterly mistaken because he was not trained as a classical philologist and makes untenable linguistic claims. Again, see Walbank, "Hannibal's Pass" and *Polybius, Rome and the Hellenistic World*, 24, 164–68ff.

2. Polybius, *Histories*, bk. 3, 49.6.

3. Lancel, *Hannibal*, 74.

4. Jean-Pascal Jospin, "Grenoble de Cularo à Gratianopolis," in *Atlas culturel des Alpes occidentales*, ed. C. Jourdain-Annequin (Paris: Picard, 2004), 128–29; Jospin, *Allobroges, Gaulois et Romains des Alpes*.

5. Polybius, *Histories*, bk. 3, 49.5.

6. Hunt, "Rhône," 5843–44.

7. Polybius, *Histories*, bk. 3, 49.10–11.

8. Polybius, *Histories*, bk. 3, 49.7.

9. Jean-Pascal Jospin. "Des Allobroges Alpins: Souverainetés, Résistances et Autonomies," *Rester Libres! Les expressions de la liberte des Allobroges a nos jours* (Grenoble, Fr.: Musee Dauphinois, 2006), 13–21.

10. Polybius, *Histories*, bk. 3, 50.3.

11. Geoffroy de Galbert, *Hannibal en Gaule* (Grenoble, Fr.: Editions Belledone, 2007); Patrick Hunt, "Hannibal in the Alps: Alpine Archaeology, 1994–2006," chap. 8 in *Alpine Archaeology* (New York: Ariel Books, 2007), 97–108. Carefully researched by French historian de Galbert and others, this newly found probable Celtic *oppidum* is the focus of a planned joint French-American collaboration, including a team from Stanford directed by this author.

12. Barry Cunliffe, *The Ancient Celts* (Oxford: Oxford University Press, 1997), 76.

13. Stephen Allen. *Celtic Warrior 300 BC–AD 100* (Oxford: Osprey, 2001), 44.

14. Polybius, *Histories*, bk. 3, 52.1.

EIGHT: THE SECOND AMBUSH

1. Polybius, *Histories*, bk. 3, 34.2.

2. Ibid., 48.1–3.

3. Ibid., 34.6.

4. Walbank, "Hannibal's Pass," 37. Walbank says that too much ink has been wasted on this problem and that the past half century of research has not solved it.

5. Polybius, *Histories*, bk. 3, 52.3–6.

6. This is plausible where the French national road D215 runs today between Modane, Fort Saint-Gobain, Villarodin-Bourget, and Aussois, at which point an army could easily descend eastward back to the Arc River at a much shallower topography somewhat following the French national D83 road, but exiting the low plateau near the Ruisseau d'Ambin-Arc River confluence around Les Glières just west of Bramans.

7. The local Musée Archéologique at Sollières has accumulated some of this material (much from the Grotte des Balmes, spanning a minimum of six thousand years of antiquity); French archaeologist René Chemin of the Société d'Histoire et d'Archéologie de Maurienne has documented a high degree of Celtic activity in the region of the Val Cenis between Bramans and Lansvillard. This society has sponsored many archaeological projects in

the region and has presented exhibitions and lectures. The author attended one such lecture in Lanslebourg in August 2013 by René Chemin on Celtic activity in the local region; another 2013 exposition was Jean Barthélémy's "L'expédition d'Hannibal dans les Alpes: Etat des hypothèses"; another exposition in 2013 was by Jean-Pascal Jospin of the Musée Dauphinois, Grenoble.

8. Livy, *History of Rome*, bk. 21, 32.

9. Polybius, *Histories*, bk. 3, 53.6. The Greek word for "white rock" is *leukopetron*. While this landscape of white rock might be expected in many places in the Alps, it is most likely a more dramatic topographic feature of vast rock framed by dark forest. This suggests that the second ambush took place still below the tree line—normally between six thousand and seven thousand feet in the Alps—and snow would be redundant if a place is so named "white [or bare] rock."

10. Our Stanford team has verified the antiquity of this gorge as an exposed anticline of layered dolomite and gypsum for at least 2,500 years based on chemical solubility rates of the stone. Richard A. Jolly, "Hannibal's Pass: Results of an Empirical Test," *Alpine Journal* 67, nos. 304/305 (1962): 246, 248, suggests that the *leukopetron* "white rock" location is the nearby L'Echeillon Gorge, one and a half miles west of the Bramans Gorge, although both share geological circumstances.

11. Livy, *History of Rome*, bk. 21, 35.

12. Shean, "Hannibal's Mules," 175.

13. Polybius, *Histories*, bk. 9, 24.4–8.

14. Giovanni Brizzi, "Carthage and Hannibal in Roman and Greek Memory," chap. 27 in *A Companion to the Punic Wars,* ed. Dexter Hoyos (Malden, MA: Wiley-Blackwell, 2011), 483–98.

NINE: SUMMIT OF THE ALPS

1. Lazenby, *Hannibal's War*, 45.

2. Polybius, *Histories*, bk. 3, 53.6. The phrase "highest pass of the Alps" has caused near endless contention. One of the weakest arguments some use since Gavin de Beer is that Polybius must have intended the Col de la Traversette, but this is specious if the Romans and, furthermore, Polybius had no knowledge of its existence. The ancients, especially Romans, were limited in their montane geography, and the Col de la Traversette might not even be that ancient geologically, based on the current rate of its deterioration: its tiny window of no more than 100 feet wide is strewn with fresh rockfall, and inscriptions there

since its first known foray in late medieval times are half eroded away. Even in the late medieval period, a tunnel had to be made under it for "safer" passage. Its tiny summit makes it impossible for an army to encamp there, as Polybius says, and its lack of any vegetation at its height (9,600 feet.) makes it extremely unlikely that animals—especially elephants with capacious appetites—could manage to find anything to eat for the several days necessary, as Polybius also states. Much more reasonable is the grassy Lac du Savine summit valley of the Col du Clapier-Savine Coche Pass. These are only a few of many possible arguments against Col de la Traversette, not even including philology, as argued by Walbank, "Hannibal's Pass," 37–45, esp. 43–45. When our Stanford team of twenty, including engineering students, as always, crossed the Col de la Traversette on foot in 2006, none found it a credible match for Polybian criteria.

3. Polybius, *Histories*, bk. 3, 54.9–54.1.

4. In 2000 our Stanford team found this to be fact in a field season at the 2,450-meter-high (8,300 feet) Gran San Bernardo, in conjunction with the Soprintendenza of the Valle da Aosta, codirected by Dr. Cinzia Joris and Davide Casagrande. Along the old Roman road Via Alpis Poenina, a partial burial had covered the torso of a man with scattered stone but left the arms and legs covered only with soil. Wolves had dug up the arms and legs and carried away bones; only one upper arm (the squarish humerus bone) we found within a few meters' radius had deep canine fang puncture holes. Also see P. Framarin, "La ripresa defli scavi e l'aggiornamento della topographia del sito di Plan de Jupiter. I sondaggi 2000 e 2007," in *Alpis Poenina, Grand Saint-Bernard: Une Voie À Travers l'Europe*, ed. L. Appolonia, F. Wiblé, and P. Framarin (Aosta, It.: Interreg IIIA, Italia-Svizzera, 2008), 33–39; for context, also see fig. 2 in Stefano Galloro, 40.

5. M. Arnold. "The Radiative Effects of Clouds and Their Impact on Climate," *Bulletin of the American Meteorological Society* 72 (June 1991): 795–813; Patrick Hunt, "Alpine Climate and Its Effects on Archaeology," chap. 2 in *Alpine Archaeology* (New York: Ariel Books, 2007), 19–28; also Hunt, "Alpine Archaeology: Some Effects of Climate and Altitude," Archaeolog, a website of Stanford University, last modified December 5, 2005, https://web.stanford.edu/dept/archaeology/cgi-bin/archaeolog/?p=17.

6. Polybius, *Histories*, bk. 3, 54.2.

7. Livy, *History of Rome*, bk. 21, 35.

8. Polybius, *Histories*, bk. 3, 54.2–3.

9. Ibid., 54.7. Kuhle and Kuhle argue capably from the Greek that this is not

a scree slope of tiered avalanche deposit from above but a sheer drop-off of broken-away rock. See "Hannibal Gone Astray?," 591–601, and "Lost in Translation," 759–71.

10. Livy, *History of Rome*, bk. 21, 37.
11. Lancel, *Hannibal*, 78–79; Patrick Hunt, "Hannibal's Engineers and Livy (XXI.36-7) on Burned Rock—Truth or Legend?," Archaeolog, a website of Stanford University, last modified June 6, 2007, https://web.stanford.edu /dept/archaeology/cgi-bin/archaeolog/?p=127; Erin Wayman, "On Hannibal's Trail: The Clues Are in the Geology," *Earth* (2010).
12. Polybius, *Histories*, bk. 3, 54.8.
13. Livy, *History of Rome*, bk. 21, 37.2; Lancel, *Hannibal*, 78–79.
14. Polybius, *Histories*, bk. 3, 56.1; Lazenby, *Hannibal's War*, 46.
15. Ibid., 60.5.
16. Ibid., 60.6.
17. Louis Rawlings, "The War in Italy, 218–203," chap. 17 in *A Companion to the Punic Wars*, ed. Dexter Hoyos (Malden, MA: Wiley-Blackwell, 2011), 299–319, esp. 305.

TEN: TICINUS

1. Lazenby, *Hannibal's War*, 47–48, aptly suggests that this fifteen-day alpine passage should be reevaluated, that it is perhaps only a partial numbering of the total time it took through the entire mountain region. He also writes that Polybius might have intended that this was the time needed for summiting the difficult pass from its approach to its descent.
2. Livy, *History of Rome*, bk. 21, 43.
3. Andreas Kluth, *Hannibal and Me: What History's Greatest Strategist Can Teach Us About Success and Failure* (New York: Riverhead Books, 2011), 92–93.
4. Polybius, *Histories*, bk. 3, 56.4.
5. Lazenby, *Hannibal's War*, 48.
6. Enrica Culasso Gastaldi and Giovanella Cresci Marrone, "I Taurini ai piedi delle Alpi," in *Storia di Torino dalla Preistoria al commune medievale*, vol. 1, ed. Giulio Einaudi Editore (Torino, It.: Accademia della Scienze di Torino, 1997), 95–134, esp. Gastaldi, "Annibale e i Taurini," 116–21. Also see F. Landucci Gattinoni, "Annibale sulle Alpi," *Aevum* 43 (1984): 38ff.

Also see the collections of the Museo Archeologico Piemonte (Museo di Antichità di Torino); also see Walter Finsinger and Willy Tinner, "Holocene Vegetation and Land-Use Changes in Response to Climatic Changes in the Forelands of the Southwestern Alps, Italy," *Journal of Quaternary Science* 21, no. 3 (March 2003): 243–58, esp. 254, discussing anthropogenic change in the history of the region; also see Martha D. Pollak, "From Castrum to Capital: Autograph Plans and Planning Studies of Turin, 1615–1673. *Journal of the Society of Architectural Historians* 47, no. 3 (September 1988): 263–80.

7. Livy, *History of Rome*, bk. 21, 38.6.

8. Polybius, *Histories*, bk. 3, 60.9.

9. John Prevas, *Hannibal Crosses the Alps: The Invasion of Italy and the Punic Wars* (Cambridge, MA: Da Capo Press, 2001), 178.

10. A. E. Astin, "The Second Punic War," *Cambridge Encyclopedia of Ancient History*, vol. 8 (Cambridge: Cambridge University Press, 1977), 76.

11. Gastaldi, "Annibale e i Taurini," 118–20.

12. O'Connell, *Ghosts of Cannae*, 90, 107.

13. Polybius, *Histories*, bk. 3, 64.1–11.

14. Ibid., 62.1–14; Livy, *History of Rome*, bk. 21, 44.9.

15. Livy, *History of Rome*, bk. 21, 45.

16. Polybius, *Histories*, bk. 3, 61.1–6.

17. Bradford, *Hannibal*, 69–70.

18. Livy, *History of Rome*, bk. 21, 46.

19. Lancel, *Hannibal*, 84.

20. Ibid.

21. "Placentia-Piacenza, Italy," in *Princeton Encyclopedia of Classical Sites*, ed. Richard Stillwell, William L. MacDonald, and Marian Holland McAlister (Princeton, NJ: Princeton University Press, 1976).

22. Livy, *History of Rome*, bk. 21, 47.1.

23. Polybius, Histories, bk. 3, 68.8.

24. John T. Koch, *Celtic Culture: A Historical Encyclopedia* (Santa Barbara, CA: ABC-Clio, 2006), 895: "Severed heads were proof of a warrior's valor, confirming the number of enemies he had slain in a battle." But judging by the frequency of decapitation in Celtic literary accounts, it was more than fascination with verifying an enemy death and clearly tied to Celtic ritual. Also see Cunliffe, *Ancient Celts*, 127–28: "A recurring theme is the cult of the severed head [as displayed in the columnar sculptures] of Roquepertuse with niches for severed heads."

25. Thomas George Eyre Powell, *The Celts,* repr. (London: Thames and Hudson, 1995), 130; Gerhard Herm, *The Celts* (New York: St. Martin's Press, 1976), 54: "The most hideous Celtic custom, in Greek historians' eyes,

was head-hunting." Herm also notes, "Diodorus once saw Celtic warriors with whole wreaths of victims' heads hanging on their bridles," quoted in Herm, 55.

26. Also note Miranda Green, "A Carved Stone Head from Steep Holm," *Britannia* 24 (1993): 241–42. According to Galbert (pers. comm., 2009), there is also a circa 1909 cache of at least nineteen decapitated skeletal heads, presumably victims of Celtic raids, found at the Grotte de Fontabert in the Grenoble area of Savoie. Also see Galbert, *Hannibal et César dans les Alpes* (Grenoble, Fr.: Editions de Belledonne, 2008), 158–59; H. Müller, "Tombes gauloises de la Tène II, découvertes au pied des Balmes de Voreppe," *Bibliothèque municipal de Grenoble, Fonds Dauphinois*, 1909; Stephen Fliegel, "A Little-Known Celtic Stone Head," *Bulletin of the Cleveland Museum of Art* 77, no. 3 (March 1990): 89, 91: "It is known from the classical literary sources as well as the representational and archaeological evidence that the Celts practiced ritualistic head-hunting, that is to say, the act of severing the head from the body after death" and "The Celts placed considerable importance on their collections of heads, particularly from distinguished enemies. Diodorus [*Library of History*, vol. 29] explains that their owners displayed them to strangers with great pride."

27. Astin, "Second Punic War," 76.

ELEVEN: TREBIA

1. Polybius, *Histories*, bk. 3, 68.9; Michael P. Fronda, "Hannibal: Tactics, Strategy, and Geostrategy," chap. 14 in *A Companion to the Punic Wars*, ed. Dexter Hoyos (Malden, MA: Wiley-Blackwell, 2011), 243.

2. Polybius, *Histories*, bk. 3, 68.11.

3. A maniple (*speira* in Polybian Greek) is a term for a fighting military unit of sixty to a hundred men and is often confused with the Latin word *cohors* (cohort). See M. J. V. Bell. "Tactical Reform in the Roman Republican Army," *Historia: Zeitschrift für Alte Geschichte* 14, no. 4 (October 1965): 404–22.

4. William O'Connor Morris, *Hannibal: Soldier, Statesman, Patriot, and the Crisis of the Struggle Between Carthage and Rome*, 1937), 127.

5. Livy, *History of Rome*, bk. 21, 53; Lazenby, *Hannibal's War*, 55; O'Connell, *Ghosts of Cannae*, 112.

6. Livy, *History of Rome*, bk. 21, 51.6ff.

7. O'Connell, *Ghosts of Cannae*, 111, with good reason, as the time of year would be long beyond the safe sailing season in the Mediterranean, which

generally closes in late September. This is another one of those Livian versions of the story that reduce his credibility compared with Polybius'.

8. J. A. Cramer, *A Dissertation on the Passage of Hannibal over the Alps* (London: J. W. Parker and G. and W. B. Whittaker, 1820), *xix.*

9. Goldsworthy, *Punic Wars*, 173.

10. Livy, *History of Rome*, bk. 21, 17.

11. Livy, *History of Rome*, bk. 21, 53.6–15.

12. Millennia later, Napoléon I tried to follow this same Hannibalic strategy in the Padana and along the Trebia as well. See John Peddie, *Hannibal's War* (Thrupp, Stroud, Gloucestershire, UK: Sutton Publishing, 1997), 32.

13. Polybius, *Histories*, bk. 3, 70.12.

14. Ibid., 70.11.

15. Rivergaro is approximately where many of the most credible historians place the combined Roman camp of Scipio and Sempronius on the east Trebia side (about 5.5 miles from the battlefield near Canneto). The likeliest Trebia battlefield lies just north of Canneto on the west side of the river, with Hannibal's camp slightly farther northwest (about 1.75 miles) of the Canneto battlefield near Campremoldo di Sopra on the west Trebia side. See map, Goldsworthy, Punic Wars, 174.

16. Goldsworthy, *Punic Wars*, 177.

17. Polybius, *Histories*, bk. 3, 72.13.

18. Hannibal seems to have often used his Celt allies this way, putting them at the center, where they would absorb the greatest damage. It is possible that he was exploiting them as cannon fodder, although he no doubt promised them great reward for their feckless bravery at taking the very brunt of the battle.

19. Polybius, *Histories*, bk. 3, 74.11.

20. Bradford, *Hannibal*, 79.

21. Goldsworthy, *Punic Wars*, 180.

22. Polybius, *Histories*, bk. 3, 77.5–6.

23. Polybius, *Histories*, bk. 3, 75.1–2.

24. Peddie, *Hannibal's War*, 58.

25. Livy, *History of Rome*, bk. 21, 15 and 63. Note bk. 23, *Hannibal at Cannae*, 37, where Livy says that Sempronius helped in a successful battle against Hannibal's brother and forced him out of Lucania. Sempronius' son, of the same name, was made consul in 194 and, redeeming the family name somewhat, oversaw Roman colonists in parts of Gaul. (See, by way of comparison, Livy, *History of Rome*, bk. 34, *Close of the Macedonian War*, 42.)

TWELVE: THE APPENNINES AND THE ARNO MARSHES

1. Lancel, *Hannibal*, 91; Miles, *Carthage Must Be Destroyed*, 270.
2. Polybius, *Histories*, bk. 3, 78.1–4; Livy, *History of Rome*, bk. 22, 1.
3. Lancel, *Hannibal*, 90; Goldsworthy, *Punic Wars*, 181–82.
4. While Polybius is our best source, his historical lens is at times imperfect, being after the fact.
5. Giovanni Brizzi, *Scipione e Annibale: La Guerre per Salvare Roma.* (Rome: Bari: Editore Giuseppe Laterza e Figli, 2007), 48: "*il quale partiva per raggiungere il fratello Cneo in Spagna.*"
6. Livy, *History of Rome*, bk. 21, 57. It includes the fortified town Victumulae, belonging to Roman ally the Celts. Livy says that Hannibal even had another battle with Sempronius, but this is not taken as fact.
7. Lancel, *Hannibal*, 91.
8. Livy, *History of Rome*, bk. 21, 58.
9. Colin Hardie, "The Origin and Plan of Modern Florence," *Journal of Roman Studies* 55, nos. 1/2 (1965): 122–40.
10. Livy, *History of Rome*, bk. 21, 62.
11. Ibid.
12. Lazenby, *Hannibal's War*, 60.
13. Polybius, *Histories*, bk. 3, 78.6.
14. Lazenby, *Hannibal's War*, 11. Lazenby also suggests that Hannibal took the internal route through Etruria hoping that the Etruscans might defect to him.
15. This pass, or the Porretta Pass, according to Lazenby, *Hannibal's War*, 61; Goldsworthy, *Punic Wars*, 184; and O'Connell, *Ghosts of Cannae*, 117.
16. Technically, both the Porretta and the Collina Passes mostly follow the Italian Trans-Apennine national road SS-64 and the Reno River (Fiume Reno) much of their route until the Commune Granaglione. Then the Reno River follows the SP-632 road mostly the rest of the way to the source of the Reno River. The Porretta Pass is on the north half of the Apennine route (Emilia Romagna), and the Collina on the south portion (Tuscany). Near Collina, the SS-64 is roughly 13 miles west of the main Italian primary north-south autostrada A1, which goes from modern Bologna to modern Prato. Although the modern autostrada A1 partly follows the Reno River Valley, leaving Bologna it diverges from the Reno River while still in Emilia Romagna. The Reno River's source is around 2,390 feet high (745 meters), about 3 miles west of the Collina Pass. So if Hannibal followed the Porretta-Collina

Pass route, he would have traveled along the Reno River watershed until cresting the Apennines at a slightly higher place.

17. Mark Healy, *Cannae 216 BC: Hannibal Smashes Rome's Army* (Oxford: Osprey, 1994), 52.

18. Polybius, *Histories*, bk. 3, 79.4–5.

19. O'Connell, *Ghosts of Cannae*, 117.

20. Polybius, *Histories*, bk. 3, 79.1–12.

21. Atkins, 270.

22. Shean, "Hannibal's Mules," 159–87.

23. Livy, *History of Rome*, bk. 22, 2.

24. Ibid.

25. Justin Denholm and Patrick Hunt, "Hannibal's Ophthalmia" (unsubmitted article manuscript under peer review in various medical journals, 2014). Denholm is a medical doctor in Australia with the Victorian Infectious Disease Service, Royal Melbourne Hospital and University of Melbourne. The authors suggest any number of possible infections from bacterial or viral agents, including but not limited to conjunctivitis, each of which is known to cause blindness. "Hippocrates tells us *ophthalmia* is more common in spring, at the time when Hannibal went through the marshes; Herodotus (VII.229ff.) reports two Spartans afflicted before the battle at Thermopylae."

26. Thomas W. Africa, "The One-Eyed Man Against Rome: an Exercise in Euhemerism," *Historia: Zeitschrift für Alte Geschichte* 19, no. 5 (1970): 528–38.

27. Robert Garland, *Hannibal*, Ancients in Action Series (London: Bristol Classical Press, 2010), 75.

28. Pliny the Elder, *Natural History*, vol. 8, 5.11.

29. De Beer, 96.

30. Polybius, *Histories*, bk. 3, 79; Livy, *History of Rome*, bk. 22, 2.

31. Goldsworthy, *Punic Wars*, 184.

32. There is considerable debate over Hannibal's route after the Arno. On the one hand, if Hannibal were trying to avoid meeting Flaminius and his army, he could have followed the abundantly fertile plains of the Val di Pesa and Val d'Elsa route (although this would have been the easier, expected route) from modern Scandicci to Poggibonsi and Siena west of Arezzo, and then turned east toward modern Sinalunga and the Valdichiana. Or, after Faesulae, he could have followed south from modern Bagno a Ripoli

to San Donati in Collina or the curving Arno Valley southeast from Pontassieve through to Figline Valdarno, Montevarchi, Pergine Valdarno, and so on (mostly parallel to the modern A1 autostrada after Bagno a Ripoli) to the Valdichiana—although it too had a fair share of marshes that weren't drained until the nineteenth century.

The Val di Pesa and Val d'Elsa routes were laden with rich farmland, and he could have leisurely bypassed south of Arretium altogether without any need to engage Flaminius. On the other hand, the Arno Valley route was not at all the expected passage due to its spring flooding, but it would have led Hannibal directly to Arretium unless he marched covertly at the end and crossed southwest from near modern Bucine to Rapolano Terme around the Monte San Savino Hills. Placed strategically at Arretium, Flaminius could have either gone west to meet Hannibal crossing the Etrurian plains after the Apennines or north to aid Servilius Geminus at Ariminum if Hannibal had marched east instead along the Po Valley to the Adriatic coast. The author notes that the year 2013 was a wet year for much of the Arno reaches between Florence and Arezzo, and many of the river's channels and oxbows flooded considerably, even though civil engineering draining projects throughout the last several centuries has mitigated much of the former flooding.

33. Michael P. Fronda. *Between Rome and Carthage: Southern Italy During the Second Punic War* (Cambridge: Cambridge University Press, 2010), 14.

34. Lazenby, *Hannibal's War*, 60.

THIRTEEN: TRASIMENE

1. Bettina Diana, "Annibale e il Passagio degli Apennini," *Aevum* 61 (1987): 108–12.

2. Polybius, *Histories*, bk. 3, 82.1–3.

3. O'Connell, *Ghosts of Cannae*, 118.

4. Healy, *Cannae 216 BC*, 52.

5. Lancel, *Hannibal*, 93.

6. Timothy P. Wiseman, *New Men in the Roman Senate, 139 B.C. to A.D. 14* (London: Oxford University Press, 1971); also see Andrew W. Lintott, "Novi Homines," *Classical Review* 24, no. 2 (1974): 261–63.

7. Lily Ross Taylor, *Roman Voting Assemblies: From the Hannibalic War to the Dictatorship of Caesar*, Jerome Lectures, 8th series (Ann Arbor: University

of Michigan, 1966); also see (although it concentrates on the first century BCE) Fergus Millar, *The Crowd in Rome in the Late Republic* (Ann Arbor: University of Michigan Press, 1998).

8. Andrew W. Lintott, *The Constitution of the Roman Republic* (Oxford: Oxford University Press, 1999), 1–4. At the outset, Lintott connects Polybius' association of Rome's ultimate "phenomenal military success with the excellence of her constitution" as well as the "constitutional innovations that the [Second Punic] war brought about" and unwritten tradition and precedent.

9. A censor was a Roman officer in charge of the census and some financial duties as well as oversight of public morality.

10. Livy, *History of Rome*, bk. 21, 62.

11. Ibid.

12. Goldsworthy, *Punic Wars*, 185. Without necessarily agreeing, Goldsworthy notes the "tradition which places the sole blame for the disaster on the commander."

13. Polybius, *Histories*, bk. 3, 80.3–4.

14. Garland, *Hannibal*, 75.

15. Livy, *History of Rome*, bk. 22, 4.

16. Polybius, *Histories*, bk. 3, 83.3–4.

17. Ovid, *Fasti*, bk. 6, 767–68. Lancel, *Hannibal*, 93, keeps to June 21, although, before Julian calendar reform, this actual day might have been in May, not the summer solstice, according to Briscoe, "Second Punic War," 49.

18. Goldsworthy, *Punic Wars*, 187, notes, however, that advancing Roman armies able to see their enemy—in this case, the only visible contingent of African and Spanish heavy infantry at the end of the valley—rarely "reconnoiter" just before battle.

19. Peddie, *Hannibal's War*, 69.

20. O'Connell, *Ghosts of Cannae*, 119.

21. Polybius, *Histories*, bk. 3, 84.4–5.

22. Ibid.

23. O'Connell, *Ghosts of Cannae*, 119.

24. Polybius, *Histories*, bk. 3, 84.9–10. Polybius also stated that the Roman soldiers, seeing the merciless death all around, also begged their own comrades to dispatch them, no doubt in fear of Hannibal's army and knowing Celtic customs of decapitation.

25. Livy, *History of Rome*, bk. 22, 6.1.

26. Polybius, *Histories*, bk. 3, 84.6.

27. Livy, *History of Rome*, bk. 22, 6.1–2.

28. Ibid, 6.4–6.

29. Lazenby, *Hannibal's War*, 64.

30. Livy, *History of Rome*, bk. 22, 6. The 75 percent casualty rate is correct only if I am accurately extrapolating the thirty thousand dead and captured alongside the ten thousand escapees.

31. O'Connell, *Ghosts of Cannae*, 118.

32. Polybius, *Histories*, bk. 3, 85.5; Livy, *History of Rome*, bk. 22, 7.

33. Briscoe, "Second Punic War," 49.

34. Lazenby, *Hannibal's War*, 65.

35. Sabin, "Face of Roman Battle," 4, notes that a 14 percent casualty rate for the loser is more in keeping with earlier classical Greek hoplite defeats but that a casualty/capture rate of more than 50 percent is not unusual for Roman infantry battles. But the Trasimene Roman casualty figures of up to 75 percent—and 100 percent of the following cavalry encounter—are simply catastrophic. Lazenby, *Hannibal's War*, 65, claims that Hannibal's army at Trasimene was around sixty thousand, including allies.

36. Livy, *History of Rome*, bk. 22, 7.

37. Ibid.

FOURTEEN: FABIUS MAXIMUS AND ESCAPE

1. Lazenby, *Hannibal's War*, 67.

2. Goldsworthy, *Punic Wars*, 191.

3. Garland, *Hannibal*, 78.

4. Ibid.

5. Polybius, *Histories*, bk. 3, 90.4–6.

6. Hoyos, *Hannibal's Dynasty*, 117.

7. B. H. Liddell Hart, *Strategy: The Classic Book on Military Strategy*, 2nd rev. ed. (New York: Meridian, 1991), 26–27.

8. Polybius, *Histories*, bk. 3, 89.9.

9. Walter Scheidel, "Human Mobility in Roman Italy, I: The Free Population," *Journal of Roman Studies* 94 (2004): 1–26, esp. 4. Noting problems with demographic data, Scheidel qualifies his quantitative estimates with several caveats and reservations about his and others' extrapolations while showing the harmony with Polybian accounts; also see D. W. Baronowski, "Roman Military Forces in 225 BC (Polybius 2.23–24)," *Historia: Zeitschrift für Alte Geschichte* 42 (1993): 183–202. Walter Scheidel also notes Italian historian

Elio Lo Cascio's contribution to this demographic problem, "Recruitment and the Size of the Roman Population from the Third to First Century BCE," in *Debating Roman Demography*, ed. Walter Scheidel (Leiden, Neth.: E. J. Brill, 2001), 111–38.

10. Polybius, *Histories*, bk. 3, 90.11ff.

11. Fronda, "Hannibal: Tactics, Strategy, and Geostrategy," 250.

12. Rawlings, "War in Italy, 218–203," 305.

13. Paul Erdkamp, "Manpower and Food Supply in the First and Second Punic Wars," chap. 4 in *A Companion to the Punic Wars,* edited by Dexter Hoyos (Malden, MA: Wiley-Blackwell, 2011), 68–69.

14. Livy, *History of Rome*, bk. 21, 23.4.

15. O'Connell, *Ghosts of Cannae*, 127.

16. "Casilinum," in *Brill's Encyclopaedia of the Ancient World (Brill's New Pauly)*, ed. H. Cancik, H. Schneider, and M. Landfester (Leiden, Neth: E. J. Brill, 2012); cross-referenced to Livy, *History of Rome*, bk. 23, 17.

17. Peddie, *Hannibal's War*, 83.

18. Polybius, *Histories*, bk. 3, 93.2.

19. Livy, *History of Rome*, bk. 22, 17.

20. Ibid., 18; Lazenby, *Hannibal's War*, 71.

21. Lancel, *Hannibal*, 100, suggests that Hannibal had also previously tried this stratagem successfully in the Alps against the Celts, possibly after one of the mountain ambushes.

22. Polybius, *Histories*, bk. 3, 94.4–5.

23. Bradford, *Hannibal*, 99.

24. Kluth, *Hannibal and Me*, 149.

25. Fronda, *Between Rome and Carthage*, 41.

FIFTEEN: CANNAE

1. Polybius, *Histories*, bk. 3, 113.5.

2. Livy, *History of Rome*, bk. 22, 41.

3. Gregory Daly, *Cannae: The Experience of Battle in the Second Punic War* (London: Routledge, 2002), 16.

4. Back in Rome in 219, Paullus was said to have not shared the spoils equally, and although charges were brought against him, along with his fellow leader Marcus Livius Salinator, Aemilius Paullus was acquitted (Livy, *History of Rome*, bk. 22, 35).

5. Goldsworthy, *Punic Wars*, 198–99.

6. Lancel, *Hannibal*, 103.

7. Goldsworthy, *Punic Wars*, 199.

8. Lancel, *Hannibal*, 103, quoting Livy's vilification, *non humilis solum, sed etiam sordido loco ortus*, or "not only humble but also foul and impure."

9. Livy, *History of Rome*, bk. 22, 39.

10. Polybius, *Histories*, bk. 3, 110.3, 116.13.

11. Erdkamp, "Manpower and Food Supply," 69.

12. Polybius, *Histories*, bk. 3, 108.3–109.13; Livy, *History of Rome*, bk. 22, 39. Livy places the essence of this exhortation not in the mouth of Paullus to his men, like Polybius does, but in the mouth of Fabius Maximus to Paullus back in Rome.

13. As related by Bradford, *Hannibal*, 115.

14. Livy, *History of Rome*, bk. 22, 43.

15. Silius Italicus asserts it in his epic poem *Punica*, vol. 1, trans. J. D. Duff (Cambridge, MA: Harvard Loeb Classical Library, 1961), bk. 8, 663–64 and bk. 9, 495, as well as in his notes, 440.

16. Lancel, *Hannibal*, 105.

17. Polybius, *Histories*, bk. 3, 110.2.

18. Goldsworthy, *Punic Wars*, 200.

19. Polybius, *Histories*, bk. 3, 110.3.

20. Lazenby, *Hannibal's War*, 77ff.

21. Polybius, *Histories*, bk. 3, 113.3.

22. Goldsworthy, *Punic Wars*, 205.

23. This figure does not include the ten thousand soldiers who were guarding the Roman camp and therefore were out of the battle.

24. Livy, *History of Rome*, bk. 22, 46, says Maharbal, but Polybius, *Histories*, bk. 3, 114.7, says that Hanno commanded the Numidian cavalry.

25. Goldsworthy, *Punic Wars*, 207.

26. Ibid., 208.

27. Livy, *History of Rome*, bk. 22, 47.

28. Fernando Quesada Sanz, pers. comm., February 21, 2011. Also see Sanz, "Patterns of Interaction: 'Celtic' and 'Iberian' Weapons in Iron Age Spain," in *Celtic Connections: Papers of the Tenth International Congress of Celtic Studies, Edinburgh, 1995*, vol. 2, *Archaeology, Numismatics, Historical Linguistics*, ed. W. Gillies and D. W. Harding (Edinburgh, Scot.: International

Congress of Celtic Studies, 2006), 56–78. Quesada Sanz noted the "falcata was accepted as the 'national' weapon of the Iberians," 58. Note in his fig 2. the high concentration of falcata finds distribution in Andalucia and around Cartagena, where the Carthaginians were concentrated.

29. Polybius, *Histories*, trans. Paton, bk. 3, 114.3.

30. Ibid., 115.3.

31. O'Connell, *Ghosts of Cannae*, 141.

32. Dexter Hoyos, "The Age of Overseas Expansion," in *A Companion to the Roman Army*, ed. Paul Erdkamp (Malden, MA: Wiley-Blackwell, 2010), 63–80. Hoyos discusses Cannae especially in 66–69 and notes the old phalanx on 68.

33. William Desmond, "Lessons of Fear: A Reading of Thucydides," *Classical Philology* 101, no. 4 (2006): 359–79; speaking in general of a climate of fear as a political current but also in specifics, Thucydides, *History of the Peloponnesian War*, bk. 3, 82.2, where "war is a violent master (or teacher)."

34. Daly, *Cannae*, 167–68.

35. Lazenby, *Hannibal's War*, 83.

36. O'Connell, *Ghosts of Cannae*, 91.

37. The presence and impact of the falcata at Cannae is still debated. Iberian Iron Age weapons expert Fernando Quesada Sanz (pers. comm.) at the Universidad Autonóma de Madrid notes that the falcata was not any more important at Cannae than other weapons were, also publishing on this elsewhere in addition to the above note (for instance, Fernando Quesada Sanz, *Arma y Símbolo: la Falcata Iberica*, Instituto de Cultura Juan Gil-Albert, Diputación de Alicante, 1992). Also see John Gibson Warry, *Warfare in the Classical World: An Illustrated Encyclopedia of Weapons, Warriors, and Warfare in the Ancient Civilisations of Greece and Rome* (London: Salamander Books, 1993), 103, 218. A modern weapons maker from Los Angeles, Dave Baker, has reconstructed in his studio foundry the Iberian falcata that some scholars maintain (for example, Lancel, *Hannibal*, 36, 107; Healy, *Cannae 216 BC*, 22–25) was used at Cannae. I have held and swung one of these vicious blades and have seen it chop through entire pig necks and watched the flesh fly off—easily cleaved and flensed because the incredibly sharp piercing blade of Spanish steel flares out behind a center of gravity that makes its lethal force even greater as its drops. I shudder to think of it at Cannae in experienced hands if it was used at all there. It might be interesting to

note a ceramic relief of a falcata-like blade from the third century BCE on an underground tomb pier in Cerveteri's Etruscan Necropolis, Tomb of the Shields.

38. Daly, *Cannae*, 167; he also mentions that this could equally exhaust the heavy infantry Libyans on the other side.

39. Polybius, *Histories*, bk. 3, 117.6, says 4,000 Celts, 1,500 Spaniards and Africans, and 200 cavalry; Lancel, 2000, 108. I might be tempted to side with Polybius here because Livy quotes the same number of Carthaginians (55,000) to perish later at Metaurus, and he may have tried to create parity for justification of a Roman triumph equal to the Cannae loss.

40. Livy, *History of Rome*, bk. 22, 49. He numbers as Roman prisoners the 10,000 guarding the larger camp who had been kept out of battle, the 7,000 who had fled to the smaller camp only to be captured, and the 2,000 who had fled and sought refuge in the fortified village of Cannae itself and were taken prisoner there.

41. Patrick Hunt, *When Empires Clash: Twelve Great Battles in Antiquity*, 88.

42. O'Connell, *Ghosts of Cannae*, 160.

43. Healy, *Cannae 216 BC*, 69, also notes how much Polybius needed to preserve the honor of the Aemilii family name, his ultimate sponsors.

44. Livy, *History of Rome*, bk. 22, 51.6ff.

45. Goldsworthy, *Punic Wars*, 215.

46. Livy, *History of Rome*, bk. 22, 51.2.

47. Bernard Montgomery (Field-Marshal Viscount Montgomery, Victor of El Alamein), *A History of Warfare* (Cleveland: World, 1968), among them.

48. Lazenby, *Hannibal's War*, 88, referring to Livy, *History of Rome*, bk. 23, 14.7, and bk. 24, 2.8, respectively.

49. O'Connell, *Ghosts of Cannae*, 174.

50. Fronda, *Between Rome and Carthage*, 46, suggests that Hannibal could have drawn different conclusions from Pyrrhus' example, such as the need to fight in Italy and remain there, and additionally that Rome might capitulate if none came to its aid; also see Kluth, *Hannibal and Me*, 123.

51. Polybius, *Histories*, bk. 3, 117.4.

SIXTEEN: THE CAMPAIGN FOR SOUTH ITALY

1. Polybius, *Histories*, bk. 3, 118.5.

2. Healy, *Cannae 216 BC*, 94.

3. Lancel, *Hannibal*, 110.

4. Livy, *History of Rome*, bk. 22, 61.

5. Elena Isayev, "Identity and Culture," chap. 2 in "Inside Ancient Lukania, Dialogues in History and Archaeology," supp. 90, *Bulletin of the Institute of Classical Studies*, 2007: 25–26.

6. Livy, *History of Rome*, bk. 22, 58.6–7.

7. Bradford, *Hannibal*, 129. While seemingly desperate, this type of recruitment has been a not-infrequent conscription method in history, especially with people convicted of minor crimes but unable to secure freedom, partly due to poverty, and Rome needed able bodies more than moral right.

8. O'Connor Morris, *Hannibal*, 194–95.

9. Livy, *History of Rome*, bk. 25, 5.

10. Jean-Michel David, *The Roman Conquest of Italy*, trans. Antonia Nevill (Oxford: Blackwell, 1996), 61.

11. Lancel, *Hannibal*, 113.

12. Healy, *Cannae 216 BC*, 87.

13. Cassius, fragment 57.30; Appian, *Punica*, 63; Valerius, *Factorum ac dictorum memorabilium*, 9.6.

14. Livy, *History of Rome*, bk. 23, 15.

15. Goldsworthy, *Punic Wars*, 222.

16. Polybius, *Histories*, bk. 3, 118.10.

17. Miles, *Carthage Must Be Destroyed*, 16.

18. Livy, *History of Rome*, trans. Aubrey de Selincourt, bk. 23, 45.3–4, says of the Punic army, "[They] have lost their sap in luxury and Campanian vice— worn out by a winter of drinking and whoring and every other excess . . . melted away is that strength of limb and staunchness of heart that brought them over the Alps and Pyrenees. Those were men, these but their relics and shadows . . . in Capua was put out the name of their valour, their discipline, their former fame, their hope of things to come."

19. Lancel, *Hannibal*, 116.

20. Goldsworthy, *Punic Wars*, 225–26.

21. Lancel, *Hannibal*, 112–13.

22. Bradford, *Hannibal*, 124–25.

23. Kluth, *Hannibal and Me*, 174.

24. Healy, *Cannae 216 BC*, 87.

25. Plutarch, *Life of Marcellus*, 10.1.

26. Livy, *History of Rome*, bk. 23, 32.

27. Lorena Jannelli and Fausto Longo, eds., *The Greeks in Sicily* (San Giovanni Lupatoto, It.: Arsenale Editrice, 2004), 61; Lancel, *Hannibal*, 118.

28. This is interesting because Bradford, *Hannibal*, 136, makes the case that the changing landscape of individual farm owners in South Italy—whose livelihood was destroyed in the Second Punic War, leaving them as spoils of war for the *ager publicus*—led to a land policy that may have paved the way for subsequent vast *latifundia* estates in later years in Magna Graecia. Some historians have challenged aspects of this assumption. These *latifundia* also drew a despairing comment from Pliny the Elder, *Natural History*, bk. 18, 35, in the first century CE: that what had been the backbone of an army made up of independent farmers in the Republic working the land had reverted in his day to the work of slaves. "[T]he *latifundial*," he claims, "destroyed Italy."

    Also see Christopher Francese, *Ancient Rome in So Many Words* (New York: Hippocrene Books, 2007), 79, on *fundus*. This is also intriguing because even today, Apulia is by far the largest producer of grapes in Italy on huge agribusiness estates. But new studies argue against this large devastation of Apulia and nearby regional loss of individual farmers: see Nathan Rosenstein, "Italy: Economy and Demography After Hannibal's War," chap. 23 in *A Companion to the Punic Wars*, ed. Dexter Hoyos (Malden, MA: Wiley-Blackwell, 2011), 412–29, esp. 416–19.

29. Erdkamp, *Hunger and the Sword*, 161.

30. Cicero, *De Divinatione (On Divination)*, bk. 1, 24.49, trans. W. A. Falconer, repr. (Cambridge, MA: Loeb Classical Library, 1996), 277–78.

31. Pliny the Elder, *Natural History*, bk. 3, 103; Appian, *The Hannibalic War*, bk. 7, 43, in *History of Rome*.

32. Lancel, *Hannibal*, 124; Gabriel, *Hannibal*, 14.

33. Polybius, *Histories*, bk. 8, 24–34.

34. Timothy W. Potter, *Roman Italy: Exploring the Roman World* (Berkeley: University of California Press, 1987), 127–30; Patrick Hunt, "Via Appia," in *Encyclopedia of Ancient History*, ed. Roger S. Bagnall et al. (Malden, MA: Wiley-Blackwell, 2012).

35. Livy, *History of Rome*, bk. 25, 9.

36. Lancel, *Hannibal*, 129, aptly suggests it was the old Taranto avenue now called Corso Due Mari; also see Livy, *History of Rome*, bk. 25, 11. This avenue is also now the border of the new island where the original peninsula has been divided with a more recent late-nineteenth-century north-south

channel, connected by the Ponte Girevole. The Aragonese Castello di Taranto on the peninsular-island side immediately west of the newer channel is too far east from the original natural channel to be in the same location as the old acropolis of Taras and the Roman citadel farther to the west that guarded the natural waterway.

37. Livy, *History of Rome*, bk. 25, 11.

SEVENTEEN: THE MARCH ON ROME

1. Plutarch, *Life of Marcellus*, 9.4. Here Plutarch says he quotes Poseidonius.

2. Ibid., 13.2. The most thorough account and analysis of this is O'Connell, *Ghosts of Cannae*.

3. A team led by 1978 Nobel laureate physicist Arno Penzias, mathematician and computer scientist Rob Cook, and this author has reconstructed some of this defense of Siracusa by Archimedes, beginning in 2009 and with collaborative on-site research in Siracusa since 2012. Cook, incidentally, a pioneer at Pixar, was a cowinner of the 2001 Academy Award for significant advancements to the field of motion picture rendering.

4. Polybius, *Histories*, bk. 8, 5–6. This passage provides details about Siracusa defended by Archimedes by various war mechanisms. Among others, he names an "iron hand" attached to a chain, capsizing Roman ships when it was dropped after raising them vertically. Polybius also describes unknown war machines of Archimedes as "small scorpions."

5. Plutarch, *Marcellus*, 17.1.

6. Livy, *History of Rome*, bk. 25, 31.

7. Nigel Bagnall, *The Punic Wars: Rome, Carthage, and the Struggle for the Mediterranean* (London: Macmillan, 2005), *vii*; Lancel, *Hannibal*, 133.

8. Chester G. Starr, *A History of the Ancient World*, 4th ed. (New York: Oxford University Press, 1991), 486; Starr also notes that the year 212 was the "high point of Roman drafts."

9. Michael P. Fronda, "Hegemony and Rivalry: The Revolt of Capua Revisited," *Phoenix* 61, nos. 1/2 (Spring/Summer 2007): 83–108.

10. Livy, *History of Rome*, bk. 26, 7; Lancel, *Hannibal*, 130.

11. Gregory K. Golden, "Emergency Measures: Crisis and Response in the Roman Republic (From the Gallic Sack to the Tumultus of 43 BC)" (PhD diss., Classics, Rutgers University, 2008), 163.

12. Livy, *History of Rome*, bk. 26, 9.

13. Erdkamp, *Hunger and the Sword*, 178.

14. Livy, *History of Rome*, bk. 26, 10.
15. Augustine of Hippo, *De Civitate Dei*, bk. 3, 20.
16. Polybius, *Histories*, bk. 9, 7.3.
17. Bagnall, *Punic Wars*, 259.
18. Livy, *History of Rome*, bk. 27; *Scipio in Spain*, 16.
19. Caven, *Punic Wars*, 201.
20. Dexter Hoyos, *The Carthaginians* (New York: Routledge, 2010), 67.
21. Barry Strauss, *Masters of Command: Alexander, Hannibal, Caesar, and the Genius of Leadership* (New York: Simon & Schuster, 2012), 7–8.

EIGHTEEN: WAR IN SPAIN

1. O'Connor Morris, *Hannibal: Soldier, Statesman, Patriot*, 259.
2. Hoyos, *Hannibal's Dynasty*, 117–18. Hoyos also notes that, from the beginning, Fabian strategy alarmed Hannibal. This must also be true partly because it would take away his blitzkrieg field advantage as an invader against cumbersome armies with split leadership. Time and attrition were not in his favor; he needed battles where he could win by cunning and by exposing and exploiting Roman weaknesses.
3. Fronda, *Between Rome and Carthage*, 235.
4. Hunt, "Ebro River."
5. Roman fleets had taken and then lost Pantelleria between 255 and 254 BCE in the First Punic War but recaptured it in 217. At least 30 anchors quickly abandoned with a treasure hoard of 3,500 bronze coins from this period have been found at Punta Tracino and in the sheltered harbor of Cala Levant on Pantelleria; see, by way of comparison, Dr. Leonardo Abelli, University of Sassari. L. Abelli, ed. *Archeologia subaquea a Pantelleria*, " . . . de Cossurensibus et Poenis navalem egit . . ." Ricerca series maijor 3. (Ante Quem, Sicilia:, 2012, esp. 55–62, 107–120.
6. Polybius, *Histories*, bk. 3, 97.3; also see Howard Hayes Scullard, "The Carthaginians in Spain," chap. 2 in *Cambridge Ancient History*, 2nd ed., vol. 8, *Rome and the Mediterranean to 133 BC*, ed. A. E. Astin et al. (Cambridge: Cambridge University Press, 1989), 56.
7. Lancel, *Hannibal*, 135, although Livy, *History of Rome*, bk. 24, 49, claims he was seventeen.
8. Livy, *History of Rome*, bk. 25, 33. This story may or may not be true. Hasdrubal certainly had the means to do so with Cartagena silver.
9. Ibid., 36.

10. Howard Hayes Scullard, *A History of the Roman World 753–146 BC* (London: Routledge, 2004), 225.

11. Livy, *History of Rome*, bk. 26, 17.

NINETEEN: SCIPIO CAPTURES CARTAGENA

1. *Paulys Real-Encyclopädie der classischen Altertumwissenschaft*, ed. G. Wissowa et al. [n.d.] (Stuttgart), 7, cols 1462–70.

2. Polybius, *Histories*, bk. 10, 3.3–6.

3. Livy, *History of Rome*, bk. 22, 53.

4. R. T. Ridley, "Was Scipio Africanus at Cannae?," *Latomus* 34, no. 1 (1975): 161–65.

5. The epigraphic evidence in the *Corpus Inscriptorum Latinarum* is without a definable year date: *CIL* I,1, 280 (201) [P. Cornelius P. f.] *Scipio Africanus cos bis censor aedilis curulis trib mil.*

6. Livy, *History of Rome*, bk. 26, 19; Polybius, *Histories*, bk. 10, 2.

7. Among many others, see Theodor Mommsen, *History of Rome*, 5 vols., trans. William Purdie Dickson (1901), vol. 2, 160; Arnold, 300–302; Theodore Ayrault Dodge, *Hannibal*, new introduction by Ian M. Cuthbertson, repr. (New York: Barnes & Noble Books, 2005), 571–72; O'Connor Morris, *Hannibal: Soldier, Statesman, Patriot*, 256; B. H. Liddell Hart, *Scipio Africanus: Greater Than Napoléon*, repr. (Cambridge, MA: Da Capo Press, 2004), 7; Lazenby, *Hannibal's War*, 136–37; Bradford, *Hannibal*, 170; Lancel, *Hannibal*, 138; Goldsworthy, *Punic Wars*, 271, among many others.

8. Livy, *History of Rome*, bk. 26, 19, names as absurd the sightings of huge serpents and other prodigies at Scipio's birth in his mother Pomponia's bedroom.

9. Liddell Hart, *Scipio Africanus*, 5.

10. Polybius, *Histories*, bk. 10, 2.12–13.

11. Goldsworthy, *Punic Wars*, 270.

12. Livy, *History of Rome*, bk. 26, 20.6, says near Saguntum, but this would have deterred Scipio from marching south of the Ebro to Cartagena, as Lazenby, *Hannibal's War*, 134, rightly points out.

13. Polybius, *Histories*, bk. 10, 2.13; Ridley, "Was Scipio Africanus at Cannae?," 161.

14. Peter van Dommelen, "Carthago Nova (Cartagena)," in *Encyclopedia of Ancient History*, ed. Roger S. Bagnall et al. (Malden, MA: Wiley-Blackwell, 2012).

15. Polybius, *Histories*, bk. 10, 8.1.

16. Peddie, *Hannibal's War,* 149.

17. Goldsworthy, *Punic Wars,* 271.

18. Polybius, *Histories,* bk. 10, 9.7; Livy, *History of Rome,* bk. 26, 42.6.

19. Polybius, *Histories,* bk. 10, 11.4, making it about thirteen thousand feet in circumference.

20. Lazenby, *Hannibal's War,* 136–37.

21. Polybius, *Histories,* bk. 10, 8.4.

22. Polybius, *Histories,* bk. 10, 10.10–12; Livy, *History of Rome,* bk. 26, 45.

23. A. Lillo and M. Lillo, "On Polybius X.10.12: The Capture of New Carthage," *Historia: Zeitschrift für Alte Geschichte* 37 (1988): 477–80; Dexter Hoyos, "Sluice-gates or Neptune at New Carthage, 209 BC?," Historia: *Zeitschrift für Alte Geschichte* 41 (1992): 124–28; Benedict J. Lowe. "Polybius 10.10.2 and the Existence of Salt Flats at Carthago Nova," *Phoenix* 54, nos. 1/2 (2000): 39–52.

24. Lowe, "Polybius 10.10.2," 49.

25. Sheldon, *Intelligence Activities in Ancient Rome,* 7 and esp. chaps. 12–13.

26. Polybius, *Histories,* bk. 10, 15.4–6.

27. Ibid., 18.1–2.

28. Jan Libourel, "Galley Slaves in the Second Punic War," *Classical Philology* 68, no. 2 (1973): 116–19, esp. 117.

29. Lazenby, *Hannibal's War,* 139; Livy, *History of Rome,* bk. 26, 50.

30. Garland, *Hannibal,* 102.

31. R. Bruce Hitchner, "Review: Roman Republican Imperialism in Italy and the West," *American Journal of Archaeology* 113, no. 4 (October 2009): 651–55, esp. 654. Hitchner notes the "striking intentionality" that these three venues were also the main ethnic communities—Celtiberian in Tarraco, Punic in Carthago Nova, and Greek in Emporion—but also that initial Roman interest was military and strategic.

32. Miles, *Carthage Must Be Destroyed,* 301.

33. Scullard, *History of the Roman World,* 227.

34. J. S. Richardson, *Hispaniae: Spain and the Development of Roman Imperialism, 218–82 BC* (Cambridge: Cambridge University Press, 2004), 60–61; S. J. Keay, *Roman Spain: Exploring the Roman World* (Berkeley: University of California Press, 1988), 50; Keay, review of *Roman Spain: Conquest and Assimilation,* by L. A. Curchin, *Brittania* 24 (1993): 332–33.

35. Naturally, this should also be factored by Roman recall of any Punic coins from circulation to remint them as Roman. See Paolo Visona, "The Punic

Coins in the Collection of Florence's Museo Archeologico: Non nulla Notanda," *Rivista di Studi Fenici* 27 (1999): 147–49; Visona, "A New Wrinkle
in the Mid-Carthaginian Silver Series," *Numismatic Chronicle* 166 (2006):
15–23; Visona, "The Serrated Silver Coinage of Carthage," *Schweizerische
Numismatische Rundschau* 86 (2007): 31–62.

36. Miles, *Carthage Must Be Destroyed*, 49–54, 110, 116–17, 229.

37. The Archaeological Museum of Cartagena (Museo Arqueologico Municipal, Cartagena) has a highly useful permanent exhibition on the economic
history of mining in the region from Punic through Roman periods; where
silver is or was once found, lead ore is a corollary metal source (silver and
lead pairing in igneous sulfide metal deposition), and Rome also fully exploited this metal too, as historic traces of lead oxide even in Greenland ice
demonstrate.

TWENTY: METAURUS

1. Bradford, *Hannibal*, 186.

2. The number of Hasdrubal's troops is greatly disputed both en route and at
Metaurus. Bagnall, *Punic Wars*, 263, says they numbered thirty thousand
before the Battle of Metaurus. En route, Hasdrubal picked up Celtic recruits
passing through Gaul, possibly swelling his numbers to forty-eight thousand if Appian, *Roman History*, bk. 8, 52, is trustworthy, although many
doubt this high figure. Goldsworthy, *Punic Wars*, 239, suggests that Hasdrubal had "significantly less than the Roman troop strength of forty thousand soldiers at Metaurus" and goes on to say that while Hasdrubal spent
gold lavishly to acquire Celtic mercenaries, he did not have the numerical
advantage. Lazenby, *Hannibal's War*, 190, also suggests there were twenty
thousand to thirty thousand soldiers in Hasdrubal's army. Livy, *History of
Rome*, bk. 27, 49, seems more unreliable than usual, suggesting far more
than sixty thousand Hasdrubal soldiers, a number that Bradford, *Hannibal*,
193, calls "fanciful."

3. Polybius, *Histories*, bk. 11, 1.1.

4. Appian, *Hannibal's War*, 52.

5. Patrick Hunt, "Rubicon," in *Encyclopedia of Ancient History*, ed. Roger S.
Bagnall et al. (Malden. MA: Wiley-Blackwell, 2012).

6. Livy, *History of Rome*, bk. 27, 39; this may be debatable, Lazenby, *Hannibal's
War*, 189.

7. "Grumentum," in *Princeton Encyclopedia of Classical Sites.*

8. Livy, *History of Rome*, bk. 27, 44.

9. Garland, *Hannibal*, 105.

10. According to Austin and Rankin, *Exploration*, 90–91, the Romans were learning to copy Hannibal's military intelligence gathering.

11. Goldsworthy, *Punic Wars*, 239.

12. Bagnall, *Punic Wars*, 263.

13. Livy, *History of Rome*, bk. 27, 38.

14. A *propraetor* was an appointed chief administrator of a province, serving after fulfilling his office of *praetor*, usually as a military commander or an elected magistrate. Also see Pat Southern, *The Roman Army: A Social and Institutional History* (New York: Oxford University Press, 2007), 331, 339.

15. Pauly-Wissowa, *Realencyclopädie der classischen Altertumswissenschaft*, vol. 4, ed. G. Wissowa et al. (Stuttgart, Ger., n.d.), 7, 246.

16. Plutarch, *Life of Marcellus*, 11.3–12.3.

17. Livy, *History of Rome*, bk. 27, 41, claims that Hannibal lost eight thousand men and six elephants. Although he identifies these soldiers as Carthaginian, it is far more probable they were Bruttians or the like.

18. Ibid., 46. Livy doesn't fully indicate the route after the Piceni (of *Picenum)* and the *Praetuti* people (around *Aprutium* or the region of *Praetutium?*, roughly modern Abruzzo). Also see Colin Adams and Ray Laurence, eds, *Travel and Geography in the Roman Empire* (London: Routledge, 2001), 74, although far later, also see Sonia Antonelli, *Il Territorio di Aprutium, Aspetti e forme delle dinamiche insediative tra Ve XI seculo* (Palombi Editore, 2010).

19. Strabo, *Geography*, bk. 5, 4.2.

20. Lancel, *Hannibal*, 147.

21. Potter, *Roman Italy*, 135–37.

22. N. Alfieri, "Sena Gallica," in *Princeton Encyclopedia of Classical Sites*.

23. Warry, *Warfare in the Classical World*, 128.

24. Elizabeth Keitel, "The Influence of Thucydides 7.61–71 on Sallust Cat. 20–21," *Classical Journal* 82, no. 4 (1987): 293–300, esp. 295n8. She points out five distinctive narrative rhetorical elements: reflections, harangues, exhortations, summaries, and repetition.

25. Livy, *History of Rome*, bk. 27, 47.

26. Bradford, *Hannibal*, 192.

27. Caven, *Punic Wars*, 214, suggests that the battle was near or above Sant-Angelo.

28. Lazenby, *Hannibal's War*, 188.

29. Peddie, *Hannibal's War*, 179.

30. Livy, *History of Rome*, bk. 27, 47.

31. Polybius, *Histories*, bk. 11, 3.1.

32. Ibid., 1.12; Livy, *History of Rome*, bk. 27, 49.

33. Polybius, *Histories*, bk. 11, 1.11.

34. Bagnall, *Punic Wars*, 263–67.

35. Although Polybius, *Histories*, bk. 11, 3.2–3, does not give statistics for the number of Hasdrubal's original troops, he estimates just ten thousand casualties at Metaurus. Livy, *History of Rome*, bk. 27, 49, on the other hand, claims that fifty-seven thousand Carthaginians died there. This is highly suspect, especially because much earlier (bk. 25, 6), he says that Cannae (where he contends fifty thousand Romans perished) is thus avenged. Livy seems to be trying to compensate with his seven thousand more Carthaginian dead at Metaurus alongside their general (Hasdrubal) than Roman dead at Cannae with their general (Aemilius Paullus). He may have wanted to mitigate the humiliation of Cannae for Rome, like an infernal balance book, but this didn't fully happen in Italy, which may have frustrated Livy.

36. Lazenby, *Hannibal's War*, 190.

TWENTY-ONE: ROMAN TRIUMPH, ITALY TO SPAIN

1. Bagnall, *Punic Wars*, 89.

2. Philip C. Schmitz, "The Phoenician Text from the Etruscan Sanctuary at Pyrgi," *Journal of the American Oriental Society* 115, no. 4 (1995): 559–75.

3. In the Aeneid, book 4, Virgil plays up the close relationship between the goddess Juno and Queen Dido of Carthage, making Dido a priestess of Juno who seems to sacrifice herself to the goddess. Juno's divine wrath then pursues Aeneas by the dying queen's curse. Virgil's partial explanation for the enmity between Carthage and Rome is that Aeneas abandoned Dido. Henry Purcell's famous mournful song "Dido's Lament" from the opera *Dido and Aeneas* relates the queen's sorrow in her suicide.

4. Livy, *History of Rome*, bk. 28; *Final Conquest in Spain*, 46.16.

5. Polybius, *Histories*, trans. Paton, bk. 3, 33.18. Polybius writes, "The fact is that I found on the Lacinian promontory a bronze tablet on which Hannibal himself had made out these lists during the time he was in Italy, and thinking this a first-rate authority, decided to follow the document."

6. Lancel, *Hannibal*, 157.

7. Mary K. Jaeger, "Livy, Hannibal's Monument and the Temple of Juno Lacinia at Croton," *Transactions of the American Philological Association (TAPA)* 136 (2006): 389–414, esp. 390; others call Livy's text here a "caesura" (390n3).

8. Livy, *History of Rome*, bk. 27, 12.

9. Polybius, *Histories*, bk. 11, 21.2.

10. Lancel, *Hannibal*, 150.

11. Liddell Hart, *Scipio Africanus*, 58.

12. Livy, *History of Rome*, bk. 27, 13.

13. Polybius, *Histories*, bk. 11, 22.3.

14. Polybius, *Histories*, trans. Robin Waterfield, notes Brian McGing (New York: Oxford University Press, 2010), *xiv*.

15. Polybius, *Histories*, bk. 11, 24.3.

16. Lancel, *Hannibal*, 150.

17. Polybius, *Histories*, bk. 11, 25–33.

18. Livy, *History of Rome*, bk. 28, 16.

19. Lancel, *Hannibal*, 159.

20. Livy, *History of Rome*, bk. 28, 18. Livy says the two generals did this to please Syphax.

21. Ibid., 18.9.

22. Richard A. Gabriel, *Scipio Africanus: Rome's Greatest General* (Washington, DC: Potomac Books, 2008), 139.

23. Livy, *History of Rome*, bk. 28, 38.

24. Lancel, *Hannibal*, 161.

25. Polybius, *Histories*, bk. 10, 5.6.

26. Andrew W. Lintott, "Electoral Bribery in the Roman Republic," *Journal of Roman Studies* 80 (1990): 1–16, esp. 4, using the word *ambitus* in relation to electoral bribery, illegal in Rome while noting Scipio's munificence; also apropos are Lintott's etymologies: *ambitus* from the verb *ambire*, "to go around" and "to canvas support," and *ambitio* was "pursuit of office and political fame (perhaps to excess)," 1.

27. Helmut Berneder, *Magna Mater-Kult und Sibyllinen* (Innsbruck, Aus.: Institut für Sprachen und Literaturen der Universität Innsbruck, 2004).

28. Livy, *History of Rome*, bk. 29, 10, 14.

29. For example, see Juvenal, *Satires*, bk. 3, 126ff; Appian, *Hannibalic War*, 56 (a source for the story of Claudia pulling the boat stuck in the river).

30. Livy, *History of Rome*, bk. 29, 14.9; Lancel, *Hannibal*, 163.

31. Liddell Hart, *Scipio Africanus*, 83.

TWENTY-TWO: ZAMA

1. Livy, *History of Rome*, bk. 28, 44.

2. F. W. Walbank, *Selected Papers: Studies in Greek and Roman History and Historiography* (Cambridge: Cambridge University Press, 2010), 328.

3. Polybius, *Histories*, bk. 12, 56.

4. Goldsworthy, *Punic Wars*, 287–88. It seems Scipio's numbers at Zama were closer to thirty-four thousand if counting Massinissa's reinforcements of Numidian cavalry and men.

5. Bradford, *Hannibal*, 206.

6. Frontinus, *Strategemata*, bk. 1, 12.1.

7. Hunt, "Locus of Carthage," 137–38.

8. Polybius, *Histories*, bk. 14, 3.

9. Livy, *History of Rome*, bk. 21, 4.9; bk. 22, 6.12; bk. 28, 44.4; also see Erich S. Gruen, *Rethinking the Other in Antiquity*, Martin Classical Lectures (Princeton, NJ: Princeton University Press, 2012), 13ff.

10. Azedine Beschaouch, "De l'Africa latino-chrétienne à l'Ifriqiya arabo-musulmane: questions de toponymie," *Comptes-rendus des séances de l'Académie des Inscriptions et Belles-Lettres (CRAI)* 130, no. 3 (1986): 530–49.

11. P. G. Walsh, "Massinissa," *Journal of Roman Studies* 55, nos. 1/2 (1965): 149–60; Haley. "Livy, Passion and Cultural Stereotypes," 375–81. Wife stealing was apparently not unusual for Numidians, a people considered as *tribal* rather than as a *nation* by the Romans. While it was reputedly practiced by barbarians (how the Romans saw the Numidians), Roman writers such as Livy are implying that Numidians are inherently very different than *lawful* Romans in their accepted mores.

12. Appian, *Punic Wars*, 28.

13. Fronda, *Between Rome and Carthage*, 36–37.

14. Diodorus, *Library of History*, bk. 27, 9, says Hannibal slaughtered three thousand horses; also see Garland, *Hannibal*, 108.

15. Livy, *History of Rome*, bk. 30, 20.

16. D. L. Stone, D. J. Mattingly, and N. Ben Lazreg, eds., *Leptiminus (Lamta): The Field Survey, Report No. 3*, supp. 87, *Journal of Roman Archaeology* (2011).

17. Paul Davis, *100 Decisive Battles: From Ancient Times to the Present* (Oxford: Oxford University Press, 2001), 51.

18. Fronda, *Between Rome and Carthage*, 237. Along with most reasonable historians, Fronda doubts Livy's dramatic assertion in *History of Rome*,

bk. 30, 20, that the Italians in the sacred shrine of Juno Lacinia who re-fused to accompany Hannibal were then butchered, deducing that oth-ers who repeat this (Diodorus, *Library of History*, bk. 27, 9.1; Appian, *Hannibalic War*, 59) are only attempting to reinforce Hannibal's alleged brutality.

19. Livy, *History of Rome*, bk. 30, 20.

20. Davis, *100 Decisive Battles*, 47, maintains that Hannibal had forty-five thou-sand infantry and three thousand cavalry at Zama. Others, such as Lancel, *Hannibal*, 175, suggest he had an army of fifty thousand, possibly count-ing his cavalry, in agreement with G. C. Picard, *Hannibal* (Paris: Hachette, 1967), 206, who adjusts the number upward to fifty thousand, based on Appian. The best estimates seem closer to forty thousand if we can trust Polybius, as suggested by Goldsworthy, *Punic Wars*, 307.

21. Nowhere is this better told than in O'Connell, *Ghosts of Cannae*, 13, 245–52.

22. Polybius, *Histories*, bk. 15, 5.

23. P. S. Derow, "Polybius, Rome and the East," *Journal of Roman Studies* 69 (1979): 1–15, esp. 3–4.

24. Davidson, "Gaze in Polybius' Histories," 10–24, esp. 12.

25. Liddell Hart, *Sherman: Soldier, Realist, American*, Boston: Da Capo, 1993 (originally Dodd, Mead & Co., 1929), x.

26. Livy, *History of Rome*, bk. 22, 53.

27. Polybius, *Histories*, bk. 14, 9.6; Davidson, "Gaze in Polybius' Histories," 20.

28. Livy, *History of Rome*, bk. 30, 30.

29. Polybius, *Histories*, bk. 15, 7.

30. Livy, *History of Rome*, bk. 30, 31.

31. Ibid., bk. 31–32.

32. Hoyos, *Hannibal's Dynasty*, 177.

33. Polybius, *Histories*, bk. 15, 10–11.

34. F. M. Russell, "The Battlefield of Zama," *Archaeology* 23, no. 2 (1970): 120–29; "Zama ('Aelia Hadriana Augusta') Tunisia," in *Princeton Encyclopedia of Classical Sites*, 1976.

35. T. A. Dorey, "Macedonians at the Battle of Zama," *American Journal of Phi-lology* 78, no. 2 (1957): 185–87; unless they were possibly there without of-ficial Macedonian sanction.

36. Gabriel, *Scipio Africanus*, 187–88.

37. Peddie, *Hannibal's War*, 212.

38. Hoyos, *Hannibal's Dynasty*, 177–78.

39. Gabriel, *Scipio Africanus*, 188.

40. Caven, *Punic Wars*, 251.

41. Livy, *History of Rome*, bk. 30, 33.

42. Polybius, *Histories*, bk. 3, 112–13, 115–16. Polybius details how Aemilius Paullus was not happy with the potential battleground at Cannae (112.2); how close the Romans were to the River Aufidus (113.3), how crowded the Roman maniples were (115.6), and how impossible movement became for the Romans finally compressed on all sides (116.10–12).

43. Livy, *History of Rome*, bk. 30, 34.

44. Polybius, *Histories*, bk. 15, 12.

45. Livy, *History of Rome*, bk. 30, 33.

46. Polybius, *Histories*, bk. 15, 14.

47. Howard Hayes Scullard, *Scipio Africanus: Soldier and Politician* (Ithaca, NY: Cornell University Press, 1970), 154, claims instead that only 1,500 Romans perished at Zama.

48. Hoyos, *Hannibal's Dynasty*, 178.

49. Polybius, *Histories*, bk. 15, 15.

50. Picard, *Hannibal*, 208.

51. Lazenby, *Hannibal's War*, 225.

52. Jakob Seibert, 474.

53. O'Connell, *Ghosts of Cannae*, 252n93 and 286, uses 2009 estimates at $13.25 per-ounce spot price; in 2016 the per-ounce spot price was $16.62.

54. Lancel, *Hannibal*, 182.

55. Note that the Treaty of Versailles in 1919 assigned responsibility of blame for World War I to Germany. Two years later, following negotiations, the London Schedule of Payments assessed Germany 132 billion gold marks (equivalent to $33 billion) in reparations, to be paid in installments— although in the end, the actual payments were insignificant. See William N. Goetzmann and K. Geert Rouwenhorst, eds., *The Origins of Value: The Financial Innovations That Created Modern Capital* (New York: Oxford University Press, 2005), 329.

56. O'Connell, *Ghosts of Cannae*, 252, calls Hannibal without an army "a military oxymoron."

57. J. Roger Dunkle, "The Greek Tyrant and Roman Political Invective of the Late Republic," *Transactions of the American Philological Association (TAPA)* 98 (1967): 151–71, esp. 156–57.

58. Livy, *History of Rome*, bk. 28, 42. Here Fabius implies that Scipio fancies

himself more a king than a consul; if Scipio's character were different, this might have been possible, especially after Zama.

59. Lancel, *Hannibal*, 179.

60. Livy, *History of Rome*, bk. 30, 37.7.

61. Ibid., bk. 30, 44.4–11.

62. Polybius, Histories, bk. 3, 8.6–10. As mentioned at the outset of this book, even Polybius, in the first paragraph of bk. 3 (1.1), called it the "Hannibalic War" (*ton 'Annibiakon*). However, surely he was not the first.

63. Ibid., bk. 15, 15.

TWENTY-THREE: EXILE

1. Liddell Hart, *Strategy*, 33.

2. Serge Lancel, *Carthage: A History*, trans. Antonia Nevill (Oxford: Blackwell, 1995), 118–19.

3. David J. Mattingly and R. Bruce Hitchner, "Roman Africa: An Archaeological Review," *Journal of Roman Studies* 85 (1995): 165–213, esp. 200 and 204.

4. Aurelius Victor, *De Caesaribus*, 37.2–3.

5. Virgil, *Aeneid*, bk. 4, 60ff.

6. Walter Ameling, *Karthago: Studien zu Militär, Staat und Gesellschaft. Vestigia: Beiträge zur Alten Geschichte* 45. Munich: C. H. Beck Verlag, 1993, 82.

7. E. Lipinski, ed. (dir.), "Suffète," *Dictionnaire de la civilisation phénicienne et punique* (Paris: Brepols, [Turnhout] 1992), 429. Lipinski also references an earlier Semitic word in *shapitum* from Akkadian.

8. F. Brown, S. R. Driver, and C. A. Briggs, *Hebrew and English Lexicon of the Old Testament* (Oxford: Clarendon Press, 1951), 1047: "judge, lawgiver" with Punic cognate *sufet* noted.

9. Robert Drews, "Phoenicians, Carthage and the Spartan Eunomia," *American Journal of Philology* 100, no. 1 (Spring 1979): 45–58, esp. 54.

10. G. C. Picard, "Hannibal," in *Dictionnaire de la civilisation phénicienne et punique*, ed. (dir.) E. Lipinski (Paris: Brepols, [Turnhout] 1992), 207.

11. Cornelius Nepos, *Life of Hannibal*, 7.4. The Roman biographer also equates the office with a Roman praetor.

12. Hoyos, *Hannibal's Dynasty*, 210.

13. Livy, *History of Rome*, bk. 33, 46.

14. Bradley, 228.

15. Nepos, *Life of Hannibal*, 7. 7.

16. Hoyos, *Hannibal's Dynasty*, 129ff.; Fronda, *Between Rome and Carthage*, 298.

17. Livy, *History of Rome*, bk. 33, 47.

18. Lancel, *Hannibal*, 192.

19. Nepos, *Life of Hannibal*, 7.10ff. Undermining some of Nepos' credibility is that he follows these details with Hannibal returning to Cyrene with five ships within three years of flight (8.1–3).

20. John Ray, *The Rosetta Stone and the Rebirth of Ancient Egypt* (Cambridge, MA: Harvard University Press, 2007), 133–34; Patrick Hunt, *Ten Discoveries That Rewrote History* (New York: Penguin/Plume, 2007), 4–5.

21. Gabriel, *Hannibal*, 221.

22. While in *qinah* (lament) poetic form over its future destruction, *Ezekiel* 27 surveys one of Tyre's great periods in the early sixth century BCE. See I. M. Diakonoff. "The Naval Power and Trade of Tyre." *Israel Exploration Journal* 42, nos. 3/4 (1992) 168–93; its purple dye murex trade and Carthaginian connections are noted on 176.

23. Roger Batty, "Mela's Phoenician Geography," *Journal of Roman Studies* 90 (2000): 70–94, esp. 79–83.

24. Fergus Millar, "The Phoenician Cities: A Case-Study of Hellenization," *Proceedings of the Cambridge Philological Society* 209 (1983): 55–71; Andrea J. Berlin, "From Monarchy to Markets: The Phoenicians to Hellenistic Palestine," *Bulletin of the American Schools of Oriental Research* 306 (May 1997): 75–88, esp. 76–77.

25. Lancel, *Hannibal*, 193.

26. Aulus Gellius, *Noctes Atticae (Attic Nights)*, V.v.5: *Satis, plane satis esse credo Romanis haec omnia, etiamsi avarissimi sunt.*

27. Lancel, *Hannibal*, 203.

28. Among others, see Livy, *History of Rome*, bk. 35, 14; Plutarch *Flamininus*, 21.3–4; Appian, *The Syrian Wars*, bk. 11 in *Roman History*.

29. Arthur M. Eckstein, *Rome Enters the Greek East: From Anarchy to Hierarchy in the Hellenistic Mediterranean 230–170 BC* (Malden, MA: Wiley-Blackwell, 2012).

30. R. M. Errington, "Rome Against Philip and Antiochus," chap. 8 in *Cambridge Ancient History*, 2nd ed., vol. 8, *Rome and the Mediterranean to 133 BC*, ed. A. E Astin et al. (Cambridge: Cambridge University Press, 1990), 285–86.

31. Nepos, *Life of Hannibal*, 9; Justin (Marcus Junianus Justinus), *Epitome of Pompeius Trogus*, bk. 32, 4.3–5; Horace (Quintus Horatius Flaccus), *Epode* 9. Lancel, *Hannibal*, 205, however, suggests the story should be taken with a considerable grain of salt.

32. Francis Cairns, "Horace Epode 9: Some New Interpretations, *Illinois Classical Studies* 8, no. 1 (1983): 80–93; Bradley, 235.

33. Tullia Linders, *Studies in the Treasure Records of the Temple of Artemis Brauronia Found in Athens* (Stockholm: Svenska Institutet i Athen, 1972); Linders. "The Treasures of Other Gods in Athens and Their Functions," *Beiträge zur klassischen Philologie* 62 (1975); Meisenheim; Georges Roux, "Trésors, Temples, Tholos," in *Temples et Sanctuaires,* ed. Roux (Lyon, Fr.: Travaux de la Maison de l'Orient 7, 1984), 153–72; Josephine Shaya, "The Greek Temple as Museum: The Case of the Legendary Treasure of Athena from Lindos," *American Journal of Archaeology* 109, no. 3 (2005): 423–42, esp. 425–27ff. on temple treasury and ensuing record lists of votive gifts. "Hellenistic" refers to the culture fusing Greek and Oriental influences in the Greek cities after the reign of Alexander the Great.

34. Joan R. Mertens, "Greek Bronzes in the Metropolitan Museum of Art," *Metropolitan Museum of Art Bulletin,* 43, no. 2 (1985): 5–66, esp. 13; Bruce Christman, "The Emperor as Philosopher," *Bulletin of the Cleveland Museum of Art* 74, no. 3 (1987): 100–13; Carol Mattusch, *Greek Bronze Statuary: From the Beginnings Through Fifth Century B.C.,* Ithaca, NY: Cornell University Press, 1989, 15–17ff.; Alessandra Giumlia-Mair, "Techniques and Composition of Equestrian Statues in Raetia," in *From the Parts to the Whole,* vol. 2, *Acta of the 13th International Bronze Congress at Cambridge, Massachusetts, 1996,* supp. 39, *Journal of Roman Archaeology* (2002): 93–97, esp. 95.

35. Strabo, *Geography,* bk. 11, 14.6; Plutarch, *Life of Lucullus,* 31.4–5

36. Pliny the Elder, *Natural History,* bk. 5, 148.

37. Nepos, *Life of Hannibal,* 10; Justin, *Epitome,* bk. *32,* 4.6.

38. Gavin de Beer, *Hannibal: The Struggle for Power in the Mediterranean* (London: Thames and Hudson, 1969), 299; James W. Martin, George W. Christopher, and Edward M. Eitzen, "History of Biological Weapons: From Poisoned Darts to Intentional Epidemics," in *Medical Aspects of Biological Warfare,* ed. Z. F. Dembek (Washington DC: Borden Institute, Walter Reed Army Medical Center, 2007), 1–20, esp. 2; also see Adrienne Mayor, *Greek Fire, Poison Arrows, and Scorpion Bombs: Biological Warfare in the Ancient World* (London: Duckworth, 2009), 188: "the Carthaginian general had many ad hoc animal tricks."

39. Plutarch, *Flamininus,* 2.1–2.

40. Eckstein, 89; Prusias' wife, Apama, was the half sister of Philip V of Macedon.

41. Livy, *History of Rome*, bk. 39, 51.2.

42. Flavius Eutropius (or Victor), *De Viris Illustribus*, 4.42.

43. Pliny the Elder, *Natural History*, bk. 5, 43.

44. Lancel, *Hannibal*, 210.

45. Livy, *History of Rome*, bk. 39, 51.9–11; Plutarch, *Flamininus*, 20.5, 21.1–3; Appian, *Syrian Wars*, 11; Nepos, Life of *Hannibal*, 13.

TWENTY-FOUR: HANNIBAL'S LEGACY

1. Vegetius (Publius Flavius Vegetius Renaus), *De Re Militari (The Military Institutions of the Romans)*, bk. 1, 1.

2. Valerius, *Factorum ac dictorum memorabilium*, V.3.2b: *"Ingrata patria, ne ossa quidem habebis."* He continues: *"Cineres ei suos negavit quam in cinerem collabi passus non fuerat."* ("Ungrateful fatherland, you will not have my bones." "He denied his ashes to her whom he had not let collapse into ash.")

3. Seneca, *De Ira (On Anger)*, bk. 2, 5.4.

4. Horace, *Ode* 3, 6.36; Juvenal, *Satires*, bk. 7, 161.

5. Ovid, *Fasti*, bk. 3, 148, bk. 6, 242.

6. Miles, *Carthage Must Be Destroyed*, 375n2.

7. Plutarch, *Life of Flamininus*, 21.2, *Life of Fabius*, 5.3, *Life of Marcellus*, 24.6.

8. Diodorus, *Library of History*, bk. 36, 14.2; bk. 27, 9.1–10.1.

9. Cassius, fragment, 15.57.25.

10. Polybius, *Histories*, bk. 9, 24.4–8; Rawlings, "Hannibal the Cannibal?," 1–30.

11. Brizzi, "Carthage and Hannibal in Roman and Greek Memory," 483–98, esp. 484.

12. Garland, *Hannibal*, 136–37; Virgil, *Aeneid*, bk. 4, 622–26. Some of this interpretation of Virgil is from Fairclough; other parts are my own. (I had to translate this passage as part of my graduate Latin assignment at the University of California, Berkeley, in the summer of 1982.) The phoenix allusion and metonymy between ashes and bones is a wordplay device called subtle or concealed paronomasia. See Patrick Hunt, "Subtle Paronomasia in the *Canticum Canticorum*: Hidden Treasures of the Superlative Poet," *Goldene Äpfel in silbernen Schalen. Beiträge zur Erforschung des Alten Testaments und des Antiken Judentums* 20 (1992): 147–54. The phoenix was known from Greek writers, including Hesiod, fragment, 171.4, and Herodotus, 2.73. The phoenix building a funeral pyre—like Dido—is also known in the first century to Statius (*Silvae* II.4.22 *ducite flammis funera*). That the phoenix progeny emerges from the bones only every few hundred years, see Ovid,

Metamorphoses, bk. 15, 393; Pliny the Elder, *Natural History,* bk. 10, 2.4; also *"phoenix"* in Charlton T. Lewis and Charles Short, *A Latin Dictionary,* 1372. That both the actual phoenix and Hannibal are unnamed reinforces the brilliant wordplay, also because Virgil knows that it would be anachronistic for Dido to mention Hannibal.

13. Valerius, *Factorum ac dictorum memorabilium,* bk. 5, 1.6, putting these honorable acts in a different light than Livy, *History of Rome,* bk. 22, 52.6 (Aemilius Paullus), bk. 35, 17.4–7 (Tiberius Gracchus), and bk. 27, 28.2ff. (M. Marcellus).

14. Frontinus, *Strategemata,* bk. 1, 5.28 (Volturnus), bk. 1 7.2 (Rhone?), bk. 1, 8.2 (slander Fabius), bk. 2, 2.6 (choosing topography at Numistro against Marcellus), bk. 2, 3.7 (Cannae), bk. 2, 3.9 (topography against Marcellus), bk. 2, 3.16 (Zama), bk. 2, 5.13 (against Romans gorging), bk. 2, 5.21 (against Fulvius), bk. 2, 5.22 (against Minucius), bk. 2, 5.23 (Trebia), bk. 2, 5.24 (Trasimene), bk. 2, 5.25 (against Junius), bk. 2, 5.27 (Numidians at Cannae), bk. 2, 6.4 (Trasimene), bk. 2, 7.7 (Carpetani in Italy), bk. 3, 2.3 (Hannibal spies), bk. 3, 3.6 (Tarentum), bk. 3, 9.1 (Cartagena), bk. 3, 10.3 (Himera), bk. 3, 10.4 (Saguntum), bk. 3, 16.4 (deserters), bk. 4, 3.7 (Hannibal's self-discipline), bk. 4, 3.8 (Hannibal's self-discipline), bk. 4, 7.10 (vipers in sea battle), bk. 4, 7.25 (Hannibal at Trasimene), to name but a few.

15. Valerius, *Factorum ac dictorum memorabilium,* bk. 7, 4.2.

16. Ibid., bk. 3, 7.6.

17. Colonel John R. Elting, *The Super-Strategists: Great Captains, Theorists and Fighting Men Who Have Shaped the History of Warfare* (New York: Charles Scribner's Sons, 1985), 17.

18. Albert Merglen, *Surprise Warfare: Subversive, Airborne and Amphibious Operations,* trans. K. Morgan (London: George Allen and Unwin, 1968), 11.

19. Frontinus, *Strategemata,* bk. 1, 1.9.

20. Valerius, *Factorum ac dictorum memorabilium,* bk. 7, 3.8.

21. Valerius, *Factorum ac dictorum memorabilium,* bk. 6.1b.

22. Michael Grant, *The Army of the Caesars* (New York: Evans Books, 1974), 4.

23. Polybius, *Histories,* bk. 3, 117.4–5.

24. Leslie J. Worley, *Hippeis: The Cavalry of Ancient Greece* (Oxford: Westview Press, 1994), 59.

25. A. Hyland, *Equus: The Horse in the Roman World* (New Haven, CT: Yale University Press, 1990), 74, 123, 129, 174–75. Hyland also copiously notes that "the Numidians were most effective at Ticinus where they swamped the Roman

Gallic flanks," 175; how Hannibal used Numidians at Trebia to cross the icy river to harass and goad the Romans, 129, 175; how he employed cavalry at Trasimene, 123, 175; and how Hannibal's envelopment at Cannae successfully implemented Numidian and other cavalry from the rear, 166, 175, 189. Hyland also explains the Numidian charge and disperse tactics on smaller, nimbler horses, and how Numidians rode without a bridle, using a long, flexible willow or wood sapling around the horse's neck for control, 174–75.

26. Liddell Hart, *Strategy*, 40.

27. Harold Winters, *Battling the Elements: Weather and Terrain in the Conduct of War* (Baltimore: Johns Hopkins University Press, 1998), 47, 164.

28. Valerius, *Factorum ac dictorum memorabilium*, bk. 7, 4.2.

29. Cassius, fragment, bk. 15, 57.25.

30. Frontinus, *Strategemata*, bk. 3, 9.1.

31. Valerius, *Factorum ac dictorum memorabilium*, bk. 7, 4.4.

32. O'Connell, *Ghosts of Cannae*, 212.

33. Frontinus, *Strategemata*, bk. 3, 2.3.

34. R. M. Sheldon, "Hannibal's Spies," *Espionage* 2, no. 3 (August 1986): 149–52; Sheldon, "Hannibal's Spies," *International Journal of Intelligence and Counterintelligence (IJIC)* 1, no. 3 (1987): 53–70.

35. Paul Kennedy, *Grand Strategies in War and Peace* (New Haven, CT: Yale University Press, 1991), 79.

36. Fronda, *Between Rome and Carthage*, 330.

37. Juvenal, *Satires*, bk. 10, 147–48, 161–62.

38. Dexter Hoyos, "Hannibal," in *Encyclopedia of Ancient History*, ed. Roger S. Bagnall et al. (Malden, MA: Wiley-Blackwell, 2012), 3057. Hoyos notes correctly other critical assessments such as Jakob Seibert, *Hannibal* (Darmstadt, Ger.: Wissenschaftliche Buchgesellschaft, 1993) and lists these as generally admiring: Lazenby, *Hannibal's War*; Lancel, *Hannibal*; Goldsworthy, *The Fall of Carthage* (Phoenix, 2003); and Barceló, *Hannibal*—with Picard's 1967 *Hannibal* as adulatory.

39. Gianni Granzotto, *Annibale* (Milan, It.: Arnoldo Mondadori Editore, 1980), 310: "*Annibale, tutto sommato, non poteva vincere. Di questo occorre rendersi conto, pur considerando che egli era indubbiamente un uomo di genio superior . . . Se Annibale fu grande, Roman fu ancora piu grande di lui.*" ("Hannibal, after all, could not win. Of this you have to realize, even considering that he was undoubtedly a man of superior genius . . . If Hannibal was great, Rome was far greater.")

BIBLIOGRAPHY

ANCIENT SOURCE TEXTS

Ammianus Marcellinus. *Res Gestae (History of Rome) vols. 1–3.* Translated by J. C. Rolfe. Cambridge, MA: Harvard Loeb Classical Library, 1939–50.

Appian of Alexandria (Appianus Alexandreus, Appianus Alexandrinus). *Roman History 1.* Bk. 6, *The Wars in Spain*; bk. 7, *The Hannibalic War*, 52–58; bk. 8, *The Punic Wars*, 28, 70–136; bk. 11, The *Syrian Wars*, 9–11. Translated by Horace White. Cambridge, MA: Loeb Classical Library, Reprint of Cambridge, MA: Harvard University Press, 1912 edition.

Augustine of Hippo (Aurelius Augustinus Hipponensis), *De Civitate Dei*, bk. 3, 20. Translated by Henry Bettenson, 1972. New York, New York: Penguin Books, 1984 edition.

Aulus Gellius. *Noctes Atticae (Attic Nights).* 5.v.5. Translated by J. C. Rolfe. Cambridge, MA: Loeb Classical Library, Reprint of Cambridge, MA: Harvard University Press, 1927 edition.

Sextus Aurelius Victor. *De Caesaribus* 37.2–3. Translated by H. W. Bird. Liverpool University Press, 1994.

Caesar, Julius. *The Gallic Wars.* Bk. 4, 35. Translated by H. J. Edwards. Cambridge,

MA: Loeb Classical Library, 1966, 224–5, Reprint of Cambridge, MA: Harvard University Press, 1946 edition.

Cato (Marcus Porcius Cato). *Origines.* Translated by M. Chassignet. *Caton: Les Origines.* Fragments. Paris: Collection Budé, les Belles Lettres, 1986.

Cicero (Marcus Tullius Cicero). *De Divinatione (On Divination).* Translated by W. A. Falconer. Cambridge, MA: Loeb Classical Library, 1996), 277–78. Reprint of Cambridge, MA: Harvard University Press, 1923 edition.

———. *de Oratore (On the Orator).* 2.18.74–75. Translated by J. S. Watson. Published by George Bell, London, 1896, text in Perseus Digital Library, Tufts University.

Lucius Coelius Antipater. *Second Punic War* (fragmentary, mainly lost), referenced at times by Cicero, among others. Hans Beck. "Lucius Coleus Antipater" in *Wiley-Blackwell Encyclopaedia of Ancient History,* 2012.

Dio Cassius (Cassius Dio). Fragments, Book 11. 10–13, 15 Translated by Earnest Cary. Cambridge, MA: Loeb Classical Library, Reprint of Cambridge, MA: Harvard University Press, 1914 edition.

Diodorus Siculus. *Bibliotheca Historia (Library of History).* 12 vols. Translated by C. H. Oldfather, Charles Sherman, Russell Geer, C. Bradford Welles, Frances Walton. Cambridge, MA: Loeb Classical Library, Reprint of Cambridge, MA: Harvard University Press, 1933–1963.

Frontinus, Sextus Julius. *Strategems, Aqueducts of Rome.* Translated by C. E. Bennett. Cambridge, MA: Loeb Classical Library, Reprint of Cambridge, MA: Harvard University Press, 1925.

———. *Stratagemata.* Bks. 1–4. Translated by Charles E. Bennett. New York, New York: Palatine Press, 2015.

Horace (Quintus Horatius Flaccus). *Epode* 9, *Ode* 3. Translated by C. E. Bennett. Cambridge, MA: Loeb Classical Library, 1995). Reprint of Cambridge, MA: Harvard University Press, 1968.

Justin (Marcus Junianus Justinus). *Epitome of Pompeius Trogus.* 29.3.7, 30.3.2, 4.14, 31.1–7.9, 32.4.1–12. Translation by J. C. Yardley. American Philological Association Classical Resources 1st Edition, Book 3. Atlanta: Scholars Press and Oxford University Press, 1994.

Juvenal. *Satires.* Bk. 3, 126ff.; bk. 7, 161; bk. 10, 147–188. Juvenal, *The Sixteen Satires.* Translated by Peter Green, 1982 reprinting. New York, New York: Penguin Books, 1967 edition.

Livy (Titus Livius). *Ab Urbe Condita (The History of Rome).* Bks. 21–22, edited by T. A. Dorey. Leipzig, Ger.: Teubner, 1971.

———. *Ab Urbe Condita*. Bks. 23–25, edited by T. A. Dorey. Leipzig, Ger.: Teubner, 1976.

———. *Ab Urbe Condita*. Bks. 26–27, edited by P. G. Walsh. Leipzig, Ger.: Teubner, 1989.

———. *Ab Urbe Condita*. Bks. 27–30, edited by P. G. Walsh. Leipzig, Ger.: Teubner, 1986.

———. *Hannibal's War*. Bks. 21–30. Translated by J. C. Yardley. Introduction and notes by Dexter Hoyos. Oxford: Oxford University Press, 2009.

———. Livy. *The War with Hannibal*. Translated by Aubrey de Selincourt. Middlesex, UK: Penguin Books, 1983. Reprint of Baltimore: Penguin Books, 1965 edition.

Lucan (*Marcus Annaeus Lucanus*), *Pharsalia*. Bk. 1, line 38. Translation by Jane Wilson Joyce. Ithaca: Cornell University Press, 1993, 4.

Nepos, Cornelius (Cornelius Nepos). *Vitae (Life of Hannibal 1–13)*. Albert Fleckeisen, ed. Leipzig, Ger.: Teubner, 1886.

Ovid (P. Ovidius Naso). *Fasti*. Translated by Sir James G. Frazer. Cambridge, MA: Loeb Classical Library, 1987). Reprint of Cambridge, MA: Harvard University Press, 1931 edition.

———. *Metamorphoses*, 1983 reprinting. Translation by Mary Innes. New York, New York: Penguin Books, 1955 edition.

Plato (Platon). *Laws* I.625e. Translated by Thomas Pangle. Chicago: University of Chicago Press, 1988.

Pliny the Elder (Gaius Plinius Secundus). *Naturalis Historia* (*The Natural History*). *Natural History: A Selection*. Translated by John F. Healy. New York: Penguin Classics, 1991 reprint.

———. Translated by H. Rackham, vols, 1–5, 9; W. H. S. Jones, vols. 6–8; D. E. Eichholz, vol 10. Cambridge, MA: Loeb Classical Library, Reprint of Cambridge, MA: Harvard University Press, 1938–62.

Plutarch (Plutarchos, later Lucius Mestrius Plutarchus). Plutarch, *Lives*, vol. 6. *Life of Aemilius Paullus*. Translated by Bernadotte Perrin. Cambridge, MA: Loeb Classical Library, Reprint of Cambridge, MA: Harvard University Press, 1918.

———. *Life of Fabius Maximus*. Plutarch, *Lives*, vol. 3. Translated by Bernadotte Perrin. Cambridge, MA: Loeb Classical Library, Reprint of Cambridge, MA: Harvard University Press, 1916.

———. *Life of Flamininus. Maximus*. Plutarch, *Lives*, vol. 10. Translated by Bernadotte Perrin. Cambridge, MA: Loeb Classical Library, Reprint of Cambridge, MA: Harvard University Press, 1921.

———. *Life of Lucullus.* Plutarch, *Lives,* vol. 2. Translated by Bernadotte Perrin. Cambridge, MA: Loeb Classical Library, Reprint of Cambridge, MA: Harvard University Press, 1914.

———. *Life of Marcellus.* Plutarch, *Lives,* vol. 5. Translated by Bernadotte Perrin. Cambridge, MA: Loeb Classical Library, Reprint of Cambridge, MA: Harvard University Press, 1917.

———. *Plutarch's Lives.* Vol. 1. Edited by Arthur Hugh Clough. New York: Modern Library, 1992.

Polybius (Polybios). *The Histories.* Bks. 3–12. Translated by W. R. Paton. Revised by F. W. Walbank and Christian Habicht. Cambridge, MA: Harvard Loeb Classical Library, 2010.

———. *The Histories.* Translated by Robin Waterfield. Notes by Brian McGing. New York: Oxford University Press, 2010.

Seneca. *De Ira (On Anger).* Seneca: Moral and Political Essays. Translated by John M. Cooper. Cambridge Texts in the History of Political Thought. Cambridge: Cambridge University Press, 1995.

Silenus Calatinus (of Caelacte). *Frag.Gr.H.*175 (preserved mostly via Cicero). Felix Jacoby. *Die Fragmente der greichischen Historiker,* 1923–59 (also on http://www.attalus.org/translate/fgh.html#175.0).

Silius Italicus. *Punica.* Bks. 1–17. vols. 1–2. Translated by J. D. Duff. Cambridge, MA: Harvard Loeb Classical Library, Reprint of Cambridge, MA: Harvard University Press,1934.

Sosylus of Lacedaemon. *Frag.Gr.H* 176. Felix Jacoby. *Die Fragmente der greichischen Historiker,* 1923–59 (also on http://www.attalus.org/translate /fgh.html#176.0).

Stesichorus. Frag. 4. *Greek Lyric,* vol. 3. Translated by David A. Campbell. Cambridge, MA: Loeb Classical Library, Reprint of Cambridge, MA: Harvard University Press, 1991 edition.

Strabo (Strabon). *Geography.* Bks. 5 and 11. *The Geography of Strabo.* Translated by Duane Roller. Cambridge: Cambridge University Press, 2014.

Thucydides (Thoukudides). *History of the Peloponnesian War.* Bks. 3, 7, and 8. Translated by Rex Warner. London: Penguin Classics, 1954.

Valerius Antias. Fragments. T. J. Cornell ed. *The Fragments of the Roman Historians.* Oxford: Oxford University Press, 2014.

Valerius (Valerius Maximus). *Factorum ac dictorum memorabilium. (Memorable Doings and Sayings)* Bks. 1–9. (vols, 1–2). Translated D. R. Shackleton Baily.

Cambridge, MA: Loeb Classical Library, Reprint of Cambridge, MA: Harvard University Press, 2000.

Vegetius (Publius Flavius Vegetius Renaus. *De Re Militari (The Military Institutions of the Romans)*, 1. John Clarke, tr. 1767. M. Brevik update, 2001 (http://www.digitalattic.org/home/war/vegetius/).

Marcus Velleius Paterculus. *History of Rome (Res Gestae Divi Augusti)* 1.2.3. Translated by Frederick W. Shipley. Cambridge, MA: Loeb Classical Library, Reprint of Cambridge, MA: Harvard University Press, 1924.

Virgil (Publius Vergilius Maro). *Eclogues, Georgics, Aeneid 1–6. Aeneid.* Bk. 4. Translated by H. R. Fairclough. Cambridge, MA: Loeb Classical Library, Reprint of Cambridge, MA: Harvard University Press, 1916.

Xenophon. *Hipparchikos.(The Art of Horsemanship).* Translated by Morris H. Morgan. Mineola, New York: Dover Publications 2006 revised edition (originally Boston: Little Brown and Company 1893).

MODERN TEXTS

Abelli, Leonardo, ed. " . . . *de Cossurensibus et Poenis navalem egit* . . ." *Archeologia subaquea a Pantelleria*, Ricerca series maijor 3. Ante Quem, Sicilia, 2012.

Adams, Colin, and Ray Laurence, eds. *Travel and Geography in the Roman Empire*. London: Routledge, 2001.

Adkins, Roy, and Leslie Adkins. *Dictionary of Roman Religion*. New York: Oxford University Press, 2001.

Adcock, F. E. *The Greek and Macedonian Art of War*. Sather Classical Lectures. Berkeley: University of California Press, 1957. See esp. chap. 4, "Cavalry, Elephants, and Siegecraft."

Ager, Derek. "From Where Did Hannibal's Elephants Come?" *New Scientist* 103, no. 1420 (September 6, 1984): 37.

Alfieri, N. "Sena Gallica." In *Princeton Encyclopedia of Classical Sites*, edited by Richard Stillwell, William L. MacDonald, and Marian Holland McAlister. Princeton, NJ: Princeton University Press, 1976.

Africa, Thomas W. "The One-Eyed Man Against Rome: An Exercise in Euhemerism." *Historia: Zeitschrift für Alte Geschichte* 19, no. 5 (1970): 528–38.

Allan, Nigel J. R. "Accessibility and Altitudinal Zonation Models of Mountains." *Mountain Research and Development* 6, no. 3 (1986): 185–94.

Allen, Stephen. *Celtic Warrior 300 BC–AD 100*. Oxford: Osprey, 2001.

Ameling, Walter. *Karthago: Studien zu Militär, Staat und Gesellschaft. Vestigia: Beiträge zur Alten Geschichte* 45. Munich: C. H. Beck Verlag, 1993.

Amoros, J. L., R. Lunar, and P. Tavira. "Jarosite: A Silver-Bearing Mineral of the Gossan of Rio Tínto (Huelva) and La Unión (Cartagena)." *Mineralium Deposita* 16 (1981): 205–13.

Annequin, C., and G. Barruol. "Les grandes traversées des Alpes: l'itinéraire d'Hannibal." In *Atlas Culturel des Alpes Occidentales: de la Préhistoire à la fin du Moyen Age*, edited by C. Annequin and M. Le Berre. Paris: Picard, 2004.

Arnold, M. "The Radiative Effects of Clouds and Their Impact on Climate." *Bulletin of the American Meteorological Society* 72 (June 1991): 795–813.

Arnold, Thomas. *The Second Punic War Being Chapters of the History of Rome.* Edited by William T. Arnold. London: Macmillan, 1886.

Ascoli, Albert R. "Pyrrhus' Rules: Playing with Power from Boccaccio to Machiavelli." *Modern Language Notes* 114, no. 1 (1999): 14–57.

Astin, A. E. "Saguntum and the Origins of the Second Punic War." *Latomus* 26, no. 3 (July–September 1967): 577–96.

Aubet, M. E. *The Phoenicians and the West: Politics, Colonies and Trade.* 2nd ed. Cambridge: Cambridge University Press, 1991.

Austin, N. J. E., and N. B. Rankov. *Exploration: Military and Political Intelligence in the Roman World from the Second Punic War to the Battle of Adrianopole.* London: Routledge, 1998.

Azan, Paul. *Hannibal dans les Alpes.* Paris, 1902.

Bagnall, Nigel. *The Punic Wars: Rome, Carthage, and the Struggle for the Mediterranean*, London: Macmillan, 2005.

Baker, G. P. *Hannibal.* New York: Cooper Square Press, 1999.

Bamford, Andrew. *Sickness, Suffering, and the Sword: The British Regiment on Campaign, 1808–1815.* Norman: University of Oklahoma Press, 2013.

Barceló, Pedro. *Hannibal: Stratege und Staatsman.* Stuttgart, Ger.: Klett-Cotta, 2004.

Baronowski, D. W. "Roman Military Forces in 225 BC (Polybius 2.23–24)." *Historia: Zeitschrift für Alte Geschichte* 42 (1993): 183–202.

Bath, Tony. *Hannibal's Campaigns.* Cambridge: Patrick Stephens, 1981.

Batty, Roger. "Mela's Phoenician Geography." *Journal of Roman Studies* 90 (2000): 70–94.

Beck, Hans. "The Reasons for the [Second Punic] War." Chap. 13 in *A Companion to the Punic Wars*, edited by Dexter Hoyos. Malden, MA: Wiley-Blackwell, 2011.

Bell, M. J. V. "Tactical Reform in the Roman Republican Army." *Historia: Zeitschrift für Alte Geschichte* 14, no. 4 (October 1965): 404–22.

Ben Khader, Aicha Ben Abed, and David Soren. *Carthage: A Mosaic of Ancient Tunisia*. New York: American Museum of Natural History in association with W. W. Norton, 1987.

Benz, Franz. *Personal Names in the Phoenician and Punic Inscriptions*. Rome: Pontifical Institute, 1982.

Berlin, Andrea J. "From Monarchy to Markets: The Phoenicians to Hellenistic Palestine." *Bulletin of the American Schools of Oriental Research* 306 (May 1997): 75–88.

Berneder, Helmut. *Magna Mater-Kult und Sibyllinen: Kulttransfer und annalistische Geschichtsfiktion*. Innsbruck, Aus.: Institut für Sprachen und Literaturen de Universität Innsbruck, 2004.

Berrocal Caparros, María del Carmen. "Poblamiento romano en la Sierra Minera de Cartagena," *Pallas* 50 (1999): 183–93.

Beschaouch, Azedine. "De l'Africa latino-chrétienne à l'Ifriqiya arabo-musulmane: questions de toponymie." *Comptes-rendus des séances de l'Académie des Inscriptions et Belles-Lettres (CRAI)* 130, no. 3 (1986): 530–49.

Bickerman, Elias J. "An Oath of Hannibal." *Transactions and Proceedings of the American Philological Association (TAPA)* 75 (1944): 87–102.

Billot, Frances. "Representations of Hannibal: A Comparison of Iconic Themes and Events from the Life and Times of Hannibal." PhD diss., University of Auckland, 2009.

Blanco, A., and J. M. Luzón. "Pre-Roman Silver-Miners at Riotinto." *Archaeology* 43 (1969): 124–31.

Boardman, John, Jasper Griffin, and Oswyn Murray, eds. *The Oxford History of the Roman World*. Oxford: Oxford University Press, 2001. Reprint of New York: Oxford University Press, 1986 edition.

Boccaccio, Giovanni. *De Casibus Virorum Illustrium*. Vol. 9. *Tutte le opere di Giovanni Boccaccio* under guidance of Pier Giorgio Ricci and Vittorio Zaccaria, ed. Vittore Branca, 12 vols. I Classici Mondadori. Milan, It.: Arnoldo Mondadori, 1983.

———. "Hannibal." *The Fates of Illustrious Men*. Bk. 5. Translated by Lewis Brewer Hall. New York: Frederick Ungar, 1965.

Bocquet, Aimé. *Hannibal chez les Allobroges (Le grand traversée des Alpes, deuxième partie)*. Montmélian, Fr.: La Fontaine de Siloé, 2009.

Bonnet, Corinne. "On Gods and Earth: The Tophet and the Construction of a New Identity in Punic Carthage." In *Cultural Identity in the Peoples of the Ancient Mediterranean,* edited by Erich Gruen. Los Angeles: Getty Research Institute, 2011.

Booms, Dirk, Belinda Crerar, and Susan Raikes. *Roman Empire: Power and People.* London: British Museum Press, 2013.

Boularès, Habib. *Hannibal.* Paris: Librairie Académique Perrin, 2000.

Bradford, Ernle. *Hannibal.* London: Folio Society, 1998. Reprint of New York: McGraw-Hill, 1981 edition.

Brizzi, Giovanni. "Carthage and Hannibal in Roman and Greek Memory." Chap. 27 in *A Companion to the Punic Wars,* edited by Dexter Hoyos. Malden, MA: Wiley-Blackwell, 2011.

———. *I sistemi informativi dei Romani.* Historia Einzelschriften 39. Wiesbaden, Ger., 1982.

———. "L'armée et la guerre." In *La civilization phénicienne et punique: Manuel de recherche.* Handbuch der Orientalistik, sec. 1: Near and Middle East. Vol. 20. Edited by V. Krings. Leiden, Neth.: E. J. Brill, 1995.

———. *Scipione e Annibale.* Rome: Editori Laterza, 2007.

Brody, Aaron. "From the Hills of Adonis Through the Pillars of Hercules: Recent Advances in the Archaeology of Canaan and Phoenicia." *Near Eastern Archaeology* 65, no. 1 (2002): 69–80.

Brown, F., S. R. Driver, and C. A. Briggs. *A Hebrew and English Lexicon of the Old Testament.* Oxford: Clarendon Press, 1951.

Brown, S. *Late Carthaginian Child Sacrifice and Sacrificial Monuments in Their Mediterranean Context.* Sheffield: JSOT Press, 1981.

Bruscino, Thomas. "Naturally Clausewitzian: U.S. Army Theory and Education from Reconstruction to the Interwar Years." *Journal of Military History* 77, no. 4 (2013): 1251–75, esp. 1252–53.

Cairns, Francis. "Horace Epode 9: Some New Interpretations." *Illinois Classical Studies* 8, no. 1 (1983): 80–93.

"Casilinum." In *Brill's Encyclopaedia of the Ancient World (Brill's New Pauly),* edited by H. Cancik, H. Schneider, and M. Landfester. Leiden, Neth: E. J. Brill, 2012.

Casson, Lionel. *Travel in the Ancient World.* Baltimore: Johns Hopkins University Press, 1994.

Caven, Brian M. "Hannibal." In *The Oxford Companion to Classical Civilization,* edited by Simon Hornblower and Antony Spawforth. Oxford: Oxford University Press, 1998.

——. *The Punic Wars.* London: Weidenfeld and Nicholson, 1980.

Chamorro, Javier G. "Survey of Archaeological Research on Tartessos." *American Journal of Archaeology* 91, no. 2 (April 1987): 197–232.

Champion, Craige B. "Polybius and the Punic Wars." Chap. 6 in *A Companion to the Punic Wars,* edited by Dexter Hoyos. Malden, MA: Wiley-Blackwell, 2011.

Charles, Michael B., and Peter Rhodan. "*Magister Elephantorum*: A Reappraisal of Hannibal's Use of Elephants." *Classical World* 100, no. 4 (2007): 363–89.

Chevallier, Raymond. Review of *Hannibal,* by G. C. Picard. *L'Antiquité Classique* 36, no. 2 (1967): 730–33.

Christ, Karl, ed. *Hannibal.* Darmstadt, Ger.: Wissenschaftliche Buchgesellschaft, 1974.

——. "Probleme um Hannibal." In *Hannibal,* edited by Karl Christ. Darmstadt, Ger.: Wissenschaftliche Buchgesellschaft, 1974.

——. "Zur Beurteilung Hannibals." *Historia: Zeitschrift fur Alte Geschichte* 17 (1968): 463–65.

Christman, Bruce. "The Emperor as Philosopher." *Bulletin of the Cleveland Museum of Art* 74, no. 3 (1987): 100–13.

Claerhout, Inge, and John Devreker. *Pessinous: Sacred City of the Anatolian Mother Goddess—An Archaeological Guide.* Istanbul: Homer Kitabevi, 2008.

Clifford, Richard, "Phoenician Religion," *Bulletin of the American Society of Oriental Religion* 279 (1990).

Colin, Jean Lambert Alphonse. *Annibal en Gaule.* Charleston, SC: Nabu Press, 2010. Reprint of Paris: Librairie Militaire R. Chapelot et cie, 1904 edition.

Collins, Roger. *Spain: An Oxford Archaeological Guide.* Oxford: Oxford University Press, 1998.

Connolly, Peter. *Greece and Rome at War.* London: Greenhill Books, 2006. Reprint of Greenhill Books, 1998 edition.

Cooke, George Albert. *A Textbook of North Semitic Inscriptions: Moabite, Hebrew, Phoenician, Aramaic, Nabataean, Palmyrene, Jewish.* "Suffete." Oxford: Clarendon Press, 1903.

Cooper, Emmanuel. *Ten Thousand Years of Pottery.* 45th ed. Philadelphia: University of Pennsylvania Press, 2000.

Cornell, T., B. Rankov, and P. A. G. Sabin, eds. "The Second Punic War: A Reappraisal." Special issue, *Bulletin of the Institute of Classical Studies* 41, no. S67 (February 1996): *vii–xv,* 1–117.

Coss, Edward J. "Review of A. Bamford. *Sickness, Suffering and the Sword,* Oklahoma, 2013." *Journal of Military History* 78. no. 1 (2014): 366–67.

Cramer, J. A. *A Dissertation on the Passage of Hannibal over the Alps*. London: J. W. Parker and G. and W. B. Whittaker, 1820, *xix*.

Crocq, Marc-Antoine, and Louis Crocq. "From Shell Shock and War Neuroses to Posttraumatic Stress Disorder: A History of Psychotraumology." *Dialogues in Clinical Neuroscience* 2, no. 1 (2000): 47–55.

Croke, Vicki Constantine. *Elephant Company*. New York: Random House, 2014.

Cunliffe, Barry. *The Ancient Celts*. Oxford: Oxford University Press, 1997.

———, ed. *The Oxford Illustrated Prehistory of Europe*. Oxford: Oxford University Press, 1994.

D'Amico, Robert, Dennis Lynn, and Eric S. Wexler. "Munitions of the Mind: Strategic Information Operations." *Strategic Review* 29, no. 1 (2001): 49–57.

Dalaine, Laura, and Jean-Pascal Jospin. *Hannibal et les Alpes: une traversée, un mythe*. Grenoble, Fr.: Musée Dauphinois, 2011. (Also see Jospin.)

———. "Mais par où est donc passé Hannibal?" *L'Alpe* 54 (Autumn 2011): 70–76.

Daly, Gregory. *Cannae: The Experience of Battle in the Second Punic War*. London: Routledge, 2002.

Dangréaux, Bernard. "Irréductibles Gaulois des Alpes." *L'Alpe* 54 (Autumn 2011): 18–21.

David, Jean-Michel. *The Roman Conquest of Italy*. Translated by Antonia Nevill. Oxford: Blackwell, 1996. First published 1994 by Paris: Aubier.

Davidson, James. "The Gaze in Polybius' Histories." *Journal of Roman Studies* 81 (1991): 10–24.

Davies, Penelope J. E. "Pollution Propriety and Urbanism in Republican Rome." In *Rome, Pollution and Propiety: Dirt, Disease and Hygiene in the Eternal City from Antiquity to Modernity*, edited by M. Bradley. Cambridge: Cambridge University Press for the British School at Rome, 2012.

Davis, Paul K. *100 Decisive Battles: From Ancient Times to the Present*. Oxford: Oxford University Press, 2001.

———. *Masters of the Battlefield: Great Commanders from the Classical Age to the Napoleonic Era*. Oxford: Oxford University Press, 2013.

Dawson, A. "Hannibal and Chemical Warfare." *Classical Journal* 63, no. 3 (1967): 117–25.

de Beer, Gavin. *Alps and Elephants: Hannibal's March*. London: Bles, 1955.

———. *Hannibal: The Struggle for Power in the Mediterranean*. London: Thames and Hudson, 1969.

Delbruck, Hans. *Warfare in Antiquity.* Vol. 1. Lincoln: University of Nebraska Press, 1990.

Denholm, Justin, and Patrick Hunt. "Hannibal's Ophthalmia." Unsubmitted article under peer review by various medical journals, 2014.

Derow, P. S. "Polybius, Rome and the East." *Journal of Roman Studies* 69 (1979): 1–15.

Desmond, William. "Lessons of Fear: A Reading of Thucydides." *Classical Philology* 101, no. 4 (2006): 359–79.

Diakonoff, I. M. "The Naval Power and Trade of Tyre." *Israel Exploration Journal* 42, nos. 3/4 (1992): 168–93.

Diana, Bettina. "Annibale e il Passagio degli Apennini." *Aevum* 61 (1987): 108–12.

Dietler, Michael, and Carolina López-Ruiz. *Colonial Encounters in Ancient Iberia: Phoenician, Greek and Indigenous Relations.* Chicago: University of Chicago Press, 2009. See esp. chaps 7–9 on Phoenicians.

Dixon, K. R., and Pat Southern. *The Roman Cavalry: From the First to the Third Century AD.* London: Batsford, 1992.

Dodge, Theodore Ayrault. *Hannibal.* New introduction by Ian M. Cuthbertson. New York: Barnes & Noble Books, 2005. Reprint of Cambridge, MA: Riverside Press, 1891 edition.

Domergue, C. *Les mines de la Péninsule Ibérique dans l'antiquité romaine.* Collection de l'École française de Rome, 127, Rome, 1990.

Dommelen, Peter van. "Carthago Nova (Cartagena)." In *The Encyclopedia of Ancient History,* edited by Roger S. Bagnall, Kai Brodersen, Craige B. Champion, Andrew Erskine, and Sabine R. Huebner. Malden, MA: Wiley-Blackwell, 2012.

Dorey, T. A. "Macedonians at the Battle of Zama." *American Journal of Philology* 78, no. 2 (1957): 185–87.

Drews, Robert. "Phoenicians, Carthage and the Spartan Eunomia." *American Journal of Philology* 100, no. 1 (Spring 1979): 45–58.

Clausewitz, General Carl von. *On War.* Berlin, Ferdinand Dümmler, 1832.

Dunbabin, T. J. *The Western Greeks: The History of Sicily and South Italy from the Foundation of the Greek Colonies to 480 BC.* Oxford: Oxford University Press, 1999. Reprint of Oxford: Clarendon Press, 1948 edition.

Dunkle, J. Roger. "The Greek Tyrant and Roman Political Invective of the Late Republic." *Transactions of the American Philological Association* (*TAPA*) 98 (1967): 151–71, esp. 156–57.

Dvornik, Francis. *Origins of Intelligence Services: The Ancient Near East, Persia,*

Greece, Rome, Byzantium, the Arab Muslim Empires, the Mongol Empire, China, Muscovy. New Brunswick, NJ: Rutgers University Press, 1974.

Eckstein, A. M. Review of *Hannibal's Dynasty*, by B. D. Hoyos. *Classical Review* 55, no. 1, new series (2005): 263–66.

———. "Hannibal at New Carthage: Polybius 3.15 and the Power of Irrationality." *Classical Philology* 84, no. 1 (1989): 1–15.

———. *Rome Enters the Greek East: From Anarchy to Hierarchy in the Hellenistic Mediterranean 230–170 BC*. Malden, MA: Wiley-Blackwell, 2012.

———. "Rome, Saguntum and the Ebro Treaty." *Emerita* 55 (January 1, 1984): 51–68.

Edmonson, J. C. *Two Industries in Roman Lusitania: Mining and Garum Production*. International Series 362. Oxford: British Archaeological Reports (BAR), 1987.

Edwards, Jacob. "The Irony of Hannibal's Elephants." *Latomus* 60, no. 4 (2001): 900–905.

Elting, Colonel John R. *The Super-Strategists: Great Captains, Theorists and Fighting Men Who Have Shaped the History of Warfare*. New York: Charles Scribner's Sons, 1985.

Elton, Hugh. *Frontiers of the Roman Empire*. Bloomington: Indiana University Press; London: Batsford, 1996.

Engels, Donald. *Alexander the Great and the Logistics of the Macedonian Army*. Berkeley: University of California Press, 1978.

Ennabli, A. *Carthage: Le site archéologique*. Tunis: Cérès, 1993.

———, ed. *Pour Sauver Carthage: Exploration et conservation de la cité punique, romaine et byzantine*. Tunis: UNESCO, 1992.

Erdkamp, Paul, ed. *A Companion to the Roman Army*. Oxford: Wiley-Blackwell, 2010. First published 2007 by Malden, MA: Blackwell.

———. *Hunger and the Sword: Warfare and Food Supply in the Roman Republican Wars 264–30 BC*. Dutch Monographs on Ancient History and Archaeology 20. Leiden, Neth.: E. J. Brill, 1998.

———. "Manpower and Food Supply in the First and Second Punic Wars." Chapter 4 in *A Companion to the Punic Wars*, edited by Dexter Hoyos. Malden, MA: Wiley-Blackwell, 2011.

———. "Polybius, the Ebro Treaty and the Gallic Invasion of 225 BCE." *Classical Philology* 104 (2009): 495–510.

Errington, R. M. "Rome Against Philip and Antiochus." Chap. 8 in *The Cambridge Ancient History*. 2nd ed. Vol. 8, *Rome and the Mediterranean to 133*

BC. Edited by A. E Astin, F. W. Walbank, M. W. Frederiksen, and R. M. Ogil-vie. Cambridge: Cambridge University Press, 1990.

Erskine, Andrew. "Hannibal and the Freedom of the Italians." *Hermes* 121, no. 1 (1993): 58–62.

Evans, Harry B. *Water Distribution in Ancient Rome: The Evidence of Frontinus.* Ann Arbor: University of Michigan Press, 1997.

Fagan, Garrett, and Matthew Trundle, eds. *New Perspectives on Ancient Warfare.* History of Warfare 59. Leiden, Neth.: E. J. Brill, 2010.

Fantar, M'hamed-Hassine. *Carthage: Approche d'une civilization.* Vols. 1 and 2. Tunis: ALIF, 1993.

———. *Carthage: La cité punique.* Túnez/ALIF: les Éditions de la Méditerranée, 1995.

———. "Death and Transfiguration: Punic Culture After 146." Chap. 25 in *A Companion to the Punic Wars,* edited by Dexter Hoyos. Malden, MA: Wiley-Blackwell, 2011.

Fields, Nic. *Carthaginian Warrior 264–146 BC.* Oxford: Osprey, 2010.

———. *Hannibal.* Oxford: Osprey, 2010.

———. *The Roman Army of the Punic Wars 264–146 BC.* Oxford: Osprey, 2007.

Finsinger, Walter, and Willy Tinner. "Holocene Vegetation and Land-Use Changes in Response to Climatic Changes in the Forelands of the Southwestern Alps, Italy." *Journal of Quaternary Science* 21, no. 3 (March 2003): 243–58.

Fliegel, Stephen. "A Little-Known Celtic Stone Head." *Bulletin of the Cleveland Museum of Art* 77, no. 3 (March 1990): 82–103.

Framarin, P. "La ripresa defli scavi e l'aggiornamento della topographia del sito di Plan de Jupiter. I sondaggi 2000 e 2007." In *Alpis Poenina, Grand Saint-Bernard: Une Voie À Travers l'Europe,* edited by L. Appolonia, F. Wiblé, and P. Framarin. Aosta, It.: Interreg IIIA, Italia-Svizzera, 2008.

Francese, Christopher. *Ancient Rome in So Many Words.* New York: Hippocrene Books, 2007.

Freedman, Lawrence. *Strategy: A History.* Oxford: Oxford University Press, 2013.

———, ed. *War.* Oxford Readers. Oxford: Oxford University Press, 1994.

Fronda, Michael P. *Between Rome and Carthage: Southern Italy During the Second Punic War.* Cambridge: Cambridge University Press, 2010.

———. "Hannibal: Tactics, Strategy, and Geostrategy." Chap. 14 in *A Companion to the Punic Wars,* edited by Dexter Hoyos. Malden, MA: Wiley-Blackwell, 2011.

———. "Hegemony and Rivalry: The Revolt of Capua Revisited." *Phoenix* 61, nos. 1/2 (Spring/Summer 2007): 83–108.

———. Review of *Hannibal,* by Robert Garland. *Mouseion: Journal of the Classical Association of Canada* 10, no. 3 (2010): 454–56.

Gabriel, Richard. *Hannibal: The Military Biography of Rome's Greatest Enemy.* Washington, DC: Potomac Books, 2011.

———. *Scipio Africanus: Rome's Greatest General.* Washington, DC: Potomac Books, 2008.

Galbert, Geoffroy de. *Hannibal en Gaul.* Grenoble, Fr.: Éditions de Belledonne, 2006.

———. *Hannibal et César dans les Alpes.* Grenoble, Fr.: Éditions de Belledonne, 2008.

———. *Hannibal, Scipion et les Guerres Puniques dans l'Art et L'Archéologie.* La Buisse, Fr.: Edition La Magnanerie, 2013.

Garland, Robert. *Hannibal.* Ancients in Action. London: Bristol Classical Press, 2010.

Gascó, C. A. "Saguntum [Sagunto]." In *The Encyclopedia of Ancient History.* Malden, MA: Wiley-Blackwell, 2012.

Gastaldi, Enrica Culasso, and Giovanella Cresci Marrone. "I Taurini ai piedi delle Alpi." In *Storia di Torino dalla Preistoria al commune medievale,* vol. 1, ed, Giuseppe Sergi (Torino, It: Accademia della Scienze di Torino, 1997), 95–134, esp. Gastaldi, "Annibale e i Taurini," 116–21.

Gattinoni, F. Landucci. "Annibale sulle Alpi." *Aevum* 43 (1984): 38ff.

Gibbon, Edward. *The History of the Decline and Fall of the Roman Empire.* Vols. 1–4. New York: Harper & Brothers, 1836. First published 1776–1788 by London: Strahan & Cadell.

Gibbons, Wess, and Teresa Moreno. *Geology of Spain.* Bath, UK: Geological Society of London, 2002.

Giumlia-Mair, Alessandra. "Techniques and Composition of Equestrian Statues in Raetia." In *From the Parts to the Whole,* vol. 2, *Acta of the 13th International Bronze Congress at Cambridge, Massachusetts, 1996,* supplement 39, *Journal of Roman Archaeology* (2002): 93–97, esp. 95.

Glover, R. F. "The Tactical Handling of the Elephant." *Greece & Rome* 17 (1948): 1–11.

Golden, Gregory K. "Emergency Measures: Crisis and Response in the Roman Republic (From the Gallic Sack to the Tumultus of 43 BC)." PhD diss., Classics, Rutgers University, 2008.

Goetzmann, William N. and K. Geert Rouwenhorst, eds. *The Origins of Value: The Financial Innovations That Created Modern Capital.* New York: Oxford University Press, 2005.

Goldsworthy, Adrian. *Cannae: Hannibal's Greatest Victory.* London: Cassell, 2001.

———. *The Fall of Carthage.* Phoenix, 2003.

———. *The Punic Wars.* London: Cassell, 2000.

Goukowsky, P. *Appien, Livre Hannibal.* Paris: CUF (Collection des Universités de France), 1998.

Grant, Michael. *The Army of the Caesars.* New York: Evans, 1974.

Granzotto, Gianni. *Annibale.* Milan, It.: Arnoldo Mondadori Editore, 1980.

Gray, Colin S. *Modern Strategy.* Oxford: Oxford University Press, 1999.

Green, Miranda. "A Carved Stone Head from Steep Holm." *Britannia* 24 (1993): 241–42.

———. "The Religious Symbolism of Llyn Cerrig Bach and Other Early Sacred Water Sites." *Holy Wells Journal* 1 (1994).

Green, Peter. *Alexander of Macedon, 356–323 B.C.: A Historical Biography.* Berkeley: University of California Press, 1992. Reprint of Pelican Books, 1974 edition.

Grimal, Pierre. *Le siècle des Scipions: Rome et l'hellénisme au temps des guerres puniques.* 2nd ed. Paris: Aubier, 1975.

Grossman, Janet B. *Greek Funerary Sculpture: Catalogue of the Collections at the Getty Villa.* Los Angeles: J. Paul Getty Museum (Getty Trust), 2002.

Gruen, Erich S. "The Advent of the Magna Mater." Chap. 1 in *Studies in Greek Culture and Roman Policy.* Berkeley: University of California, 1996. First published 1990 by E. J. Brill.

———, ed. *Cultural Identity in the Peoples of the Ancient Mediterranean,* Los Angeles: Getty Research Institute, 2011.

———. *Rethinking the Other in Antiquity.* Martin Classical Lectures. Princeton, NJ: Princeton University Press, 2012.

Haley, S. P. "Livy, Passion and Cultural Stereotypes." *Historia: Zeitschrift für Alte Geschichte* 39, no. 3 (1990): 375–81.

Handel, Michael I. *Masters of War: Classic Strategic Thought.* 3rd ed. London: Routledge, 2000.

Hanson, Victor Davis. *Carnage and Culture: Landmark Battles in the Rise of Western Power.* New York: Anchor Books, 2002. See esp. chap. 4 on Cannae.

Hardie, Colin. "The Origin and Plan of Modern Florence." *Journal of Roman Studies* 55, nos. 1/2 (1965): 122–40.

Hardie, Philip. *Ovid's Poetics of Illusion.* Cambridge: Cambridge University Press, 2002.

Healy, Mark. *Cannae 216 BC: Hannibal Smashes Rome's Army.* Oxford: Osprey, 1994.

Herm, Gerhard. *The Celts*. New York: St. Martin's Press, 1976.

Herschel, Clemens. *Frontinus and the Water Supply of Rome*. New York: Longmans, Green, 1913.

Hitchner, R. Bruce. "Review: Roman Republican Imperialism in Italy and the West." *American Journal of Archaeology* 113, no. 4 (2009): 651–55. See esp. 654.

Hoyos, Dexter. "The Age of Overseas Expansion." In *A Companion to the Roman Army*, edited by Paul Erdkamp. Oxford: Wiley-Blackwell, 2010. First published 2007 by Malden, MA: Blackwell.

――――. "Cannae, Battle of." In *The Encyclopedia of Ancient History*. Malden, MA: Wiley-Blackwell, 2012.

――――. *The Carthaginians*. New York: Routledge, 2010.

――――, ed. *A Companion to the Punic Wars*. Malden, MA: Wiley-Blackwell, 2011.

――――. "Crossing the Durance with Hannibal and Livy: The Route to the Pass." *Klio: Zeitschrift für Alte Geschichte* 88 (2006): 408–65.

――――. "Hannibal." In *The Encyclopedia of Ancient History*. Malden, MA: Wiley-Blackwell, 2012.

――――. *Hannibal: Rome's Greatest Enemy*. Liverpool: Liverpool University Press, 2008.

――――. "Hannibal: What Kind of Genius?" *Greece & Rome* 30, no. 2 (1983): 171–80.

――――. *Hannibal's Dynasty: Power and Politics in the Western Mediterranean, 247–183 BC*. London: Routledge, 2003.

――――. *Mastering the West: Rome and Carthage at War*. Oxford: Oxford University Press, 2015.

――――. "Sluice-gates or Neptune at New Carthage, 209 BC?" *Historia: Zeitschrift für Alte Geschichte* 41 (1992): 124–28.

――――. "Trasimene, Battle of." In *The Encyclopedia of Ancient History*. Malden, MA: Wiley-Blackwell, 2012.

――――. "Zama, Battle of." In *The Encyclopedia of Ancient History*. Malden, MA: Wiley-Blackwell, 2012.

Hoyte, John. *Trunk Road for Hannibal: With an Elephant over the Alps*. London: Geoffroy Bles, 1960.

Hunt, Patrick. *Alpine Archaeology*. New York: Ariel Books, 2007.

――――. "Alpine Archaeology: Some Effects of Climate and Altitude." Archaeolog, a website of Stanford University, last modified December 5, 2005, https://web.stanford.edu/dept/archaeology/cgi-bin/archaeolog/?p=17.

———. "Alps." In *The Encyclopedia of Ancient History*. Malden, MA: Wiley-Blackwell, 2012, 340–41.

———. "Battle of Trasimene." In *Encyclopaedia Britannica*, 2014.

———. "Battle of the Trebbia River." In *Encyclopaedia Britannica*, 2014.

———. "Celtic Iron Age Sword Deposits and Arthur's Lady of the Lake." Archaeolog, a website of Stanford University, last modified February 26, 2008, https://web.stanford.edu/dept/archaeology/cgi-bin/archaeolog/?p=181.

———. "Ebro River." In *The Encyclopedia of Ancient History*, edited by Roger S. Bagnall. Malden, MA: Wiley-Blackwell, 2012.

———. "Gaius Claudius Nero." In *Encyclopaedia Britannica*, 2014.

———. "Hannibal's Engineers and Livy (XXI.36–7) on Burned Rock—Truth or Legend?" Archaeolog, a website of Stanford University, last modified June 6, 2007, https://web.stanford.edu/dept/archaeology/cgi-bin/archaeolog/?p=127.

———. "Hannibal's Theophoric Destiny and the Alps." Archaeolog, a website of Stanford University, 2006.

———. "Lichenometry Dating in the Alps with Hannibal Route Implications."*Atti Accademia Roveretana degli Agiati, a 265*. Series 9. Vol. 5. B. Rovereto, Italy: 2015.

———. "The Locus of Carthage: Compounding Geographical Logic." *African Archaeology Review* 26, no. 2 (2009): 137–54.

———. "Maharbal." In *Encyclopaedia Britannica*, 2014.

———. "Mt. Saphon in Myth and Fact." In *Studia Phoenicia XI: Orientalia Lovaniensia Analacta* 44, edited by E. Lipinski. Leuven, Bel.: Peeters, 1991.

———. "Quintus Fabius Maximus Verrucosus." In *Encyclopaedia Britannica*, 2014.

———. "Rhône." In *The Encyclopedia of Ancient History*. Malden, MA: Wiley-Blackwell, 2012.

———. "Rubicon." In *The Encyclopedia of Ancient History*. Malden, MA: Wiley-Blackwell, 2012.

———. "Scipio Africanus the Elder." In *Encyclopaedia Britannica*, 2014.

———. "Subtle Paronomasia in the *Canticum Canticorum*: Hidden Treasures of the Superlative Poet." *Goldene Äpfel in silbernen Schalen. Beiträge zur Erforschung des Alten Testaments und des Antiken Judentums* 20 (1992): 147–54.

———. "Summus Poeninus on the Grand St. Bernard Pass." *Journal of Roman Archaeology* 11 (1998): 265–74.

———. *Ten Discoveries That Rewrote History*. New York: Penguin/Plume, 2007.

———. "Via Appia." In *The Encyclopedia of Ancient History*. Malden, MA: Wiley-Blackwell, 2012.

———. *When Empires Clash: Twelve Great Battles in Antiquity*. Newport, RI: Stone Tower Books, 2015.

Hunt, Patrick, and Andreea Seicean. "Alpine Archaeology and Paleopathology: Was Hannibal's Army Also Decimated While Crossing the Alps?" Archaeolog, a website of Stanford University, 2007.

Hurst, Henry. "The Sanctuary of Tanit at Carthage in the Roman Period: A Reinterpretation," supplementary series 30, *Journal of Roman Archaeology* (1999).

Hyde, W. W. *Roman Alpine Roads*. Philadelphia: American Philosophical Society, 1935.

Hyland, A. *Equus: The Horse in the Roman World*. New Haven, CT: Yale University Press, 1990.

Isayev, Elena. "Identity and Culture." Chap. 2 in "Inside Ancient Lukania: Dialogues in History and Archaeology," supplement 90, *Bulletin of the Institute of Classical Studies* (2007).

Jaeger, Mary K. "Livy, Hannibal's Monument and the Temple of Juno Lacinia at Croton." *Transactions of the American Philological Association (TAPA)* 136 (2006): 389–414.

Jannelli, Lorena, and Fausto Longo, eds. *The Greeks in Sicily*. San Giovanni Lupatoto, It.: Arsenale Editrice, 2004.

Jiménez-Martínez, J., L. Candela, J. L. García-Aróstegui, and R. Aragón. "Campo de Cartagena, SE Spain 3D Hydro-geological Model: Hydrological Implications." *Geologica Acta* 10, no. 1 (2012): 49–62.

Jolly, A. Richard. "Hannibal's Pass: Results of an Empirical Test." *Alpine Journal* 67, nos. 304/305 (1962): 243–49.

Jospin, Jean-Pascal. *Allobroges, Gaulois et Romains des Alpes*. Grenoble, Fr.: Les Patrimoines, Dauphiné Libéré, 2009.

———. "Des Allobroges Alpins: Souverainetés, Résistances et Autonomies." *Rester Libres! Les expressions de la liberte des Allobroges a nos jours*. Grenoble, Fr.: Musee Dauphinois, 2006.

———. "Les Allobroges: des Gaulois d'Italie du Nord?" *Un air d'Italie: La présence italienne en Isère*. Grenoble, Fr.: Musée Dauphinois, 2011.

———. "Grenoble de Cularo à Gratianopolis." In *Atlas culturel des Alpes occidentales*, edited by C. Jourdain-Annequin. Paris: Picard, 2004.

Jospin, Jean-Pascal, and Laura Dalaine. *Hannibal et les Alpes: une traversée, un mythe*. Grenoble, Fr.: Musée Dauphinois, 2011. (Also see Dalaine.)

Keay, S. J. Review of *Roman Spain: Conquest and Assimilation*, by L. A. Curchin. *Britannia* 24 (1993): 332–33.

———. *Roman Spain: Exploring the Roman World*. Berkeley: University of California Press, 1988.

Keegan, John. *A History of Warfare*. London: Hutchinson, 1993.

Keitel, Elizabeth. "The Influence of Thucydides 7.61–71 on Sallust Cat. 20–21." *Classical Journal* 82, no. 4 (1987): 293–300.

Kennedy, Paul. *Grand Strategies in War and Peace*. New Haven, CT: Yale University Press, 1991.

Keppie, Lawrence. *The Making of the Roman Army: From Republic to Empire*. Norman: University of Oklahoma, 1998. First published 1984 by London: B. T. Batsford.

Kimyongür, A. "The Beast Never Dies: Maurice Gouiran and the Uses of War Memory." *Journal of War and Culture Studies* 4, no. 3 (2011): 372–81.

Kleu, Michael. "Prusias I of Bithynia." In *The Encyclopedia of Ancient History*. Malden, MA: Wiley-Blackwell, 2012.

Kluth, Andreas. *Hannibal and Me: What History's Greatest Military Strategist Can Teach Us About Success and Failure*. New York: Riverhead Books, 2011.

Koch, John T. *Celtic Culture: A Historical Encyclopedia*. Santa Barbara, CA: ABC-Clio, 2006.

Koon, Sam. *Infantry Combat in Livy's Battle Narratives*. British Archaeological Reports (BAR) International Series 2071. Oxford: Archaeopress, 2010.

Koortbojian, Michael. "A Painted Exemplum at Rome's Temple of Liberty." *Journal of Roman Studies* 92 (2002): 33–48.

Kuhle, M., and S. Kuhle. "Hannibal Gone Astray? A Critical Comment on W. C. Mahaney Et Al: 'The Traversette (Italia) Rockfall: Geomorphological Indicator of the Hannibalic Invasion Route' (*Archaeometry* 52, 1 [2010]: 156–72)." *Archaeometry* 54, no. 3 (June 2012): 591–601.

———. "Lost in Translation *or* Can We Still Understand What Polybius Says About Hannibal's Crossing of the Alps?—A Reply to Mahaney (*Archaeometry* 55 [2013]: 1196–204)." *Archaeometry* 57, no. 4 (August 2015): 759–71.

Lancel, Serge. *Carthage: A History*. Translated by Antonia Nevill. Oxford: Blackwell, 1995.

———. *Hannibal*. Translated by Antonia Nevill. Oxford: Blackwell, 1998. First published 1995 by Paris: Librairie Arthème Fayard.

Laufer, Robert S., M. S. Gallops, and Ellen Frey-Wouters. "War Stress and Trauma:

The Vietnam Vet Experience." *Journal of Health and Social Behavior* 25, no. 1 (1985): 65–85.

Laursen, Larry, and Marc Bekoff. "Loxodonta Africana." *Mammalian Species* 92 (January 6, 1978): 1–8.

Lavis-Trafford, M. A. de. *Le Col Alpin Franchi par Hannibal: son identification topographic.* St. Jean-de-Maurienne, Fr.: Libr. Termignon, 1958.

Lazenby, John F. *Hannibal's War: A Military History of the Second Punic War.* Warminster, UK: Aris and Phillips, 1978.

———. "Was Maharbal Right?" In "The Second Punic War: A Reappraisal," edited by T. J. Cornell, B. Rankov, and P. Sabin. Special issue, *Bulletin of the Institute of Classical Studies* 41, no. S67 (February 1996): 39–48.

Lendon, J. E. "The Rhetoric of Combat: Greek Military Theory and Roman Culture in Julius Caesar's Battle Descriptions." *Classical Antiquity* 18, no. 2 (1999): 273–329.

Lewis, Charlton T., and Charles Short. *A Latin Dictionary: Founded on Andrews' Edition of Freund's Latin Dictionary.* Oxford: Oxford University Press, 1956.

Libourel, Jan. "Galley Slaves in the Second Punic War." *Classical Philology* 68, no. 2 (April 1973): 116–19.

Liddell Hart, B. H. "Roman Wars, Hannibal, Scipio, and Caesar." Chap. 3 in *Strategy: The Classic Book on Military Strategy.* 2nd rev. ed. New York: Meridian, 1991. First published 1954 by London: Faber & Faber.

———. *Scipio Africanus: Greater Than Napoleon.* Cambridge, MA: Da Capo Press, 2004. Reprint of Edinburgh: W. Blackwood & Sons, 1926 edition.

Liddell, H. G., and R. Scott. *Greek-English Lexicon.* Oxford: Clarendon Press, 1996.

Lillo, A., and M. Lillo. "On Polybius X.10.12: The Capture of New Carthage." *Historia: Zeitschrift für Alte Geschichte* 37 (1988): 477–80.

Linders, Tullia. *Studies in the Treasure Records of the Temple of Artemis Brauronia Found in Athens.* Stockholm: Svenska Institutet i Athen, 1972.

———. "The Treasures of Other Gods in Athens and Their Functions." *Beiträge zur klassischen Philologie* 62 (1975).

Lintott, Andrew W. *The Constitution of the Roman Republic.* Oxford: Oxford University Press, 1999.

———. "Electoral Bribery in the Roman Republic." *Journal of Roman Studies* 80 (1990): 1–16.

———. "Novi Homines." *Classical Review* 24, no. 2 (1974): 261–63.

Ligt, Luuk de. "Roman Manpower and Recruitment During the Middle Republic." In *A Companion to the Roman Army*, edited by P. Erdkamp. Oxford: Wiley-Blackwell, 2010. First published 2007 by Malden, MA: Blackwell.

Lipinski, E., ed. dir. *Dictionnaire de la civilisation phénicienne et punique.* Paris: Brepols (Turnhout), 1992.

———. *Itineraria Phoenicia.* Leuven, Bel.: Peeters, 2004.

———, ed. *Studia Phoenicia VI: Carthago.* Orientalia Lovaniensia Analecta 26. Leuven, Bel.: Peeters, 1988.

———, ed. *Studia Phoenicia XI: Phoenicians and the Bible.* Orientalia Lovaniensia Analecta 44. Leuven, Bel.: Peeters, 1991.

Lo Cascio, E. "Recruitment and the Size of the Roman Population from the Third to First Century BCE." In *Debating Roman Demography*, edited by Walter Scheidel. Leiden, Neth.: E. J. Brill, 2001.

Lowe, Benedict J. "Polybius 10.10.2 and the Existence of Salt Flats at Carthago Nova." *Phoenix* 54, nos. 1/2 (2000): 39–52.

Ludwig, Emil. *Napoléon.* Translated by Eden and Cedar Paul. New York: Boni and Liveright, 1926.

MacDonald, Eve. *Hannibal: A Hellenistic Life.* New Haven, CT.: Yale University Press, 2015.

Machiavelli, Niccolò. "Of Cruelty and Clemency, and Whether It Is Better to Be Feared Than Loved," chap. 17 in *The Prince.* Cambridge, MA: Harvard Classics, 1914.

Madden, Thomas F., *Empires of Trust: How Rome Built—and America Is Building—a New World.* New York: Penguin, 2008.

Mahaney, William. *Hannibal's Odyssey: Environmental Background to the Alpine Invasion of Italia.* Piscataway, NJ: Gorgias Press, 2009.

Mahaney, William, Barbara Kapran, and Pierre Tricart. "Hannibal and the Alps: Unraveling the Invasion Route." *Geology Today* 24, no. 6 (2008): 223–30.

Mahaney, W., V. Kalm, R. W. Dirszowsky, M. W. Milner, R. Sodhi, R. Beukens, R. Dorn, P. Tricart, S. Schwartz, E. Chamorro-Perez, S. Boccia, R. W. Barendregt, D. H. Krinsley, E. R. Seaquist, D. Merrick, and B. Kapran. "Hannibal's Trek Across the Alps: Geomorphological Analysis of Sites of Geoarchaeological Interest." *Mediterranean Archaeology and Archaeometry* 8, no. 2 (2008): 39–54.

Mahaney, W. C., C. C. R. Allen, P. Pentlavalli, A. Kulakova, J. M. Young, R. W. Dirszowsky, A. West, B. Kelleher, S. Jordan, C. Pulleyblank, S. O'Reilly, B. T. Murphy, K. Lasberg, P. Somelar, M. Garneau, S. A. Finkelstein, M. K. Sobol,

V. Kalm, P. J. M. Costa, R. G. V. Hancock, K. M. Hart, P. Tricart, R. W. Bar-endregt, T. E. Bunch, and M.W. Milner. "Biostratigraphic Evidence Relating to the Age-Old Question of Hannibal's Invasion of Italy, I: History and Geologic Reconstruction." *Archaeometry* (March 8, 2016): 1–15.

Marconi, Clemente. "Sicily and South Italy." In *A Companion to Greek Art.* Blackwell Companions to the Ancient World. Vol. 1. Edited by T. J. Smith and D. Plantzos. Malden, MA: Wiley-Blackwell, 2012.

Martin, James W., George W. Christopher, and Edward M. Eitzen. "History of Biological Weapons: From Poisoned Darts to Intentional Epidemics." In *Medical Aspects of Biological Warfare,* edited by Z. F. Dembek. Washington DC: Borden Institute, Walter Reed Army Medical Center, 2007.

Mattingly, David J., and R. Bruce Hitchner. "Roman Africa: An Archaeological Review." *Journal of Roman Studies* 85 (1995): 165–213. See esp. 200 and 204.

Mattusch, Carol. *Greek Bronze Statuary: From the Beginnings Through Fifth Century B.C.* Ithaca, NY: Cornell University Press, 1989.

Matusiak, Frederick Charles. *Polybius and Livy: The Causes of the Second Punic War.* PhD diss., University of Nebraska, 1992.

Mayor, Adrienne. *Greek Fire, Poison Arrows, and Scorpion Bombs: Biological Warfare in the Ancient World.* London: Duckworth, 2009.

———. *The Poison King: The Life and Legend of Mithradates, Rome's Deadliest Enemy.* Princeton, NJ: Princeton University Press, 2011.

McCall, Jeremiah B. *The Cavalry of the Roman Republic: Cavalry Combat and Elite Reputations in the Middle and Late Republic.* London: Routledge, 2002.

McDonald, A. H. "Hannibal's Passage of the Alps." *Alpine Journal* 61 (1956): 93–101.

McGing, Brian. "Polybius and Herodotus." In *Imperialism, Cultural Politics and Polybius,* edited by Christopher Smith and Liv Mariah Yarrow. Oxford: Oxford University Press, 2012.

Meijer, F. J. "Cato's African Figs." *Mnemosyne: A Journal of Classical Studies* 37, nos. 1/2 (1984): 117–24.

Meister, K. "Annibale in Sileno." *Maia* 22 (1971): 3–9.

Meredith, Martin. *Elephant Destiny: Biography of an Endangered Species in Africa.* New York: Public Affairs, 2001.

Merglen, Albert. *Surprise Warfare: Subversive, Airborne and Amphibious Operations.* Translated by K. Morgan. London: George Allen and Unwin, 1968. First published as *La Guerre de l'Inattendu* 1966 by Paris: Arthaud.

Mertens, Joan R. "Greek Bronzes in the Metropolitan Museum of Art." *Metropolitan Museum of Art Bulletin*, 43, no. 2 (1985): 5–66, esp. 13.

Meyer, Ernst. "Hannibal and Propaganda." Chap. 15 in *A Companion to the Punic Wars*, edited by Dexter Hoyos. Malden, MA: Wiley-Blackwell, 2011.

———. "Hannibals Alpenübergang." In *Hannibal,* edited by Karl Christ. Darmstadt, Ger.: Wissenschaftliche Buchgesellschaft, 1974. Reprint of 1964 and 1958 editions. (Also see Christ.)

———. "Hasdrubal." In *The Encyclopedia of Ancient History*. Malden, MA: Wiley-Blackwell, 2012. "Hannibals Alpenübergang." *Museum Helveticum* 15 (1958): 227–41.

———. "Noch einmal Hannibals Alpenübergang." *Museum Helveticum* 21 (1964): 99–102.

Miles, Richard. *Carthage Must Be Destroyed: The Rise and Fall of an Ancient Civilization.* New York: Viking, 2011.

Millar, Fergus. *The Crowd in Rome in the Late Republic.* Ann Arbor: University of Michigan Press, 1998.

———. "The Phoenician Cities: A Case-Study of Hellenization." *Proceedings of the Cambridge Philological Society* 209 (1983): 55–71.

Mineo, Bernard. "Principal Literary Sources for the Punic Wars (Apart from Polybius)." Chap. 7 in *A Companion to the Punic Wars,* edited by Dexter Hoyos. Malden, MA: Wiley-Blackwell, 2011.

Minunno, G. "Sul passaggio del Rodano da parte degli elefanti di Annibale." *Révue des Études militaires anciennes (RÉMA)* 5 (2005–08).

Mommsen, Theodor. *History of Rome.* 5 vols. Translated by William Purdie Dickson. 1901. First published 1854–56 as *Römische Geschichte.*

Montgomery, Bernard (Field-Marshal Viscount Montgomery, Victor of El Alamein). *A History of Warfare.* Cleveland: World, 1968.

Mosca, P. G. *Child Sacrifice in Canaanite and Israelite Religion.* Cambridge, MA: Harvard University Press, 1975.

Moscati, Sabatino. *I Cartagi nesi in Italia.* Milan: A. Montadori, 1977.

———. "Il sacrificio punico dei fanciulli: realta o invenzione?" *Quaderni dell'Accademia Nazionale dei Lincei* 261 (1987): (Problemi attuali di scienza e di cultura) 4–15.

Müller, H. "Tombes gauloises de la Tène II, découvertes au pied des Balmes de Voreppe," *Bibliothèque municipal de Grenoble, Fonds Dauphinois,* 1909.

Negbi, Ora. "Early Phoenician Presence in the Mediterranean Islands: A

Reappraisal." *American Journal of Archaeology* 96, no. 4 (October 1992): 599–615.

Norman, Naomi. "Carthage." In *An Encyclopedia of the History of Classical Archaeology,* edited by Nancy Thomson de Grummond. Westport, CT: Greenwood Press, 1996.

Ober, Josh. "Hannibal: How to Win Battles and Lose Wars." *Military History Quarterly* 2, no. 4 (1990): 50–59.

O'Bryhim, S. "Hannibal's Elephants and the Crossing of the Rhone." *Classical Quarterly* 41, no. 1 (1991): 121–25.

O'Connell, Robert. *The Ghosts of Cannae: Hannibal and the Darkest Hour of the Roman Republic.* New York: Random House, 2011.

O'Connor Morris, William. *Hannibal: Soldier, Statesman, Patriot, and the Crisis of the Struggle Between Carthage and Rome.* 1937. Reprint of New York: G. P. Putnam's Sons, 1897 edition.

O'Gorman, Ellen. "Cato the Elder and the Destruction of Carthage." *Helios* 31 (2004): 97–122.

Orejas, A., and F. J. Sanchez-Palencia. "Mines, Territorial Organization and Social Structure in Roman Iberia: The Example of Carthago Nova and the Peninsular Northwest." *American Journal of Archaeology* 106, no. 4 (2002): 581–99.

Pauly-Wissowa. *Realencyclopädie der classischen Altertumswissenschaft.* Vols. 4, 5. Edited by G. Wissowa, W. Kroll et al. Stuttgart, Ger. (n.d.).

Peddie, John. *Hannibal's War.* Thrupp, Stroud, Gloucestershire, UK: Sutton, 1997.

Pedley, John Griffiths, ed. *New Light on Ancient Carthage.* Ann Arbor: University of Michigan Press, 1980.

Perez-Juez, Amalia. "Gades/Gadir." In *The Encyclopedia of Ancient History.* Malden, MA: Wiley-Blackwell, 2012.

Perrin, M. *Marche d'Annibal des Pyrenees au Po.* Paris, 1887.

Picard, G. C. *Hannibal.* Paris: Hachette, 1967.

Plácido, Domingo, ed. *Historia de Espana, Hispania Antigua.* Vol. 1. Madrid: Critica / Marcial Pons, 2009.

Pollak, Martha D. "From Castrum to Capital: Autograph Plans and Planning Studies of Turin, 1615–1673." *Journal of the Society of Architectural Historians* 47, no. 3 (September 1988): 263–80.

Pollard, Nigel, and Joanne Berry. *The Complete Roman Legions.* London: Thames and Hudson, 2012.

———. "Hannibal." In *Dictionnaire de la civilisation phénicienne et punique,* edited by E. Lipinski. Paris: Brepols [Turnhout], 1992.

Pomeroy, Arthur J. "Hannibal at Nuceria." *Historia: Zeitschrift für Alte Geschichte* 38, no. 2 (1989): 162–76.

Potter, Timothy W. *Roman Italy: Exploring the Roman World*. Berkeley: University of California Press, 1987.

Powell, Thomas George Eyre. *The Celts*. London: Thames and Hudson, 1995. Reprint of London: Thames and Hudson, 1958 edition.

Prevas, John. *Hannibal Crosses the Alps: The Invasion of Italy and the Punic Wars*. Cambridge, MA: Da Capo Press, 2001. Reprint of Rockville Centre, NY: Sarpedon, 1998 edition.

Proctor, Dennis. *Hannibal's March in History*. Oxford: Clarendon Press, 1971.

Quinn, Josephine Crawley. "The Cultures of the Tophet: Identification and Identity in the Phoenician Diaspora." In *Cultural Identity in the Peoples of the Ancient Mediterranean*, edited by Erich Gruen. Los Angeles: Getty Research Institute, 2011.

Rawlings, Louis. "The Carthaginian Navy: Questions and Assumptions." Chap. 8 in *New Perspectives on Ancient Warfare*. History of Warfare. Vol. 59. Edited by Garrett Fagan and Matthew Trundle. Leiden, Neth.: E. J. Brill, 2010.

———. "Hannibal the Cannibal? Polybius on Barcid Atrocities." *Cardiff Historical Papers* 9 (2007): 1–30.

———. "The War in Italy, 218–203." Chap. 17 in *A Companion to the Punic Wars*, edited by Dexter Hoyos. Malden, MA: Wiley-Blackwell, 2011.

Ray, John. *The Rosetta Stone and the Rebirth of Ancient Egypt*. Cambridge, MA: Harvard University Press, 2007.

Rey, Fernando Echeverría. "Weapons, Technological Determinism, and Ancient Warfare." Chap. 1 in *New Perspectives on Ancient Warfare*. History of Warfare. Vol. 59. Edited by Garrett Fagan and Matthew Trundle. Leiden, Neth.: E. J. Brill, 2010.

Richardson, J. S. *Hispaniae: Spain and the Development of Roman Imperialism, 218–82 BC*. Cambridge: Cambridge University Press, 2004. First published 1986 by Cambridge: Cambridge University Press.

———. Review of *Roman Spain: Conquest and Assimilation*, by L. A. Curchin. *Brittania* 24 (1993): 332–33.

———. "The Spanish Mines and the Development of Provincial Taxation in the Second Century BC." *Journal of Roman Studies* 66 (1976): 139–52.

Richmond, J. A. "Spies in Ancient Greece." *Greece & Rome* 45, no. 1 (April 1998): 1–18.

Ridley, R. T. "Was Scipio Africanus at Cannae?" *Latomus* 34, no. 1 (1975): 161–65.

Roberts, Paul. "Mass-Production of Roman Finewares." In *Pottery in the Making: World Ceramic Traditions*, edited by Ian Freestone and David Gaimster. London: British Museum Press, 1997.

Rosenstein, Nathan. "Italy: Economy and Demography After Hannibal's War." Chap. 23 in *A Companion to the Punic Wars*, edited by Dexter Hoyos. Malden, MA: Wiley-Blackwell, 2011.

———. *Rome at War: Farms, Families, and Death in the Middle Republic*. Chapel Hill: University of North Carolina Press, 2004.

Rossi, Andreola. "Parallel Lives: Hannibal and Scipio in Livy's Third Decade." *Transactions of the American Philological Association (TAPA)* 134, no. 2 (2004): 359–81.

Roux, Georges. *L'Amphictionie, Delphes et le temple d'Apollon au IVe siecle*. Collection de la Maison de l'Orient méditerranéen. Serie archéologique, vol. 8, 1979.

Russell, F. M. "The Battlefield of Zama." *Archaeology* 23, no. 2 (1970): 120–29.

Sabin, Philip. "The Face of Roman Battle." *Journal of Roman Studies* 90 (2000): 1–17.

Sanctis, Gaetano De. *Storia dei Romani*. Florence, It.: La Nuova Italia, 1964.

Sage, Michael M. "The De Viris Illustribus: Chronology and Structure." *Transactions of the American Philological Association (TAPA)* 108 (1978): 217–41, esp. 219, 222.

Sanz, Fernando Quesada. *Arma y Símbolo: la Falcata Iberica*, Instituto de Cultura Juan Gil-Albert, Diputación de Alicante, 1992.

———. "Patterns of Interaction: 'Celtic' and 'Iberian' Weapons in Iron Age Spain." In *Celtic Connections. Papers from the Tenth International Congress of Celtic Studies, Edinburgh 1995*. Vol. 2: *Archaeology, Numismatics, Historical Linguistics*, edited by W. Gillies and D. W. Harding. Edinburgh, Scot.: International Congress of Celtic Studies, 2006.

Scarborough, John. *Arma y Símbolo: la Falcata Iberica*. Instituto de Cultura Juan Gil-Albert, Diputación de Alicante, 1992.

———. Review of *The Elephant in the Greek and Roman World*, by H. H. Scullard. *Classical Journal* 72, no. 2 (1976): 174–76.

Scheidel, Walter. "Human Mobility in Roman Italy I: The Free Population." *Journal of Roman Studies* 94 (2004): 1–26.

———. "Progress and Problems in Roman Demography." Chap. 1 in *Debating Roman Demography*, edited by Walter Scheidel. Leiden, Neth.: E. J. Brill, 2001.

Schmitz, Philip C. "The Phoenician Text from the Etruscan Sanctuary at Pyrgi." *Journal of the American Oriental Society* 115, no. 4 (1995): 559–75.

———. "A Research Manual of Phoenician and Punic Civilization." *Journal of the American Oriental Society* 121, no. 4 (2001): 623–36.

Schwartz, Jeffrey H., Frank Houghton, Roberto Machiarelli, and Luca Bondioli. "Skeletal Remains from Punic Carthage Do Not Support Systematic Sacrifice of Infants." *Public Library of Science* 5, no. 2 (February 17, 2010): e9177.

Scullard, Howard Hayes. "The Carthaginians in Spain." Chap. 2 in *The Cambridge Ancient History*. 2nd ed. Vol. 8, *Rome and the Mediterranean to 133 BC*, edited by A. E. Astin, J. Boardman, F. W. Walbank, M. W. Frederikson, and R. M. Ogilvie. Cambridge: Cambridge University Press, 1989.

———. *The Elephant in the Greek and Roman World*. Ithaca, NY: Cornell University Press, 1974.

———. "Hannibal's Elephants." *Numismatic Chronicle* 6, no. 8 (1948): 158–68.

———. *A History of the Roman World 753–146 BC*. London: Routledge, 2004. First published 1935 by London: Methuen.

———. *Scipio Africanus: Soldier and Politician*. Ithaca, NY: Cornell University Press, 1970.

Seibert, Jakob. *Hannibal*. Darmstadt, Ger.: Wissenschaftliche Buchgesellschaft, 1993.

———. *Hannibal: Feldherr und Staatsman*. Mainz, Ger.: Philip von Zabern, 1997.

Servadio, Gaia. *Motya: Unearthing a Lost Civilization*. London: Weidenfeld and Nicolson, 2000.

Shaya, Josephine. "The Greek Temple as Museum: The Case of the Legendary Treasure of Athena from Lindos." *American Journal of Archaeology* 109, no. 3 (2005): 423–42.

Shean, John. "Hannibal's Mules: The Logistical Limitations of Hannibal's Army and the Battle of Cannae, 216 BC." *Historia: Zeitschrift für Alte Geschichte* 45, no. 2 (1996): 159–87.

Sheldon, R. M. "Hannibal's Spies." *Espionage* 2, no. 3 (August 1986): 149–52.

———. "Hannibal's Spies." *International Journal of Intelligence and Counterintelligence (IJIC)* 1, no. 3 (1987): 53–70.

———. *Intelligence Activities in Ancient Rome: Trust in the Gods but Verify*. New York: Routledge, 2005, esp. chap. 3, "Hannibal's Spies."

Shoshani, Jeheskal, and J. K. Eisenberg. "Elephas Maximus." *Mammalian Species* 182 (1982): 1–8.

Silver, Morris. "Antonine Plague and the Deactivation of Spanish Mines." *Arctos: Acta Filologica Fennica* 45 (2011): 133–42.

Smith, Christopher, and Liv Mariah Yarrow, eds. *Imperialism, Cultural Politics, & Polybius.* Oxford: Oxford University Press, 2012.

Smith, Gene. *Mounted Warriors: From Alexander the Great and Cromwell to Stuart, Sheridan, and Custer.* Hoboken, NJ: John Wiley & Sons, 2009.

Smith, Patricia and Gal Avishai. "The Use of Dental Criteria for Estimating Postnatal Survival in Skeletal Remains of Infants." *Journal of Archaeological Science* 32, no. 1 (2005): 83–89.

Soren, David, Aicha Ben Abed Ben Khader, and Hedi Slim. *Carthage: Uncovering the Mysteries and Splendors of Ancient Tunisia.* New York: Simon & Schuster, 1990.

Southern, Pat. *The Roman Army: A Social and Institutional History.* New York: Oxford University Press, 2007.

Spaeth, John W. "Hannibal and Napoleon." *Classical Journal* 24, no. 4 (January 1929): 291–93.

Spence, I. G. *The Cavalry of Classical Greece.* Oxford: Clarendon Press, 1993.

Stager, Lawrence. E. "Excavations at Carthage 1975. The Punic Project: First Interim Report." *Annual of the American Schools of Oriental Research* 43 (1978): 151–90.

———. "The Rite of Child Sacrifice at Carthage." In *New Light on Ancient Carthage,* edited by John Griffiths Pedley. Ann Arbor: University of Michigan Press, 1980.

———. "A View from the Tophet." In *Phönizier im Westen,* edited by H. G. Niemeyer. Mainz, Ger.: Philip von Zabern, 1982.

Stager, Lawrence E., and Samuel R. Wolff. "Child Sacrifice at Carthage: Religious Rite or Population Control?" *Biblical Archaeology Review* 10 (1984): 30–51.

Starks, John H. "Fides Aeneia: The Transference of Punic Stereotypes in the Aeneid." *Classical Journal* 94 (1999): 255–83.

Starr, Chester G. *A History of the Ancient World.* 4th ed. New York: Oxford University Press, 1991. First published 1965 by New York: Oxford University Press.

———. "Political Intelligence in Classical Greece," supplement 31, *Mnemosyne: A Journal of Classical Studies* (1974).

Stephenson, Ian P. *Hannibal's Army.* Stroud, UK: Tempus, 2008.

Stevens, Susan T. "Carthage." In *The Encyclopedia of Ancient History.* Malden, MA: Wiley-Blackwell, 2012.

Stillwell, Richard, William L. MacDonald, and Marian Holland McAlister, eds.

Princeton Encyclopedia of Classical Sites. Princeton, NJ: Princeton University Press, 1976.

Stoll, Oliver. "For the Glory of Athens: Xenophon's Hipparchikos 'Logos'—A Technical Treatise and Instruction Manual on Ideal Leadership." *Studies in History and Philosophy of Science* 43, no. 2 (2012): 250–57.

Strauss, Barry. *Masters of Command: Alexander, Hannibal, Caesar, and the Genius of Leadership.* New York: Simon & Schuster, 2012.

Strauss, Barry, and Josiah Ober. *The Anatomy of Error: Ancient Military Disasters and Their Lessons for Modern Strategists.* New York: St. Martin's Press, 1992.

Sumida, Jon. "A Concordance of Selected Subjects in Carl von Clausewitz's *On War.*" *Journal of Military History* 78, no. 1 (2014): 271–331.

Sun Tzu. *The Art of War.* Translated by S. B. Griffith. New York: Oxford University Press, 1979.

Tarpin, M. "L'héroique et la quotidian. Hannibal et les autres dans les Alpes." Société d'Histoire du Valais Romand, Sion, Bibliotheque Cantonale: *Annales valaisannes* (2002): 7–19.

Taylor, Lili Ross. *Roman Voting Assemblies: From the Hannibalic War to the Dictatorship of Caesar.* Jerome Lectures, 8th series. Ann Arbor: University of Michigan, 1966.

Toynbee, Arnold J. *Hannibal's Legacy: The Hannibalic War's Effect on Roman Life.* 2 vols. Oxford: Oxford University Press, 1965.

Visona, Paolo. "A New Wrinkle in the Mid-Carthaginian Silver Series." *Numismatic Chronicle* 166 (2006): 15–23.

———. "The Punic Coins in the Collection of Florence's Museo Archeologico: Nonnulla Notanda." In *Rivista di Studi Fenici* 27 (1999): 147–49.

———. "The Serrated Silver Coinage of Carthage." *Schweizerische Numismatische Rundschau* 86 (2007): 31–62.

Walbank, F. W. *A Historical Commentary on Polybius.* Vol. 1 (1957), vol. 2 (1967), vol. 3 (1979). Oxford: Clarendon Press.

———. *Polybius, Rome and the Hellenistic World: Essays and Reflections.* Cambridge: Cambridge University Press, 2002.

———. "The Scipionic Legend." *Proceedings of the Cambridge Philological Society* 13 (1967): 54–69.

———. *Selected Papers: Studies in Greek and Roman History and Historiography.* Cambridge: Cambridge University Press, 2010.

———. "Some Reflections on Hannibal's Pass." *Journal of Roman Studies* 46 (1956): 37–45.

Waldman, C., and C. Mason. "Allobroges," "Tricorii," "Voconti," and "Volcae." *Encyclopedia of European Peoples*. New York: Facts on File, 2006.

Walsh, P. G. "Massinissa." *Journal of Roman Studies* 55, nos. 1/2 (1965): 149–60.

Warmington, Brian H. *Carthage*. London: Penguin, 1960.

Warmington, Brian H., William Nassau Weech, and Roger J. A. Wilson. "Carthage." In *Oxford Companion to Classical Civilization*. Oxford: Oxford University Press, 1998, 141–44.

———. "Carthage." In *The Oxford Classical Dictionary*, 4th ed., edited by Simon Hornblower, Antony Spawforth, and Esther Edinow. Oxford: Oxford University Press, 2012.

Warry, John Gibson. *Warfare in the Classical World: An Illustrated Encyclopedia of Weapons, Warriors, and Warfare in the Ancient Civilisations of Greece and Rome*. London: Salamander Books, 1993.

Wayman, Erin. "On Hannibal's Trail: The Clues Are in the Geology." *Earth* (2010).

Wheeler, Everett L. "Methodological Limits and the Mirage of Roman Strategy, Part I." *Journal of Military History* 57, no. 1 (1993): 7–41.

———. "The Modern Legality of Frontinus' Stratagems." *Militärgeschichtliche Mitteilungen* 44, no. 1 (1988): 7–29.

———. "Ruses and Stratagems." In *International Military and Defense Encyclopedia*, vol. 5, edited by Trevor N. Dupuy. Washington, DC: Macmillan-Brassey's, 1993.

———. "Stratagem and the Vocabulary of Military Trickery," supplement 108, *Mnemosyne: A Journal of Classical Studies* (1988).

Wilkinson, Spencer. *Hannibal's March Through the Alps*. Oxford: Clarendon Press, 1911.

Williams, J. H. C. *Beyond the Rubicon: Romans and Gauls in Republican Italy*. New York: Oxford University Press, 2001.

Wilson, Andrew. "Water Supply in Ancient Carthage." In "Carthage Papers: The Early Colony's Economy, Water Supply, a Public Bath, and the Mobilization of the State Olive Oil," edited by J. T. Peña, J. J. Rossiter, A. I. Wilson, and C. Wells, M. Carroll, J. Freed, and D. Godden, supplement 28, *Journal of Roman Archaeology* (1998): 65–102.

Wilson, Roger J. A. "Carthage." In *The Oxford Companion to Archaeology*, edited by Brian Fagan. Oxford: Oxford University Press, 1996.

———. "Why Did the Carthaginians Sacrifice Children?" In *The Seventy Great Mysteries of the Ancient World*, edited by Brian Fagan. London: Thames and Hudson, 2001.

Winters, Harold. *Battling the Elements: Weather and Terrain in the Conduct of War.* Baltimore: Johns Hopkins University Press, 1998.

Wise, Terence. *Armies of the Carthaginian Wars 265–146 BC.* Oxford: Osprey Books, 1982.

Wiseman, Timothy P. *New Men in the Roman Senate, 139 B.C. to A.D. 14.* London: Oxford University Press, 1971.

———. "Roman Republican Road-Building." *Papers of the British School at Rome* 38 (1970): 122–52.

Woodward, Rachel. *Military Geographies.* Oxford: Blackwell / Royal Geographical Society (RGS-IBG), 2004.

Worley, Leslie J. *Hippeis: The Cavalry of Ancient Greece.* Oxford: Westview Press, 1994.

Zimmerman, Klaus. "Roman Strategy and Aims in the Second Punic War," Chap. 16 in *A Companion to the Punic Wars,* edited by Dexter Hoyos. Malden, MA: Wiley-Blackwell, 2011.

INDEX

Page numbers in *italics* refer to maps. Page numbers beginning with 275 refer to notes.